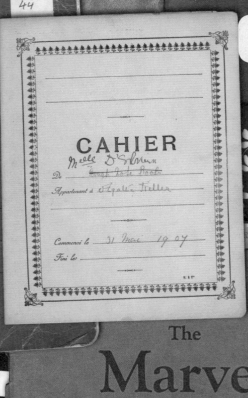

Agatha Christie's
SECRET NOTEBOOKS

By Agatha Christie

UK TITLE / US OR ALTERNATE TITLE

* UK short story collection only

Five Little Pigs / Murder in Retrospect (1943)
The Moving Finger / The Case of the Moving Finger (1943)
Towards Zero (1944)
Death Comes As the End (1945)
Sparkling Cyanide / Remembered Death (1945)
The Hollow / Murder After Hours (1946)
The Labors of Hercules (1947)
Taken at the Flood / There Is a Tide . . . (1948)
Witness for the Prosecution and Other Stories (1948)
Crooked House (1949)
Three Blind Mice and Other Stories / The Mousetrap and Other Stories (1950)
A Murder Is Announced (1950)
They Came to Baghdad (1951)
The Under Dog and Other Stories (1951)
Mrs. McGinty's Dead (1952)
Murder with Mirrors / They Do It With Mirrors (1952)
After the Funeral / Funerals Are Fatal (1953)
A Pocket Full of Rye (1953)
Destination Unknown / So Many Steps to Death (1954)
Hickory Dickory Dock / Hickory Dickory Death (1955)
Dead Man's Folly (1956)
4.50 from Paddington / What Mrs. McGillicuddy Saw! (1957)
Ordeal by Innocence (1958)
Cat Among the Pigeons (1959)
The Adventure of the Christmas Pudding (1960)*
Double Sin and Other Stories (1961)
The Pale Horse (1961)
The Mirror Crack'd from Side to Side / The Mirror Crack'd (1962)
The Clocks (1963)
A Caribbean Mystery (1964)
At Bertram's Hotel (1965)
Third Girl (1966)
Endless Night (1967)
By the Pricking of My Thumbs (1968)
Hallowe'en Party (1969)
Passenger to Frankfurt (1970)
The Golden Ball and Other Stories (1971)
Nemesis (1971)
Elephants Can Remember (1972)
Postern of Fate (1973)
Poirot's Early Cases (1974)
Curtain (1975)
Sleeping Murder (1976)

Cont. Autobiography   Jan. 1965 -

27

Recap -
     Parents' Marriage -
     Home - 3rd birthday — my
mother - San - Stores - Reading

Goldie + the Canvas Book

II. The nursery
     Servants - / Jam & / in woods
(Queer anecdote ab. "Cuci Cadi" in y early
married days)

Jesus found but about Servants?
     Census -
     Dog Tony.

Nancy Sister
Eddy - born who Granny

Notes dated 1965 in Notebook 27 summarising the early chapters of
An Autobiography, *eventually published in 1977.*

Agatha Christie's
SECRET NOTEBOOKS

———————◦———————

*Fifty Years of Mysteries
in the Making*

JOHN CURRAN

HARPER
An Imprint of HarperCollins*Publishers*
www.harpercollins.com

For
Joseph, Conor,
Francis, Oisin and Lorcan

Contents

Acknowledgements

This book has benefited greatly from the encouragement and assistance of many people whose names do not appear on the title page.

First and foremost, my thanks go to Mathew Prichard and his wife Lucy. The very existence of this book is due to Mathew's generosity. He unhesitatingly agreed to my writing about the Notebooks when I first approached him. And he not only granted me complete and unfettered access to all of his grandmother's papers but he and Lucy also extended me limitless hospitality on the many occasions when I studied them.

David Brawn, HarperCollins, for his faith in the project and Steve Gove for his eagle-eyed editing.

My brother Brendan read an early draft and his positive words gave much encouragement; and with his wife, Virginia, he provided me with a home-from-home (but with superior technical backup!).

My friend and fellow Christie devotee, Tony Medawar, made many helpful suggestions as well as sharing his research with me.

Felicity Windmill, HarperCollins Archivist; Dr Christine Faunch and her staff in Exeter University Library; Tamsen Harward and Jemma Jones at Agatha Christie Ltd.

David Headley of Goldsboro Books for his invaluable help and advice.

My many colleagues and friends in Dublin City Council for their support, especially Michael Sands, Press Officer and Jane Alger, Divisional Librarian, Readers' Services.

And, for various reasons, my thanks also to Eurion Brown, Pete Coleman, Julius Green, John Perry, John Ryan, John Timon, Andy Trott and Nigel Wollen.

Notes

I have 'tidied up' Agatha Christie's notes as little as possible. Every page of every Notebook is littered with dashes, brackets and question marks; complete sentences are the exception rather than the rule. I have removed some capital letters, brackets and dashes, solely in the interests of legibility. In some cases I have amended a paragraph of words, broken only by dashes, into separate sentences. All remaining question marks, underlining, crossing-out, exclamation marks and dashes, as well as some grammatical errors, are as they appear in the Notebooks. If I have omitted text from within extracts I indicate this by the use of dots.

Spellings have not been corrected but marked as [sic].

Square brackets are used for editorial clarification or remarks.

Dates of publication refer to the UK edition. They have been taken, for the most part, from contemporary catalogues in Collins archives. Traditionally, Crime Club titles were published on the first Monday of the month and in the few instances where actual dates were not available, I have used this guideline.

I have reinstated the title *Ten Little Niggers*, rather than the more politically correct *And Then There Were None*, throughout. This accurately reflects both the Notebooks and the book as Agatha Christie first saw it in November 1939.

At the beginning of each chapter I have included a list of titles whose solutions are revealed within. It proved impossible to discuss a title intelligently or to compare it to the Notebooks unless I disclosed some endings, and in many cases the notes mention the vital name or plot device anyway. Christie's creative ruthlessness in deciding her killer is a vital part of her genius and to try circumventing this with ambiguous verbal gymnastics cannot do her justice.

In deciding which titles to include and which to omit, I intentionally avoided an alphabetical or a chronological listing. The former is meaningless in the context of this book and the latter resulted in all the classic titles appearing together in the middle years of Christie's career. I decided on a thematic arrangement, thereby incorporating variety and simultaneously illustrating Christie's exploitation of a motif. The grouping of titles within categories is somewhat arbitrary. Some titles might fit under a few headings, e.g. *A Caribbean Mystery* could appear in either 'A Holiday for Murder' or 'Murder Abroad'; *Five Little Pigs* could fit neatly into 'The Nursery Rhyme Murders' and 'Murder in Retrospect'. I selected and arranged them with an eye to variety and balance.

Relatively few short stories have detailed notes. I have chosen those with sufficient notes to make their inclusion worthwhile.

It is not possible in a book of this size to mention every title and if your favourite is missing I apologise; I hope to remedy this situation in a subsequent and expanded edition.

It is important for readers to note that the Notebooks are not available for viewing. It is hoped in a few years to be able to grant limited access to them but at present this is not possible.

Foreword

MATHEW PRICHARD

Quite a few years ago, my first wife, Angela, and I made a trip to Calgary in western Canada to see a world premiere of a very early Agatha Christie play called *Chimneys*. At the first reception we met a quiet, bespectacled Irishman called John Curran. He took with his customary good humour my opening gambit that he must be mad to travel from Dublin to Calgary to see an Agatha Christie play and we have been friends ever since.

After my parents died at Greenway in Devon, which has recently been taken over by the National Trust (and has just been reopened), John was a frequent visitor. Most people who visit Greenway are transfixed by the gardens and the walks by the river. Not John. He spent all his time in the 'fax room', a room on the first floor about ten feet by four in which the Agatha Christie archive was kept. He had to be prised out for meals, sometimes spending 12 hours a day immersed in the history of Agatha Christie's work.

It was here that John's love affair with Agatha Christie's Notebooks blossomed, and neither he nor I could believe our (and your) good fortune when HarperCollins agreed to publish John's book about them. I think you will find that his fascination and enthusiasm for them emerge very clearly and,

13

as a bonus, he has included two very rare Agatha Christie short stories.

I never cease to be astounded that over 30 years since she died, interest in every aspect of Agatha Christie's life and work is still at fever pitch. To John's credit, he has always concentrated on her work, leaving to others more morbid fascination about the person behind the books, and here is a book which deals with the very kernel, the raw material of all this great work. It is highly personal and certainly a piece of literary history. John has produced a treat for us all – I hope you enjoy it.

MATHEW PRICHARD

PREFACE

Shadows in Sunlight – Interlude at Greenway, Summer 1954

As she watches the river below, a pleasure steamer chugs towards Dartmouth, sun glinting on the water in its wake. The laughter of the holidaymakers on board reaches her vantage point in the Battery, and the dog at her feet raises his head peering inquisitively towards the river. A drowsy bee is the only other sound that disturbs her peace. Elsewhere in this haven the gardener, Frank, is busy preparing for the flower show and Mathew is following the treasure hunt she set for him, but here in this semicircular battlement at the edge of the garden overlooking the river she has peace. And a temporary solitude to think about her next project after a wonderful period of leisure – eating the glorious produce of the garden and swimming in the sea and picnicking on the nearby moors and lazing on the lawn and enjoying the company of her family and friends.

She knows that if she lets her mind wander inspiration will come; after all, for over 35 years her imagination has never let her down and there is no reason to suppose that in this tranquil setting it will fail her. She gazes vaguely around. Just visible to her left is the roof of the Boathouse, and behind and to the right the garden continues its upward climb towards the imposing Georgian house. She can now hear

15

occasional rustles in the undergrowth as Mathew follows her trail of clues.

If he has followed them properly he should, by now, be heading in the direction of the tennis court . . . Wonder if he'll spot the tennis ball . . . it has the next clue. Very like a detective story really . . . but more fun and less planning . . . and no editing or proofreading . . . and nobody writes to you afterwards and points out mistakes . . . But if there were a few participants it would be even better – more fun and more of a contest. Perhaps next time I could arrange for some of Max's nephews to join him and that would make it more exciting. Or the next time I have a garden party for the local school . . . maybe I could work in the Battery and the Boathouse . . . although the Boathouse could seem slightly sinister . . . especially if you were there on your own . . .

She is now gazing unseeingly over the river and imagining her surroundings in a more ominous light . . .

If the lawn was a scene of light-hearted enjoyment . . . a family event . . . no, it would need more people than that . . . a garden party . . . a fund-raiser? For the Scouts or the Guides – they were always in need of funds . . . yes, possibilities there . . . There could be stalls on the lawn and teas in a tent, perhaps by the magnolia . . . people in and out of the house . . . a fortune-teller and a bottle stall . . . and confusion about where everyone was . . . And elsewhere in the grounds a darker force at work . . . unrecognised . . . unsuspected . . . What about here in the Battery? No – too open and . . . too . . . too . . . unmenacing, and you couldn't really hide a body here; but the Boathouse . . . now, that has possibilities – far enough away to be lonely, down those rickety steps, and yet perfectly accessible to anyone. And you can lock the door . . . and it can be reached from the river . . .

What about Mrs Oliver? . . . perfect for planning a treasure hunt . . . and it could go wrong for some reason and somebody dies. Let's see . . . how about a murder hunt instead of a treasure hunt . . . like Cluedo except around a real house and grounds instead of a board. Now, Poirot or Marple . . . Marple or Poirot . . . can't see Miss M walking around Greenway, bad enough for Poirot but not really credible that she would . . . and she doesn't know Mrs Oliver anyway, and I have to use her . . . So . . . Mrs O would have to bring in Poirot for some reason . . . perhaps she could call him down to the house on some pretext . . . she needs his help with some of the clues? . . . or could he know the Chief Constable . . . but I've used that a few times already . . . how about handing out the prize for the winner of the hunt . . .

She reaches into her bag and extracts a large red note-book . . .

Not really suitable for carrying around but to use the Scouts' own motto – be prepared. Now, I'm sure there's a pen here somewhere . . . Best to get this down while it is still fresh – it can be changed later but I think the basic idea has distinct possibilities.

She opens the notebook, finds an empty page and starts to write.

Basic ideas usable
Mrs Oliver summons Poirot
She is at Greenway – professional job – arranging a Treasure Hunt or a Murder Hunt for the Conservation Fete, which is to be held there –

She is totally absorbed, covering the pages with characteristically large, sprawling handwriting, getting ideas down on paper even if they are to be discarded at a later stage. The real

Greenway has disappeared as she peoples it with the children of her imagination: foreign students, girl guides, boy scouts, murder hunt solvers, policemen – and Hercule Poirot.

Some ideas
Hiker (girl?) from hostel Next door – really Lady Bannerman

*Yes, the youth hostel next door could be put to some good use . . .
foreign students . . . possibilities of disguising one of them as . . .
who? They're always coming and going and nobody knows who
they are – they could be anyone, really. A girl is easier to disguise
than a man . . . perhaps she could double as the lady of the house.
Mmmmm, that would mean nobody really knowing her well . . .
perhaps she could be ill . . . an invalid . . . always in her room . . .
or stupid and nobody pays attention to her . . . or recently married
and new to everyone. But then someone from her past arrives . . .
her real husband, maybe . . . or a lover . . . or a relative . . . and
she has to get rid of them . . .*

Young wife recognised by someone who knows she is
married already – blackmail?

*I can adapt one of the treasure hunts I've done for Mathew and
work in the Boathouse somehow . . . and invent Mrs Oliver's hunt
. . . I could use the Cluedo idea of weapons and suspects . . . but
with a real body instead of a pretend one . . .*

Mrs Oliver's plan
The Weapons
Revolver – Knife – Clothes Line

*Who will I murder? The foreign student . . . no, she has to be part
of the plan . . . someone very unexpected then . . . how about the
lord of the manor? . . . no, too clichéd . . . needs to have impact . . .*

what about a stranger? . . . but who . . . and that brings a lot of problems . . . I'll leave that for next year maybe . . . How about a child? . . . needs to be handled carefully but I could make it a not-very-nice child . . . perhaps the pretend body, could be one of the scouts, turns out to be really dead . . . or, better again, a girl guide . . . she could be nosy and have seen something she shouldn't . . . Don't think I've had a child victim before . . .

Points to be decided – Who first chosen for victim?
(?a) 'Body' to be Boy Scout in boat house – key of which has to be found by 'clues'

She gazes abstractedly into the distance, blind to the panoramic view of the river and the wooded hillside opposite. She is Poirot, taking afternoon tea in the drawing room, carefully exiting through the French windows and wandering down through the garden. She is Hattie, intent on preserving her position and money at all costs. She is Mrs Oliver, distractedly plotting, discarding, amending, changing . . .

Next bits – P at house – wandering up to Folly – Finds?

Hattie goes in as herself – she changes her clothes and emerges (from boathouse? Folly? fortune teller's tent?) as student from Hostel

Now, I have to provide a few family members . . . how about an elderly mother . . . she could live in the Gate Lodge. If I make her mysterious, readers will think she is 'it' . . . little old ladies are always good as suspects. Could she know something from years earlier? . . . perhaps she knew Hattie from somewhere . . . or thinks she does . . . or make Poirot think she does, which is almost as good . . . Let's see . . .

Mrs Folliat? suspicious character – really covering up for
something she saw. Or an old crime – a wife who 'ran away'

She stops writing and listens as a voice approaches the
Battery calling 'Nima, Nima.'

'Here, Mathew,' she calls and a tousled 12-year-old runs
down the steps.

'I found the treasure, I found the treasure,' he chants
excitedly, clutching a half-crown.

'Well done. I hope it wasn't too difficult?'

'Not really. The clue in the tennis court took me a while
but then I spotted the ball at the base of the net.'

'I thought that one would puzzle you,' she smiles.

She closes the notebook and puts it away in her bag.
Hercule Poirot's questioning of Mrs Folliat and the identity
of a possible second victim will have to wait.

'Come on,' she says. 'Let's see if there is anything nice to
eat in the house.'

Agatha Christie, Queen of Crime, is finished for the day
and Agatha Christie, grandmother, climbs the steps from the
Battery in search of ice-cream for her grandson.

And the Christie for Christmas 1956 was *Dead Man's Folly*.

Introduction

Julia leaned back and gasped. She stared and stared and stared . . .

Cat among the Pigeons, Chapter 17

I first saw the Notebooks of Agatha Christie on Friday 11 November 2005.

Mathew Prichard had invited me to spend the weekend at Greenway to experience it in its current state before the National Trust began the extensive renovations necessary to restore it to its former glory. He collected me at Newton Abbot railway station, scene of the radio play *Personal Call*, and we drove through the gathering dusk to Galmpton village, past the school of which Dame Agatha had been a governor and the cottage where her friend Robert Graves, the dedicatee of *Towards Zero*, had lived. We drove up the coal-dark road beyond the village but the panoramic view of the Dart and the sea, enjoyed many years earlier by Hercule Poirot on his way to the fatal murder hunt in Nasse House, was lost to me. By now it was raining heavily and the phrase 'a dark and stormy night' was a reality and not mere atmosphere. We passed the entrance to the youth hostel, refuge of the foreign students from *Dead Man's Folly*, and eventually drove through the imposing gates of Greenway House, winding our way up the drive to arrive at the house itself. The lights were on and there was a welcoming fire in the library where we had tea. I sat in Agatha Christie's favourite armchair and forgot my manners enough to gaze avidly at the surrounding bookshelves – at the run of, appropriately, the Greenway Edition of her novels, the foreign language versions, the much thumbed and jacket-less first editions; at the crime novels of her contemporaries and the well-read books from her happy childhood in Ashfield, lovingly recalled in *Postern of Fate*.

Mathew then gave me a guided tour of the house – the imposing entrance hall complete with dinner-gong ('Dead Man's Mirror'), brass-bound trunk ('The Mystery of the Spanish Chest') and impressive family portraits (*Hercule Poirot's Christmas*); a careless collection of sports equipment in the corner beneath the stairs contained, I like to imagine, a left-handed golf-club ('Murder in the Mews'), a few tennis racquets (*Towards Zero* or, less gruesomely, *Cat among the Pigeons*) and a perfectly innocent cricket bat. The drawing room was dominated by a grand piano (*They Do It with Mirrors*) and a door that obstinately refused to remain open unless propped with a doorstop (*A Murder is Announced*); in the china cabinet reposed the set of Harlequin figures that inspired *The Mysterious Mr Quin*. The window behind the piano was the one from which Hercule Poirot delicately descended following afternoon tea in *Dead Man's Folly*.

On the top floor, up a winding wooden staircase, were the bathrooms still with the names of the child refugees (*Ordeal by Innocence*) from the Second World War taped to the cupboard shelves, while a bookcase contained signed copies from some of her fellow writers ('To Agatha with blushes – Ngaio Marsh'). The following morning, there were panoramic views of the river and the Devon hills with glimpses of the Boathouse (*Dead Man's Folly*) and the Battery (*Five Little Pigs*).

On the first-floor landing was a revolving bookcase (*Curtain*) with multiple paperback editions and just down the corridor was Dame Agatha's bedroom, commandeered by her creation for the duration of *Dead Man's Folly*. Around the corner hung the tea-gown worn by Dame Agatha's mother in a photograph in *An Autobiography* and further along this corridor were the back stairs, similar to those used by Miss Marple at the climax of *Sleeping Murder*.

At the top of the stairs were two locked rooms, silent guardians of unimaginable literary treasure and heart's desire for every Agatha Christie enthusiast (but in reality accessible to very few). The bigger of the two contained a complete run of UK and US jacketed first editions, all signed, many with personal inscriptions, as well as the books published about the Queen of Crime and her work. The second room was long and narrow, with nothing but shelves and cupboards containing more books – hardback and paperback, first and Book Club editions, many signed; typescripts and manuscripts, letters and contracts, posters and playbills, photos and dust-jackets, scrapbooks and diaries. On a bottom shelf was an ordinary cardboard box with a collection of old exercise copybooks . . .

I lifted the box on to the floor, knelt down and removed the top exercise book. It had a red cover and a tiny white label with the number 31. I opened it and the first words that I read were 'The Body in the Library – People – Mavis Carr – Laurette King'. I turned over pages at random . . . 'Death on Nile – Points to be brought in . . . Oct 8th – Helen sequence from girl's point of view . . . The Hollow – Inspector comes to Sir Henry – asks about revolver . . . Baghdad Mystery May 24th . . . 1951 Play Act I – Stranger stumbling into room in dark – finds light – turns it on – body of man . . . A Murder has been arranged – Letitia Bailey at breakfast'.

All these tantalising headings were in just one Notebook and there were over 70 more still stacked demurely in their unprepossessing box. I forgot that I was kneeling uncomfortably on the floor of an untidy, dusty room, that downstairs Mathew was waiting for me to begin dinner, that outside in the November darkness the rain was now spattering the shuttered window. I knew now how I would spend the rest of the evening and most of the weekend. And, as it transpired, the next four years . . .

It was very late when I eventually, and reluctantly, went to bed that night. I had systematically gone through every page of every Notebook and as I climbed the winding stairs in the silent house I tried to retain as much of the fascinating information as I could remember from such a brief read-through. The fact that *Death on the Nile* was to have been a Marple story . . . that there were more than ten characters in the early stages of *Ten Little Niggers* . . . that I now knew her intentions for the ending of *Death Comes as the End* . . . that she toyed with various solutions for *Crooked House* . . .

Next morning Mathew took me walking in Greenway Gardens. We began at what used to be the stable block (and then a National Trust office and gift shop), past the tennis court (*Dead Man's Folly*) and walled garden with a view of the extensive greenhouses; past the croquet lawn and up behind the house and along the path to the High Garden with a magnificent view of the River Dart. Then we wound our way down to the Boathouse, the setting for ill-fated Marlene Tucker's death in *Dead Man's Folly*, and ended up in the Battery looking out over the river with the low wall where the vibrant Elsa Greer (*Five Little Pigs*) posed for the already-dying Amyas Crale many years earlier (see page 127). We walked back to the house along the path taken by doomed Caroline Crale from the same novel. As we approached the front of the house I remembered that this was Agatha Christie's holiday home, where she came to relax with her extended family. I could imagine those summers of 50 years earlier when there was tea on this very lawn, the thwack of ball on racquet from the tennis court, the click of ball on croquet mallet; where dogs sprawled lazily in the afternoon sun and rooks soared and cawed in the trees; where the sun glinted on the Dart and Cole Porter drifted over the lawn from the turntable as the butler prepared the table for dinner; and where the faint click of a typewriter could be heard through an upstairs window . . .

I spent almost 24 hours of that weekend in the fascinating room at the top of the stairs, emerging only to eat (and that at Mathew's insistence!) and sleep. I refused offers of lunch in Dartmouth and tea in the library with family friends; I eschewed polite after-dinner conversation and lingering breakfasts and Mathew's amused indulgence tacitly encouraged such bad-mannered behaviour. As carefully as Hercule Poirot in Roger Ackroyd's study I scrutinised the typescripts of *Curtain* and *Sleeping Murder*; the original and deleted scenes for the first draft of *The Mousetrap*; the extensively annotated manuscript of *Endless Night*; the original magazine appearance of 'The Disappearance of Mr Davenby' [sic]; the signed first-night programmes of *Death on the Nile* and *Appointment with Death*; the official scrapbook for the fiftieth book celebrations for *A Murder is Announced*; the Royal Premiere memorabilia for *Murder on the Orient Express*; and all the time, as Miss Lemon to her filing, I kept returning to the mesmerising Notebooks.

Among Agatha Christie's papers there still remains much work from her early days as a writer – some non-crime, some light-hearted, some borderline crime and her pre-Styles novel *Snow Upon the Desert*. Among the original typescripts of her short stories (some with textual differences from the printed versions) there was also 'The Incident of the Dog's Ball'. The existence of this story was known to Christie scholars, including my friend and fellow Christie enthusiast Tony Medawar, editor of *While the Light Lasts*, but its similarity to an already published work had always militated against its inclusion in any of the posthumous collections. I was convinced that this very resemblance, albeit with a major difference, made it of intense interest. You can now judge for yourself.

It was on a subsequent visit the following year that I made what I now think of as The Discovery. I spent the month of August 2006 in Greenway sorting and organising Dame Agatha's papers in preparation for their removal from the house before the restoration work began. Weekdays were often scenes of boisterous activity as surveyors and architects, workmen and volunteers could be found in any and every corner of the house, but weekends tended to be quiet and, although the gardens were open to the public on Saturdays, life in the house itself was more tranquil; indeed, so quiet was it, that it was possible to imagine that there was nobody else on the entire estate. On the afternoon of Saturday 19 August I was checking the collection of manuscripts and typescripts preparatory to listing them before storage. The only bound typescript of a short story collection, as distinct from novels, was *The Labours of Hercules* and I idly wondered how, if at all, it differed from the published version, knowing that stories that have been first published in magazines are often amended slightly when collected between hard covers. The Foreword and the early stories all tallied with the known versions but when I got to the twelfth, 'The Capture of Cerberus', the opening line ('Hercule Poirot sipped his aperitif and looked out across the Lake of Geneva . . .') was not familiar to me. As I read on, I realised that I was looking at something unimaginably unique – an unknown Poirot short story, one that had lain silently between its covers for over 60 years, had been lifted and carried and moved and re-shelved numerous times over that period, had been handled by more than one person and had still managed to evade attention until a summer afternoon almost 70 years after its creation. My self-imposed task of listing and sorting was abandoned and I sat down to read, for the first time since October 1975 and his last poignant words in *Curtain* ('Yes, they have been good days . . .'), an unknown and forgotten adventure of Hercule Poirot.

When, earlier in 2006, I had approached Mathew about the possibility of a book based on his grandmother's Notebooks, with his customary generosity he immediately agreed. And, shortly afterwards, HarperCollins was equally enthusiastic. The question of how to treat the two unpublished stories remained. I had gone through the Notebooks slowly and carefully and I realised that there were notes for both stories within their pages. Mathew agreed to their publication and I am very honoured that the initial appearance of two new stories from the Queen of Crime has been entrusted to me.

At the end of *The Mysterious Affair at Styles* Poirot tells Hastings, 'Never mind. Console yourself, my friend. We may hunt together again, who knows? And then . . .' Who knew, indeed, that almost a century after those words were written we would join Hercule Poirot in one more hunt . . . and then, unbelievably, just one more . . .

1

A Murder is Announced:
The Beginning of a Career

That was the beginning of the whole thing. I suddenly saw
my way clear. And I determined to commit not one murder,
but murder on a grand scale.

Ten Little Niggers, Epilogue

---◄○►---

SOLUTIONS REVEALED

Death on the Nile • *Evil under the Sun* • *The Hollow* • *Lord
Edgware Dies* • *The Murder at the Vicarage* • *The Mysterious
Affair at Styles* • *Ordeal by Innocence* • *Witness for
the Prosecution*

---◄○►---

The Golden Age of British detective fiction is generally
regarded as roughly the period between the end of the
First World War and that of the Second, i.e. 1920 to 1945.
This was the era of the country house weekend enlivened
by the presence of a murderer, the evidence of the ade-
noidal under-housemaid, the snow-covered lawn with no
footprints and the baffled policeman seeking the assistance
of the gifted amateur. Ingenuity reached new heights with
the fatal air embolism via the empty hypodermic, the

poison-smeared postage stamp, and the icicle dagger that evaporates after use.

During these years all of the names we now associate with the classic whodunit began their writing careers. The period ushered in the fiendish brilliance of John Dickson Carr, who devised more ways to enter and leave a locked room than anyone before or since; it saluted the ingenuity of Freeman Wills Crofts, master of the unbreakable alibi, and Anthony Berkeley, pioneer of multiple solutions. It saw the birth of Lord Peter Wimsey, created by Dorothy L. Sayers, whose fiction and criticism did much to improve the literary level and acceptance of the genre; the emergence of Margery Allingham, who proved, with her creation Albert Campion, that a good detective story could also be a good novel; and the appearance of Ngaio Marsh, whose hero, Roderick Alleyn, managed to combine the professions of policeman and gentleman. Across the Atlantic it welcomed Ellery Queen and his penultimate chapter 'Challenge to the Reader', defying the armchair detective to solve the puzzle; S.S. Van Dine and his pompous creation Philo Vance breaking publishing records; and Rex Stout's overweight creation Nero Wolfe, solving crimes while tending his orchid collection.

Cabinet ministers and archbishops extolled the virtues of a good detective story; poets (Nicholas Blake, otherwise Cecil Day Lewis), university dons (Michael Innes, otherwise Professor J.I.M. Stewart), priests (Rev. Ronald Knox), composers (Edmund Crispin, otherwise Bruce Montgomery) and judges (Cyril Hare, otherwise Judge Gordon Clark) contributed to and expanded the form. R. Austin Freeman and his scientific Dr John Thorndyke sowed the seeds of the modern forensic crime novel; Gladys Mitchell introduced a psychologist detective in her outrageous creation Mrs Bradley; and Henry Wade prepared the ground for the police procedural with his Inspector Poole. Books were presented in the form of correspondence in Sayers' *The Documents in the Case*, as verbatim question-and-answer evidence in Philip Macdonald's *The Maze* and, ultimately, as actual police dossiers complete with physical clues in the shape of telegrams and train tickets in Dennis Wheatley's *Murder off Miami*. Floor plans, clue-finders, timetables and footnotes proliferated; readers became intimately acquainted with the properties of arsenic, the interpretation of train timetables and the intricacies of the 1926 Legitimacy Act. Collins Crime Club and the Detection Club were founded; Ronald Knox issued a Detective Story Decalogue and S.S. Van Dine wrote his Rules.

And Agatha Christie published *The Mysterious Affair at Styles*.

Poirot Investigates . . .

In her *Autobiography* Christie gives a detailed account of the genesis of *The Mysterious Affair at Styles*. By now the main facts are well known: the immortal challenge – 'I bet you can't write a good detective story' – from her sister Madge, the Belgian refugees from the First World War in Torquay who inspired Poirot's nationality, Christie's knowledge of poisons from her work in the local dispensary, her intermittent work on the book and its eventual completion during a two-week seclusion in the Moorland Hotel, at the encouragement of her mother. This was not her first literary effort, nor was she the first member of her family with literary aspirations. Both her mother and sister Madge wrote, and Madge actually had a play, *The Claimant*, produced in the West End before Agatha did. Agatha had already written a long dreary novel (her own words) and a few stories and sketches. She had even had a poem published in the local newspaper. While the story of the bet is plausible, it is clear that this alone would not be spur enough to plot, sketch and write a successful book.

There was obviously an inherent gift and a facility with the written word.

Although she began writing the novel in 1916 (*The Mysterious Affair at Styles* is actually set in 1917), it was not published for another four years. And its publication was to demand consistent determination on its author's part as more than one publisher declined the manuscript. Until, in 1919, John Lane, The Bodley Head asked to meet her with a view to publication. But, even then, the struggle was far from over.

The contract, dated 1 January 1920, that John Lane offered Christie took advantage of her publishing naivety. (Remarkably, the actual contract is for *The Mysterious Affair of Styles*.) She was to get 10 per cent only after 2,000 copies were sold in the UK and she was contracted to produce five more titles. This clause led to much correspondence over the following years. Possibly because she was so delighted to be published or because she had no intention then of pursuing a writing career, it is entirely possible that she did not read the small print carefully.

When she realised what she had signed, she insisted that if she *offered* a book she was fulfilling her part of the contract whether or not John Lane accepted it. When John Lane expressed doubt as to whether *Poirot Investigates*, as a volume of short stories rather than a novel, should be considered part of the six-book contract, the by now confident writer pointed out that she had offered them a novel, the non-crime *Vision*, as her third title. The fact that the publishers refused it was, as far as she was concerned, their choice. It is quite possible that if John Lane had not tried to take advantage of his literary discovery she might have stayed longer with the company. But the prickly surviving correspondence shows that those early years of her career were a sharp learning curve in the ways of publishers – and that Agatha Christie was a star pupil. Within a relatively short space of time she is transformed from an awed and inexperienced neophyte perched nervously on the edge of a chair in John Lane's office into a confident and businesslike professional with a resolute interest in every aspect of her books – jacket design, marketing, royalties, serialisation, translation and cinema rights, even spelling.

Despite favourable readers' reports a year earlier, in October 1920 Christie wrote to Mr Willett of John Lane wondering if her book was 'ever coming out' and pointing out that she had almost finished her second one. This resulted in her receiving the projected cover design, which she approved. Ultimately, after a serialisation in 1920 in *The Weekly Times*, *The Mysterious Affair at Styles* was published later that year in the USA. And, almost five years after she began it, Agatha Christie's first book went on sale in the UK on 21 January 1921. Even after its appearance there was much correspondence about statements and incorrect calculations of royalties as well as cover designs. In fairness to John Lane, it should be said that cover design and blurbs were also a recurring feature of her correspondence with Collins throughout her career.

Verdict . . .

The readers' reports on the Styles manuscript were, despite some misgivings, promising. One gets right to the commercial considerations: 'Despite its manifest shortcomings, Lane could very likely sell the novel . . . There is a certain freshness about it.' A second report is more enthusiastic: 'It is altogether rather well told and well written.' And another speculates on her potential future 'if she goes on writing detective stories and she evidently has quite a talent for them'. They were much taken with the character of Poirot, noting 'the exuberant personality of M. Poirot who is a very welcome variation on the "detective" of romance' and 'a jolly little man in the person of has-been famous Belgian detective'. Although Poirot might take issue with the use of the description 'has-been', it was clear that his presence was a factor in its acceptance. In a report dated 7 October 1919 one very perceptive reader remarked, 'but the account of the trial of John Cavendish makes me suspect the hand of a woman'. (Because her name on the manuscript had appeared as A.M. Christie, another reader refers to Mr Christie.) All the reports agreed that Poirot's contribution to the Cavendish trial did not convince and needed revision.

They were referring to the denouement of the original manuscript, where Poirot's explanation of the crime comes in the form of his evidence given in the witness box during the trial of John Cavendish. This simply did not work, as Christie herself accepted, and Lane demanded a rewrite. She obliged and, although the explanation of the crime itself remains the same, instead of giving it in the form of evidence from the witness box Poirot holds forth in the drawing room of Styles, in the type of scene that was to be replicated in many later books.

Sutherland Scott, in his 1953 history of the detective story, *Blood in their Ink*, perceptively calls *The Mysterious Affair at Styles* 'one of the finest firsts ever written'. It contained some of the features that were to distinguish many of her later titles.

Poirot and The Big Four

Hercule Poirot

There is an irony in the fact that although Agatha Christie is seen as a quintessentially British writer, her most famous creation is 'foreign', a Belgian. The existence of detective figures with which she would have been familiar may have been a contributing factor. Poe's Chevalier Dupin, Robert Barr's

Eugène Valmont, Maurice Leblanc's Arsène Lupin and A.E.W. Mason's Inspector Hanaud of the Sûreté were already, in 1920, established figures in the world of crime fiction. And a title Christie specifically mentions in her *Autobiography* is Gaston Leroux's 1908 novel *The Mystery of the Yellow Room*, with its detective, Monsieur Rouletabille. Although largely forgotten nowadays, Leroux was also the creator of *The Phantom of the Opera*.

At the time it was also considered necessary for the detective figure to have a distinguishing idiosyncrasy, or, even better, a collection of them. Holmes had his violin, his cocaine and his pipe; Father Brown had his umbrella and his deceptive air of absent-mindedness; Lord Peter Wimsey had his monocle, his valet and his antiquarian book collection. Lesser figures had other no less distinctive traits – Baroness Orczy's Old Man in the Corner sat in an ABC Teashop and tied knots, Ernest Bramah's Max Carrados was blind and Jacques Futrelle's Professor Augustus S.F.X. Van Dusen was known as The Thinking Machine. So Poirot was created Belgian with his moustaches, his little grey cells, his over-weening vanity, both intellectual and sartorial, and his mania for order. Christie's only mistake was in making him, in 1920, a *retired* member of the Belgian police force; this, in turn, meant that by 1975 and *Curtain*, he was embarking on his thirteenth decade. Of course, in 1916 Agatha Christie had no idea that the fictional little Belgian would outlive herself.

Readability

As early as this first novel one of Christie's great gifts, her readability, was in evidence. At its most basic, this is the ability to make readers continue from the top to the bottom of the page and then turn that page; and then make them do that 200 times in the course of any, and in her case, every, book. This facility deserted her only in the very closing chapter of her writing career, *Postern of Fate* being the most challenging example. This gift was, with Christie, innate; and it is doubtful whether it can be learned anyway. Thirty years after *The Mysterious Affair at Styles* the reader at Collins, reporting on *They Came to Baghdad*, wrote in an otherwise damning report: 'It is eminently readable and passes the acid test of holding the interest throughout.'

Christie's prose, while by no means distinguished, flows easily, the characters are believable and differentiated, and much of each book is told in dialogue. There are no long-winded scenes of question-and-answer, no detailed scientific explanations, no wordy descriptions of people or places. But there is sufficient of each to fix the scene and its protagonists clearly in the mind. Every chapter, indeed almost every scene, pushes the story on towards a carefully prepared solution and climax. And Poirot does not alienate the reader with either the irritating facetiousness of Dorothy L. Sayers' Lord Peter Wimsey, the pedantic arrogance of S.S. Van Dine's Philo Vance or the emotional entanglements of E.C. Bentley's Philip Trent.

A comparison with almost any other contemporaneous crime title shows what a chasm existed between Christie and other writers, most of them long out of print. As illustration, the appearance of two other detective-story writers also coincided with the publication of *The Mysterious Affair at Styles*. Freeman Wills Crofts, a Dubliner, published *The Cask* in 1920 and H.C. Bailey published *Call Mr Fortune* the previous year. Crofts' detective, Inspector French, showed painstaking attention in following every lead, and specialised in the unbreakable alibi. However, this very meticulousness militated against an exciting reading experience. H.C. Bailey began his career as a writer of historical fiction but turned to crime fiction and issued his first collection of long short stories, *Call Mr. Fortune*, featuring his detective, Reginald

Fortune, in 1919. The two writers, although skilled plot tech-
nicians in both novel and short story form, lacked the vital
ingredient of readability. Nowadays their names are known
and admired only by aficionados of the genre.

Plotting

Christie's plotting, coupled with this almost uncanny readability, was to prove, over the next 50 years, a peerless combination. I hope to show, by an examination of her Notebooks,
that although this gift for plotting was innate and in profusion, she worked at her ideas, distilling and sharpening and
perfecting them, and that even the most inspired titles (e.g.
Crooked House, Endless Night, The A.B.C. Murders) were the
result of painstaking planning. The secret of her ingenuity
with plot lies in the fact that this dexterity is not daunting.
Her solutions turn on everyday information – some names
can be male or female, a mirror reflects but it also reverses, a
sprawled body is not necessarily a dead body, a forest is the
best hiding place for a tree. She knows she can depend on
our erroneous interpretation of an eternal triangle, an overheard argument or an illicit liaison. She counts on our
received prejudice that retired Army men are harmless buf-
foons, that quiet, mousy wives are objects of pity, that all
policemen are honest and all children innocent. She does
not mystify us with the mechanical or technical; or insult us
with the clichéd or the obvious; or alienate us with the terrifying or the gruesome.

In almost every Christie title the mise-en-scène features a
closed circle of suspects – a strictly limited number of potential murderers from which to choose. A country house, a
ship, a train, a plane, an island – all of these provided her
with a setting that limits the number of potential killers and
ensures that a complete unknown is not unmasked in the last
chapter. In effect, Christie says, 'Here is the flock of suspects

from which I will choose my villain. See if you can spot the black sheep.' It can be as few as four (*Cards on the Table*) or five (*Five Little Pigs*) or as many as the coach full of travellers in *Murder on the Orient Express*. *The Mysterious Affair at Styles* is typical of the country-house murders beloved of Golden Age writers and readers – a group of assorted characters sharing an isolated setting long enough for murder to be committed, investigated and solved.

Although an element of the solution in *The Mysterious Affair at Styles* turns on a scientific fact, it is not unfair as we are told from the outset of the investigation what the poison is. Admittedly, anyone with knowledge of toxicology has a distinct advantage, but the information is readily available. Other than this mildly controversial item, all the information necessary to arrive at the solution is scrupulously given – the coffee cup, the scrap of material, a fire lit during a July heatwave, the medicine bottle. And, of course, it is Poirot's passion for neatness that gives him the final proof – and in a way that was to be reused, ten years later, in the play *Black Coffee*. But how many readers will notice that Poirot has to tidy the mantelpiece twice, thereby discovering a vital link in the chain of guilt (Chapters 4 and 5)?

Fairness

Throughout her career Christie specialised in giving her readers the clues necessary to the solution of the crime. She was quite happy to provide the clue, firm in the knowledge that, in the words of her great contemporary R. Austin Freeman, 'the reader would mislead himself'. After all, how many readers will properly interpret the clue of the calendar in *Hercule Poirot's Christmas*, or the fur stole in *Death on the Nile*, or the love letters in *Peril at End House*? Or who will correctly appreciate the significance of the wax flowers in *After the Funeral*, or Major Palgrave's glass eye in *A Caribbean Mystery*, or the telephone call in *Lord Edgware Dies*, or the beer bottle in *Five Little Pigs?*

While not in the same class of 'surprise solution' as *Murder on the Orient Express*, *The Murder of Roger Ackroyd* or *Crooked House*, the solution to *The Mysterious Affair at Styles* still manages to surprise. This is due to the use of one of Christie's most effective ploys – the double-bluff. It is the first example in her work of this powerful weapon in the detective-story writer's armoury. Here the most obvious solution, despite an initial appearance of impossibility, transpires to be the correct one after all. In her *Autobiography* she explains that 'The whole point of a *good* detective story was that it must be somebody obvious but at the same time for some reason, you would then find that it was not obvious, that he could not possibly have done it. Though really, of course, he *had* done it.' She returned throughout her career to this type of solution; and particularly when the explanation revolves around a murderous alliance – *The Murder at the Vicarage*, *Evil under the Sun*, *Death on the Nile*. Lethal partnerships aside, *Lord Edgware Dies* and *The Hollow* also feature this device. And she can take the bluff one step further, as with *Ordeal by Innocence* and, devastatingly, *Witness for the Prosecution*.

In *The Mysterious Affair at Styles* we are satisfied that Alfred Inglethorp is both too obvious and too dislikeable to be the murderer; and, on a more mundane level, he was absent from the house on the night of his wife's death. So we discount him. As a further strengthening of the double-bluff, part of his plan depends on being suspected, arrested, tried and acquitted, thus ensuring his perpetual freedom. Unless carefully handled this solution runs the risk of producing an anticlimax. Here it is skilfully avoided by uncovering the presence of an unexpected co-conspirator in the person of hearty Evelyn Howard, who, throughout the novel, has denounced her employer's husband (her unsuspected lover) as a fortune hunter – as indeed he is.

Productivity

Although no one, least of all Christie herself, knew it at the time, *The Mysterious Affair at Styles* was to be the first in a substantial corpus of books that were to issue from her typewriter over the next 50-odd years. She was equally successful in the novel and the short story form and alone among her contemporaries she also conquered the theatre. She created two famous detectives, a feat not duplicated by other crime writers. During the height of her powers publication could hardly keep pace with creation – 1934 saw the publication of no fewer than four crime titles and a Mary Westmacott, the name under which she wrote six non-crime novels published between 1930 and 1956. And this remarkable output is also a factor in her continuing success. It is possible to read a different Christie title every month for almost seven years; and at that stage it is possible to start all over again safe in the knowledge that you will have forgotten the earliest. And it is possible to watch a different Agatha Christie dramatisation every month for two years. Very few writers, in any field, have equalled this record.

And so Christie's work continues to transcend every barrier of geography, culture, race, religion, age and sex; she is read as avidly in Bermuda as in Balham, she is read by grandparents and grandchildren, she is read on e-book and in graphic format in this twenty-first century as eagerly as in the green Penguins and *The Strand* magazine of the last. Why? Because no other crime writer did it so well, so often or for so long; no one else has ever matched her combination of readability, plotting, fairness and productivity.

And no one ever will.

Dumb Witness: The Evidence
of the Notebooks

Like a conjuror, he whipped from a drawer in the desk two
shabby exercise books.

The Clocks, Chapter 28

Although mentioned by both of her biographers, Janet
Morgan and Laura Thompson, Agatha Christie's Notebooks
remain a closely protected, and largely unknown, treasure.
After the death of her mother, Rosalind Hicks ensured their
safety in Greenway House and, with the exception of Torquay
Museum, they have never been publicly displayed. But
Christie does briefly mention them in her *Autobiography*:

*Of course, all the practical details are still to be worked out, and the
people have to creep slowly into my consciousness, but I jot down my
splendid idea in an exercise book. So far so good – but what I
invariably do is lose the exercise book. I usually have about half a
dozen on hand, and I used to make notes in them of ideas that had
struck me, or about some poison or drug, or a clever little bit of
swindling that I had read about in the paper. Of course, if I had
kept all these things neatly sorted and filed and labelled, it would
save me a lot of trouble. However, it is a pleasure sometimes, when*

looking vaguely through a pile of old note-books to find something scribbled down, as: Possible plot – do it yourself – girl and not really sister – August – *with a kind of sketch of a plot. What it's all about I can't remember now; but it often stimulates me, if not to write that identical plot, at least to write something else.*

A closer examination of some of these remarks will give a clearer idea of what she meant. Using Christie's own words as a guide, we can begin to see the part these Notebooks played in her creative process.

. . . idea in an exercise book . . .

Considered as the notes, drafts and outlines for the greatest body of detective fiction ever written (and in many cases, unwritten) these Notebooks are unique and priceless literary artefacts. Viewed as physical objects they are somewhat less impressive. They are before me as I write these words and, at a passing glance, look like the piles of exercise books gathered by teachers at the end of class in schools the world over. Because most of them are just that – exercise books. Red and blue and green and grey exercise books, coverless copybooks ruled with wide-spaced blue lines, small black pocket-sized notebooks: The Minerva, The Marvel, The Kingsway, The Victoria, The Lion Brand, The Challenge, The Mayfair exercise books, ranging in price from The Kingsway (Notebook 72) for 2d to The Marvel (Notebook 28) for a shilling (5p); Notebook 5 represented particularly good value at 4 for 7½d (3p). Inside covers often have 'useful' information – a map of the UK, capitals of the world, decimal conversion rates (obviously bought just before or after the introduction of decimal coinage in February 1971). There are covers illustrated by the New York skyline (Notebook 23) or a Mexican volcano (Notebook 18).

Some of them are more worthy recipients of their contents – hard-backed multi-paged notebooks with marbled covers or spiral binding with embossed covers; some are even grandly inscribed on the cover 'Manuscript'. Notebook 7 is described inside the back cover as 'spongeable PVC cover from WHS', and Notebook 71 is a 'Cahier' with 'Agatha Miller 31 Mai 1907' written on the cover and containing French homework from her time in Paris as a young woman. Notebook 31 is an impressive wine-coloured hardback from Langley and Sons Ltd., Tottenham Court Rd. and costing 1s 3d (6p).

In a few cases the very availability and unpretentiousness of the Notebooks are now a liability as some of them have suffered on their journey down the years – they have lost their covers (and perhaps some pages – who knows?), staples have become rusted, pencil has faded and in some cases the quality of the paper, combined with the use of a leaky biro, has meant that notes written on one page have seeped on to the reverse also. And, of course, as many of them date from the war years, paper quality was often poor.

It would seem that some Notebooks originally belonged to, or were temporarily commandeered by, Christie's daughter Rosalind, as her name and address in her own neat handwriting appears on the inside cover (Notebook 41). And Notebook 73, otherwise blank, has her first husband Archie Christie's name in flowing script inside the front cover. The name and address lines on the front cover of Notebook 19 have been filled in: 'Mallowan, 17 Lawn Road Flats'.

The number of pages Christie used in each Notebook varies greatly – Notebook 35 has 220 pages of notes while Notebook 72 has a mere five. Notebook 63 has notes on over 150 pages but Notebook 42 uses only 20. The average lies somewhere between 100 and 120.

Although they are collectively referred to as 'The Notebooks of Agatha Christie', not all of them are concerned with her literary output. Notebooks 11, 40 and 55 consist solely of chemical formulae and seem to date from her days as a student dispenser; Notebook 71 contains French homework and Notebook 73 is completely blank. Moreover, she often used them for making random notes, sometimes on the inside covers – there is a list of 'furniture for 48' [Sheffield Terrace] in Notebook 59; Notebook 67 has reminders to ring up Collins and make a hair appointment; Notebook 68 has a list of train times from Stockport to Torquay. And her husband Max Mallowan has written accurately in his small, neat hand, '*The Pale Horse*' on the front of Notebook 54.

what I invariably do is lose the exercise book . . .

In a career spanning over 55 years and two world wars, some loss is inevitable but the reassuring fact is that it seems to have happened so seldom. Of course, we cannot be sure how many Notebooks there should be, but the 73 we still have are an impressive legacy.

Nevertheless, nothing in the way of notes or outlines exists for *The Murder on the Links* (1923), *The Murder of Roger Ackroyd* (1926), *The Big Four* (1927) or *The Seven Dials Mystery* (1929). From the 1920s we have notes only for *The Mysterious Affair at Styles* (1920), *The Man in the Brown Suit* (1924), *The Secret of Chimneys* (1925) and *The Mystery of the Blue Train* (1928). When we remember that *The Murder of Roger Ackroyd* was published just before Christie's traumatic disappearance and subsequent divorce it is perhaps not surprising that these notes are no longer extant. The same applies to *The Big Four*, despite the fact that this episodic novel had appeared earlier as individual short stories. And there is nothing showing the genesis of the first adventure of Tommy and Tuppence in *The*

Secret Adversary (1922); for the 1929 collection *Partners in Crime*, there are only the sketchiest of notes. This is a particular disappointment as it might have given us an insight into the thoughts of Agatha Christie on her fellow writers, who are affectionately pastiched in this collection.

From the 1930s onwards, however, the only missing book titles are *Murder on the Orient Express* (1934), *Cards on the Table* (1936) and *Murder is Easy* (1939). (The latter appears merely as a passing reference in Notebook 66.) This would seem to suggest that very few notebooks were, in fact, lost. Apart from *Murder is Easy*, the other titles date from the mid-1930s and may well have been written up in the same notebook. But as the novels on either side of *Murder is Easy* all appear, why this title should be missing is something of a mystery in itself.

In some cases the notes are sketchy and consist of little more than a list of characters (*Death on the Nile* – Notebook 30). And some titles have copious notes – *They Came to Baghdad* (100 pages), *Five Little Pigs* (75 pages), *One, Two, Buckle my Shoe* (75 pages). Other titles outline the course of the finished book so closely that I am tempted to assume that there were earlier, rougher notes that have not survived. A case in point is *Ten Little Niggers* (aka *And Then There Were None*). In her *Autobiography* she writes: 'I had written the book *Ten Little Niggers* because it was so difficult to do that the idea fascinated me. Ten people had to die without it becoming ridiculous or the murderer becoming obvious. I wrote the book after a tremendous amount of planning.' Unfortunately, none of this planning survives. What there is in Notebook 65 (see Chapter 4) follows almost exactly the progress of the novel. It is difficult to believe that this would have been written straight on to the page with so few deletions or so little discussion of possible alternatives. Nor are there, unfortunately, any notes for the

It is a major disappointment that there remains nothing from the creation of two of Christie's most famous titles – *The Murder of Roger Ackroyd* and *Murder on the Orient Express*. These are among her most audacious constructions and a behind-the-scenes look could have been fascinating. About the latter we know absolutely nothing, as it is not mentioned even in passing. Notebook 67 does have a list of characters from *The Murder of Roger Ackroyd* but nothing more. There is, however, some background to its creation contained in an intriguing correspondence with Lord Mountbatten of Burma.

In a letter dated 28 March 1924 Mountbatten wrote to 'Mrs Christie, Author of The Man who was No. 4, c/o The Sketch' (this was a reference to the recently finished serial publication of *The Big Four* in that magazine). Writing in the third person, he expressed his admiration for Poirot and Christie and begged to offer an idea for a detective story. He explained that, although he had had a few stories published under a pseudonym, his career at sea did not leave a lot of time for writing.

Briefly, his idea was that Hastings, before he leaves for South America, should introduce a friend, Genny, to

dramatisation of this famous story. For the rest of her career we are fortunate to have notes on all of the novels. In the case of most of the later titles the notes are extensive and detailed – and legible.

Fewer than 50 of almost 150 short stories are discussed in the pages of the Notebooks. This may mean that, for many of them, Christie typed directly on to the page without making any preliminary notes. Or that she worked on loose pages that she subsequently discarded. When she wrote the

Poirot. When a murder occurs Poirot writes to inform Hastings and explains that Genny will write subsequent letters keeping him abreast of developments. The plot involves the drugging of the victim to appear dead; when the body is 'discovered', the murderer stabs him. Genny's alibi appears impeccable as he is with Poirot until the discovery. Only in the final chapter is Genny unmasked as the killer. As can be seen, Christie retained the underlying suggestion, the narrator/murderer idea. All the surrounding detail, however, was her embroidery on his basic pattern.

On 26 November 1969 Mountbatten wrote again to congratulate Christie on *The Mousetrap*'s seventeenth birthday. She replied within the week and apologised in case she had not acknowledged his suggestion of 45 years earlier (he subsequently assured her that she had), thanked him for his kind words and enclosed her latest book, *Hallowe'en Party* ('not as good as Roger Ackroyd but not too bad'). She also mentioned that her brother-in-law, James, had suggested a similar narrator/murderer plot to her around the same time, although she had thought then that it would be very difficult to carry off.

early short stories she did not consider herself a writer in the professional sense of the word. It was only after her divorce and the consequent need to earn her living that she realised that writing was now her 'job'. So the earliest adventures of Poirot as published in 1923 in *The Sketch* magazine do not appear in the Notebooks at all, although there are, thankfully, detailed notes for her greatest Poirot collection, *The Labours of Hercules* (see Chapter 11). And many of the ideas that she sketched for short stories did not make it

Newspapers
Toilet Paper
Salt, Pepper
Saucepan cleaner. ++
...
Casserole — ?

Electric Fire —

Sweep, brush
Dusters
Glass cloths
Teapot
Plates etc
Cedar Mop
Brass Polish
Funnel

Teapot
Plates etc
Tooth Glass

Saucepan Cleaners
Cedar Mop —
Brass Polish
...
...
Knives + forks
Salt & Pepper Castors.
Glass cloths.
Dusters —

L... wooden Spoons.

Mirror
Mats
Table ?

London   Car   Hair
Great Bag.
Marmalade —
Anthony's Picture —
Library book
Decanter
white wine
Cash P.O's

Wall-to —
Elephant Picture?
New Purse —
+ Travelling Jar.
Navy Sweater.
a hat?
Tweed 2 piece
Grey coat & skirt?
Yellow wool dress.
Books etc — Peter
Go through drawers.
Send Car in morning.
Selected clothes.
Small cloak.

Two examples of Agatha Christie, the housekeeper. The heading
'Wallingford' on the lower one confirms that they are both lists of items
to bring to or from her various homes.

any further than the pages of the Notebooks (see 'The House of Dreams', page 303).

There are notes on most of her stage work, including unknown, unperformed and uncompleted plays. There are only two pages each of notes for her most famous and her greatest play, *Three Blind Mice* (as it still was at the time of writing the notes) and *Witness for the Prosecution* respectively. But these are disappointingly uninformative, as they contain no detail of the adaptation, merely a draft of scenes without any of the usual speculation.

And there are many pages devoted to her *Autobiography*, her poetry and her Westmacott novels. Most of the poetry is of a personal nature as she often wrote a poem as a birthday present for family members. And, in the case of these poems, having little prior knowledge of the subject matter does not help when deciphering near-illegible handwriting. There are only 40 pages in total devoted to the Westmacott titles and no detailed planning. Of that relatively small number many are taken up with quotations that included possible titles. Many of these were not used but make for fascinating reading. And the notes for the *Autobiography* are, for the most part, diffuse and disconnected, consisting of what are, in effect, reminders to herself.

. . . I usually have about half a dozen on hand . . .

It could reasonably be supposed that each Agatha Christie title has its own Notebook. This is emphatically not the case. In only five instances is a Notebook devoted to a single title. Notebooks 26 and 42 are entirely dedicated to *Third Girl*; Notebook 68 concerns only *Peril at End House*; Notebook 2 is *A Caribbean Mystery*; Notebook 46 contains nothing but extensive historical background and a rough outline for *Death Comes as the End*. Otherwise, every Notebook is a fascinating record of a productive brain and an industrious professional. Some examples should make this clear.

Notebook 53 contains:
Fifty pages of detailed notes for *After the Funeral* and *A Pocket Full of Rye* alternating with each other every few pages
Rough notes for *Destination Unknown*
A short outline of an unwritten novel
Three separate and different attempts at the radio play *Personal Call*
Notes for a new Mary Westmacott
Preliminary notes for *Witness for the Prosecution* and *The Unexpected Guest*
An outline for an unpublished and unperformed play, *Miss Perry*
Some poetry

Notebook 13 contains:
Death Comes as the End – 38 pages
Taken at the Flood – 20 pages
Sparkling Cyanide – 20 pages
Mary Westmacott – 6 pages
Foreign Travel Diary – 30 pages
The Hollow, Curtain, N or M? – 4 pages each

Notebook 35 contains:
Five Little Pigs – 75 pages
One, Two, Buckle my Shoe – 75 pages
N or M? – 8 pages
The Body in the Library – 4 pages
25 pages of ideas

. . . if I had kept all these things neatly sorted . . .

One of the most appealing yet frustrating aspects of the Notebooks is the lack of order, especially dates. Although there are 73 Notebooks, we have only 77 examples of dates. And in many cases what dates we do have are incomplete. A page can be headed 'October 20th' or 'September 28th' or just '1948'. There are only six examples of complete (day/month/year) dates and they are all from the last ten years. In the case of incomplete dates it is sometimes possible to work out the year from the publication date of the title in question, but in the case of notes for an unpublished or undeveloped idea, this is almost impossible. This uncertainty is compounded for a variety of reasons.

First, use of the Notebooks was utterly random. Christie opened a Notebook (or, as she says herself, any of half a dozen contemporaneous ones), found the next blank page and began to write. It was simply a case of finding an empty page, even one between two already filled pages. And, as if that wasn't complicated enough, in almost all cases she turned the Notebook over and, with admirable economy, wrote from the back also. In one extreme case, during the plotting of 'Manx Gold' she even wrote sideways on the page! (Remember that many of these pages were filled during the days of rationing in the Second World War.) In compiling this book I had to devise a system to enable me to identify whether or not the page was an 'upside-down' one.

Second, because many of the pages are filled with notes for stories that were never completed, there are no publication dates as a guideline. Deductions can sometimes be made from the notes immediately preceding and following, but this method is not entirely flawless. A closer look at the contents of Notebook 13 (listed above) illustrates an aspect of this

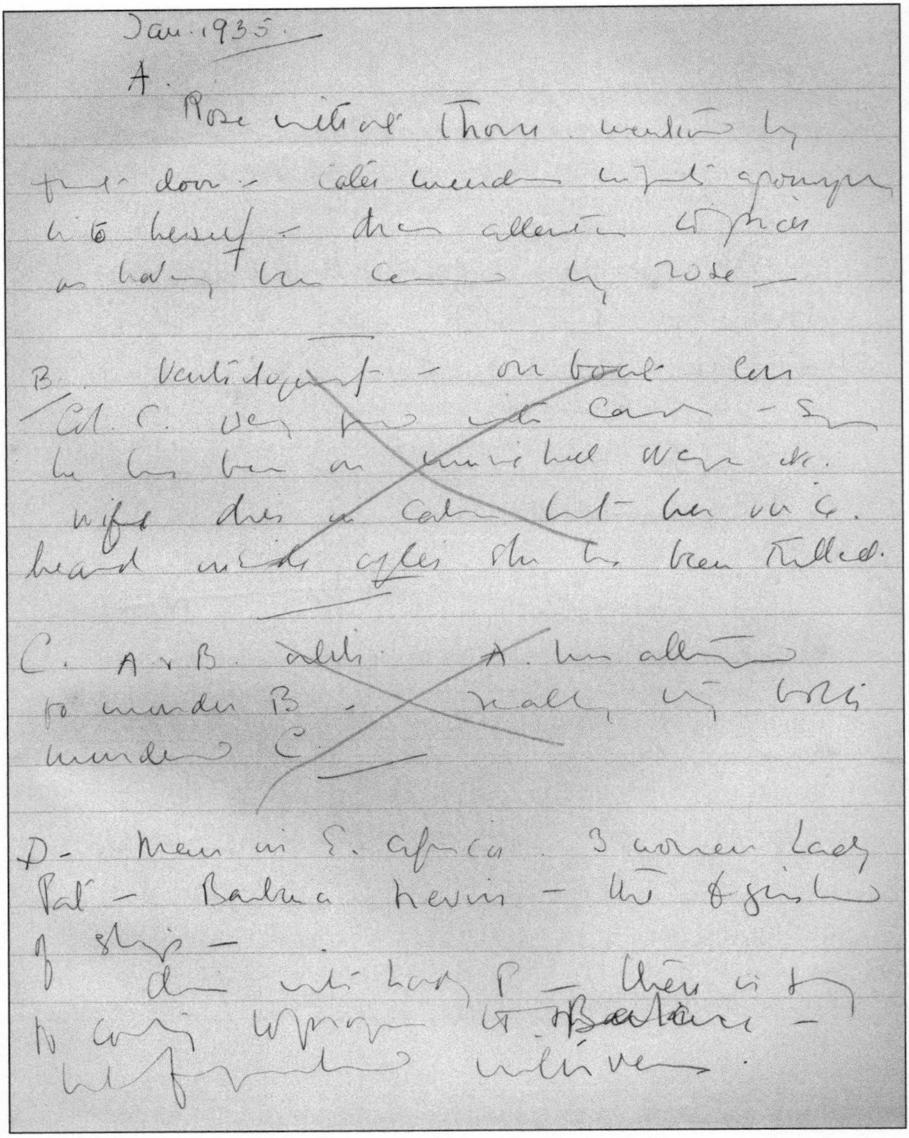

Jan. 1935.

A.
Rose without Thorn. *[handwritten text largely illegible]* by
front door — *[illegible]* gramophone
[illegible] to herself — then *[illegible]* to *[illegible]*
[illegible] the *[illegible]* by rose —

B. Ventriloquist — on board *[illegible]*
Col. C. *[illegible]* into cabin — *[illegible]*
he has been *[illegible]* *[illegible]*
wife dies in cabin but has *[illegible]* C.
heard *[illegible]* *[illegible]* she has been killed.

C. A + B decide *[illegible]* A has *[illegible]*
to murder B. *[illegible]* *[illegible]*
murder C. —

D. Men in E. Africa. 3 women Lady
Pat — Barbara Nevins — the *[illegible]* girl *[illegible]*
of ship —
[illegible] with Lady P — then *[illegible]*
[illegible] *[illegible]* *[illegible]* —
[illegible] *[illegible]* *[illegible]* .

This page, in Notebook 66, is from Christie's most prolific and ingenious period and list ideas that became Sad Cypress, 'Problem at Sea' *and* They Do It With Mirrors. *It was one of very few pages in the Notebooks to bear a date, and the stories were published between 1936 and 1952.*

nov 2nd 1973

Book of Stories

The White Horse stories.
First one

The White Horse Party
(Rather Similar to Jan Marple's Tuesday Night
Club)
Each story might be based on a
particular white Horse in England –
The White Horse in question plays a part in
Some Particular Incident – or Problem, or
Some Criminal happening – a likeness
to Mr Quin – – A White Horse always
partakes – a ghostly Side to it

*Another rare page with a date, demonstrating a marked change in
handwriting, these are among the last notes that Christie wrote and appear
in Notebook 7. Although she continued making notes, no new material
appeared later than* Postern of Fate, *published in October 1973.*

random chronology. Leaving aside *Curtain*, the earliest novel listed here is *N or M?* published in 1941 and the latest is *Taken at the Flood* published in 1948. But many of the intervening titles are missing from this Notebook – *Five Little Pigs* is in Notebook 35, *Evil under the Sun* in Notebook 39 and *Towards Zero* in Notebook 32.

Third, in many cases jottings for a book may have preceded publication by many years. The earliest notes for *The Unexpected Guest* are headed '1951' in Notebook 31, i.e. seven years before its first performance; the germ of *Endless Night* first appears, six years before publication, on a page of Notebook 4 dated 1961.

The pages following a clearly dated page cannot be assumed to have been written at the same time. For example:

page 1 of Notebook 3 reads 'General Projects 1955'
page 9 reads 'Nov. 5th 1965' (and there were ten books
  in the intervening period)
page 12 reads '1963'
page 21 reads 'Nov. 6 1965 Cont.'
page 28 is headed 'Notes on Passenger to Frankfort
  [sic] 1970'
page 36 reads 'Oct. 1972'
page 72 reads 'Book Nov. 1972'

In the space of 70 pages we have moved through 17 years and as many novels and, between pages 9 and 21, skipped back and forth between 1963 and 1965.

Notebook 31 is dated, on different pages, 1944, 1948 and 1951, but also contains notes for *The Body in the Library* (1942), written in the early days of the Second World War. Notebook 35 has pages dated 1947, sketching *Mrs McGinty's Dead*, and 1962, an early germ of *Endless Night*.

... and filed ...

Although the Notebooks are numbered from 1 through to 73, this numbering is completely arbitrary. Some years before she died, Christie's daughter Rosalind arranged, as a first step towards analysing their contents, that they should be numbered and that the titles mentioned within be listed. The analysis never went any further than that, but in the process every Notebook was allocated a number. This numbering is completely random and a lower number does not indicate an earlier year or a more important Notebook. Notebook 2, for instance, contains notes for *A Caribbean Mystery* (1964) and Notebook 3 for *Passenger to Frankfurt* (1972), while Notebook 37 contains a long, deleted extract from *The Mysterious Affair at Styles* (1920). As can be seen, therefore, the numbers are nothing more than an identification mark.

... and labelled ...

Some of the Notebooks show attempts on the part of the elderly Agatha Christie to impose a little order on this chaos. Notebook 31 has a loose-page listing inside the front cover in her own handwriting; others have typewritten page-markers indicating where each title is discussed. These brave attempts are rudimentary and the compiler (probably not Christie herself) soon wearied of the enormous task. Most Notebooks contain notes for several books and as three novels can often jostle for space among 20 pages, the page markers soon become hopelessly cumbersome and, eventually, useless.

To give some idea of the amount of information contained, randomly, within their covers, for the purposes of this book I created a table to index the contents of all of the Notebooks. When printed, it ran to 17 pages.

. . . something scribbled down . . .

Before discussing the handwriting in the Notebooks, it is only fair to emphasise that these were notes and jottings written as *aides-mémoire*. There was no reason to make an effort to maintain a certain standard of calligraphy as no one but Christie herself was ever intended to read it. As evidenced elsewhere (see Chapter 3) these were personal journals and not written for any purpose other than to clarify her thoughts.

Our handwriting changes as we age. The scrambled notes from college or university soon overtake the copperplate efforts of our early school days. Accidents, medical conditions and age all take their toll on our writing. In most cases it is safe to assert that as we get older our handwriting deteriorates. In the case of Agatha Christie the opposite is the case. At her creative peak (roughly 1930 to 1950) her handwriting is almost indecipherable. It looks, in many cases, like shorthand and it is debatable if even she could read some sections of it. I have no doubt that the reason for the scrawl was that, during these hugely prolific years, her fertile brain teemed with ideas for books and stories. It was a case of getting them on to paper as fast as possible. Clarity of presentation was a secondary consideration.

The conversion of the Notebooks into an easily readable format, for the purposes of this book, took over six months. A detailed knowledge of all of Dame Agatha's output was not just an enormous help but a vital necessity. It helped to know, for instance, that a reference to 'apomorphine' is not a misprint, a mistake or a mis-spelling but a vital part of the plot of *Sad Cypress*. But it did not help in the case of notes for an unpublished title or for ideas for a published work that she later discarded. As the weeks progressed I was surprised how used to her handwriting I became and I found converting the last batch of Notebooks considerably quicker than the first. I also discovered that if I left a seemingly indecipherable page and returned to it a few days later, I could often make sense of it. But some words or sentences still defied me and in a number of cases I had to resort to an educated guess.

From the late 1940s onwards her handwriting steadily 'improved' so that by the early 1950s and, for example, *After the Funeral* in Notebook 53, the notes could be read straight off by someone seeing them for the first time. She was ruefully aware of this herself. In November 1957, in a letter about *Ordeal by Innocence,* she writes, 'I am asking Mrs. Kirwan [her secretary Stella Kirwan] to type this to you knowing what my handwriting is like', and again in August 1970 she describes her own handwriting as 'overlarge and frankly rather illegible'. And she writes this *after* the improvement!

For some years, there has been a theory in the popular press that Agatha Christie suffered from dyslexia. I have no idea where this originated but even a cursory glance at the Notebooks gives the lie to this story. The only example that could be produced in evidence is her struggle with 'Caribbean' and 'Carribean' throughout the notes for *A Caribbean Mystery* – and I think in that she would not be alone!

. . . *a kind of sketch of a plot* . . .

Dotted irregularly throughout the Notebooks are brief jottings dashed down and often not developed any further at the time. This is what Christie means by 'a sketch of a plot'; these jottings were all she needed to stimulate her considerable imagination. The ideas below are reproduced exactly as they appear on the page of the Notebooks, and some of them occur in more than one Notebook (examples of similar jottings are given later in this book). All of them were to appear, to a greater or lesser degree, in her titles. The first two are major plot devices and the remaining two are minor plot features:

Poirot asks to go down to country – finds a house and various fantastic details [see *The Hollow* in Chapter 12]

Saves her life several times [see *Endless Night* in Chapter 12]

Dangerous drugs stolen from car [see Exhibit F: 'The House of Dreams']

Inquire enquire – both in same letter [see *A Murder is Announced* in Chapter 5]

. . . it often stimulates me, if not to write that identical plot at least to write something else . . .

Throughout her career one of Christie's greatest gifts was her ability to weave almost endless variations on seemingly basic ideas. Murderous alliances, the eternal triangle, victim-as-murderer, disguise – down the years she used and reused all these ploys to confound reader expectation. So when she writes about being stimulated to write 'something else' we know that she could do this effortlessly. Something as seemingly unimportant or uninspiring as the word 'teeth' could inspire her and, in fact, she used that very idea in at least two novels – *One, Two, Buckle my Shoe* and, as a minor plot element, in *The Body in the Library.*

Identical twins (one killed in railway smash) survivor – claims to be the rich one (teeth?)

Poor little rich girl – house on hill – luxury gadgets etc. – original owner

Stamp idea – man realises fortune – puts it on old letter – a Trinidad stamp on a Fiji letter

Old lady in train variant – a girl is in with her – later is offered a job at the village – takes it

As we shall see, the 'Stamp idea' features in a short story and a play over 15 years apart; the 'Old lady in train' ploy appears in two novels almost 20 years apart; and the 'Poor little rich girl' inspired a short story and, 25 years later, a novel.

EXHIBIT A:
THE DETECTION CLUB

'It's rather early to ring you up but I want to ask you a favour.'
'Yes?'
'It is the annual dinner of our Detective Authors' Club.'
Third Girl, Chapter 2

The Detection Club, as its name suggests, is a club for writers of detective stories. Although the exact date is uncertain, it was probably founded in 1929. Anthony Berkeley and Dorothy L. Sayers were two of the founders and by the early 1930s all of the major writers of detective fiction of the day, including Agatha Christie, were members. Only writers of classical detective fiction, as distinct from crime writers in general, were eligible to join. It was not a professional body campaigning to improve the lot of crime writers; rather it was a glorified dining club with G.K. Chesterton, creator of Father Brown, as its first President, followed in 1936 by E.C. Bentley, author of the famous *Trent's Last Case*, and, from 1958 to her death in 1976, Agatha Christie. She agreed to this role on the understanding that she would never have to give a speech. Membership was by invitation only and all new members had to undergo an initiation ceremony (designed by Dorothy L. Sayers), involving the President in ceremonial robes, a procession with candles and the initiate swearing an oath, while placing a hand on Eric the Skull, to uphold the club's rules.

Although these rules were unwritten and the ritual itself, designed by Sayers, light-hearted, the intentions behind them were serious and admirable. In an effort to raise the literary level of the detective story and to distinguish it from the thriller or 'shocker', candidates had to promise:

* to honour the King's English;
* never to conceal a vital clue from the reader;
* to adhere to detection as distinct from 'Divine Revelation, Feminine Intuition . . . Coincidence or Acts of God';
* to observe 'a seemly moderation in the use of Gangs, Death-Rays, Ghosts, Mysterious Chinamen and Mysterious Poisons unknown to Science';
* never to steal or disclose the plots of other members.

In the early days the Detection Club produced collaborative novels and, in more recent times, short story collections. In the early ventures different hands wrote succeeding chapters, each subsequent writer taking cognisance of the plot developments of his or her predecessor. Agatha Christie contributed to the three earliest publications, *The Scoop* in 1930, *Behind the Screen* the following year and the full-length novel *The Floating Admiral* in 1932. The first two shorter efforts were read in instalments on BBC radio and subsequently published in *The Listener*, finally appearing in book form in 1983. Apart from Christie, the collaborators on *The Scoop* were Dorothy L. Sayers, Anthony Berkeley, E.C. Bentley, Freeman Wills Crofts and Clemence Dane; Ronald Knox and Hugh Walpole replaced Crofts and Dane for *Behind the Screen*.

In the case of *The Floating Admiral* each contributor had to include a proposed solution as well as a chapter in an effort to prevent complications being introduced merely to make life difficult for the following contributor. Christie's contribution is, unfortunately, the shortest in the book, but her proposed solution is a typically ingenious one. However, she decided that the time and effort that went into one of these productions could be more profitably spent on her own writing and she politely declined to involve herself in any further titles.

The Detection Club in the Notebooks

The main reference to the Detection Club in the Notebooks is in Notebook 41, the first page of which is headed 'Ideas 1931' (despite the uncertainty about its date of foundation, by the time of this note the club was well established):

The 13 at Dinner

Detective story Club (?)
Miss Sayers and her husband – Poisons
Mr Van Dine and
Mr Wills Crofts and wife – Alibis
Mrs Christie
Mr Rhode
Mr and Mrs Cole
Mr Bentley
Miss Clemence Dane
Mr Berkeley and wife – fantastic writer

Coincidentally, the title *Thirteen at Dinner* was used in America two years later for Christie's 1933 novel *Lord Edgware Dies*. The US title refers to Chapter 15 of the book, where a character remarks that there were 13 guests at the dinner table on the evening of Lord Edgware's death, thereby giving Lady Edgware 12 witnesses. It is unlikely, however, that this is what Christie had in mind when she sketched the Detection Club idea.

Of the 13 people she lists who would have composed this party, most of them were her fellow-writers. 'Miss Sayers' is Dorothy L. Sayers – writer, dramatist, anthologist, theologian and scholar – Christie's great contemporary and one of the founders of the Detection Club. Although listed in Notebook 41 as 'Miss', Sayers had married Oswald Fleming in April 1926 but retained her maiden name for her professional activities.

'Mr Van Dine' was known to the reading public as S.S. Van Dine, creator of Philo Vance. The gap after his name would seem to indicate that Christie was not sure if he was married (he was), but the inclusion of his partner would have given 14 dinner guests – which perhaps accounts for the uncertainty. It is odd that Christie should have included Van Dine at all. She certainly read his novels – a few are on the shelves in Greenway House – as they were enormous bestsellers in their day, but he was not a member of the Detection Club as he lived in America.

'Mr Wills Crofts' was Freeman Wills Crofts, creator of Inspector French of Scotland Yard, a painstaking and thorough policeman whose speciality (as indicated) is the unbreakable alibi. Like Christie his first novel, *The Cask*, appeared in 1920 and is still considered a classic. He continued to write until his death in 1955, producing over 40 novels.

'Mr Rhode' is John Rhode, whose real name was Major Cecil John Charles Street and who also wrote as Miles Burton. Like Christie he was a Crime Club author for most of his career and altogether he wrote almost 150 novels under both names.

'Mr and Mrs Cole' was the husband-and-wife team of G.D.H. and Margaret Cole, detective novelists and Socialists. Although the pair were prolific, with 30 novels to their credit, their books are verbose, lifeless and long out of print.

'Mr Bentley' was E.C. Bentley, whose reputation as a detective novelist rests almost entirely on one novel, the classic *Trent's Last Case*. He also issued a book of short stories and co-wrote another title, *Trent's Own Case*, both featuring Philip Trent.

Clemence Dane is largely forgotten as a crime writer. *Enter Sir John*, filmed by Hitchcock as *Murder*, is her best-known title.

'Mr Berkeley' is Anthony Berkeley, who also wrote as Francis Iles. A very influential writer, he foresaw the emergence of the crime novel, as distinct from the detective novel, and his contribution to both branches of the genre is impressive. Alfred Hitchcock memorably filmed his Iles novel *Before the Fact* as *Suspicion*.

In addition to this list, Christie makes various allusions to her fellow Detection Club members in a range of works. *Partners in Crime*, Christie's 1929 Tommy and Tuppence collection of short stories, sees the Beresfords investigating their cases in the style of various detectives. She pastiches Berkeley in 'The Clergyman's Daughter' and Crofts in 'The Unbreakable Alibi' although, oddly, none of the other writers mentioned in Notebook 41 is featured.

An article Christie wrote for the Ministry of Information in 1945, 'Detective Writers in England', is also of note. Here the writers featured are Dorothy L. Sayers, John Dickson Carr, H.C. Bailey, Ngaio Marsh, Austin Freeman and Margery Allingham – Sayers being the only writer common to the article and Notebook 41, although all were members of The Detection Club. This may be due to the fact that Christie had more dealings with Sayers, mostly during the planning of the collaborative titles *The Floating Admiral*, *The Scoop* and *Behind the Screen*, all of which were masterminded by Sayers.

Chapter 6 of *The Body in the Library* also mentions Sayers, H.C. Bailey and John Dickson Carr (as well as Christie herself); and 'The Flock of Geryon', the tenth *Labour of Hercules*, mentions Sherlock Holmes, Mr Fortune, the creation of Bailey, and Sir Henry Merrivale, the creation of Dickson Carr. Dickson Carr's *The Burning Court* is also a minor clue in *Evil under the Sun* and the same writer gets a further mention in *The Clocks*.

A single sentence each in Notebooks 18 and 35 also mentions the Detection Club, both with the same idea:

Guest night at the Det[ection] Club during ritual –
Mrs. O[liver]'s 6 guests

Detection Club Murder – Mrs Oliver – her two guests –
someone killed when the Ritual starts

Guest Night was, not surprisingly, an evening when members of the club could invite a guest for dinner. The 'ritual' was the ceremony, involving the swearing of an 'oath' with Eric the Skull standing in for the Bible, at which new members were initiated. As a detective novelist Mrs Oliver would, of course, have been a member of the club.

3

The Moving Finger:
Agatha Christie at Work

'I mean, what *can* you say about how you write your books?
What I mean is, first you've got to think of something, and
then when you've thought of it you've got to force yourself
to sit down and write it. That's all.'

Dead Man's Folly, Chapter 17

◄○►

SOLUTIONS REVEALED
Crooked House • *Endless Night* • *Mrs McGinty's Dead* •
A Murder is Announced • *Murder in Mesopotamia* •
One, Two, Buckle my Shoe

◄○►

How did Agatha Christie produce so many books of such a
high standard over so many years? A close examination of
her Notebooks will reveal some of her working methods,
although, as will be seen, 'method' was not her strong suit.
But that, I contend, *was* her secret – even though she was
unaware of this paradox herself.

Dumb Witnesses

In February 1955, on the BBC radio programme *Close-Up*, Agatha Christie admitted, when asked about her process of working, that 'the disappointing truth is that I haven't much method'. She typed her own drafts 'on an ancient faithful typewriter that I've had for years' but she found a Dictaphone useful for short stories. 'The real work is done in thinking out the development of your story and worrying about it until it comes right. That may take quite a while.' And this is where her Notebooks, which are not mentioned in the interview, came in. A glance at them shows that this is where she did her 'thinking and worrying'.

Up to the mid-1930s her Notebooks are succinct outlines of the novels with relatively little evidence of rough notes or speculation, deletions or crossing-out. And, unlike later years, when each Notebook contains notes for a few titles, at this early stage the bulk of the notes for any title is contained within one Notebook. These outlines follow closely the finished novel and would seem to indicate that the 'thinking and worrying' was done elsewhere and subsequently destroyed or lost. Notes for *The Mysterious Affair at Styles* (Notebook 37), *The Man in the Brown Suit* (Notebook 34), *The Mystery of the Blue Train* (Notebook 54), *The Murder at the Vicarage* (Notebook 33), *The Sittaford Mystery* (Notebook 59), *Peril at End House* (Notebook 68) and *Lord Edgware Dies* (Notebook 41) are accurate reflections of the novels. But from the mid-1930s and *Death in the Clouds* on, the Notebooks include all her thoughts and ideas, accepted or rejected.

She did all her speculating on the page of the Notebook until she knew, in her own mind at least, where she was going with a plot, although it is not always obvious from the Notebook alone which plan she has adopted. She worked out variations and possibilities; she selected and discarded; she explored and experimented. She 'brainstormed' on the page, and then sorted the potentially useful from the probably useless. Notes for different books overlap and intersect; a single title skips throughout a Notebook or, in extreme cases, through 12 Notebooks.

When asked by Lord Snowdon in a 1974 interview how she would like to be remembered, Agatha Christie replied, 'I would like to be remembered as a rather good writer of detective stories.' This modest remark, coming after a lifetime as a bestseller in bookshop and theatre, is unconscious confirmation of another aspect of Christie evident from the Notebooks – her lack of self-importance. She saw these unpretentious jotters as no more precious a tool in her working life than the pen or pencil or biro she grabbed to fill them. She employed her Notebooks as diaries, as scribblers, as telephone-message pads, as travel logs, as household accounts ledgers; she used them to draft letters, to list Christmas and birthday presents, to scribble to-do reminders, to record books read and books to read, to scrawl travel directions. She sketched maps of Warmsley Heath (*Taken at the Flood*) and St Mary Mead in them; she doodled the jacket design for *Sad Cypress* and the stage setting for *Afternoon at the Seaside* in them; she drew diagrams of the plane compartment from *Death in the Clouds* and the island from *Evil under the Sun* in them. Sir Max used them to do calculations, Rosalind used them to practise her handwriting and everyone used them as bridge-score keepers.

Pigeon among the Cats

Part of the pleasure of working with the Notebooks is derived from the fact that when you turn a page you never know what you will read. The plotting of the latest Poirot novel can be interrupted by a poem written for Rosalind's birthday; a page headed, optimistically, 'Things to do' is sandwiched between the latest Marple and an unfinished stage play. A phone number and message break the flow of a new radio play; a list of new books disrupts the intricacies of a murderer's timetable; a letter to *The Times* disturbs the new Westmacott novel.

You could discover the original ending to *Death Comes as the End* or you could try solving a crossword clue ('– I – T – –'); you might stumble across the draft of an unfinished Poirot story or a list of tulips ('Grenadier – Really scarlet, Don Pedro – good bronze purple'); you could read a letter to *The Times* ('I have read with great interest the article written by Dr. A. L. Rowse on his discovery of the identity of Shakespeare's Dark Lady of the Sonnets') or a sketch for *Mousetrap* II.

A random flick through the Notebooks illustrates some of these points. A page of jottings – a short list of books (all published in 1970), arrangements for Christmas shopping and a quotation that caught her attention – interrupts the notes for *Nemesis*:

At some place in (Ireland?) (Scotland?) (Cornwall?) a family lives – writes her to stay for a day or two or weekend – rejoin tour later – (Has she been taken slightly ill? fever? Sickness – some drug administered)

Notes on books
Deliverance – James Dickey
The Driver's Seat – Muriel Spark
A Start in Life – Alan Sillitoe

Let's go to Syon Lodge Ltd. (Crowthers) – 20 mins. by car from Hyde Park Corner – on way to airport – Xmas shopping? Collingwood in Conduit St

Remark made by McCauley 'To be ruled by a busybody is more than human nature can bear'

One of the many lists of books scattered throughout the Notebooks, this one across two pages lists crime novels from the late 1930s/early 1940s, including titles by Simenon, Wentworth, Innes, Ferrars and Sayers . . .

From Collins

Poetry of Paderewsky.
Pamela Frankau Wright
  Disappearing Masterpieces.
  Caroline of England:
  The Dark Star
  Brief Return

Buy The Idea of a Christian Society

Give a Corpse a Bad Name.
The Clock Strikes Twelve.
Mr Skeffington. Knobel.
Maid No More. Helen Simpson.
Idle Apprentice.
Good Night, Sweet Ladies.
The Edge of Running Water.
Mansion for Souls.

. . . Her publishers would send Agatha books to read, and indeed the page above is headed 'From Collins'.

What is this focal point of (an accused person imprisoned) –
R's son – a failure – R. always knew when he was lying

The plotting of *One, Two, Buckle my Shoe* and a listing of possible short story ideas is interrupted by a social message from her great friend Nan Gardner:

H.P. not satisfied – asks about bodies – at last – one is found

All away weekend – can we go Thursday Nan

Ideas (1940)
A. 2 friends – arty spinsters – <u>one</u> a crook – (other camouflage) they give evidence – possible for Miss Marple

A list of ideas, some of which became *Death in the Clouds, The A.B.C. Murders* and 'Problem at Sea', is put on hold for three pages of Christmas presents:

C. Stabbed by an arrow – Stabbed by dart (poison) from blow pipe

Jack [her brother in law] – Dog?
Mrs E – Menu holders
Aunt Min – blotter and notepaper stand
Barbara – bag and scarf
Joan – Belt?

D. Ventriloquist

E. Series of murders – P gets letter from apparent maniac – First – an old woman in Yorkshire

Three Act Tragedy is preceded by an address and phone number:

Toby, 1 Granville Place, Portman Street Mayfair 1087

P suggests Egg should tackle Mrs Dacres

Travel details appear in the middle of 'The Capture of Cerberus' ('Robin' was possibly Robin McCartney, who drew the jacket designs for *Death on the Nile*, *Murder in Mesopotamia* and *Appointment with Death*):

> Young widow – husband missing believed killed – P sees him in 'Hell'
>
> Any Thursday by afternoon train Robin
>
> Combine with idea of man who has gone under – Dead? A waiter in Hell?

As can be seen, Christie's creativity was not exclusive – she was able to plot a murder while making a social appointment, or consider a murder weapon while compiling a reading list, or mull over a motive while transcribing travel directions. Throughout the Notebooks she is Agatha Christie, Queen of Crime while always remaining Agatha, the family member.

Motive and Opportunity

One of her most personal creations, Ariadne Oliver, is generally accepted as Christie's own alter ego. Mrs Oliver is a middle-aged, successful and prolific writer of detective fiction and creator of a foreign detective, the Finnish Sven Hjerson. She hates literary dinners, making speeches, or collaborating with dramatists; she has written *The Body in the Library* and doesn't drink or smoke. The similarities are remarkable. There can be little doubt that when Mrs Oliver speaks we are listening to Agatha Christie.

In Chapter 2 of *Dead Man's Folly* Mrs Oliver shrugs off her ingenuity:

> *'It's never difficult to think of things,' said Mrs Oliver. 'The trouble is that you think of too many, and then it all becomes too*

complicated, so you have to relinquish some of them and that is rather agony.'

And again, later in Chapter 17 she says:

'I mean, what can you say about how you write your books? What I mean is, first you've got to think of something, and then when you've thought of it you've got to force yourself to sit down and write it. That's all.'

It was as simple as that and, for 55 years, exactly what her creator did.

The process of production was, as we have seen, random and haphazard. And yet, this seeming randomness was transformed into an annual bestseller and, for many years, into more than one bestseller. For over 50 years she delivered the latest 'Christie for Christmas' to her agent; for 20 years she presented London's West End with one box-office success after another; she kept magazine editors busy editing her latest offering. And all of them – novels, short stories and plays – flow with the fluid precision of the Changing of the Guard.

So although it is true that she had no particular method, no tried and true system that she brought with her down the long years of her career, we know this appearance of indiscriminate jotting and plotting is just that – an appearance. And eventually we come to the realisation that, in fact, this very randomness *is* her method; this is how she worked, how she created, how she wrote. She thrived mentally on chaos, it stimulated her more than neat order; rigidity stifled her creative process. And it explains how the Notebooks read from both ends, how they leap from one title to another on the same page, how different Notebooks repeat and develop the same ideas and why her handwriting can be impossible to read.

Notebook 15 and the plotting of *Cat Among the Pigeons* illustrate some of these points. She talks to herself on the page:

> How should all this be approached? – in sequence? Or followed up backwards by Hercule Poirot – from disappearance . . . at school – a possibly trivial incident but which is connected with murder? – but murder of whom – and why?

She wonders and speculates and lists possibilities:

> Who is killed?
> Girl?
> Games mistress?
> Maid?
> Foreign Mid East ?? who would know girl by sign?
> Or a girl who ?
>
> Mrs. U sees someone out of window – could be
>   New Mistress?
>   Domestic Staff?
>   Pupil?
>   Parent?
>
> The Murder –
> Could be   A girl (resembles Julia/resembles Clare?
>   A Parent – sports Day
>   A Mistress
>
> Someone shot or stalked at school Sports?
> Princess Maynasita there –
> or – an actress as pupil
> or – an actress as games mistress

She reminds herself of work still to be done:

> Tidy up – End of chapter
>
> Chapter III – A good deal to be done –
>
> Chapter IV – A good deal to be worked over – (possibly end chapter with 'Adam the Gardener' – listing mistresses – (or next chapter)
>
> Chapter V – Letters fuller
>
> Notes on revision – a bit about Miss B
>
> Prologue – Type extra bits
>
> Chapter V – Some new letters

And for some light relief she breaks off to solve a word puzzle. In this well-known conundrum the test is to use all of the letters of the alphabet in one sentence. In her version she has an alternate answer although she is still missing the letter Z.

A D G J̶ L M̶ P̶ S̶ V Y Z

THE QUICK BROWN FOX JUMPS over gladly

Remembered Deaths

In *Cards on the Table* Mrs Oliver is asked if she has ever used the same plot twice.

> 'The Lotus Murder,' murmured Poirot, 'The Clue of the Candle Wax.'
> Mrs Oliver turned on him, her eyes beaming appreciation.
> 'That's clever of you – really very clever of you. Because, of course, those two are exactly the same plot – but nobody else has seen it. One

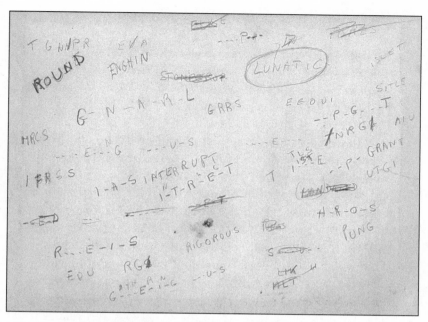

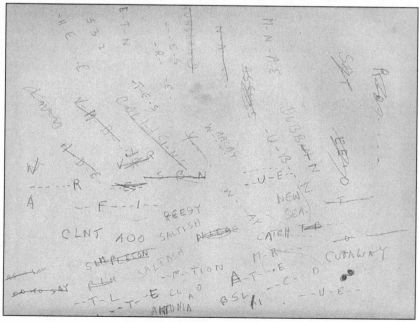

Two pages of random word puzzles, probably the rough work for a crossword.

is stolen papers at an informal weekend-party of the Cabinet, and the other's a murder in Borneo in a rubber planter's bungalow.'

'But the essential point on which the story turns is the same,' said Poirot. 'One of your neatest tricks.'

So it is with Christie. She reused plot devices throughout her career; and she recycled short stories into novellas and novels – she often speculates in the Notebooks about the expansion or adaptation of an earlier title. The Notebooks demonstrate how, even if she discarded an idea for now, she left everything there to be looked at again at a later stage. And when she did that, as she wrote in her *Autobiography*, 'What it's all about I can't remember now; but it often stimulates me.' So she used the Notebooks as an *aide-mémoire* as well as a sounding board.

The first example dates from the mid-1950s and relates to the short stories 'Third Floor Flat' and 'The Adventure of the Baghdad Chest'; it is surrounded by notes for 'Greenshaw's Folly' and *Four-Fifty from Paddington*. The second example, concerning 'The Adventure of the Christmas Pudding', is from early 1960 and the last one, concerning 'The Shadow on the Glass', probably from 1950:

Development of stories

3rd Floor Flat – murder committed earlier – return to get post and also footprints etc. accounted for – service lift idea? Wrong floor

Baghdad Chest or a screen?
Idea? A persuades B hide B
Chest or screen as Mrs B – having affair with C – C gives party – B and A drop in – B hides A – kills him – and goes out again

Extended version of Xmas Pudding – Points in it of importance
A Ruby (belonging to Indian Prince – or a ruler just married?)
in pudding

A book or a play from The Shadow on the Pane idea? (Mr Q)

The ABC of Murder

One system of creation that Christie used during her most prolific period was the listing of a series of scenes, sketching what she wanted each to include and allocating to each individual scene a number or a letter; this neat idea, in the days before computers with a 'cut and paste' facility, may have been inspired by her play-writing experience. She would subsequently reorder those letters to suit the purposes of the plot. In keeping with her creative and chaotic process, this plan was not always followed and even when she began with it, she would sometimes abandon it later for a more linear approach (see *Crooked House* below). And sometimes the pattern in the finished book would not exactly follow the sequence she had originally mapped out, perhaps due to subsequent editing.

The following, from Notebook 32, is a perfect example of this method in practice. It is part of the plotting of *Towards Zero* (see also Chapter 10).

E. Thomas and Audrey what's wrong? She can't tell him. He stresses I <u>know</u>, my dear – I know – But you must begin to live again. Something about 'died' a death – (meaning Adrian – somebody like N[evile] ought to be dead)
F. Mary and Audrey – suggestion of thwarted female – 'Servants even are nervous'
G. Coat buttons incident
H. Moonlight beauty of Audrey

The following are examples of Christie's reworked ideas, many of which are discussed elsewhere in this book. Some elaborations are obvious:

'The Case of the Caretaker'/*Endless Night*

'The Mystery of the Plymouth Express'/*The Mystery of the Blue Train*

'The Market Basing Mystery'/'Murder in the Mews'

'The Submarine Plans'/'The Incredible Theft'

'The Mystery of the Baghdad Chest'/'The Mystery of the Spanish Chest'

'Christmas Adventure'/'The Adventure of the Christmas Pudding'

'The Greenshore Folly' (unpublished)/*Dead Man's Folly*

In other cases she challenged herself when adapting and expanding by changing the killer:

The Secret of Chimneys/Chimneys

'The Second Gong'/'Dead Man's Mirror'

'Yellow Iris'/*Sparkling Cyanide*

'The Incident of the Dog's Ball'/*Dumb Witness* (see Appendix)

Some stage versions differ from their source novels . . .

Appointment with Death presents a new villain with a compelling and daring solution.

The Secret of Chimneys introduces many variations on the original novel, including a new killer.

Ten Little Niggers unmasks the original killer within a very different finale.

Meanwhile, there are more subtle links between certain works:

The Mysterious Affair at Styles, Death on the Nile and *Endless Night* are all essentially the same plot.

The Man in the Brown Suit, The Murder of Roger Ackroyd and *Endless Night* all share a major plot device.

Evil under the Sun and *The Body in the Library* feature a common ploy.

After the Funeral and *They Do It with Mirrors* are both based on the same trick of misdirection.

Murder on the Orient Express, At Bertram's Hotel and, to a lesser extent, *The Hollow* are all built on a similar foundation.

Three Act Tragedy, Death in the Clouds and *The A.B.C. Murders* all conceal the killer in similar surroundings.

And there are other examples of similarities between short stories and novels that have escaped notice in previous studies of the Queen of Crime:

'The Tuesday Night Club'/*A Pocket Full of Rye*

'A Christmas Tragedy'/*Evil under the Sun*

'Sing a Song of Sixpence'/*Ordeal by Innocence*

'The Love Detectives'/*The Murder at the Vicarage*

Points

Mr T – A. Talk with Lady T – asks about Mary
B. The story of murder led up to how?
C. Royde and justice (after Mr T has said: Many
murders known to police)
D. Hotel – his rooms are on top floor

Work out sequence of evening
G. H. A. D. C. B. ~~G. H.~~

It is notable how the E F G H scenes appear on an earlier page and the A B C D scenes on a later one. After they have all been tabulated, she then rearranges them to give the sequence she desires. At first, she intended the G and H scenes to follow A D C B but changed her mind, crossed them out and transposed them, squeezing them in, in front, at the left-hand margin of the page. A study of the relevant second section of the novel – 'Snow White and Red Rose' – will show that she followed this plan exactly:

G. Coat buttons	V
H. Moonlight	V
A. Lady T	VI
D. Hotel	VI
C. Royde	VI
B. Lead up	VI
F. Mary and Audrey	VII
E. Thomas and Audrey	VIII

Work out sequence of evening G. H. A. D. C. B. ~~G. H.~~ [F E]

She follows this scheme in the plotting of, among others, *Sparkling Cyanide, One, Two, Buckle my Shoe* and *Crooked House*. But with her chaotic approach to creativity and creative approach to chaos, she sometimes abandons it.

Middle Sequence.

Points

Mr T — A/ Talk with Lady T —
Anxious about Mary. She says
need companion &
B/ The story of murder dealt proved
false.

Led up to — How?

C Royde Hypersice (after
Mr T has said: Many
murderers known to police)

D Hotel — His rooms are
on Top floor —

Work out Sequence of Evening.
G.H.A. D.. C. B. G.H.
Drinks etc. Girls go to bed — Nevile Come
off. up. — He a Ted — Royde. has some off.

Detailed plotting for Towards Zero *– see opposite page.*

Notebook 14 shows this scheme, up to a point, in use for *Crooked House* (see also Chapter 4). But this time she has added further complications – AA and FF. Ultimately she dispensed with the reordering of the letters and just reordered the scenes without the alphabetical guideline. And the AA and FF were merely afterthoughts to be inserted at a later stage.

A. Inquires into Ass[ociated] Cat[ering] – discreet at first – Chartered Accountant will get us what we want [Chapter 10/11]

AA Also Brenda – femme fatale – are sorry for etc. [Chapter 9]

B. Later? – ~~on its~~ In Queer St. – Get Roger there – Roger – his story – etc. [Chapter 11]

C. Child's evidence – best evidence – there is – no good in court – children don't like being asked direct questions. To you she was showing off [Chapter 12]

D. Charles and Josephine – asks about letters – I was making it up – won't tell you – you shouldn't have told police [Chapter 13]

E. Charles and Eustace – (Listens outside door – really a boring teacher) Eustace – his views – scornful of Josephine [Chapter 16]

F. Charles and Edith – this side idolatry – asks Philip – you mustn't be deterred by his cold manner – really cared for his father – Philip is jealous of Roger [Chapter 14]

FF. Question as to saving Ass. Cat. Roger refuses – Clemency backs him up – Is very definite about it

[Chapter 14. There are indications in Notebook 14 that she intended this to form part of H below]

G. Magda and Charles – Edith didn't hate him – in love with him – would have liked to marry him [Chapter 15]

H. Charles and Clemency – her total happiness in marriage – how Roger would have been happy away from it all – Josephine writing in her book [Chapter 14]

I. A.C. says – be careful of the child – there's a poisoner about [Chapter 12]

J. The weight over the door (if J) or definitely dies – little black book missing [Chapter 18]

K. Charles and Sophia Murder – what does murder do to anyone? [Chapter 4]

The notes for *Crooked House* also illustrate a seemingly contradictory and misleading aspect of the Notebooks. It is quite common to come across pages with diagonal lines drawn across them. At first glance it would seem, understandably, that these were rejected ideas but a closer look shows that the exact opposite was the case. A line across a page indicates Work Done or Idea Used. This was a habit through her most prolific period although she tended to leave the pages, used or not, unmarked in her later writing life.

Ten Little Possibilities

In 'The Affair at the Bungalow', written in 1928 and collected in *The Thirteen Problems* (1932), Mrs Bantry comes up with reasons for someone to steal their own jewels:

> *'And anyway I can think of hundreds of reasons. She might have wanted money at once . . . so she pretends the jewels are stolen and sells them secretly. Or she may have been blackmailed by someone who threatened to tell her husband . . . Or she may have already sold the jewels . . . so she had to do something about it. That's done a good deal in books. Or perhaps he was going to have them reset and she'd got paste replicas. Or – here's a very good idea – and not so much done in books – she pretends they are stolen, gets in an awful state and he gives her a fresh lot.'*

the A. B. C. Murder.

Chapter I.

Hastings — his return to the
Argentine — Poirot — as young
as ever — Kadee chair. P. explains
false mustaches! P. replies — idea
in honour.

not really working. my case etc.
Hastings family prepares itself!
The Letter.
a robbery.
he — a murder.

Chapter II.
Japp — he comes round.
The 14th notes happens suddenly.
telephone — an old woman —
Mrs Archer — head bashed in —

The opening of The A. B. C. Murders *(note the reference to a
single 'Murder'), illustrating the use of crossing-out as an indication
of work completed.*

AGATHA CHRISTIE AT WORK

In *Third Girl* (1966) Norma Restarick comes to Poirot and tells him that she might have committed a murder. In Chapter 2, Mrs Ariadne Oliver, that well-known detective novelist, imagines some situations that could account for this possibility:

> *Mrs Oliver began to brighten as she set her ever prolific imagination to work. 'She could have run over someone in her car and not stopped. She could have been assaulted by a man on a cliff and struggled with him and managed to push him over. She could have given someone else the wrong medicine by mistake. She could have gone to one of those purple pill parties and had a fight with someone. She could have come to and found she'd stabbed someone. She . . . might have been a nurse in the operating theatre and administered the wrong anaesthetic . . .'*

In Chapter 8 of *Dead Man's Folly* (1956) Mrs Oliver again lets her imagination roam when considering possible motives for the murder of schoolgirl Marlene Tucker:

> *'She could have been murdered by someone who just likes murdering girls . . . Or she might have known some secrets about somebody's love affairs, or she may have seen someone bury a body at night or she may have seen somebody who was concealing his identity – or she may have known some secret about where some treasure was buried during the war. Or the man in the launch may have thrown somebody into the river and she saw it from the window of the boathouse – or she may have even got hold of some very important message in secret code and not known what it was herself . . .' It was clear that she could have gone on in this vein for some time although it seemed to the Inspector that she had already envisaged every possibility, likely or unlikely.*

These extracts from stories, written almost 40 years apart, illustrate, via her characters, Christie's greatest strength –

her ability to weave seemingly endless variations around one idea. There can be little doubt that this is Agatha Christie herself speaking; Mrs Oliver is, after all, a very successful detective novelist. And as we can now see from the Notebooks, this is exactly what Christie did. Throughout her career her ideas were consistently drawn from the world with which her readers were familiar – teeth, dogs, stamps (as below), mirrors, telephones, medicines – and upon these foundations she built her ingenious constructions. She explored universal themes in some of her later books (guilt and innocence in *Ordeal by Innocence*, evil in *The Pale Horse*, international unrest in *Cat among the Pigeons* and *Passenger to Frankfurt*), but they were still firmly rooted in the everyday.

Although it is not possible to be absolutely sure, there is no reason to suppose that listings of ideas and their variations were written at different times; I have no doubt that she rattled off variations and possibilities as fast as she could write, which probably accounts for the handwriting. In many cases it is possible to show that the list is written with the same pen and in the same style of handwriting. The outline of *One, Two, Buckle my Shoe* (see also Chapter 4) provides a good example of this. She is considering possible motives to set the plot in motion.

> Man marries secretly one of the twins
> Or
> Man was really already married [this was the option adopted]
> Or
> Barrister's 'sister' who lives with him (really wife)
> Or
> Double murder – that is to say – A poisons B – B stabs A – but really owing to plan by C

Or
Blackmailing wife finds out – then she is found dead
Or
He really likes wife – goes off to start life again with her
Or
Dentists killed – 1 London – 1 County

A few pages later in the same Notebook, also in connection with *One, Two, Buckle my Shoe*, she tries further variations on the same theme, this time introducing 'Sub Ideas'.

Pos. A. 1st wife still alive –
A. (a) knows all – co-operating with him
   (b) does not know – that he is secret service

Pos. B 1st wife dead – someone recognises him – 'I was a great friend of your wife, you know –'

In either case – crime is undertaken to suppress fact of 1st marriage and elaborate preparations undertaken

C. Single handed

D. Co-operation of wife as secretary

Sub Idea C

The 'friends' Miss B and Miss R – one goes to dentist
Or
~~Does wife go to a certain dentist?~~
Miss B makes app[ointment] – with dentist – Miss R keeps it
Miss R's teeth labelled under Miss B's name

Also from Notebook 35, but this time in connection with *Five Little Pigs*, we find a few very basic questions and possibilities under consideration:

❧ *Murder Made Easy* ❧

Dotted throughout the Notebooks are dozens of phrases that show Agatha Christie the resourceful creator, Agatha Christie the critical professional, Agatha Christie the sly humorist at work. In many cases she 'thought' directly on to the page and there are many instances where she addresses herself in this way.

Sometimes it is idle speculation as she toys with various ideas before settling on just one:

'How about this' . . . as she works out the timetable of 'Greenshaw's Folly'

'A good idea would be' . . . this, tantalisingly, is on an otherwise blank page

'or – a little better' . . . firming up the motive in *Hercule Poirot's Christmas*

'How about girl gets job' . . . from early notes for *A Caribbean Mystery*

'Who? Why? When? How? Where? Which?' . . . the essence of a detective story from *One, Two, Buckle my Shoe*

'Which way do we turn?' . . . in the middle of *Third Girl*

'A prominent person – such as a minister – (Aneurin Bevan type?) – on holiday? Difficulties as I don't know about Ministers' . . . rueful while looking for a new idea in the mid-1940s

When she has decided on a plot she often muses about the intricacies and possibilities of a variation:

'Does Jeremy have to be there then' . . . pondering on character movements for *Spider's Web*

'Contents of letter given? Or Not' . . . in the course of *Cat among the Pigeons*

'How does she bring it about . . . What drug' . . . while planning *A Caribbean Mystery*

'Yes – better if dentist is dead' . . . a decision reached during *One, Two, Buckle my Shoe*

'Why? Why??? Why?????' . . . frustration during *One, Two, Buckle my Shoe*

'He could be murderer – if there is a murder' . . . a possibility for *Fiddlers Three*

Like a true professional she is self-critical:

'unlike twin idea – woman servant one of them – NO!!' . . . a decision during *The Labours of Hercules*

'NB All v. unlikely' . . . as she approaches the end of *Mrs McGinty's Dead*

'All right – a little elaboration – more mistresses?' . . . not very happy with *Cat among the Pigeons*

continued overleaf

She includes reminders to herself:

'Look up datura poisoning . . . and re-read Cretan Bull'
. . . as she writes *A Caribbean Mystery*

'Find story about child and other child plays with him'
. . . probably her short story 'The Lamp'

'Possible variant – (read a private eye book first before typing)' . . . a reminder during *The Clocks*

'A good idea – needs working on' . . . for *Nemesis*

Things to line up' . . . during *Dead Man's Folly*

And there are the odd flashes of humour:

'Van D. pops off' . . . during *A Caribbean Mystery*

'Pennyfather is conked' . . . a rather uncharitable description from *At Bertram's Hotel*

'Elephantine Suggestions' . . . from, obviously, *Elephants Can Remember*

'Suspicion of (clever!) reader to be directed toward Nurse'
. . . a typically astute observation from *Curtain* when the nurse is completely innocent (note the use of the exclamation mark after 'clever'!)

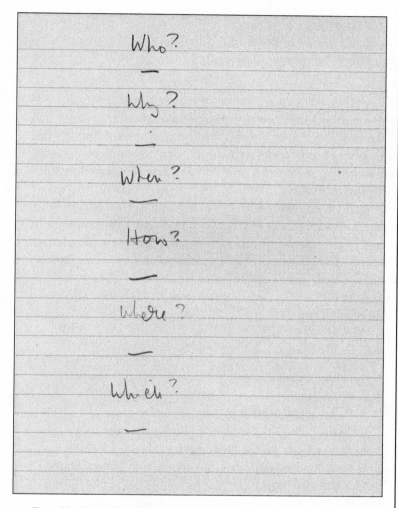

From Notebook 35 and One, Two, Buckle my Shoe – *the essence of detective fiction distilled into six words.*

Did mother murder –
  A. Husband
  B. Lover
  C. Rich uncle or guardian
  D. Another woman (jealousy)

Who were the other people

During the planning of *Mrs McGinty's Dead* (see also Chapter 7), the four murders in the past, around which the plot is built, provided Christie with an almost infinite number of possibilities and she worked her way methodically through most of them. More than almost any other novel, this scenario seemed to challenge her mental fertility as she considered every character living in Broadhinny, the scene of the novel, as a possible participant in the earlier murders. In this extract from Notebook 43 she tries various scenarios with the possible killer underlined (her underlining) in each case. As we know, it was idea 1B that she eventually settled on.

Which?

1. A. False – elderly Cranes – with daughter (girl – Evelyn)
   B. Real – Robin – son with mother <u>son</u> [Upward]
2. A. False Invalid mother (or not invalid) and son
   B. Real – dull wife of snob A.P. (Carter) <u>Dau</u>[ghter]
3. A. False artistic woman with <u>son</u>
   B. Real middle-aged wife – dull couple – or flashy Carters (daughter invalid)
4. A. False widow – soon to marry rich man
5. [A] False man with dogs – stepson – different name
   [B] Real – invalid mother and daughter – <u>dau</u>[ghter] does it [Wetherby]

And, later in the same Notebook, she considers which of her characters could fit the profiles of one of the earlier crimes, the Kane murder case:

Could be
Robin's mother   (E. Kane)
Robin   (EK's son)
Mrs Crane   (EK)
Their daughter   (EK's dau)
Mrs Carter   (EK's dau)
Young William Crane   (EK's son)
Mrs Wildfell   (EK's dau)

In Notebook 39 Christie rattles off six (despite the heading!) plot ideas, covering within these brief sketches kidnapping, forgery, robbery, fraud, murder and extortion:

4 snappy ideas for short Stories

Kidnapping? [The Adventure of] Johnnie Waverley again – Platinum blonde – kidnaps herself?

Invisible Will? Will written on quite different document

Museum robbery – celebrated professor takes things and examines them? – or member of public does

Stamps – Fortune hidden in them – gets dealer to buy them for him

An occurrence at a public place – Savoy? Dance? Debutantes tea? Mothers killed off in rapid succession?

The Missing Pekingese

The 'snappy' suggests that these were jotted down while she waited for the kettle to boil – as, indeed, they probably were.

The accurate dating of this extract is debatable. The reference 'missing Pekingese' is to 'The Nemean Lion', collected in *The Labours of Hercules* but first published in 1939. This, taken in conjunction with the reference to the 'Debutantes tea', probably indicates a late 1930s date when Christie's daughter, Rosalind, would have been a debutante. Only two of the ideas appear in print ('Invisible Will' in 'Motive Vs Opportunity' in *The Thirteen Problems* and 'Stamps' in 'Strange Jest' and *Spider's Web*), although not quite as they appear here.

In Notebook 47 Christie is in full flight planning a new short story, possibly a commission as she specifies the number of words. The following is all contained on one page and was probably written straight off:

> Ideas for 7000 word story
> A 'Ruth Ellis' . . . idea?
> Shoots man – not fatally – other man (or woman) eggs her on
>
> Say this 2nd person was –
>
> A. Sister in law? Brother's wife – her son or child would get this money and not be sent to boarding school away from her influence – a gentle soft motherly creature
> B. A mannish sister determined brother should not marry Ruby
> C. Man (with influence over Ruby) works her up while pretending to calm her. X has some knowledge concerning him. He wants to marry X's sister
> D. Man formerly Ruby's lover/husband – has it in for her <u>and</u> X

Unfortunately, she did not pursue this idea and no story resulted; she returned, four pages later, to plotting the play *The Unexpected Guest*, so the extract probably dates from the mid-1950s. (Ruth Ellis was the last woman to hang in the UK, in July 1955 after her conviction for the shooting of her lover David Blakely.)

Destinations Unknown

When she sat down to consider her next book, even before she got as far as plotting, Christie would rattle off possible settings. The next extract appears in Notebook 47 a few pages before notes for *Four-Fifty from Paddington* (and this list contains the germ of that book) and so would seem to date from the mid-1950s:

Book

Scene
Baghdad?
Hospital
Hotel [*At Bertram's Hotel*]
Flat   Third Floor Flat idea
    Baghdad Chest idea ['The Mystery of the Spanish
    Chest' and *The Rats*]
Small house in London husband and wife, children etc.
Park   Regent's Park
School   Girl's school [*Cat among the Pigeons*]
Boat   Queen Emma? Western Lady
Train   seen from a train? Through window of house or vice
    versa? [*Four-Fifty from Paddington*]
Beach   And Boarding house [possibly *Afternoon at the Seaside*]

Although difficult to date exactly, the following extract would seem to date from the very late 1940s. It is just after notes for *Mrs McGinty's Dead* (although with a totally different plot outline) and *They Do It with Mirrors* (also with a completely different plot) and is followed by a list of her books in her own handwriting, the latest title of which is *The Hollow* (1946).

> Ideas for Mise-en-scene?
>
> Conditions like The White Crow. Start with the murder –
>   a prominent person – such as a minister –
> (Aneurin Bevan type?) – on holiday? Interrogation of his
>   personnel – His wife – Female secretary
> Male [secretary] – Difficulties as I don't know about
>   Ministers
> Chief pharmacist in a Hospital? Young medical man doing
>   research on Penicillin?
> A brains trust? Local one? BBC Mrs AC arrives to broadcast
>   – Dies – not the real Mrs AC?
> A big hotel? Imperial? No – done
> Shop? Worth's during mannequin parade – Selfridges – in a
>   cubicle during Sale

Some of the references in this extract may need clarification. *The White Crow* is a 1928 novel by Crime Club writer Philip MacDonald; it concerns the murder of an influential businessman in his own office (as in *A Pocket Full of Rye*). Aneurin Bevan was UK Minister of Health, 1945–51. The position of chief pharmacist was one with which Christie would have been familiar both from her early life and from her experience in the Second World War (*The Pale Horse* contains a gesture in this direction). 'Imperial' is a reference to *Peril at End House*, although the hotel is disguised as the Majestic. And Worth's, like Selfridge's, is a famous department store.

'Mrs AC arrives to broadcast' reminds us that although Christie refused countless requests throughout her career to broadcast on either radio or television, she did, at least once, take part in a *Desert Island Discs* type programme, *In the*

Gramophone Library, broadcast in August 1946. And the rueful remark 'Difficulties as I don't know about Ministers' – my favourite comment from the entire Notebooks – shows that she abided by the old maxim – 'Write about what you know'.

Surprise, Surprise!

But the most unexpected element in the Notebooks was, to me, the fact that many of Christie's best plots did not necessarily spring from a single devastating idea. She considered all possibilities when she plotted and did not confine herself to one idea, no matter how good it may have seemed. In very few cases is the identity of the murderer a given from the start of the plotting.

The most dramatic example is *Crooked House* (see also Chapter 4). With its startling revelation that the killer is a child, it remains one of the great Christie surprises, in the same class as *The Murder of Roger Ackroyd, Murder on the Orient Express, Curtain* and *Endless Night*. (To be entirely fair, at least two other writers, Ellery Queen in *The Tragedy of Y* and Margery Allingham in *The White Cottage Mystery* had already exploited this idea but far less effectively.) At that stage she had already used the narrator-murderer gambit, the policeman-murderer gambit, the everybody-did-it gambit, the everybody-as-victim gambit. Before reading the Notebooks, I had visualised Agatha Christie at her typewriter smiling craftily as she sat down in 1948 to write the next 'Christie for Christmas' and weaving a novel around the device of an 11-year-old girl as a cold-blooded murderer. Not so, however. Even a cursory glance at Notebook 14 shows that Christie considered Sophia, Clemency and Edith as well as Josephine when it came to potential murderers. It was not a case of arranging the entire plot around Josephine as the one unalterable fact. It was not the raison d'être of this novel; the shattering identity of the murderer was only one element under consideration and not necessarily the key element.

Again, at no point in the notes for her last devastating surprise, *Endless Night* (see Chapter 12), is there mention of the narrator-killer. It was not a case of thinking 'I'll try the Ackroyd trick again but this time with a working-class narrator. And I'll begin with the meeting and courtship, which is all part of the plot, rather than after the marriage.' Indeed, there is brief mention in Notebook 50 of one of the characters being a friend of Poirot, who was, presumably, to investigate the case; and at only one point is there mention of telling the story in the first person. The inspiration for the shock ending came to her as she plotted rather than the other way round.

Arguably the last of the ingeniously clued detective novels, *A Murder is Announced* (see Chapter 5), would seem to allow of only one solution, and yet at one stage Letitia Blacklock is pencilled in as the second victim of Mitzi, who has already murdered her own husband Rudi Sherz. It was not a case of deciding to write a novel featuring a supposed victim actually murdering her blackmailer during a carefully devised game. Nor did *Murder in Mesopotamia* (see Chapter 8) begin life featuring a wife-killing husband with a perfect alibi; she also considered Miss Johnston and, in fact, Mrs Leidner herself was a strong contender for the role of killer for much of the plotting. The setting, the archaeological dig, would seem to have been the fixed idea for this novel and the rest of the plot was woven around it rather than vice versa.

Although this still seems surprising, it is in keeping with her general method of working. Her strengths lay in her unfettered mental fertility and her lack of system. Her initial inspiration could be as vague as a gypsy's curse (*Endless Night*), an archaeological dig (*Murder in Mesopotamia*) or a newspaper advertisement (*A Murder is Announced*). After that, she let her not inconsiderable imagination have free rein with the idea and hey, presto! a year later the latest Christie appeared on the bookshelves. And some of the ideas that did not make it into that masterpiece might well surface in the one to be published the following year – or ten years hence.

We now have a clearer idea of Christie's approach to the construction of her stories. Using the Notebooks as a combination of sounding board and literary sketchpad, she devised and developed; she selected and rejected; she sharpened and polished; she revisited and recycled. And, as I hope to show by a more detailed analysis in the following chapters, out of this seeming chaos she produced a unique and immortal body of work.

EXHIBIT B:
OTHER CRIME WRITERS IN THE NOTEBOOKS

'Do you like detective stories. I do. I read them all and I've got autographs from Dorothy Sayers and Agatha Christie and Dickson Carr and H. C. Bailey.'

The Body in the Library, Chapter 6

Apart from the '13 at Dinner' list in Notebook 41, Agatha Christie makes various references to her fellow crime writers throughout the Notebooks. The following is a selection of those mentioned:

✳ E.C. Bentley

Apart from his appearance in connection with the Detection Club, he is also referred to in Notebook 41. The following concerns a contribution to Bentley's anthology *A Second Century of Detective Stories*, published in 1938, where 'The Case of the Distressed Lady' from *Partners in Crime* represents Christie; she did not write a story specifically for inclusion.

A HP story for Bentley

✳ G.K. Chesterton

The creator of Father Brown, the immortal priest detective, and first president of the Detection Club, Chesterton contributed to their collaborative novel *The Floating Admiral*. The reference in Notebook 66 is a reminder to provide a short story for him, presumably for his 1935 anthology *A Century of Detective Stories*. She did not write a new one but instead provided 'Sing a Song of Sixpence'.

Ideas for G.K.C.

* John Creasey

In Notebook 52 there are two references, both very similar, to John Creasey, British crime writer of almost 600 books. Hugely prolific under a variety of pseudonyms, he was also a founder of the Crime Writers Association. In *The Clocks*, the typewriting agency, which is the focus of much of the novel, does some work for Creasey-like authors. He did not write detective fiction.

Miss M[artindale] is chief agent – Sec[retary] to Creasey – who wrote spy stories

* Rufus King

Twice in Notebook 35, during the plotting of *Mrs McGinty's Dead*, Christie mentions *Murder by Latitude*, the title of a novel by this largely forgotten writer, although his name itself does not appear. *Murder by Latitude* features a typical Christie setting, aboard a ship from which contact with land has been severed. There are a few King titles in the library at Greenway House.

Atmosphere like Murder by Latitude – some people – amongst them a Murderer

* A.E.W. Mason

Mason was the creator of Inspector Hanaud. The reference in Notebook 35 is to *At the Villa Rose*, published in

1910, a case involving the death of an elderly woman and the suspicion surrounding her companion. While plotting *One, Two, Buckle my Shoe* Christie reminds herself of it:

A murder discovered (woman? Elderly? Like Villa Rose) Clue – a shoe buckle

＊ Edgar Allan Poe

The 'inventor' of the detective story when he published 'The Murders in the Rue Morgue' in 1841, 'The Purloined Letter' is another famous case for his detective Auguste Dupin, turning on the idea of hiding in plain sight. Christie's reference is in connection with a fortune hidden not *in* but *on* an envelope – as stamps. She used this plot device in the short story 'Strange Jest' and also much later, in *Spider's Web*. The concept of hiding in plain sight is also used in 'The Nemean Lion'.

Stamps – fortune left in them – on old letters in desk – 'Purloined Letter' mentioned – they look in obvious envelope – really stamps on it

＊ Dorothy L. Sayers

Sayers' creation Lord Peter Wimsey made his debut in 1923 in *Whose Body*. In addition to the writer herself, Wimsey is mentioned in Notebook 41 – this time in a reference to Ronnie West in *Lord Edgware Dies*. It is also possible that the naming of Dr Peter Lord in *Sad Cypress* is homage to Christie's great contemporary.

Ronnie West (debonair Peter Wimseyish)

4

Cat among the Pigeons:
The Nursery Rhyme Murders

'I adore nursery rhymes, don't you? Always so tragic and
macabre. That's why children like them.'

The Mousetrap, I, i

◄○►

SOLUTIONS REVEALED

Crooked House • *Five Little Pigs* • 'Four and Twenty
Blackbirds' • *Hickory Dickory Dock* • 'How Does Your
Garden Grow?' • *Ordeal by Innocence* • *A Pocket Full of Rye* •
'Sing a Song of Sixpence' • *Ten Little Niggers* •
'The Tuesday Night Club'

◄○►

The attraction of children's literature, either as titles or
themes, has often provided crime writers with inspiration.
Dickson Carr's *The Arabian Nights Murder*, Douglas Browne's
The Looking Glass Murders, McBain's *Snow White and Rose Red*
and *Rumpelstiltskin*, Queen's *There Was an Old Woman*, Smith's
This Is the House, Witting's *There Was a Crooked Man* and Fuller's
With My Little Eye are all drawn from the playroom, while S.S.
Van Dine's *The Bishop Murder Case* uses Mother Goose as a
theme. The attraction is obvious – the juxtaposition of the

childlike and the chilling, the twisting of the mundane into the macabre.

But it was Agatha Christie who made it her own and exploited it more comprehensively than any other writer. There are numerous references to nursery rhymes scattered throughout the Notebooks. Sometimes the idea went no further than a brief jotting (see 'Miscellaneous' on page 129); others provided her with some of her greatest works – *Ten Little Niggers*, *Five Little Pigs* and *Three Blind Mice/The Mousetrap*. In some cases it provides no more than a title, *Hickory Dickory Dock* and *One, Two, Buckle my Shoe*; in some cases, *Ten Little Niggers* and *A Pocket Full of Rye*, it provides the book with an overall schema; while the use of *Crooked House* and *Three Blind Mice* is more symbolic than actual. The most successful are undoubtedly *Five Little Pigs* and *Ten Little Niggers*, where the rhyme is convincingly and ingeniously followed. The dramatic impact of an innocent nursery rhyme transforming into a killer's calling card is irresistible to an imaginative crime writer such as Agatha Christie.

> *Sing a song of sixpence, a pocket full of rye,*
> *Four and twenty blackbirds, baked in a pie,*
> *When the pie was opened, the birds began to sing,*
> *Was not that a dainty dish to set before the king?*

> *The king was in his counting-house, counting out his money,*
> *The queen was in the parlour, eating bread and honey,*
> *The maid was in the garden, hanging out the clothes*
> *When down came a blackbird and pecked off her nose.*

The most fruitful nursery rhyme was 'Sing a Song of Sixpence', which provided no less than three titles: the novel *A Pocket Full of Rye*, and the short stories 'Sing a Song of Sixpence' and

106

'Four and Twenty Blackbirds'. In the case of the short stories, only the title has been inspired by the rhyme, whereas the novel follows the pattern of the rhyme very closely.

'Sing a Song of Sixpence'
December 1929

────────────◄○►────────────

A sixpenny piece helps to solve a brutal murder that has left a family divided with mutual suspicion.

────────────◄○►────────────

Although there are no surviving notes for 'Sing a Song of Sixpence' – unsurprisingly, since it made such an early appearance in the Christmas 1929 edition of *Holly Leaves* – there is a reference to it in Notebook 56. Appearing as it does among the notes for *A Pocket Full of Rye*, this is unusual in, puzzlingly, also appearing to make reference to the already published *Crooked House*.

Sing a Song of Sixpence
The crooked sixpence found (a Crooked man Crooked wife Crooked house)

An aspect of this short story that has escaped the attention of Christie commentators is its similarity to *Ordeal by Innocence* (see Chapter 7). 'Sing a Song of Sixpence' features the arrival of an outside investigator, Sir Edward Palliser, at the home of Miss Crabtree, who has been murdered by a blow to the head administered by a member of her own household. Because no one has been arrested for the crime, her family describe how 'they sit there every day looking at each other surreptitiously and wondering'. In this atmosphere of mutual suspicion he reaches a solution which explicitly foreshadows the 1958 novel.

'How Does Your Garden Grow?'
August 1935

---◀○▶---

A plea for help to Poirot is too late to save Amelia Barrowby, but he is determined to get to the truth.

---◀○▶---

Mary, Mary, quite contrary
How does your garden grow?
With silver bells and cockle-shells
And pretty maids all in a row.

This short nursery rhyme features no less than five times throughout the Notebooks, even though its words gave the title of just one short story, 'How Does Your Garden Grow?'. But it seems to have made an impression on Christie's mind as she often referred to it in the course of plotting other titles. And there are similarities between this short story and a novel she planned but never wrote. The story was first published in the UK in *The Strand*, having appeared some months earlier in *Ladies' Home Journal* in the USA. This story's connection to the nursery rhyme is stronger than 'Sing a Song of Sixpence' or 'Four and Twenty Blackbirds', as it includes the shells, the garden and the killer's name. Mary Delafontaine poisons her aunt and hides the shells of the fatal oysters among the other cockle shells used as decoration in her garden. She tries, unsuccessfully, to incriminate the foreign companion:

The old lady – the foreign girl – Mary – the 'weak' husband

The final plot is encapsulated in Notebook 20:

> Oyster story – Man dies after dinner – strychnine in oyster –
> swallowed – shells out in garden or in shell box – food
> analysed – nothing. Possibly some complication about a
> cachet he took – or someone gave him – if so, unjustly
> accused

It is another example of one of Christie's favourite early plot
devices – the summoning of Poirot to the scene of a suspected
crime only to discover when he arrives that he is too late. As
early as 1923 she first used this idea in *The Murder on the Links*,
and subsequently in 'The Cornish Mystery', *Dumb Witness* and
'The Incident of the Dog's Ball' (see the Appendix). It can be
seen why – it has an emotional and a practical impact. The
summoner, who has promised to explain the situation in
detail, is now unable to do so and Poirot has a moral, as well
as a practical, imperative to solve the crime. There is also the
plot device of the victim having known 'too much', always a
good way to start a detective story. In 'How Does Your Garden
Grow?', the appearance of a Russian character would have
been very unusual in detective fiction of the day. In fact, the
appearance of any foreigner (including Poirot) is always
viewed with suspicion by the inhabitants of small villages
throughout the Christie canon. And, of course – as can be
seen in *Dumb Witness* – this allowed Christie to subvert, yet
again, the readers' prejudices.

The eponymous main character, Mary Delafontaine,
became a byword in Christie's shorthand, appearing in
abbreviated form in the course of plotting *Third Girl* and
Ordeal by Innocence respectively, even though she was used in
the final plot of neither novel:

Mary Del. – Arthur (innocent husband) – Katrina – suspicious, passionate – for money looks after old boy

Olivia (The Mary Delafontaine wife)

The name was also used for one of the victims in *The Pale Horse*, she is a friend of Mrs Oliver in Chapter 1 and she appears on Father Gorman's doomed list in the following chapter.

Ten Little Niggers
6 November 1939

◄○►

Ten strangers are invited to a weekend on an island off the coast of Devon. Their host fails to appear and a series of deaths among their fellow-guests make them realise that one of them is a killer following the macabre nursery rhyme that hangs in each bedroom.

◄○►

Ten little nigger boys went out to dine
One choked his little self and then there were nine;
Nine little nigger boys sat up very late
One overslept himself and then there were eight;
Eight little nigger boys travelling in Devon
One said he'd stay there and then there were seven;
Seven little nigger boys chopping up sticks
One chopped himself in half and then there were six;
Six little nigger boys playing with a hive
A bumble bee stung one and then there were five;
Five little nigger boys going in for law
One got in Chancery and then there were four;

110

Four little nigger boys going out to sea
A red herring swallowed one and then there were three;
Three little nigger boys walking in the Zoo
A big bear hugged one and then there were two;
Two little nigger boys sitting in the sun
One got frizzled up and then there was one;
One little nigger boy left all alone
He went and hanged himself and then there were none.

Ten Little Niggers (also known as *And Then There Were None*) is Agatha Christie's most famous novel, her greatest technical achievement and the best-selling crime novel of all time. Of all the 'nursery rhyme' titles this is the one that sticks closest to its origins. Although Christie adopted the 'He got married and then there were none' ending for the stage adaptation, she used the original ending for the climax of the novel. The existence of the rhyme is a constant theme throughout the novel, especially when the characters realise what is happening. The manner of each death cleverly echoes the rhyme, the only slightly jarring note being the death of Blore where the difficult Zoo idea is somewhat stretched.

With the writing of this book Christie set herself a challenge and in her *Autobiography* she describes how the difficulty of the central idea attracted her: 'Ten people had to die without it becoming ridiculous. I wrote the book after a tremendous amount of planning . . . It was clear, straightforward, baffling and yet had a perfectly reasonable explanation . . . the person who was really pleased with it was myself, for I knew better than any critic how difficult it had been.'

As we saw in Chapter 2, this 'tremendous planning' is not evident from Notebook 65, the only one to feature this novel. This Notebook does, however, include interesting details of various characters that did not make it into the completed book. And, on the evidence of the Notebooks alone, it would seem to be the characters themselves that gave most trouble. At no stage are ten characters listed. At first there are eight (I have added probable names to both lists, although Vera Claythorne, Emily Brent, Philip Lombard and General MacArthur appear in the novel as listed in the Notebook, although minor background details were to change):

When Collins began to advertise *Ten Little Niggers* in *Booksellers Record* in July 1939, they called it, quite simply, 'the greatest story Agatha Christie has ever written'. But their item in the *Crime Club News* incurred the wrath of the writer herself and she wrote from Greenway House on 24 July to William Collins to protest. She felt that too much of the plot was revealed, pointing out that 'any book is ruined when you know exactly what is going to happen all the way along'. She also includes a veiled threat when she reminds him that she is just about to sign a contract for her next four books and is unwilling to do so unless they can guarantee that this error of judgement will not be repeated. Despite the fact that Collins declared it to be 'certainly the greatest detective story that the Crime Club has ever published and probably, we believe, the world will declare it the greatest detective story ever written', they included too many revelations. It is obvious what she means. They write about the island, the rhyme, the disappearing china figures, the realisation that the killer is among them and, most damning of all, the fact that the last one to die is not necessarily the villain. One's sympathies are entirely with Agatha Christie; all they omitted was the name of the killer.

Ten Niggers

Doctor – drunk at op – or careless [Dr Armstrong]
Judge – unjust Summing Up [Judge Wargrave]
Man and Wife – Servants (did in old lady) [Mr and Mrs
    Rogers]
Girl – ~~whose lover shot himself~~ [Vera]
Husband and wife – Blackmailing
Allenby – Youngish man – dangerous alert [Lombard]

At a later stage, to judge from the change from pencil to pen and the slightly different handwriting, she tries again. This time she includes 12 characters:

1. Vera Claythorne – Secretary at school – has applied at agency for holiday post
2. Mr Justice Swettenham in first class carriage [Judge Wargrave]
3. Doctor – telegram from Gifford – Can you join us – etc. [Dr Armstrong]
4 5. Capt and Mrs Winyard – Letters – mutual friend Letty Harrington – Come for weekend
6. Lombard – visited by solicitor or confidential agent – offered one hundred guineas – take it or leave it
7. University student who runs over children – a bit tight – arrives in car [Anthony Marston]
8. Llewellyn Oban – Committed perjury in murder case – man executed [Blore]
9. Emily Brent – turned out maidservant – later drank oxalic acid – letter from someone starting guest house and is a friend of hers – free stay
10 11. Man and wife servant [Mr and Mrs Rogers]
12. General MacArthur – killed 30 men unnecessarily in war

Each of the lists includes a husband-and-wife combination, Capt. and Mrs Winyard in the latter list, and these were the ones to be dropped. The second listing is much nearer to that of the novel although it is possible to discern the germ of the characters in the first tentative listing.

Two further refinements to the plot are included between characters 8 and 9 in the Notebook. Most of the guests to the island are lured by arrangements or invitations made by a Mr or Mrs Owens, sometimes with the initials 'U.N.' or, as Justice Wargrave says at the end of Chapter 3, 'by a slight stretch of fancy: UNKNOWN'. The initials undergo a few variations and the first note below is probably the seed of this idea. The second note refers to the diminishing collection of china figurines on the dining-room table:

Ulick Noel Nomen

Ten Little Niggers on dinner table

After a blank page the notes begin with Chapter 9 and, over the next six pages, trace the course of the rest of the novel including the scene at Scotland Yard. This means that the last seven murders (from Rogers onwards) are all covered in this relatively short space, lending further support to the theory that the plotting for the book was done elsewhere and Notebook 65 represents the almost-finished plot.

Chapter IX
Judge takes charge – exhibits a good deal of quickwittidness [sic] – Armstrong and Wargrave – Judge has an idea. The storm comes on – all of them huddled into a room – nerves crackling. Next morning – no Rogers – no sign of him – breakfast not laid. Men search island – at breakfast – suddenly Vera sees – ~~Seven~~ Six niggers. Growing suspicion

of Emily – a face watches her – a wasp stings her – dead bee
on floor. Everyone terrified – all keep together. Where's old
Wargrave – they find him dressed up in red robe and wig.
He and Blore carry him up – the dining room – still 5 niggers.
The 3 of them – criminal <u>must</u> be Armstrong. Finally: body
washed up Armstrong! Blore crushed by falling rock. Vera and
Lombard – one of us – her fears – self preservation – she gets
his revolver – finally she shoots him – at last – safe – Hugo

The investigation –
The other deaths Owen? V and L last? Mrs R[ogers] and
    AM [Marston] all dead –
Morris dead too – he did all arrangements – committed
    suicide – dead –
Young man suggests Wargrave – Edward Seton was guilty –
    Old Wargrave was queer

Epilogue – Letter in bottle – he describes how it was done

One idea that was abandoned was that of a 'watcher' throughout the action. After the death of Emily Brent we read in the
Notebook that 'A face watches her'; and at the climax of the
story, when Vera goes up to her room the notes read 'Goes up
to her bedroom – the noose – man steps out of darkness'. In
retrospect the reader can imagine the killer 'watching' the

> An interesting footnote is provided by Christie's great
> American contemporary fellow crime-writer Ellery
> Queen. In his *In the Queen's Parlor* (1957) he discloses
> how, twice during his writing career, he had to abandon
> a book-in-progress when he read the latest Agatha
> Christie. Francis M. Nevins in his study of Queen, *Royal
> Bloodline*, confirms that one of these was a plot based on
> the same idea as *Ten Little Niggers*.

unfolding of his plan, both before and after his supposed death, but it appears from these brief references that Christie toyed with the idea of mentioning the nameless 'watcher'. Far more effective and less melodramatic, however, is the concept she adopted at the end of Chapter 11, and again in Chapter 13, when she allows us to share the thoughts of the six remaining characters, including the killer's, but without identifying the thinker.

∽⚘∾

One, Two, Buckle my Shoe
4 November 1940

---◀◦▶---

Hercule Poirot's dentist's appointment coincides with the murder of his dentist. A shoe buckle, a disappearance and more deaths follow before he can say 'Nineteen, twenty, My plate's empty.'

---◀◦▶---

One, two, buckle my shoe
Three, four, shut the door
Five, six, pick up sticks
Seven, eight, lay them straight
Nine, ten, a big fat hen
Eleven, twelve, men must delve
Thirteen, fourteen, maids are courting
Fifteen, sixteen, maids in the kitchen
Seventeen, eighteen, maids in waiting
Nineteen, twenty, my plate's empty . . .

The notes for this novel are contained in four Notebooks with the majority (over 75 pages) in Notebook 35. They alternate for much of that Notebook with the notes for *Five Little Pigs*. *One, Two, Buckle my Shoe* is Christie's most complicated novel. It features a triple impersonation and a complex murder plot with its beginnings in the distant past. The novel turns on the identity of a dead body but, unlike *Four-Fifty from Paddington*, it is a tantalising, rather than an aggravating, question.

The only aspect of this novel that does not ring true is, ironically, the use of the nursery rhyme. It is strained and unconvincing and, apart from the all-important shoe buckle, the rhyme has little or no significance other than providing chapter titles. This is confirmed by the following extract from Notebook 35 where Christie jots down the rhyme and tries to match ideas to each section. As can be seen, they are not very persuasive and in fact few of them, apart from the shoe buckle, went into the novel:

One Two Buckle my Shoe – the Shoe Buckle – think of it – the start of this case

The Closed Door – something about a door – either room locked or something not heard through closed door when it should have been.

Picking up sticks – assembling clues

Lay them Straight – order and method

A good fat hen – the will – read – rich woman it was who died – murdered woman – fat elderly – two girls – man recently coming to live with rich relative?

Men must Delve – Digging up garden – another body – discovered buried in garden – wrong owner of shoe buckle?

Maids a courting – 2 girls – heiresses of Fat Hen? Or would have been connected by husband of fat hen – in collusion with maid servant

Maids in the kitchen – servant's gossip

Maids in Waiting?

My Plate is Empty
End

Clue – a shoe buckle

An example of the type of organised listing that occurs throughout the Notebooks, the plot of *One, Two, Buckle my Shoe* occurs as Idea H on a list from A to U. This list looks to have been written straight off with three or four ideas to a page in the same handwriting and with the same pen. Most of them have more detail included but Idea H below is exactly as it appears (the possibility of combining it with the twins or chambermaid idea – see also 'The House of Dreams', page 303 – was not pursued).

Ideas

A. Poirot's Last Case – history repeats itself – Styles now a guest house [*Curtain*]
B. Remembered Death – Rosemary dead [*Sparkling Cyanide*]
C. Dangerous drug stolen from doctor's car. [See *Hickory Dickory Dock* below and 'The House of Dreams']
D. Legless man – sometimes tall – sometimes short
E. Identical twins (one killed in railway smash)
F. Not identical twins
G. A murderer is executed – afterwards is found to be innocent [*Five Little Pigs/Ordeal by Innocence*]
H. Dentist Murder Motive? Chart substitution? Combine with E? or F? or J?
I. Two women – arty friends – ridiculous – one is crook
J. Chambermaid in hotel accomplice of man
K. Stamps – but stamps on letter ['Strange Jest']

L. Prussic acid

M. Caustic potash in cachet

N. Stabbed through eye with hatpin

O. Witness in murder case – quite unimportant – offered post abroad

P. Third Floor Flat idea

Q. Figurehead of ship idea

R. Prussic acid – 'Cry' in bath

S. Diabetic idea – insulin (substitute something else) [*Crooked House*]

T. Body in the Library – Miss Marple [*The Body in the Library*]

U. Stored blood idea, wrong blood

A few pages later, the germ of the plot emerges although, as can be seen from the question marks, the idea was hazy. As we saw in Chapter 3, Christie considered a multitude of possibilities in working out its plot. But apart from a name change this short musing is the basis of the novel:

Dead woman supposed to be actress? Rose Lane – (really is Rose Lane) but body shown to be someone else –
Why?
Why???
Why?????

From the (admittedly unscientific) evidence that the word 'dentist' occurs 65 times in the Notebooks against a mere 13 appearances for the word 'buckle', it would seem that the background came before the all-important clue, or, even the nursery rhyme. But this combination of dentist – his family, patients, surgery and, vitally, files – together with the rhyme and its accompanying main clue, gave Christie the ideal situation for creating confusion about the identification of an unrecognisable body. She could now get down to serious plot development:

Dentist Murder
H.P. in dentist's chair – latter talking while drilling
Points:
  (1) Never forget a face – patient – can't remember where I saw him before – it will come back to me
  (2) Other angles – a daughter – engaged to a rip of a young man – father disapproves
  (3) Professional character – his partner

Much hinges on evidence of <u>teeth</u> (death of dentist)

Dentist murdered – H.P. in waiting room at time – patients charts removed or substituted

Dentist – HP in waiting room – sent away

Rings Japp – or latter rings him

Do you remember who was in waiting room?

She begins to develop the novel's characters, sketching in tentative notes about names and backgrounds, in a well-ordered list of the scenes that would introduce them:

Latest dentist ideas

Little silhouettes of the people going to Mr Claymore that day

1 Mr Claymore himself at breakfast
2 Miss D – mentions a day off or just gets telephone call
3 Miss Cobb or Miss Slob at breakfast – Miss C saying much better – not aching

4 Mr Amberiotis – talk of his landlady – about his tooth –
   careful English
5 Caroline – (young swindler?) or Mr Bell (dentist's
   daughter lover – American? Trying to see father)
6 Dentist's partner – rings – can he come up to see him –
   a service lift – unprofessional conduct?
7 Mr. Marron Levy – a board meeting – a little snappy –
   admits at end – toothache – gets into Daimler –
   29 Harley St.
8 H.P. His tooth – his conversation with dentist – meets on
   the stairs – woman with very white teeth?
Later Japp – suspicious foreigner

Not all of the characters that she sketched made it into the
novel and those that did appeared under different names.
The dentist victim became Morley instead of Claymore,
Miss D became Gladys Neville, and Marron Levy became
Alistair Blunt. Mr Bell possibly became Frank Carter, the
boyfriend of Gladys, and Miss Cobb's conviction that her
toothache is improving is similar to our eventual introduction to Miss Sainsbury Seale. Miss Slob and Caroline were
abandoned after this listing. Oddly, the shoe buckle is not
mentioned at all here and the white-toothed woman mentioned in item 8 has replaced or, more likely, foreshad-
owed, Miss Sainsbury Seale.

Throughout the notes Christie continued trying to fit her
ingenious plot into the plan of the nursery rhyme:

1 – 2
Miss S going to dentist
Mr Mauro
Miss Nesbit
Mr Milton
H.P. in waiting room – shoe buckle – loose – annoys him

3 – 4
Japp comes – P. goes with him – interview partner's wife? – secretary etc.

5 – 6
The body – evidence of identity destroyed – but identified from clothes. Mrs Chapman's flat – the shoes – either a buckle missing or one found there

9 – 10
Julia Olivera – married not in love – Aunty Julia – 'the daughter is attractive'

11 – 12
Men Must Delve – dentist's secretary had been crying because young man has lost his job. In garden next morning – the gardener – P goes round a bush – Frank Carter – digging

13 – 14
Mrs Adams – that conversation – then – in park Jane and Howard

15 – 16
Final Maids in the Kitchen touch – one of the maids upstairs looked over – saw Carter – watched Carter went in – saw dentist dead

17 – 18
Miss Montressor – dark – striking – gardening – her footprint in bed

19 – 20
P outlines case – smart patent new shoe – foot and ankle strap – buckle torn off. Later woman found – shoe and buckle sewn on. It was a woman's shabby shoe – other was <u>new</u>

But it just doesn't work. The early sections – the buckle, picking up sticks (clues) and laying them straight (interpreting them) – are acceptable. But the gardening motif ('men must delve') and the maids looking over the banisters are simply unconvincing. The dauntingly clever plot does not need this window-dressing and the book can stand, without any references to the rhyme, as a supreme example of detective fiction.

If, however, any further proof were necessary of the ingenuity and fertility of Agatha Christie, a glance at almost any page of Notebook 35 would supply it. The following ideas are scattered throughout the notes for *One, Two, Buckle my Shoe.* None of them was used.

> Idea of two women – <u>one</u> criminal working with man goes to dentist – simply in order to give man alibi

> Harvey – rich, unscrupulous – married to young wife –
> a widow when he married her – had she murdered first husband?

> <u>Or</u> Double suicide man and woman – one of them not the person – therefore suicide not murder – dentist could have identified her

> M. wants to get rid of someone – (his wife?) therefore he kills his wife and another man but it proves not to be his wife but another woman

Four and Twenty Blackbirds
March 1941

---◄○►---

Poirot investigates the mysterious death of an elderly man
when his suspicions are aroused – by the man's diet.

---◄○►---

The title of 'Four and Twenty Blackbirds' appears for the first
time in Notebook 20:

4 and 20 blackbirds

Located ahead of Christie's reminder to herself ('To be
added – Sketch of Leatheran career – Chapter II') to amend
Murder in Mesopotamia, this dates it to the mid-1930s, at least
six years before the story first appeared. A rough sketch of
the story itself appears in Notebook 66 just ahead of a sketch
for 'Triangle at Rhodes':

Impersonation of old man – he eats a different meal on the
Tuesday – nothing else noticed. Died later.

Mr P Parker Pyne – They talk – points out elderly man with a
horn beamed ~~and spectacles~~ eye-glass – bushy eyebrows

Old fellow hasn't turned up – waiter says he is upset – first
noticed it a fortnight ago – when he wouldn't have his jam
roll – had blackberry tart instead. Sees body – teeth – no
blackberry tart. Empty house – fell downstairs – dead –
open letter

There is one particularly surprising aspect of the jottings in
Notebook 66 – the allocation of this case to Parker Pyne

instead of Hercule Poirot. In fact this change could be quite easily imagined; this is not one of the more densely plotted Poirot stories, and it is probable that market forces dictated the substitution of the Belgian. And as we shall see, this is not an isolated example of the interchangeability of characters.

It has to be said that the connection to the nursery rhyme is very tenuous. For the purposes of the story the blackbirds of the rhyme become blackberries: the main clue is the lack of discoloration of the victim's teeth ('Sees body – teeth – no blackberry tart') despite the fact that he was seen to eat blackberry pie shortly before his supposed death. The rather obvious disguise is the other important element of the tale. A more fitting title is that used on the story's first US appearance in *Colliers Magazine* in November 1940, 'The Case of the Regular Customer'.

Five Little Pigs
11 January 1943

This little piggy went to market
This little piggy stayed at home
This little piggy ate roast beef
This little piggy had none
This little piggy cried wee-wee-wee all the way home.

――――――◄○►――――――

Carla Lemarchant approaches Hercule Poirot and asks him to vindicate her mother, who died in prison 16 years earlier while serving a sentence for the murder of her husband. Poirot approaches the five other suspects and asks them to write accounts of the events leading up to the fatal day.

――――――◄○►――――――

125

Published in the UK in January 1943, having already appeared in the US six months earlier, *Five Little Pigs* is the apex of Christie's career as a detective novelist; it is her most perfect combination of detective and 'straight' novel. The characters are carefully drawn and the tangle of relationships more seriously realised than in any other Christie title. It is a cunning and scrupulously clued formal detective novel, an elegiac love story and a masterly example of story-telling technique with five individual accounts of one devastating event. And in this novel at least, the use of the admittedly short rhyme is not forced. Each of the five main characters is perfectly reflected in the words of the verse. And perhaps because there are no further verses, the analogy does not seem strained (as, for instance, it does in the case of *One, Two, Buckle my Shoe*). But, as the Notebooks reveal, the journey to the book we now know was neither straightforward nor obvious.

From the technical point of view the test Christie sets herself in this novel is daunting. As well as the 16-year gap between the crime and its investigation she limits herself to just five possible murderers. Seven years earlier she had first experimented with the device of a small circle of suspects; in *Cards on the Table* she limits herself to just four bridge-players. She attempts a similar problem with *Five Little Pigs*, although this time she allows herself some physical clues in the shape of a glass, a beer bottle and a crushed pipette.

It is also the greatest of Christie's 'murder in the past' plots. In fact if we don't count *Dumb Witness* – the investigation of a two-month-old murder – it is also the first of such plots. Alderbury, the scene of the crime, is based closely on Christie's own Greenway House and the geography of the story corresponds exactly with its grounds. The Battery, where Elsa poses on the battlements and watches her lover die, looks out over the River Dart and the path where the crushed pipette is found leads back up to Greenway House.

This map from Notebook 35 shows the murder scene in Five Little Pigs *with the Boathouse on the left (also the scene of a murder in* Dead Man's Folly *), Greenway House in the top right-hand corner, and the positions of Miss W(illiams) and C(aroline). The photo of the Battery from the time of writing shows the wall where Elsa posed.*

The nursery rhyme is quoted in full in Notebook 35, heralding 75 pages of notes:

5 Little Pigs
One Little Piggy went to Market (Market Basing)
1 little   "   stayed at home
1 little   "   had roast beef
1 little   "   had none
1 little   "   wa-wa-wee-wee

But it was a long and frustrating process before she arrived at the masterly plot. It is not until 60 pages into the plotting that the plot she eventually used took serious shape. Before that, she had considered a different murder method, a different murderer and different suspects; in fact, a different story altogether.

Her 'five little pigs' are successful businessman Philip Blake and his stay-at-home brother Meredith, both childhood friends of the victim, artist Amyas Crale; Elsa Greer, Amyas's model and mistress; Angela Warren, sister of the convicted Caroline; and Miss Williams, Angela's governess. At the start of the notes we can clearly see the forerunners of these five main characters, although, as yet, Christie had not decided on the victim, let alone the villain:

Girl – (New Zealand) learns her mother has been tried and
    condemned for murder – possibly convicted to penal
    s[ervitude] – for life and then died
Great shock – she is an heiress uncle having left her all his
    money – gets engaged – tells man her real name and facts –
    sees look in his eye – decides then and there to do
    something about it – her mother not guilty – comes to H.P.
The past – 18 years ago? 1920–24

If not guilty who was?

4 (or 5) other people in house (a little like Bordens?)

Did mother murder
A. Husband
B. Lover
C. Rich uncle or guardian
D. Another woman (jealousy)

Who were the other people – Possibilities

Servant – Irish girl rather dumb – Ellen
Housekeeper – woman – reserved – practical – another Carlo
Girl – 15 at time (now 30 odd) (a Judy?)
Man – English gentleman – fond of gardening etc.
Woman – Actress?

❧ *Miscellaneous* ❧

Of the numerous references to nursery rhymes scattered through the Notebooks, sometimes the idea went no further than brief jottings, and in a number of cases it would seem that the rhyme defeated even Christie's fertile imagination. In Notebook 31 we find the following list:

1948 Short story for Nash's [Magazine]

A. Hickory Dickory Dock
Complex about the word Dock – a terror story –
danger – girl in job – finds out something – (the
people who wanted to pull the hall down) starts in
hotel – rich people – crooks

continued overleaf

B. Little Boy Blue
Where are you going to my pretty maid?
C. This is the way the gentlemen ride
Little Brown Jug – (My wife likes coffee and I like tea she
    says she's very fond of me)
D. Ding Dong Dell
E. Pussy Cat, Pussy Cat where have you been?
F. Town Mouse Country Mouse
G. Lucy Locket

This is one of the few examples of a dated page. Unfortunately, it is only a year, giving no indication of when during the year it was written. It is likely that Christie rattled off the list of nursery rhymes with quick, jotted and somewhat cryptic notes attached, intending to work on them later. The reference to 'Nash's' is something of a mystery: Christie published nothing in *Nash's* later than 1933, when they published the final six Parker Pyne stories. She was obviously working on the idea of a theme based around nursery rhymes but, as we will see, the idea, for the most part, came to nothing. Perhaps she, or *Nash's*, changed their minds and she subsequently abandoned the idea.

The only rhymes to appear at all, and in very different guises at that, were the first two. 'Hickory Dickory Dock', as it appears above, seems to have little, if any, connection with the rhyme. A 'complex' is an intriguing idea but apart from Helen in *Sleeping Murder* and her terrifying association of ideas at the performance of *The Duchess of Malfi*, there are no examples of 'complexes' in Christie. The *Hickory Dickory Dock* that we know is much different to the speculations above. Perhaps the last six words ('starts in hotel – rich people – crooks') foreshadow *At Bertram's Hotel.*

'Little Boy Blue' eventually appeared, although in much altered form and very briefly, in *Taken at the Flood.* Adela, the mystic of the Cloade family, receives the message 'Little Boy Blue' from her medium. She interprets this as a sign that Robert Underhay is still alive. This convoluted logic is due to the last line of the rhyme – 'under the haycock fast asleep'. Poirot wonders, not surprisingly, why the medium could not have conveyed this directly.

Despite the fact that 'Ding Dong Dell' appears in Notebook 18 and again in Notebook 35 with the added note (see below), it was never used. And, apart from a brief reference to 'Pussy-cat, Pussy-cat, where have you been' in the final page of *An Autobiography,* none of the rest appear either.

Three further references to nursery rhymes are scattered through the Notebooks:

One, two, 3 – 4 –5 Catching fishes all alive

Ding Dong Dell – Pussy's in the Well – ? An old maid murdered

Old King Cole?

Although at first glance it seems that none of these were ever used, a closer look at the last one reveals that its last line provided the title for the last play Christie wrote – *Fiddlers Three.* The complicated genesis of this final theatre offering is discussed in Chapter 9.

The early notes are a relatively accurate plan of what was to follow, but there are minor differences. Carla Lemarchant ('the Girl') is a Canadian rather than a New Zealander; and of the five sketches for possible characters one of them, 'the dumb Irish servant girl Ellen', is completely dropped. The 'Girl' and the 'Man' eventually became Angela and Meredith respectively; the 'housekeeper' is the prototype for Miss Williams and the 'woman' becomes Elsa Greer – although not a professional actress, she is in many ways the consummate performer.

There are three references that may require explanation. The reference to 'Bordens' is to the infamous Lizzie Borden murder case in Fall River, Massachusetts in August 1892 when Mr and Mrs Borden were hacked to death in the family home while their daughter Lizzie and the Irish maid Bridget were in the house. Although Lizzie was tried for the brutal murders, she was acquitted and no one was ever convicted. To this day her guilt or innocence is still a matter of debate and argument. 'Carlo' is Carlo Fisher, Agatha Christie's personal secretary and, ultimately, friend. She first came to her in 1924 and stayed for the rest of her working life. 'Judy' is in all probability Judith Gardner, the daughter of Agatha's friend Nan Gardner (née Kon).

We can immediately see a major problem with the set-up laid out above. There are four female characters and only one male. As the last three are obviously Angela, Meredith and Elsa respectively, the first two names are the ones to go. Subsequent attempts bring her closer to the final arrangement:

The 5 people

Miss Williams elderly Caro – devoted to Caroline

Mrs Sargent – Caro's elder half-sister – married money – etc.

Lucy – husband's sister – violently anti-Caro

A. (Idea) – Caro has injured a sister or brother when a child owing to her ungovernable temper – she believes this s[ister] or b[rother] did crime – therefore feels that she is expiating and gains content

Is s[ister] or b[rother] No 5 – Wee-Wee

And eventually she arrives at the five suspects in the novel itself. The following brief notes reflect accurately, apart from a name change of Carslake to Blake, the 'five little pigs' and their inter-relationships:

Philip Carslake – George's Hill – Prosperous – his best friend – Amyas – virulent against Caro – Describes how the injured step sister – as instance of her temper – induced to write an account –

Meredith – his home – takes P up to house – (now a hostel for youth) ghosts – he explains – will write – hedges about Elsa – shares picture of her – I did find she could have done it – her daughter

Elsa – rich woman – Changed from picture – frozen – virulent against Caro – vindictive – talks a little – sends her account. You want truth? You shall have it (says drama to vent spleen)

Miss Williams – elderly – room in London – Violently pro Caro – but admits she knows – about Angela – P persuades her truth is best – She agrees – will write –

Wee Wee woman of brains – character – successful archaeologist – welcomes P's intervention – quite convinced

– explains why Caro couldn't have done it – because of what she did to her

All of the details of the crime were arrived at only after numerous attempts. Through much of the notes the murder method was to be a shooting rather than a poisoning, and even though this was not pursued it is interesting to see how much of the attendant detail was retained:

A. Pistol – (Amyas's) wiped clean of prints except his – but they are wrong – also her prints in blood on table – Miss W covers for Angela? – saw her doing this – Angela in boat? But is returning)

Did someone pretend to be Wee-wee – steal up to him from behind and use her voice – press pistol against his head and fire – C thinks it is W[ee-wee] has heard voice – picks up pistol and wipes it

Caro heard Angela – speaking to Amyas pressed revolver into his back – sporty playacting – (she had peashooter) . . . she got there found him dead. Picked up pistol – wiped it – put it in his hand – but suicide not possible and one of her fingerprints on butt

Caroline went down to call Amyas for lunch – shot – but before she got there – Caro seen to take pistol from drawer of desk

Caro comes – Elsa springs up, snatches revolver – and shoots him – then rushes away – Caroline – sees her – thinks it is Angela – horrified – stunned at find – Elsa goes up to house – drops jersey on path – Miss Williams comes down – picks up jersey – then hears shot – she goes on – sees Caro – pressing his hand over revolver

In the novel the vital clue that convinces Poirot, in the course of his questioning, of Caroline's innocence is her wiping of the beer bottle and the subsequent superimposition of Amyas's fingerprints on it, as witnessed by Miss Williams. As can be seen in four of the extracts, this wiping was originally intended for a gun. And the detail of Caroline being seen taking a pistol is retained in the novel by her being seen taking the poison from Meredith's laboratory. In three of these extracts we also see the vital factor of Caroline's mistaken belief that the culprit is Angela, thereby paving the way for the ultimate sacrifice after her arrest.

The rejection of a gun in favour of poison is no surprise, as Christie knew little about the former but had a professional knowledge of the latter. She used poison more than any other murder method and more than any of her contemporaries, resorting to firearms infrequently. When Christie does decide on poison her fertility of invention is once again very evident in both the type of poison and its method of administration:

Nucleus – poison in port – husband had a glass in his room (analysed and full of it) – Caro seen washing out port decanter (by maid)

Poison – Sherry – One person poured it out, Caro took glass to Am – later cyanide found in glass, or belladonna

Possibilities of poison
A – Poison put into sherry at time when 'shut your eyes etc' is done – C has brought sherry to him – she finds him (having heard WW) later dead – wipes glass – puts dead man's fingers on it – (seen by Miss W)

B – Sherry pure – cyanide in strawberry – Caro still does her act – murderer adds cyanide to sherry – dregs with pipette – latter is found

C – Medicine – HCN – added to sherry by Caro – capsule is already taken

D – Capsule altered to AC from PC

Coniine – in capsule?
Result – he appears drunk – staggers about – double vision – (P's evidence) – E. sits down and watches him die – somebody comes – she gets up and speaks to him – joins other person – he shakes his head – or – seen sitting behind a table

A decanter – port? – Caroline washed it out afterwards

Box of cachets – <u>before</u> meals

HCN and bismuth mixture – extra HCN? Beer?

It is notable that even when she decides on coniine, the capsule idea in the above list is not used.

Other important plot points, and clues, are mentioned. The danger of a mistaken interpretation of overheard remarks is emphasised in the first two extracts; the final moving letter written by Caroline from her prison cell to her daughter, in the third extract, is another example of misinterpretation. Angela's penchant for practical jokes, as evidenced by the slug and, later, the valerian, is an important factor in Caroline's supposition of her guilt. And the all-important wiping of the glass (beer bottle in the book) surfaces again:

Case against Caroline – Quarrelled with husband that morning – said 'I'd love to kill you. Someday I will'

Don't you worry – I'll see to her packing (send her packing) heard between Caro and Amyas

A's – including parting note from C in prison my darling I
am quite content – going to Amyas – also important about
C's lover – Meredith?

Miss W – re Angela and slug

Miss W <u>saw</u> Caro wipe glass or cleaning revolver prints

After an admonition to herself, Christie eventually arrives at
the plot we know:

Go over the morning again

Dinner with Meredith night before – the drugs – Valerian –
coniine etc. – Caroline takes coniine – Elsa sees her – Talk
between Meredith and Amyas – one more day – row between
Angela and Amyas – School – next day Meredith discovers
coniine has been taken – rings up Philip – (? Is Philip
somewhere and Elsa with him – she hears?) Elsa is sitting ~~With~~
to M – says she is cold – goes up to house (gets coniine) – (Did
Caroline and Amyas have row after breakfast – ? Did Elsa hear
them – did she say to Philip 'conjugal quarrel') – sits – come
out – presently A comes out and says come down and sit.
    Elsa tests him – Caroline comes down – Elsa is cold – goes
to get jersey (gets coniine) – Caro and Amyas have row –
some of it overheard by P and M (But their evidence – I'll kill
you etc. – heard by Philip and E). 'Haven't I told you I'll send
her packing' – Comes out – sees them and says school –
Angela etc. – Elsa reappears this time <u>has</u> jersey – he drinks
off beer – Says (after looking down to sea) – they turn round
– Elsa is there – He drinks off beer – says hot and disgusting –
Caro ~~goes away~~ says she'll bring him some down iced – she
goes to get it – finds Angela at refrigerator – doing something
to beer – Caro takes bottle from her – Caro goes down with it
– she pours it out and gives it to him – he drinks it off.

~~Miss Williams~~ – Meredith looks at Elsa – sitting there –
her eyes – once or twice she speaks – (she has put some
coniine in dregs of glass – <u>not</u> bottle) – We're going to be
married aren't we? – looks up and sees Meredith – acts her
part. M sees A from door – queer expression – doesn't say
anything – one of his moods – M says I hear you were over at
my place this morning – A says Yes – I wanted – something?

Caroline and Miss W find him – C sends Miss W for ~~police~~
doctor – she then smashes his beer bottle and replaces it by
another. Findings – beer in glass had coniine in it – and his
fingers superimposed on hers – but not as they could have been

Oddly, there is little of Poirot's final scene, the explanation of
the events of 16 years ago and the revelation of the real killer
of Amyas Crale. For all practical purposes, the necessary detail
for that scene is included in the above extract and Christie
probably felt confident of writing the closing chapter without
the need for further detailed notes. And the conclusion is
somewhat ambivalent. Even though Poirot is certain he has
arrived at the truth, he realises that there is no proof . . .

Last Scene

Ph and M are there – Angela comes in – then W – finally
Lady D – M is a little dismayed. Caroline had motive – she
had means – now to hand takes coniine and it seems quite
certain she did take it – has questioned Meredith if person
could handily take it if 5 people in room – but she was last
and M in doorway had his back to room – so we take it as
proved that she took it

Three Blind Mice
(Radio Play 30 May 1947; Short Story 31 December 1948;
Play 25 November 1952)

Three blind mice, three blind mice
See how they run, See how they run
They all ran after the farmer's wife
She cut off their tails with a carving knife
Did you ever see such a thing a thing in your life
As three blind mice

◄○►

Monkswell Manor Guest House welcomes its first visitors,
including the formidable Mrs Boyle and the mysterious
Mr Paravacini, as well as amusing Christopher Wren and
enigmatic Miss Casewell. But Sergeant Trotter arrives to
warn them of a potential killer in their midst, just before
one of the guests is murdered.

◄○►

As usual, Christie's *Autobiography* is maddeningly vague about
dates, so when she writes 'About then the B.B.C. rang me up
and asked me if I would like to do a short radio play for a
programme they were putting on for some function to do
with Queen Mary', we must assume it was in 1946 as the
'function' was the eightieth birthday of Queen Mary on 30
May 1947. She duly presented them with *Three Blind Mice*, a
half-hour radio play. The following 21 October it was broadcast as a 30-minute television play with the same name and
script. She subsequently reworked it as a long short story,
which appeared in a US magazine in 1948 and a UK one
early in January 1949. It was collected, but only in the USA, in

3

An amusing rebus in Notebook 56 heads the top of the first of only two pages to feature the most famous play in the world – Three Blind Mice
(later The Mousetrap*).*

Three Blind Mice and other Stories in 1950. When the collection that ultimately appeared in the UK as *The Adventure of the Christmas Pudding* was in the planning stage, Christie made it clear that she did not want *Three Blind Mice* to be included as 'masses of people haven't seen it yet' and she did not want to spoil their enjoyment.

In her *Autobiography* she continues, 'The more I thought about *Three Blind Mice*, the more I felt that it might expand from a radio play lasting twenty minutes to a three act thriller.' So she re-reworked it as a stage play, but when it came to presenting it a new title had to be found as the original was already the name of a play. Her son-in-law, the erudite Anthony Hicks, came up with *The Mousetrap* (from Act II, Scene ii of *Hamlet*) and it opened in London on 25 November 1952. The rest is history . . .

The main changes between the different versions are in the very beginning. The radio and television versions feature the first murder, that of Mrs Lyon in Culver Street; the theatre version includes this only in sound effects on a darkened stage. The early draft of the script included an opening scene with two workmen sitting round a brazier who ask a passer-by for a match; the passer-by transpires to be the murderer on his way back from killing Mrs Lyon in nearby Culver Street and it is here that he drops the notebook containing the address of Monkswell Manor. Replacing this scene in the novella version is one set in Scotland Yard where the workmen describe the events of that evening.

There is almost nothing showing the genesis of this most famous work as a radio play. Notebook 56 does, however, have two pages headed, amusingly, 3 (an eye crossed out) (a mouse). As the following passage indicates, these few notes refer to either the novella or the stage version:

Arrival of Christopher Wren – his muffler – his dark overcoat
– his light hat (throw on bench) – weight of suitcase –
nothing in it? Some significant word between him and
Molly. Police in London – Sergeant Dawes – the workmen –
man was indistinct. The notebook – brought to S.Y. by one
of them? The identification – Monkswell Manor. H'm – get
me the Berkshire police. Mrs Bolton arrives – My dear, a
formidable woman – very Memsahib

A reference to Christopher Wren's suspicious suitcase appears
in the novella, as does the 'get me the police' phrase; the combination of these two ideas would lend support to the theory
that it is the novella version to which the Notebook refers. Also
notable is the odd reference to Mrs Bolton rather than Mrs
Boyle, the name by which she is known in every version.

∽‿∾

Crooked House
23 May 1949

◄○►

Charles Hayward falls in love with Sophia Leonides during
the war and is fascinated by her family, who live together in
a crooked house ruled over by her wealthy grandfather.
When he is poisoned, it is obvious that a member of the
family is crooked in the criminal sense.

◄○►

Crooked House remains one of the great Christie shock endings. So shocking was it considered that Collins wanted her to
change the ending (*Sunday Times* interview, 27 February
1966), but she refused. It would be reasonable, therefore, to
suppose that this solution was the book's raison d'être. At

least judging from the Notebooks we have, however, this was far from the case. As we saw in Chapter 3, several characters were considered as possible murderers before Christie arrived at the perfect solution.

In her specially written foreword to the Penguin 'Million' edition of *Crooked House* Agatha Christie writes: 'This book is one of my own special favourites. I saved it for years, thinking about it, working it out, saying to myself "One day when I have got plenty of time, and want to really enjoy myself – I'll begin it." I should say that of one's output, five books are work to one that is real pleasure. Writing *Crooked House* was pure pleasure.'

If, indeed, she spent years thinking and working it out, none of those notes have survived. Notebook 14, which contains most of the notes for this title, also contains, very exceptionally, two instances of dates. A few pages before the *Crooked House* outline the dates 'Sept. 1947' and '20th Oct [1947]' occur. The novel first appeared in an American serialisation in October 1948 and was published in the UK in May 1949. From internal evidence (a reference to Aristide's will being drafted 'last year' in November 1946) and from the evidence of the Notebooks below, the book was completed late in 1947 or early in 1948. So the years spent 'thinking about it and working it out' are, in all probability, those spent in the mental process before pen was put to paper. The more than 20 pages of notes cover the entire course of the novel.

The first page of notes in Notebook 14 is also headed 'Crooked House' so it seems to have been the title from the beginning. And, indeed, it is difficult to think of a better one. But (as we saw earlier in this chapter) Notebook 56 lists, on its opening page, the germ of *A Pocket Full of Rye*, which includes a distinct reference to a crooked house – although it is possible that the intention was to have a crooked, i.e.

dishonest, businessman and no reference to the novel of that name is intended.

> Sing a song of sixpence – the crooked sixpence found
>   (a Crooked man Crooked wife Crooked house)
> Coming home – Parlourmaid – maid and son – collusion –
>   maid killed to prevent her telling

Some pages before starting the serious plotting of this title we find two references to it:

> Crooked House
> Crippled soldier – with scarred face – old man is treating him
> for war wounds – but <u>not</u> war wounds – really a murderer

> Plans Sept. 1947
> ~~Crooked House (The Alt[erations]).~~ Done

It is not possible to date the first entry as this 'crippled soldier' scenario does not appear in any Christie title, but the next, on the following page, is headed unambiguously, showing that the bulk of the novel, if not the entire novel, was completed by this date with only the alterations to attend to. As we saw in Chapter 3, the crossing out of words is Christie's usual indication that something has been completed; here, in the same ink, we have the word 'Done' added.

Two pages later the plotting begins. The family is set out in some detail, as is the Sophia/Charles set-up:

> Old Aristide Kriston – Gnome but attractive – vitality – a
>   restaurant keeper – then marries the daughter of a fox
>   hunting squire – good looks – very fair and English.
> Roger – Greek – clever – devoted to father
> Clemency – woman scientist

Leo – fair handsome [possibly a forerunner of Philip]
Penelope – good humoured – motivated [possibly a
   forerunner of Magda]
Sophia
His second wife – Dorcas (Tabitha) [Brenda]
Laurence – the crippled tutor

[Told in] First person – Charles(?) in Foreign office – Sophia
Alexander is in his department – her talk – attraction – Oh, we
all live together in a little crooked house – he looks up nursery
rhyme – sees her in London – or arranges so to do – murder of
Grandfather. She refuses to marry him – because of murder –
because I don't know which of us did it? – anyone of us
might. His father is A.C. [Assistant Commissioner] – Charles
goes into it all – the old man – his marriage

There is a succinct, initial assertion on the second page of
notes that 'Harriet kills the old man'. However, consideration
is subsequently given to five other characters – Brenda, the
second wife; Clemency, Roger's wife; the tutor Laurence; the
formidable Edith de Haviland, Aristide's sister-in-law; and
Sophia – before eventually returning to the child-as-murderer
ploy. The idea 'Laurence – really no legs' is not pursued,
despite Christie's fascination with this as a plot device (see
'The House of Dreams', page 303), and Laurence remains
crippled only in the emotional sense. And although the killer
was eventually named Josephine, this name does not appear
until the thirteenth page of notes. She is earlier (as above)
referred to as Harriet and/or Emma:

Dorcas – No [Brenda]
Clemency? Yes her motive – Fanatical – slightly mad
Or shall it be Clemency – No gain – they will be out on
   the world

> Does Laurence do it – a cripple – Laurence – really no legs –
> therefore always different heights
> Edith – Yes – possible
> Sophia Possible Lack of moral fibre

Christie explores this idea further, although it is possible to infer – 'Yes – interesting' in the first extract and '(if J)', five pages later, in the second – that at this stage she had not definitely settled on Josephine (as she has now become) as the killer:

> Emma [Josephine] – Yes – interesting – not normal – wants power – hated her grandfather for something particular – (wouldn't let her do ballet dancing and you must start young?): Motive – adjust for <u>her</u> method – an abnormally high intelligence. If so is there a second murder – Yes – the old nurse (if Emma)

> The weight over the door (if J) or definitely dies – little black book nursery.
> Child's ending – best evidence there is – no good in court – children don't like being asked direct questions – to you she was showing off.
> Charles and Josephine – asks about letters – I was making it up – won't tell you – you shouldn't have told police.
> Josephine writing in her book. A.C. says – be careful of the child – there's a poisoner about

Although there is no mention of Josephine in the early pages, when she is mentioned she is given a page to herself and her detective work. Throughout the novel we are told of her ghoulish curiosity, her eavesdropping, her knowledge of detective fiction, and, poignantly, her little black book containing, supposedly, her detective notes:

146

Does Harriet know that Uncle Roger has been doing this?
An odious child who always knows what's going on
Josephine – the ghoul – she knows – I've been doing
  detective work
Finds Roger was going away – because I think because he'd
  embezzled money
And Edith hates Brenda – they wrote to each other – I know
  where they kept the letters
I didn't like grandfather – ballet – dancing nono.

Although it is an important Christie title, due to its shocking denouement, *Crooked House* is not a formally clued detective story. The answer is very evident in retrospect – Josephine's confident claim of her knowledge of the killer, her lack of fear, the dents on the wash-house floor from the experiments with the marble door-stop – but it is not possible to arrive at the solution by logical deduction. Despite this, the novel shows that even after a 30-year career Christie still retains her ability to surprise and entertain.

A Pocket Full of Rye
9 November 1953

Rex Fortescue is poisoned in his counting house; his wife is poisoned during afternoon tea of bread and honey; and the maid is strangled while hanging out the clothes. A macabre interpretation of the nursery rhyme brings Miss Marple to Yewtree Lodge to investigate the presence of blackbirds.

The notes for this novel are contained in five Notebooks, the bulk of them in Notebook 53, with shorter references in the other four. It would seem from internal evidence that this plot was simmering for some time before Christie refined it for the novel. *A Pocket Full of Rye* first appeared in October as a serial in the *Daily Express*. The official reader's report from Collins, dated April 1953, describes it as 'highly readable, exciting, baffling and intelligent; it is plotted and handled with a skill that makes most current detective fiction look like the work of clumsy amateurs'. Although he considered the means of the first murder too far-fetched, overall he rated it as a 'good' Christie, which seems a little lukewarm after such an effusive description.

The following cryptic reference in Notebook 56 gives the genesis of the plot, the first story, 'The Tuesday Night Club', of *The Thirteen Problems*, which had appeared 25 years earlier in December 1927:

General pattern like hundreds and thousands

Here, a housemaid, at the behest of her married lover, sprinkles 'hundreds and thousands' (the coloured sugar confection used mainly to decorate the top of trifles and small sponge cakes) liberally doped with arsenic over a dessert in order to eliminate an inconvenient wife. As if to clinch the matter, the maid in both short story and novel is called Gladys.

As can be seen from the following note in Notebook 14, the plots of *A Pocket Full of Rye* and *They Do It with Mirrors* were intertwined in the early stages of plotting (this note would seem to date from the late 1940s as it appears with notes for *Crooked House*):

Mirrors
Percival and Lancelot brothers – P good boy – L bad lad –
violent antagonism between them – actually they get
together to put Father out of the way and his young wife?
The trick – P and L fake quarrel – overheard below (actually
P. does it above) L. returns and stuns him – calls for help

The faked quarrel became the main plot device of *They Do It
with Mirrors* while the brothers Lancelot and Percival
remained with *A Pocket Full of Rye.*

A few pages later Christie sketches a plot:

The King was in his Counting House
Pompous magnate dead in (a) Office (b) Suburban house –
Blackbirds Mine
Good son Percival – bad son Lance – deadly enemies (really
in cahoots?) Motive – swindle by one of the sons? Servant
(N.A.A.F.I. girl) in league with Lance – she could alter all
clocks. Girl takes father's coffee to study – comes out
screaming? Lance first to get to him (kills him then) others
coming up. Old man drugged first – must have been at
dinner (Lance not there). Girl suspected – could have doped
him and stabbed him and put rye in man's pockets. They
argue – she is found dead – with clothes pin

This is much nearer to the one she eventually chose,
although much of the detail was to change – e.g. there is no
changing of clocks or stabbing in the finished novel and the
brothers are not 'in cahoots'. Here also is the first mention of
Blackbird Mines, the supposedly worthless mines which
prove to be a source of uranium, thereby providing the
killer's motivation. This aspect of the plot is very reminiscent
of the swindle perpetrated on his partner by Simeon Lee,
the victim in *Hercule Poirot's Christmas.* The reference to a

'N.A.A.F.I. girl' is to the Navy, Army and Air Force Institute, founded in 1921 to run recreational establishments needed by the armed forces, and to sell goods to servicemen and their families.

But it is in Notebook 53 that we find most of the plotting for the book. Although this follows the pattern of the novel closely, we can see here that various other possibilities were considered before their eventual rejection. Both Percival and his wife, and Lance and Adele, were considered as the murderers; Lance might have been either a 'good boy' or a 'bad lot'; and Christie proposed the use of strychnine or arsenic as a poison rather than taxine:

> Percival married to a girl (crook) abroad. She comes down to stay with other brother Lancelot – posing as his wife – she and Percival are the ones who do the murder

> Lance in it with Adele – Adele is engaged to father – gets her to kill father – then arrives just in time to poison her tea

> Lance is on plane returning from East. He is good son – his wife is Ruby Mackenzie

> Good son Percival – bad son Lance – deadly enemies (really in cahoots?)

> Strychnine and arsenic found later in cupboard in hall on top shelf or in dining room alcove in soup tureen on top shelf

After these speculations the plot begins to emerge. The material in the following extracts, all from Notebook 53, appears in the novel:

Lance (bad boy) is returning on plane – father has sent for
him. Before he can get home father dies – [Perci]Val's wife
is Ruby Mackenzie – Lance has got together with Marlene at
holiday camp. Gives her powder to put in early morning tea
– says it will make his father ill – he will be sent for – Marlene
is in terrible state – Lance arrives home – in time to poison
Adelaide – (in tea?) then adds it to honey

Chapter I
Tea during 11 – the newest typist makes it
Office – blond secretary – takes in the boss's tea
'Mr Fortescue is in conference – '
Scream – ill – blond rushes in – out – call for doctor – phone
    – Hospital

Tea – A[dele] eats honey off comb – son gives it to her in
tea – dies. Or son poisons her by putting stuff in meal before
he comes back officially – girl meets him outside

Maid in garden – clothes peg on nose. Miss M points out
later you wouldn't go out and hang up clothes at that time?
But you would meet young man

After death of girl Gladys – Miss M arrives in hall – sergeant
baffled – Inspector remembers her – Miss M very positive
about girl Gladys – dead – must be stopped – nose and
clothes peg – human dignity

Hickory Dickory Dock
31 October 1955

——————————◄○►——————————

A series of mysterious thefts in the student hostel run by
Miss Lemon's sister in Hickory Road culminates in the
death of one of the students. The incongruity of the
objects stolen attracts the attention of Hercule Poirot, who
visits the hostel – just before the first death.

——————————◄○►——————————

Hickory Dickory Dock
The mouse ran up the clock
The clock struck one
The mouse ran down
Hickory Dickory Dock

The notes for *Hickory Dickory Dock* are scattered over 50 pages
of Notebook 12, with two brief and unsuccessful attempts to
come to grips with it in two other Notebooks (See below and
'Miscellaneous' on page 129 – a note which dates from six
years earlier). Despite the rejection of these other ideas
Christie did not give up on utilising the rhyme, although it
supplies only the title and even that is tenuous. Apart from
the address (which itself was changed from Gillespie Road)
there is no attempt in the novel to follow the verse, one of
the few references to it coming in the closing lines when
Poirot quotes it.

The following in Notebook 12 shows that the book had
been largely finished early in the year prior to publication:

Suggestions to enlarge and improve Hic. Dic. Doc. May 1954

Some motifs from earlier novels recur. Mrs Nicoletis has a conversation with her unnamed killer much as Amy Murgatroyd did in *A Murder is Announced*; and Patricia Lane's telephone call to Poirot as the killer attacks her recalls Helen Abernethie's in *After the Funeral* and Donald Ross's in *Lord Edgware Dies*. And there is another unlikely, and unnecessary, relationship revealed towards the end of the novel. It is along the lines of similar disclosures in *Four-Fifty from Paddington* and *The Mirror Crack'd from Side to Side*. Both Morgan and Osborne refer to the fact that there were plans, in the early 1960s, to turn this title into a musical. Unlikely as this may seem, some of the music was written and a title – 'Death Beat' – had been decided upon, but the project eventually came to nothing.

The incongruity of the stolen objects presents Poirot, and the reader, with an intriguing puzzle and the explanations are satisfying. But there are arguably too many characters and some of the foreign students are little more than stereotypes.

Each of the first five pages of notes for this book is headed 'Holiday Task', suggesting that it was written at a time when Christie should have been relaxing. And the plotting of it did not come easily, as endless permutations and much repetition is included. It does not read as if she had a very clear idea of the plot when she started. The first page of the notes has the glimmering of a plot, much of which remained, although there were to be many changes before she was happy with it. By the end of the first page she had reached a possible starting point with echoes – 'one thing needed others camouflage' – of *The A.B.C. Murders*:

Things have disappeared – a rather stupid girl 'Cilly' (for Celia or Cecelia) – very enamoured of dour student – going in for psychiatry – he doesn't notice her. Valerie, a clever girl

puts her up to stealing 'He'll notice you through silly things
or rather – one really good thing'
    Stealing – things keep disappearing – really just one thing
needed others camouflage

Some early ideas were, thankfully, not pursued . . .

Hickory Dickory Dock
Complex about the word Dock – a terror story – danger –
girl in job – finds out something

H.P. in train – girl gets him to go stealing

Holiday Task (Cont.) 23 Gillespie Road
Does Miss Lemon decide to go as Matron? Bored by
retirement – asks Poirot's advice

. . . and some later ones that sounded promising were also
abandoned.

~~Hickory Dickory Dock~~
First death at one o'clock – Second at 2 o'clock

Important – 2 murders
[First] happens quite soon after P's lecture

1. Mrs. Nicoletis? Why? Blackmails? One of the gang and
   slipping?
2. Johnston? – Her trained mind has made certain deduction
   – etc. – possibly finds after with matter – a warning hold
   you tongue –
3. Aka bombo?
4. Nigel?
5. Patricia

Although she toyed with the idea of other characters as the eventual villain, Valerie was always a front-runner, either alone or with various combinations of other students:

1. Valerie – Master mind of racket – uses students – puts C up to it – Nigel in it with her? Or blackmails her or later N. one of victims
2. Nigel – finds out about racket – or in it with Valerie – childish excitable

Basic to the plot is a bet about obtaining poison and it must be admitted that some of the tactics suggested are horribly plausible, at least in the mid-1950s. The 'doctor's car' idea was one that surfaced a few times throughout the Notebooks and the white coat used in the novel as camouflage to access a hospital drug cupboard is one obviously inspired by Christie's personal experiences in University College Hospital during the Second World War:

The 4 methods – a bet is made – Argument
Nigel
Valerie
Len
Angus
They bring back
D[angerous]D[rugs] from car – Tube of morphine
Hosp. Patient – Phenobarbitol
Poison cupboard – Strych. Or Digi?

Bicarbonate bottle taken to put powder in – and bicarbonate substituted?

Then drugs destroyed but not one of them – the hospital one?

By page 50 of Notebook 12 she has the plot under control and the following extract contains most of the elements of the eventual plot:

Main arguments

V. an organiser of smuggling into this country (jewels?) (drugs?) by means of students. Mrs. N is in it – buys houses for students – also a shop on corner nearby – where rucksacks are sold – which have false bottoms (stones imbedded in glue (or powdered heroin in rouleau [roll] of canvas).
Police are on V's track – she passes something to Nigel – Bath salts – he examines this – finds heroin – replaces it with bicarbonate – and puts stuff in his bicarbonate bottle. Police come to house – V. destroys rucksack cuts it up – afterwards works on Celia.

And a few pages later she toys with some refinements (the saccharine and rucksack ideas and the involvement of Elizabeth Johnson were subsequently rejected):

Points to be resolved

Morphine (Acetate?) replaced by <u>boracic acid</u> – latter shows green flame when burned (Recognised by <u>Celia</u>?) [therefore] C. knows boracic was taken to replace morphia.

Pat found morphia – took B.[oracic] A[cid] from bathroom.

Saccharine? Did C. use this in coffee? Morphia tablets exchanged for sacchar

Val. runs smuggling racket (Killed C?)

E[lizabeth] J[ohnson] in with Val on smuggling

Akibombo – saw – what? to do with boracic? – to do with rucksack?

Smuggling Gems? Dope? Mrs. Nic V's mother? Just figurehead?

And, of course, Nigel's back-story – he was responsible for the death of his mother and his father has left a letter to this effect to be opened after his death – plays a vital part in the plot. It is not until approaching the end of the notes, however, that it is sketched in:

Argument

N. bad lot – needs money – tries to get it from his mother – forges her name – or gives her sleeping draught – she dies – he inherits – inquest – overdose – accident. But father turns him out – he cashes in on his mother's money. (Goes through it?) Pals up with Valerie – in smuggling racquet – has by then taken another name – archaeological diplomat – friends with students etc. Police come – he thinks for him – father dead? – letter left with lawyer – takes out bulbs – (or are bulbs – new ones – stolen – and one taken out in hall)

Nigel gives mother poison (Money) – Father a chemist – tests it or finds it – turns Nigel out – signs a deposition – at bank in case of his death – or if Nigel does anything dishonourable – N. is to change his name

One of the ideas that appears after the 'Suggestions to enlarge and improve' the novel noted above is Patricia's murder:

Nigel goes to police station . . . Pat (?) rings up – speaks to Nigel – breathless scared voice – Nigel – I think I know – who

> must have taken the morphia because I remember it was
> there that night . . . I don't want to say . . . Right . . . Nigel
> and Police go – Pat dead. Nigel cries like a small boy

Coming so late in the novel, however, this feels somewhat tagged on and it is an idea that enlarges rather than improves. In fact, a sketch of it had already appeared ten pages earlier:

> End sequence
> After Nigel and Pat scene Nigel goes round to Police Station.
> Pat (ostensibly) – really Valerie – rings up – knows who took
> it. They go there – Pat dead – Nigel's grief – real – H.P. arrives.

This murder is similar to the late murders in *Four-Fifty from Paddington* and *Ordeal by Innocence*, in the following years. Mrs Oliver, in Chapter 8 of *Cards on the Table*, says: 'What really matters is plenty of bodies! If the thing's getting a little dull, some more blood cheers it up. Somebody is going to tell something – and then they're killed first. That always goes down well. It comes in all my books . . .' And in Chapter 17 of the same novel: 'when I count up I find I've only written thirty thousand words instead of sixty thousand, and so then I have to throw in another murder . . .' It is difficult not to think of these remarks, tongue-in-cheek though they may be, when reading *Hickory Dickory Dock*.

EXHIBIT C:
AGATHA CHRISTIE IN THE NOTEBOOKS

'And then – there are always the old favourites.'

The Clocks, Chapter 14

Christie several times references herself and her work in the Notebooks. For some reason she twice – in Notebooks 72 and 39 – lists some of her books, although the lists are not exhaustive nor is it obvious what the titles have in common; and she often refers to earlier titles as a quick reminder.

⁕ Analysis of books so far
   Hotels – Body in Library, Evil under the Sun
   Trains Aeroplanes – Blue Train, Orient Express, Death in
      Clouds, Nile
   Private Life (country) Towards Zero, Hollow, Xmas, 3 Act
   Tragedy, Sad Cypress
            (village) Vicarage, Moving Finger
   Travel – Appointment with Death

The above list appears just after notes for *Mrs McGinty's Dead*. The fact that *Taken at the Flood* does not appear in the list may mean that it was compiled in late 1946, after *The Hollow*, or early 1947, before *Taken at the Flood* was completed. From the headings it would seem that she was considering backgrounds she had previously used.

* Ackroyd
  Murder on Nile
  Death in Clouds
  Murder in Mesopotamia
  Orient Express
  Appointment with Death
  Tragedy in 3 Acts
  Dead Man's Mirror

And the above, squeezed into the corner of a page during the plotting of *Evil under the Sun,* is even more enigmatic. Apart from the fact that they are all Poirot stories, it is difficult to see what they have in common.

The next musing appears in the notes for *Towards Zero.* Wisely, she decided against it as another mysterious death at the hotel in the space of three years could look, in Oscar Wilde's famous phrase, like carelessness:

* Shall hotel be the same as Evil Under the Sun – N[eville] has to go across in trolley because high water

The following odd, and inaccurate, reference to an earlier killer appears in the notes for *Elephants Can Remember.* It is odd because Poirot was not involved in that case and never knew Josephine:

* Calls on Poirot – asks about Josephine (Crooked House)

This was among the last notes to appear, written as it was just before the publication of *Postern of Fate.*

* Nov. 2nd 1973 Book of Stories
  The White Horse Stories
  First one – The White Horse Party (rather similar to Jane Marple's Tuesday Night Club)

Chapter 25 of *Four-Fifty from Paddington* includes a brief, cryptic reference to *A Murder is Announced*, but without mentioning the title . . .

* Somebody greedy – bit about Letty Blacklock

. . . while this reference appears during the plotting of *Third Girl*:

* Poirot worried – old friend (as in McGinty) comes to tea

Finally, the idea of reintroducing Sergeant Fletcher from *A Murder is Announced* was briefly considered during the plotting of *A Pocket Full of Rye*:

* Chapter II – Crossways – Inspector Harwell – or Murder is Announced young man

5

Blind Man's Buff: A Game of Murder

The ping of two bullets shattered the complacency of the
room. Suddenly the game was no longer a game. Somebody
screamed . . .

A Murder is Announced, Chapter 3

————————————◄○►————————————

SOLUTIONS REVEALED

The A.B.C. Murders • *Dead Man's Folly* • 'Manx Gold' • *The
Mirror Crack'd from Side to Side* • *A Murder is Announced* •
One, Two, Buckle my Shoe • *Peril at End House* • 'Strange Jest'
• *Why Didn't They Ask Evans?*

————————————◄○►————————————

'Shattering the complacency' – this is the dramatic impact of
a game going wrong in three Christie titles; while two others
are actual games, one intellectual and one physical. The dead-
liest game of the three titles is *The A.B.C. Murders*, while the
other two, *Dead Man's Folly* and *A Murder is Announced*, feature
actual games that go wrong due to the intervention of a real
murder. 'Strange Jest' and 'Manx Gold' are intellectual puzzles played by characters with a tangible prize at the end. The
latter was an actual game played in the Isle of Man in 1930,
while the former concerns the interpretation of a will. And

162

the game played by Clarissa in *Spider's Web* proves to be more dangerous than even she realises. In Christie's overall output the concept of the game-going-wrong is not a major motif, but the dramatic impact of the scene in the drawing-room at Little Paddocks in *A Murder is Announced* cannot be denied.

∼∼∼

'Manx Gold'
May 1930

────────◄○►────────

Cousins Juan and Fenella race to find a treasure as they match wits with their dead uncle – and a killer.

────────◄○►────────

A full history of this story can be found in the 1997 collection *While the Light Lasts*, thanks to sterling detective work by its editor Tony Medawar. Briefly, the chairman of a tourism committee in the Isle of Man approached Christie, in late 1929, with a view to her creating a treasure hunt on the island to boost tourist numbers. After a visit in April 1930 she wrote 'Manx Gold', for a fee of £65 (approx. £1,300 today), and it was published in five instalments, complete with clues, in the *Manchester Daily Dispatch*, in the third week of May of that year, and in a booklet distributed throughout the island. The 'treasure' was four snuffboxes hidden in separate locations around the island. (It is at an exhibition of snuffboxes that Hercule Poirot meets Mr Shaitana in *Cards on the Table*.)

Notebook 59 has 20 pages of notes for this unusual commission. Unfortunately those pages contain some of the most indecipherable notes of any of the Notebooks, including much crossing out, doodling and rough diagrams. The story is a minor entry in her literary output, remarkable mainly for the uniqueness of its creation and for the number of ideas that were to resurface in a book four years later. A snapshot and a dying man's last words as well as a villainous doctor are all features of *Why Didn't They Ask Evans?*. And, indeed, Juan and Fenella, a couple joining forces to elucidate a mystery, could be seen as forerunners of Bobby Jones and Lady Frances Derwent from the same novel. (Oddly, Juan and Fenella are both fiancés and first cousins.) The invisible ink idea first surfaced in *Motive Vs. Opportunity* two years earlier and as minor plot element in Chapter 20 of *The Secret Adversary*.

The notes accurately reflect the story as it appeared. There were however some name changes – Ronald and Celia become Juan and Fenella and Robert becomes Ewan – while the cliff fall and cuff-link clue were eventually discarded:

Story
Ronald and Celia – first cousins – letter from deceased uncle. Her annoyance about uncle – they arrive – the housekeeper – 4 snuff boxes missing. Letter left – with doggerel rhyme – call at lawyers. Then they start off – get it – on their return – meet the others – Dr ~~Crook~~ [Crookall was the name of the chairman of the Tourism Committee!] MacRae – Alan – Robert Bagshawe . . . doesn't like his smile. They decide to pool with others. Next day – the clues – housekeeper goes to get them – stolen – she admits that they asked her and she refused – a cuff link – it was Robert.

   They dash out – find R in grounds – dying – murdered – hit on head or in hospital – has fallen over cliff. They lean near him – may be conscious at end – opens eyes says 'D'ye ken – ?' – dies

The 'doggerel rhyme' referred to above appears in Notebook 59 in two forms, the one that actually appeared and the following, an earlier unused draft:

4 points of the compass so there be, South and West North
and East
A double S – No East for me Fare forth and show how clever
you be.

Two of the other clues also appear:

Excuse verbosity – I am all at sixes and sevens and Words
brought out by heat of fire

Another point of interest in this Notebook is a rough drawing of the clue that falls out of the map of the island – a cross,
a circle and a pointing arrow down to the detail of the little
lines on one side of the circle, as noticed by Fenella.

The A.B.C. Murders
6 January 1936

A series of letters to Hercule Poirot challenges him to a
deadly game. Despite these forewarnings, the letter-writer
manages to kill Alice Ascher in Andover, Betty Barnard in
Bexhill, and Sir Carmichael Clarke in Churston. As the
entire country watches, can Poirot prevent the D murder?

Thanks to Notebook 13, we have an exact date for the writing
of this novel. There, during a 15-page travel account, we read
the following, although unfortunately there are no further
references in the travelogue to the progress of the novel:

Tuesday November 6th [1934] Started *The A.B.C. Murders*.

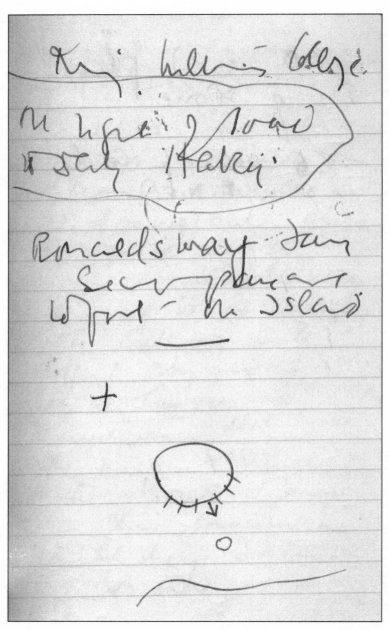

A rough sketch (and even rougher handwriting!) of a clue in the search for
Manx Gold, *from Notebook 59.*

Featuring a hugely imaginative concept – an alphabetical series both of murder victims and locations, chosen apparently at random – that was carried off with consummate skill and daring, *The A.B.C. Murders* was destined to become one of the top three Christie titles. And it is now forgotten that it was one of the earliest versions of the 'serial killer' idea that is now a staple of both the bookshelf and the screen. When this book was written the phrase did not even exist and is yet another example of Christie anticipating, without even realising it, motifs that were to dominate crime fiction in later years. (The other major anticipation was *Death Comes as the End*, set in Ancient Egypt and foreshadowing another current trend for crime novels set in various eras of the past.)

It is therefore a disappointment that there are only 15 pages of surviving notes for *The A.B.C. Murders*, scattered over three Notebooks. I suspect that there were earlier and rougher notes that have not survived, because the book's intricate premise needed detailed planning and the notes we have are relatively straightforward and organised.

Due to the elaborate plot and large cast of characters, the characterisation is slighter than usual. Dealing as it does with three separate murder investigations involving three sets of suspects, the attention to character drawing has to be somewhat perfunctory. The only people who are delineated in any detail are those who form part of Poirot's band of investigators.

The earliest jotting would seem to be Notebook 66. It appears as item E on a list that includes the plot outlines for 'Problem at Sea', 'The Dream', *Death in the Clouds*, *Dumb Witness* and *Sad Cypress*, and also includes the rudimentary germ of what was to become, almost 20 years later, *A Pocket Full of Rye*.

> Series of murders – P gets letter from apparent maniac.
> First – an old woman in Yorkshire – Second – a business

man – Third – a girl (tripper?) – Fourth – Sir McClintock
Marsh (who isn't killed – but escapes) – Fifth – Muriel Lavery
    Analysis of his house party – one person knows girl but
has absolute cast iron alibi.
    Idea of book is to prove alibi false but really Sir MM –
murdered ~~second v~~ third victim for reasons of his own – 1st
and 2nd camouflage – idea being to fasten guilt on cast iron
alibi man

It is interesting to note several points of similarity, even in
this early jotting, with the finished novel. These include the
retention of the idea of the 'old woman' as the first victim.
The novel's second victim is a young girl – 'tripper?' – at a
seaside resort, reflecting the potential third victim. The
device of two earlier murders as camouflage for a third – 'for
reasons of his own' – is retained. And the owner of the 'cast-
iron alibi' would seem to be the forerunner of Alexander
Bonaparte Cust, although a cast-iron alibi is not a feature of
his defence.

In contrast, the most surprising divergence from the finished novel is the unmasking of the fourth supposed 'victim'
of the maniac as the killer. This 'victim as killer' idea is not an
original concept; already used to great effect by Christie in
Peril at End House, it would be used again, to equally surprising effect, in *One, Two, Buckle my Shoe, A Murder is Announced*
and *The Mirror Crack'd from Side to Side*. Why she abandoned it
here we can never know, as it was by no means an overworked
plot device in her output.

The reference to 'his house party' is also puzzling. There is
no house party setting in *The A.B.C. Murders*, although the
idea does have echoes of the analysis of Sir Bartholomew
Strange's fatal house party in *Three Act Tragedy*. And, of
course, there is no mention of the alphabetical sequence,
which is the whole raison d'être of the novel. If the fifth

victim is Muriel Lavery then the sequence is certainly not alphabetical.

Notebook 20 also has a brief outline of the plot and by now the alphabetical sequence has been established. The details of the significant 'C' murder have moved nearer to those in the novel. But there are still major differences, especially at the end of the note:

> Aberystwyth – old woman Mrs. Ames – husband suspected
> Bexhill – Janet ~~Taylor~~ Blythe
> Cottersmarch – Sir Morton ~~Carmichael~~ Clarke – also a very
>   wealthy man – his brother Rudolph – anxious to help –
>   Janet Taylor's friend or sister also keen
> Doncaster – James Don – killed in a cinema
> P. gets a telegram – E. – sends it himself – man is released –
>   R[udolph] says this must be another murder

Much of the detail of the first four murders here is retained. The A murder features an old lady whose husband is suspected; the location, however, is different (this may be because Andover is easier to spell and/or pronounce than Aberystwyth!). The B murder is the same location although the victim's name is different. Note the change to a B initial, although Barnard is the surname eventually chosen. The C murder has the same set-up – a wealthy Sir Morton Clarke (note that the name as it appears in the book, Carmichael, is, interestingly, deleted here). The brother and sister of two of the victims are anxious to help, an idea pursued in Poirot's band of helpers. The D murder does take place in Doncaster and in a cinema, although in the novel it is actually a victim with the surname initial E.

A major surprise, however, and one that is, unfortunately, left unexplained, is the reference to the E murder. I would hazard a guess that in sending an ABC letter to himself

Poirot was stage-managing the release from prison of a suspect (possibly Alexander Bonaparte Cust) he knows to be innocent. He could also have been forcing the killer's hand, thereby precipitating a more dramatic unmasking in the last chapter.

Notebook 66, some 50 pages after the first reference, again takes up the novel beginning with possible locations for the murders. It goes on to consider two theories, both of which contain some elements – the existence of a 'real' victim, with an avaricious legatee, in a sequence of 'camouflage' victims – that Christie eventually adopted. Finally, it lists the questions that Poirot asks his five helpers in Chapter 32 of the novel:

A.B.C. Murder

Poirot gets letter
To Aberystwyth

Brixham or Bexhill
~~Cheadle~~ or Croydon
~~Dartmouth~~ Daneshill

Theory A
Intended victim Sir ~~Lucas~~ Oscar Dane –
It causes a stir – his fortune goes to his brother Lewis Dane

Theory B
Intended victim Janet King
3rd victim is Sir Oscar Dane – <u>but</u> he is only stabbed – not
     fatally injured – her will leaves everything to her cousin
     Vera who is the nurse attending Oscar – Vera and Oscar
     are attracted to each other

P asks a question of all of them
Megan – a passion for truth – want the truth? – NO – You

may not want the truth but you can give a truthful
answer!

Thora – would you have married Sir C if his wife had died

F[ranklin] Do you remember the news in the paper the day
you landed or [a question about] Ascot hats

J. Have you got a young man?

D[onald] When did you take your holiday

Only one of the possible locations, Bexhill, was actually used
in the book. She rejected nearby Dartmouth and both of the
C suggestions, eventually settling on somewhere else she did
know well, Churston, as the scene of the C murder. It is still
possible to get the train, like Poirot and Hastings, to
Churston and walk from there to Greenway House, although
at this point, 1934, Christie did not yet own the house.

Theory A was the eventual choice as the main plot,
although Theory B had some interesting possibilities. Sir
Oscar Dane faking an attack on himself in order to kill
another victim and inherit, through marriage, a fortune from
her is a very Christiean concept and would, no doubt, have
produced a surprise ending. It does have more than an echo,
from two years earlier, of *Peril at End House* (where Nick
Buckley fakes attacks on herself in order to kill her cousin
and inherit a fortune) and this is possibly the reason for its
rejection.

The biggest surprise at this point is that the victims are not
chosen alphabetically despite the fact that a few pages earlier
Christie is listing Brixham/Cheadle/Dartmouth. The third
'victim' is Dane and the fourth is King. While some connection between the victims would have been necessary, the
alphabetical sequence was inspired. And like many inspira-
tions it is brilliantly simple. Sadly, we will never know who or
what inspired it. Perhaps Christie remembered *Why Didn't
They Ask Evans?*, published in September 1934, two months

before she began *The A.B.C. Murders*, where an open ABC Guide is mentioned in Chapter 24 and used as a clue to a character's whereabouts?

Finally, the five questions of Chapter 32 all appear in the Notebook as they appear in the book, apart from a different initial ('J') for the Mary Drower question and the substitution of the shorter and subtler 'Ascot hat' one for the Franklin Clark.

One of the main themes of Chapter 32 and 35, that of a murderer hunted like a fox, is captured in a last cryptic note:

Bit about the fox

'Strange Jest'
July 1944

When wealthy Uncle Mathew dies and leaves very little in his will, his legatees approach Miss Marple in an attempt to uncover the whereabouts of his missing fortune.

The Miss Marple short story 'Strange Jest' was first published in the USA in November 1941 but did not appear in the UK until almost three years later. It is a slight non-crime story built around a single device, the interpretation of clues to a missing fortune. Its brevity, a mere ten pages, confirms its similarity to a rebus or literary acrostic.

The interpretation of a will appears in a few Christie short stories. Poirot deals with 'The Case of the Missing Will', Tommy and Tuppence tackle 'The Clergyman's Daughter'/'The Red House' and 'Strange Jest' is one of the Miss Marple versions, the other being 'Motive Vs. Opportunity' in *The Thirteen Problems*.

A page in Notebook 62 headed 'Short Marple Stories' goes on to list ideas that eventually appeared as 'The Case of the Perfect Maid', 'The Case of the Caretaker', 'Tape-Measure Murder', *The Moving Finger* and, oddly, *Endless Night*. There are also some unused ideas, including two that appear again and again, the twins and the chambermaid (see 'The House of Dreams', page 303). Some pages later, there are three pages of notes on 'Strange Jest' including a full outline of the plot:

> Found on love letters from abroad – cryptogram in letter? No – stamps on it.
> Old Uncle Henry – died – had money but hid it somewhere – Gold? Diamonds? Bonds? Last words – taps his eye – (glass eye like Arsene Lupin). They look through desk – secret drawer found by furniture expert – love letters from Sierra Leone signed Betty Martin

The idea of unrecognised and valuable stamps on an envelope appears again in *Spider's Web* nearly 15 years later. The main clue in the story, the phrase 'all my eye and Betty Martin', is exactly the same as the main clue in 'The Four Suspects' in *The Thirteen Problems*. The reference to Arsène Lupin is to the crime story 'The Crystal Stopper' featuring the French detective, by Maurice Leblanc.

Also of note is the glass eye idea itself. Christie decided not to use it in this story, instead adopting the idea of Uncle Henry (Mathew in the published version) tapping his eye. But it is entirely possible that the glass eye, which formed a key plot device in *A Caribbean Mystery*, almost 25 years later, has its origins here.

∽✕∾

A Murder is Announced
5 June 1950

———————◄○►———————

An advertisement in the local paper announcing a murder
brings many of the inhabitants of Chipping Cleghorn to
Little Paddocks, the home of Miss Blacklock, where the
ensuing game of Murder turns deadly. Miss Marple, who
is visiting the local vicar, investigates a triple killing.

———————◄○►———————

A Murder is Announced was Agatha Christie's fiftieth title
(although a 1939 US collection, *The Regatta Mystery,* had to be
included in order to reach this significant number) and the
occasion of a major launch and celebration party in
London's Savoy Hotel in June 1950. She happily posed for
photographs with Sir William Collins beside a cake iced with
the jacket design. Other guests included fellow crime writer
Ngaio Marsh and the actress Barbara Mullen, then appearing
in the West End as Miss Marple in *The Murder at the Vicarage.*

A Murder is Announced remains one of the best detective
novels Christie ever wrote. It qualifies effortlessly for the Top
Ten and it is easily the best of the Marple titles. The last of
the ingeniously constructed, daringly clued and perfectly
paced detective novels and a wonderful half-century title, it
shares a major plot device with both 'The Companion' in *The
Thirteen Problems* and 'The House at Shiraz' (see Chapter 8)
in *Parker Pyne Investigates.* Although we do not have extensive
notes for this title – just ten pages in total – we do have interesting ideas that were toyed with before settling on the final
plot. The following reference, in Notebook 35, is idea J in an
alphabetical list, dated 1947:

J. A Murder has been (combine with H)
    People going to meet in a Country house ~~Or at a dinner party in London~~ Like [Ten Little] Niggers – each of them thinking beforehand – about 6 people – they all have motive for killing a certain man – that is <u>why</u> they are asked – victim turns up last – host and hostess (a Mrs North) – it is often let – for parties or a London house – street numbers repainted

A death has been arranged and will take place on Monday Feb 6th at 20 Ennerly Park Gardens – friends accept this, the only intimation – no flowers by request

As we shall see, the setting changed a few times before arriving at Chipping Cleghorn, as did the wording of the invitation. And in the finished novel we do indeed meet a group of people going to a house in the country, but not all of them have a motive for murder and the reason for their invitation is very different. 'Mrs North' is possibly Christie's friend Dorothy North (the dedicatee of *One, Two, Buckle my Shoe*). The reference 'combine with H' is to an earlier jotting about a plot, never pursued, involving a divorced mother of two daughters whose first husband inherits a fortune. The children are Primrose and Lavender and the subsequent murders were to involve flowers left by the bodies; hence the 'no flowers by request' instruction.

In Notebook 31 we can see the plot that we know taking shape. These notes are inserted on four pages in the middle of extended notes for *They Came to Baghdad* dated, some pages earlier, 'May 24th'. This is, presumably, 1948; on 8 October 1948 Edmund Cork, Christie's UK agent, wrote assuring her American agent that, although she had not written a word that year, she was shortly to start on a Miss Marple story. In fact she worked on it in 1949.

Argument I, below, is the plot with which we are familiar although some fine-tuning was necessary – Harry (Patrick Simmons in the novel) is not the victim nor is he in possession of knowledge dangerous to Miss Blacklock. Apart from other name changes, as indicated, this is the plot as it finally appeared.

The really interesting passage, however, is Argument II. Here we are presented with a totally different plot and murderer with Letitia as victim rather than perpetrator:

A M[urder] has been arranged

Letitia Bailey at breakfast reading out [Letitia Blacklock]
Amy Batter – someone calls her Lottie [Dora Bunner]
young man Harry Clegg – son or nephew of old school
    friend? [Patrick Simmons]
Phillipa Hedges lodger [Phillipa Haymes]
Col and Mrs Standish [Col. and Mrs Easterbrook]
'Hinch' and 'Potts' [Hinchcliffe and Murgatroyd]
Edmund Darley and his mother [Edmund and Mrs.
    Swettenham]
Mitzi – maid?

The events

Argument I
L[etitia] is Deus ex Machina – Sister 'Charlotte' is really her
    . . . . . . Sister 'consumptive' acting I[n] P[lace]

Clue
1 Belle gives this away
2 Called Lotty by Amy instead of Letty

[therefore] L. has to remove – Harry? He knows by snapshot
– (seen it in album?) – (tie up with disappearance of album?)
– (or blank space in it) later – ostensibly photos of P and E –

176

or their mother – Phillipa is 'Pip' Recognised by L. who is however quite beneficent towards her and advances theory that H. is Pip. L. shoots ~~Pip~~ H – Later poisoning – Amy dies instead of her – Circle narrows to look for Emma or Emma's husband – or Phillipa's husband (missing) – Point anonymous letter from 'Pip' (written by L) sent to Belle.

    3rd excitement is the danger to someone who has found out something (Phillipa?) her boy friend (love interest?) Edmund or Edmund's rather mysterious friend

Argument II

Mitzi is prime mover – she is 'Emma' – Shot young man is her husband – this comes out later – she sticks to it – Harry and Phillipa arranged ambush together – second murder is Letitia – ~~(Mitzi very ill?) Poisoning~~ Mitzi suspected – persecuted Polish Girl – sulky – persecution complex – then she nearly dies – Does Leticia make new will?

How Harry and Phillipa arranging the ambush was to work is not elaborated unless it was intended to be part of the game. We shall never know.

In an undated note to Collins, Christie draws attention to the galley proofs and the correct spellings of 'Lotty' and 'enquiries', reminding them of the importance of ensuring that they are printed *incorrectly* sometimes – 'Plot depends on this'. There is just a single reference to this in the Notebooks; in Notebook 30 the following appears as an

Idea
inquire enquire – both in same letter (part of it forgery)

When she incorporated this into *A Murder is Announced* we can see how she used it in a much cleverer way than merely as a forgery. By including the different spellings, on almost

AGATHA CHRISTIE'S SECRET NOTEBOOKS

Apart from its sublime detective plot *A Murder is Announced* is also a convincing picture of an England stumbling out of post-war austerity. We are no longer in the world of butlers and cocktail receptions; there is no dressing for dinner or questioning the lady's-maid; no weekend guests or alibis provided by nights at the opera. The shadow of rationing and bartering, deserters and foreign 'help', ration books and identity cards hovers over the book. In fact, some of the clues come from that very milieu – the seemingly extravagant use of the central heating, the note with the incriminating spelling, the ease of access to houses to assist bartering. Chapter 10 iii also includes a telling conversation between Miss Marple and Inspector Craddock on the changing of the old order: 'Fifteen years ago one knew who everybody was . . . But it's not like that anymore . . . nobody knows anymore who anybody is.' And this, with customary Christie ingenuity, is also subsumed into the plot.

Another aspect of this novel that merits attention is the understated presence of the lesbian couple, Miss Hinchcliffe

consecutive pages in Chapter 18, in documents supposedly written by the same character, she defies her readers to spot the anomaly and, thereby, a major indication of the killer's identity. It remains one of her most daring clues. The use of both forms in the same letter might have been a bit *too* daring and the approach she adopts is much more subtle.

Although the Notebooks are short on detail for *A Murder is Announced*, we are fortunate to have the actual typescript – one of the few known to exist – with copious handwritten notes. An inserted handwritten page toys with changes to the name of the village – 'Chipping Burton? Chipping Wentworth?' – instead of the original Chipping Barnet, the and Miss Murgatroyd. Heretofore, the few examples of gay characters scattered through the novels have been either figures of fun (Mr Pye in *The Moving Finger* or Mr Ellsworthy in *Murder is Easy*) or menace (Lord Edgware's Greek-godlike butler or, some years later, Alec in *The Rats*). The picture of the Chipping Cleghorn couple is matter of fact and, as far as the villagers are concerned, unremarkable; and after the murder of Murgatroyd, moving. This is a distinct improvement on the representation of Christopher Wren in *Three Blind Mice,* three years earlier. He is one her campest creations and is described in the original script as having a 'pansy voice'; and he is not toned down in the stage version two years after *A Murder is Announced,* where he remarks on the attractiveness of policemen (Act I, Scene ii). Shortly after the appearance of *A Murder is Announced,* when Christie was planning *Mrs McGinty's Dead,* she intended two of the suspects to be '2 young men who live together', although she abandoned this idea.

name of the Inspector – 'Cary? Craddock?' – instead of the original Hudson and the name of the victim – 'Wiener?' – instead of the original Rene Duchamps. The original wording of the advertisement was also amended from 'A Murder has been arranged and will take place on Friday Oct. 13th at Little Paddocks at 6.p.m. Friends please accept this, the only intimation.' And the title on this typescript is the slightly more cumbersome *A Murder has been Arranged.* Puzzlingly, the name 'Laetitia' appears throughout and every example has been amended, by hand, to plain, and accurate, 'Miss (Blacklock)', leading to the assumption that this switch was a late inspiration despite its appearance in the notes – 'Sister "Charlotte" is really her' – as above. Christie would have considered it utterly unfair to refer to 'Laetitia' if, in fact, the character is actually Charlotte; hence the amendment to the accurate but ambiguous *Miss Blacklock*.

The only jarring note in this otherwise near-perfect detective novel is the unlikely denouement in the kitchen of Little Paddocks when Miss Marple practises her hitherto unknown gift for ventriloquism. A feature common to almost all of the Marple titles is the dramatic closing chapter. Like *A Murder is Announced, The Body in the Library, The Moving Finger, They Do It with Mirrors, Four-Fifty from Paddington, A Caribbean Mystery, At Bertram's Hotel, Nemesis* and *Sleeping Murder* all culminate in a theatrical action sequence where the killer incriminates him or herself, usually in a misguided attempt at another murder. In most cases this is because the case that Miss Marple outlines is somewhat short on verification and largely dependent on her intuition, which, however unerring, is not the same as legal proof. Oddly, in *A Murder is Announced*, above all her other cases, proof is abundant and there are numerous clues to complement Miss Marple's gifted insight. As Robert Barnard has pointed out in his masterly study of Dame Agatha, *A Talent to Deceive*, Miss Marple's reputation as a Great Detective is not improved by her emergence from a broom cupboard at the climax of the novel. This short two-page scene could have been easily amended to omit this embarrassment.

Spider's Web
Premiere 14 December 1954

―――――――――◄○►―――――――――

When she discovers a murdered body in her drawing
room shortly before her diplomat husband is due home
with an important politician, Clarissa devises a plan to
fool the police. She enlists the help of three houseguests,
unaware that the murderer is closer to home than
she thinks.

―――――――――◄○►―――――――――

There are 20 pages of notes for *Spider's Web*, all contained in
Notebook 12. The character of Clarissa, written specifically at
the request of the actress Margaret Lockwood, is Christie's
finest comedy creation. The play itself is a comedy thriller
with sufficient of both to make it a winning combination. It is
also a successful blend of whodunit and will-they-get-away-
with-it; a surprise killer is unmasked in the closing minutes,
maintaining Christie's reputation for shock revelations, and
there are numerous unexpected twists in the subsidiary plot.
The will-they-get-away-with-it scenario was not a regular feature of Christie's output but it is also a feature, to a greater or
lesser degree, in her next three plays – *The Unexpected Guest*,
Verdict and *The Rats*.

The first page of notes is headed:

Act III Spiders Web   Laura Finds a Body?

Christie adopts her usual method of assigning letters to the
various plot points that follow but, despite the heading, not
all refer to Act III. Some of them, as marked, appear in Act II,
Scene ii, leading to the suspicion that the acts were

rearranged (perhaps in the course of the play's production) and Act III originally included the previous scene. There are no surprises in the notes and no unexpected plot developments; those that remain reflect accurately the course of the play. With the exception of Sir Rowland Delahaye, who appears in the notes as Sir M, even the names remain the same. I assume that the disappearance of notes for the earlier acts is another casualty of the years.

Spider's Web is full of ideas from earlier works:

* Miss Peake hides the body across the top of the spare-room bed under the bolster, as does the villain in 'The Man who was No. 16', the final story in *Partners in Crime.*
* The missing playing card is a plot device of 'The King of Clubs'.
* The idea of valuable stamps on an envelope appears in 'Strange Jest'.
* Pippa's creation of a wax doll is the same course of action as Linda Marshall followed in *Evil under the Sun.*
* Clarissa taking responsibility for the murder when it seems as if Pippa is responsible has echoes of Caroline Crale's actions on behalf of her sister, Angela, in *Five Little Pigs.*
* 'The Adventure of the Cheap Flat' also has the ploy of a property made available at a discount price to the right person.
* There is also yet another clever variation on a clue involving names (see *A Murder is Announced, Mrs McGinty's Dead* and *Peril at End House*).
* There are sly references to *Ten Little Nigger Boys* [sic] in Act II, Scene ii, and to a 'body in the library' in Act I.

Points

A. Miss Peake is on spare room bed
B. Miss Peake appears – 'the body's disappeared' – she winks
C. Sir M says – 'never grown up' [Act I]
D. Inspector and Sir M – Latter puts forward idea of narcotics [Act II, Scene ii]
E. Inspector suggests he had actually found something in desk [Act II, Scene ii]
F. Clarissa (to Sir M) did one of you move it? No – all herded together in dining room
G. Cl. asks Sir M (or Hugo) name of antique dealers
H. The book – Sir M says 'What's the Inspector consulting – Who's Who' [Act II, Scene ii]
I. Sir M. says story about friend and stamps or envelope with autographs
J. Clarissa asks Elgin about references [Act II, Scene ii]
K. Pippa comes in – terrible yawns – hungry
L. Clarissa accuses Miss Peake of being Mrs. Brown

The main preoccupation for the scenes involving Pippa was the presence or absence, in retrospect for obvious reasons, of Jeremy. These scenes appear in Act I.

The Pippa bits

1. Recipe book candles, Can you eat it? Present (Sir M Jeremy? Clarissa?)
2. Priest's Hole – Place to put a body. Present Jeremy and ? ? ? [sic]
3. The autographs – Pippa shows them – puts them away in shell-box
4. Then bit about stamps – Present not Jeremy – others ad lib

One of the interesting items among Christie's papers is a suggested screen treatment, dated 1956, for a possible film version of this play. It is not entirely certain that it is by Christie herself but it looks 'unofficial', i.e. as if done by someone not directly involved in the subsequent 1960 film. It sketches out the events that have taken place prior to the start of the play – Clarissa meeting Henry, Miranda desperate for drugs, the subsequent divorce and remarriage and Pippa's acceptance of Clarissa; it also includes the sale of a stamped envelope to Mr Sellon . . .

Dead Man's Folly
5 November 1956

---◄○►---

Mrs Oliver organises a Murder Hunt in the grounds of Nasse House. When the 'body' turns out to be only too real, Hercule Poirot is on hand to discover who killed schoolgirl Marlene Tucker and what happened to Lady Folliat.

---◄○►---

Although it was published in November 1956, *Dead Man's Folly* had a complicated two-year genesis. In November 1954 Christie's agent wrote to the Diocesan Board of Finance in Exeter explaining that his client would like to see stained glass windows in the chancel of Churston Ferrers Church (Christie's local church) and was willing to pay for them by assigning the rights of a story to a fund set up for that purpose. The Diocesan Board and the local church were both very happy with the arrangement and in a letter of 3 December 1954 Hughes Massie confirmed 'Mrs Mallowan's

184

intentions to assign the magazine rights of a long short story to be entitled *The Greenshore Folly*' to such a fund. The amount involved was reckoned to be in the region of £1,000 (£18,000 in today's value).

By March 1955 the Diocesan Board was getting restive and wondering about the progress of the sale. But for the first time in 35 years, much to everyone's embarrassment, it proved impossible to sell the story. The problem was its length; it was a long novella, which was a difficult length, neither a novel nor a short story, for the magazine market. By mid-July 1955, the decision was made to withdraw the story from sale, as 'Agatha thinks [it] is packed with good material which she can use for her next full length novel'. As a compromise, it was agreed that she would write another short story for the Church, also to be called, for legal reasons, 'The Greenshore Folly', 'though it will probably be published under some other title'. So, the original and rejected novella 'The Greenshore Folly' was elaborated into *Dead Man's Folly* and Christie wrote the shorter and similarly titled 'Greenshaw's Folly' to swell the coffers of the Church authorities. 'Greenshaw's Folly' was first published in 1956 and was collected in *The Adventure of the Christmas Pudding* in 1960.

Notes relating to *Dead Man's Folly* are contained in Notebooks 45 and 47. As a result of its history, it is difficult to tell from the Notebooks whether the notes refer to the novella or the novel version, but it seems likely that Notebook 47 is the original novella and Notebook 45 the elaborated version – Notebook 47 is a discussion of basic points, which would not have been necessary if the story had already been written. In 15 pages Christie sketched the entire plot of 'The Greenshore Folly' so when it came to expanding it, she had only to elaborate actual scenes – the plot was already entire from the novella version.

Notebook 47 outlines the basic situation and sketches some ideas, all of which, with minor changes – garden fete rather than 'Conservation Fete', Girl Guide victim rather than Boy Scout – were to be included in the story:

Mrs Oliver summons Poirot – she is at Greenway – professional job – arranging a Treasure Hunt or a Murder Hunt for the Conservation Fete, which is to be held there

'Body' to be boy scout in boat house – key of which has to be found by 'clues'

or a real body is buried where tree uprooted and where Folly is to go

Some ideas
Hiker (girl?) from hostel
Next door – really Lady Bannerman [Stubbs]

It is significant that, right from the start, the story was to be set at Greenway. Perhaps because this was a personal project, written for her place of personal worship, Christie was anxious to retain a local flavour. Although she had used Greenway before for *Five Little Pigs* and would use the ferry at the bottom of the garden in a few years' time in *Ordeal by Innocence*, *Dead Man's Folly* represents an extended and detailed use of her beloved Greenway. Apart from the house itself, and its history as told by Mrs Folliat, also featured in the story are the Gate Lodge, Ferry Cottage, the Boathouse, the Battery, the Tennis Court and the Youth Hostel next door; and the internal geography of the house reflects reality even down to Poirot's bedroom and the bathroom across the corridor. The magnolia tree near the front door where Mrs Folliat and Hattie stand to talk, the winding drive ending at the big iron gates, the winding and steep path connecting the Battery and the Boathouse – all these exist to this day.

The notes that follow, all from Notebook 47, form the basis of *Dead Man's Folly*. Christie decided on a version of B below as the motivation and nobody called Lestrade features in either version:

Who wants to kill who
A. Wife wants to kill rich P Lestrade has lover – both poor
B. Young wife recognised by someone who knows she is
   married already – blackmail?
C. P Lestrade – has a first wife who is not dead – (in S.
   America?) – it is wife's sister who recognises him
Czech girl at hostel? P mentions meeting a hostel girl
   'trespassing' – angry colloquy between them seen (but not
   heard) by someone – he decides to kill her
D. Mrs Folliat – a little balmy – or young Folliat at hostel?

Mrs Folliat of original family who built it – now belongs to
Sir George Stubbs with beautiful young wife – Chilean girl? –
Italian mother – Creole? – Rich sugar people – girl is feeble
minded. Spread about that Sir G made his money in Army
Contracts – really Sir G (a pauper) is planning to kill wife
and inherit her money

The references to 'Greenshore' in the following extract would seem to confirm that Notebook 47 contains the original notes for the novella:

Does Sir George marry Hattie Deloran – she is mentally
defective – he buys place 'Greenshore' and comes here with his
wife – the night a folly has been prepared – she is buried. The
Folly goes up the next day – another Lady Dennison [Stubbs]
takes her place – servants see nothing – they go out for a stroll –

other girl comes back (from boathouse). Then for a year Sir
George and Lady Dennison are well known for guests. Then the
time comes for Lady D to disappear – she goes up and down to
London – doubles part with pretending to be a student

Sally Legge remains in the novel; the reason for the change
of first name from Peggy was highlighted by Christie herself
below. Definitely a good idea!

Points to be decided
A. Who first chosen for victim? Peggy Legge? Something
   about Old Peg Leg
B. What did Maureen [Marlene] know or do – heard
   grandfather talk about body and Sir George really
   being James?
   Or
Does she snoop? Intending to snoop on events? Really sees
Lady S change into hiker?
   Or
See Sir George and his partner together?
What does Maureen write on Comic
Mrs O's clue?
Boat house?
House boat?
Maureen's scribble on the comic – G[eorge] S[tubbs] goes
   with a girl from the YHA

The following extracts, from Notebook 45, have page references, presumably to the proofs of 'The Greenshore Folly'.
The accompanying remarks are reminders to Christie herself, as she expands the original story. She also experiments
with the details of Mrs Oliver's Murder Hunt and clarifies, for
herself, the timetable of the fatal afternoon:

P.119 – Elaborate Mrs F's remembering
P.21 – A much elaborated scene in the drawing room
  at tea
P.24 Go on to Legges after 'Hattie'

Recast order of next events
P.38 elaborate breakfast party –
P.47 Perhaps an interview with Michael Weyman at tennis
  Pavilion
Clear up point about Fortune teller's tent
p.61 much more detail after discovery of body

Mrs Oliver's plan

The Weapons
Revolver
Knife
Clothes Line

Footprint (in concrete)
Rose Gladioli or Bulb catalogue? Marked?
Shoe
Snap shot

Who?   Victim
Why?   Weapon
How?   Motive
Where?   Time
When   Place

Scheme of afternoon –

4 pm P[eggy] L[egge] leaves tent
4.5 pm H[attie] tells Miss B to take tea
4.10 pm H goes into tent – out of back into hut – dresses as
  girl – goes to boat house

4.20 Calls to Marlene – strangles her then back and arrives
as herself Italian girl – talks to young man with turtles
[turtle-shirted competitor]

4.30 leaves with Dutch girl and pack on back or with turtle –
Dutch girl goes to Dartmouth – Italian girl to Plymouth

EXHIBIT D:
TRUE CRIME IN THE NOTEBOOKS

———————— ⚓ ————————

'I have occupied myself of late in reading various real life unsolved mysteries. I apply to them my own solutions.'

The Clocks, Chapter 14

Agatha Christie wrote on two true-life murder cases, both of them very similar to her own fiction. 'The Tragic Family of Croydon' in the *Sunday Chronicle* of 11 August 1929 is an article about the then current and still unsolved Croydon poisoning case in which three members of the Sidney family were murdered, almost certainly by a member of their own household, in the space of a few months; and in October 1968 a short article by Christie appeared in the *Sunday Times* about the Charles Bravo murder, another domestic poisoning drama. And apart from fictional crime and its practitioners, Christie also refers in the Notebooks to a few real-life murder cases. Some are very well known but others are quite obscure:

Lizzie Borden
In Notebooks 5, 17 and 35 the infamous Lizzie Borden is mentioned during the plotting of *Elephants Can Remember*, *They Do it with Mirrors* and *Five Little Pigs* respectively. In 1892 in Fall River, Massachusetts, Mr and Mrs Andrew Borden were brutally murdered in their own home. Although their daughter Lizzie was tried for the murders, she was acquitted and to this day her guilt or innocence is a matter of intense speculation. In each case, as can be seen, it is the possibility of using a set-up similar to the Borden case – a domestic

crime with the killer, in all likelihood, a member of the family – that attracts Christie:

> Or Lizzie Borden family – father and mother killed – 2 daughters – devoted sister in law – boy (nephew) – Harriet Irish maid
>
> ambitious woman – rich (really a Lizzie Borden) married to 3rd husband
>
> If not guilty who was? 4 (or 5) other people in house (a little like Bordens?)

Constance Kent

Notebooks 5 and 6, during the plotting of *Elephants Can Remember* and *Nemesis* respectively, refer to this notorious case. Constance Kent served 20 years for the murder of her three-year-old half-brother on 13 June 1860. She was released in 1885.

> Constance Kent type of story – girl Emma – adored governess – mother dies. Governess who had apparently adored Emma now turns against her
>
> Case of Constance Kent – had governess she adored – mother died. Governess married Father. She had a little boy – Constance very fond of him – he is found in earth closet – killed

Crippen and Le Neve

In Notebook 43 Eva Crane from *Mrs McGinty's Dead* is compared to Ethel Le Neve, the partner of the notorious Dr Crippen. The reference to Crippen himself, in Notebook 56, appears during the planning of an unwritten book based on the discovery of a body some years after the commission of the crime. Crippen was hanged in 1910 for the murder of his wife Cora, whose body was discovered, buried in the cellar of their home – although recent forensic developments have cast some doubt on this verdict.

> Janice [Eva in the book] Crane – former Ethel Le Neve – husband – Crane a bloodless lawyer whom she adores

> Murder discovered afterwards – (5 years) (2 years) like Crippen?

Charles Bravo

In Notebooks 27 and 36, during the plotting of *Third Girl* and *By the Pricking of my Thumbs*, there is reference to this still unsolved murder. In April 1876, four months after marrying Florence Ricardo, Charles Bravo died an agonising death from antimony poisoning. A subsequent Coroner's inquest found that there was insufficient evidence to identify his murderer. Again, Christie was using the basic situation as a starting point:

> Arthur (innocent husband) – Katrina – suspicious, passionate for money – looks after old boy – she has boy friend . . . chemical research – or doctor – Bravo framework

> The Bravo idea – would entail woman (widow) having affair with a doctor. She gives up liaison – he goes back to wife – she marries again

Finally, in Notebook 2, and notes for *A Caribbean Mystery*, some unused dialogue between Miss Marple and Major Palgrave, who is discussing his own story of a murderer he knew, lists four murderers from high-profile British murder cases:

> No, No – it's a pattern all right – Smith – Armstrong – Buck – Haig[h] – chap gets away with the first one and thinks he's OK because he's so clever

Joseph Smith, who drowned three 'wives', is the infamous 'Brides in the Bath' murderer who was hanged in August 1915. Major Herbert Rowse Armstrong was convicted in May 1922 for the murder of his wife although his original arrest was for the attempted murder of a professional rival. In September 1935 Dr Buck Ruxton murdered his wife and housemaid and dismembered the bodies; his conviction owed much to the groundbreaking forensic evidence. John Haigh, the acid-bath murderer, was convicted for the murder of six people and hanged in 1949.

6

The Girl in the Train: Murder Aboard

'Trust the train, Mademoiselle, for it is le bon Dieu who drives it'

The Mystery of the Blue Train, Chapter 23

───────◄○►───────

SOLUTIONS REVEALED
Death in the Clouds • 'Death on the Nile' (short story) •
Four-Fifty from Paddington • 'Problem at Sea'

───────◄○►───────

Modes of transport provided an attractive setting for Christie throughout her career. As early as *The Secret Adversary* the sinking of the *Lusitania* is the starting point of a complicated plot and two years later, in 1924, *The Man in the Brown Suit* is set largely on a ship. Some of her most famous titles are set aboard modes of transport – trains (*Murder on the Orient Express*), ships (*Death on the Nile*) and planes (*Death in the Clouds*). The advantages with this type of setting are obvious: it provides a credible means of isolating suspects, it eliminates Scotland Yard and its technical know-how which could, in some cases, short-circuit the plot, and, in the case of Agatha Christie, it also puts to good use her personal experience. They also provide variety as a background, which, at

195

the time, tended to revolve around country houses, offices and villages.

'Death on the Nile' (short story)
July 1933

―――――――◄○►―――――――

Aboard *SS Fayoum* Lady Grayle approaches Parker Pyne with a story of being poisoned by her husband. But is it just a story?

―――――――◄○►―――――――

The notes for 'Death on the Nile' are contained in Notebook 63:

> Wife confides to P (. . . or clergyman)
>   That she thinks her husband is poisoning her. She has money – apparently duel between husband and P – really husband is victim – wife is dupe – young man paying attention to niece is engineering it all – making love to auntie

The death scene in this short story has strong echoes of *The Mysterious Affair at Styles* and the overall plot has distinct similarities with 'The Cornish Mystery'. The resemblances are so strong that this extract could indicate 'The Cornish Mystery'. But the wife in 'Death on the Nile' has money whereas Mrs Pengelly, from the former, has not, so I believe that this is a sketch for the exotic version of the plot.

One notable revelation from the above extract was that Christie intended the story to involve Hercule Poirot ('P. P.' was her shorthand for Parker Pyne). In fact it was published as a Parker Pyne story; the idea was abandoned probably because Poirot had appeared in 'The Cornish Mystery' almost ten years earlier.

And two further pages of notes in Notebook 63 also reveal that Christie considered a dramatisation of the story:

Play   PP version *Death on the Nile*

Lady Grayle – hard boiled – 45
Sir George – 50 good fellow – sportsman
Miss McNaughton – hospital nurse
Pam – lovely, nice
Michael – Sir G's secretary
Dr. Crowthorne

Act II
She is poisoned – Miss M thinks it is Sir G – Doctor takes
   charge – strychnine found on Sir G – Miss M loses her head
Act III
Young people – Pam says Miss M did it – puts it up to
   doctor – he gets to work on her – Michael and Doctor

These notes follow the story closely, with no indication of the elaboration which would have been necessary for a ten-page short story. The reason for this may be deduced from the surrounding pages of the Notebook, where Christie experimented with other possible dramatic scenarios. On either side of this sketch there are similar brief outlines for stage adaptations (none of which were pursued) of *Three Act Tragedy*, 'Triangle at Rhodes' and 'The House at Shiraz', as well as an original, *Command Performance*. And earlier, and later, in the same Notebook there are detailed notes for the dramatisation of the novel *Death on the Nile*. Interestingly, with the exception of *Three Act Tragedy*, all of the titles share a foreign setting.

Death in the Clouds
1 July 1935

◄○►

The mysterious and silent death of Madame Giselle high
over the English Channel on a flight from Paris
challenges Hercule Poirot – especially as he is a suspect.
His investigation involves a visit to Paris, a blowpipe,
a detective novelist and a wasp.

◄○►

All of the notes for this title are included in Notebook 66 and
comprise 30 pages with some fascinating diagrams. The notes
follow fairly closely the plan of the novel, although there are
some minor deviations mentioned below. Oddly, an all-
important list of the passengers' possessions, which contains
the main clue in the novel and which first draws Poirot's
attention to the killer, is not included in the notes.

The first page succinctly states the plot:

Aeroplane Murder – A special knife with thin pointed blade.
Man gets up – goes into lavatory (blue pullover) comes back
in white coat – darting like a steward – leans over talks
about menu card stabs man – gives low sneeze at same time
– goes back – returns in blue pullover and sits down again

From the beginning of the notes the killer is a man and, perhaps surprisingly, even the detail of the blue pullover he
wears is retained. The idea of a low sneeze (an echo of *The
Murder at the Vicarage*) was, however, discarded and the victim
changed to a woman.

In later pages the plot is further elaborated:

198

Chapter II

The steward – discovers the body – asks for doctor. B[ryant] comes

  HP at his elbow – the ways – the Duponts suggest it – Mr Ryder agrees – mark on neck – P picks up thorn – Mr Clancy – blowpipe – arrow poison.

  Arrival at Croydon – everyone kept in first car – Inspector – in plain clothes – another Inspector – Japp –

  Why, it's Mr Hercule Poirot – Or asks stewards who he is – they say they know him by sight etc.

Some pages earlier the idea of a blowpipe or an arrow as a murder weapon was considered. But, with typical Christie ingenuity, they were both to be used as a weapon for stabbing:

Stabbed by an arrow
  "   by dart (poison) from blow pipe

This appears as Idea C on a list of plot ideas. Idea H on the same list is 'Aeroplane murder'. When she settled down to plotting *Death in the Clouds* Christie incorporated the blow-pipe dart idea, while the arrow idea was used many years later in 'Greenshaw's Folly'. In *Mrs McGinty's Dead*, Mrs Oliver complains bitterly about pedantic readers who write to her to point out mistakes in her books. She instances the blowpipe she used in her novel *The Cat it was who Died*, 'where I made a blow-pipe a foot long and it's really six feet' (Chapter 12). This sounds very like a rueful Agatha Christie!

Most of the characters were also settled from early on although, as happens with most titles, names were to change. Some were dropped altogether and replaced. I have indicated below the probable changes:

People on the plane

Mr Salvey and Mr Rider – Business acquaintances [James
    Ryder and, possibly, Daniel Clancy]
Mr Ryder Long – a dentist [Norman Gale]
Lady Carnforth – a gambler – husband won't pay her debts
    [Countess of Horbury]
Jane Holt – a girl who has a humdrum career who has won a
    prize in the Irish Sweep [Jane Grey]
M. Duval – pere et fils – Archaeologists [the Duponts]
Venetia Carr (who wants to marry Carnforth) [Venetia Kerr]
James Leslie younger brother of Carnforth [possibly
    replaced completely by Dr. Bryant]
Madeleine Arneau – maid to Lady Carnforth ['Madeleine']

And during the subsequent investigation, the plot developments are observed, although not their final sequence:

Then Lady Carnforth – Japp and P – P stays behind and gets
her to suggest his staying behind – tells her the truth and
frightens her [Chapter 19]

Venetia Carr – P and J? – P plays on her dislike of Lady C
[apart from a brief appearance in Chapter 12 Venetia Kerr
does not feature again]

Mr Ryder – all fairly straightforward – business difficulties
etc. [Chapter 18]

The Duponts – M. Dupont is to lecture at Antiquarian
Society but perhaps they see them in Paris [Chapter 22]

Bryant – Japp interviews him – P goes as patient – may be
a drug supplier – or someone who has done an Illegal
operation – or guilty of non-professional conduct
[Chapter 20/23]

Clancy – received the little man very hospitably – very chatty [Chapter 15]

An odd point about the interrogation of witnesses is that Venetia Kerr is not questioned either by Poirot or any of his fellow-investigators. Note also her address – Little Paddocks, 15 years later the scene of a dramatic murder in *A Murder is Announced*. And the subterfuge adopted by the Countess of Horbury to disguise her cocaine – labelling it 'Boracic powder' – is the same as that adopted by the criminal 20 years later in *Hickory Dickory Dock*.

With her customary plot fertility, Christie came up with a few possibilities for Gale's partner in crime:

Motive

Inheritance of money by daughter Anne

A. Anne is Jane Holt – Jane Holt and Angell [Norman Gale] plan the murder
B. Anne is Jane Holt – she is unaware of this – but Angell determines to marry her
C. Angele Morisot is Anne – she is in it with Angell – creates disturbance by coming in and speaking to her mistress at moment of murder – also gives damaging evidence against her
D. Angele Morisot is Anne – but is not guilty – she is engaged to Angell but never sees him on liner. He gets engaged to her under a false name – James Clare – a novelist – has a flat in London
E. Real False Angele Morisot presents herself with full proofs of identity to recover fortune (Real one Jane)

The most striking is the idea of Jane Grey as a fellow criminal, which would have provided an attractive surprise element. It

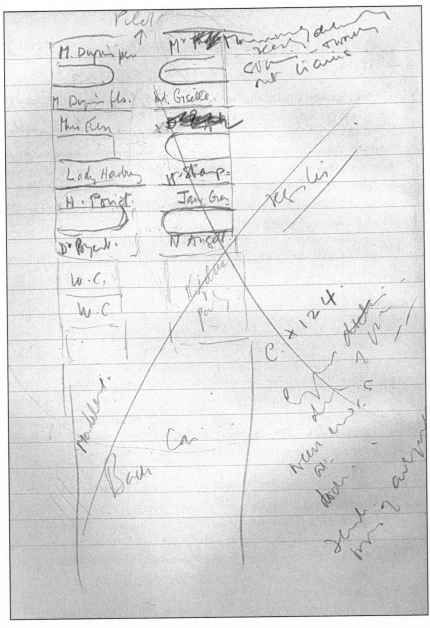

These sketches from consecutive pages of Notebook 66 show great attention to detail during the plotting of Death in the Clouds. *Vitally, Norman Angell's seat in the earliest two sketches is beside the WCs . . .*

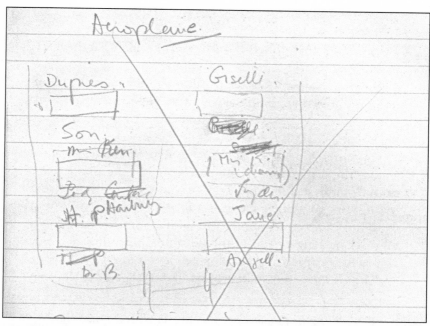

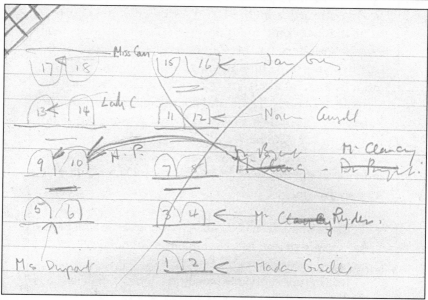

. . . but he is subsequently moved to the opposite end of the cabin, as dictated by the plot. Note the inclusion of the pilot's cabin, the kitchen and pantry, the WCs, and the fact that some seats face each other.

was however abandoned in favour of the maid, and Idea C was utilised.

The notes stop at Chapter 16, although the chapters in the notes do not correspond exactly to those in the novel. And, oddly, Norman Gale is never actually named in the notes as the killer.

The notes for *Death in the Clouds* feature diagrams illustrating the disposition of the passengers in the plane seats. Both from these and the novel as a whole, it can be seen that the interior of a plane cabin in the 1930s was very different to that of a modern plane. There are only 18 seats and a mere 11 passengers and of the possible nine aisle seats, only two are occupied. And a feature common to all three sketches is the arrangement of Jane and Angell (as Norman

---

Death in the Clouds depends for its effectiveness, both as a murder method and a detective novel, on a tactic that has come in for adverse criticism. The accusation of snobbery has been levelled because the killer, and by extension the author, takes it for granted that 'nobody looks at a servant'. This ploy is also a feature, to a greater or lesser degree and sometimes with a twist, in *Three Act Tragedy, After the Funeral, Appointment with Death, The Mystery of the Blue Train, Sparkling Cyanide* and *One, Two, Buckle my Shoe*. Christie somewhat defuses this accusation with the following exchange from Chapter 24 ii of *After the Funeral*:

'I ought to have seen it sooner – I felt in a vague kind of way I had seen you before somewhere – but of course one never looks much at –' He stopped.

'No, one doesn't bother to look at a mere companion-help . . . a drudge, a domestic drudge! Almost a servant.'

Gale was known at that stage). They are always shown sitting opposite each other in window seats, away from the aisle, as dictated by the plot. The chances of Gale being identified on his admittedly daring walk through the plane on the way to and from his commission of the crime are remote; as he reasonably guessed, Jane was likely to spend the interim checking her appearance. A greater danger, and one that has not been commented upon, was from the other stewards. It was much more likely that they would have spotted an 'extra' steward.

∽‍✤‍∽

'Problem at Sea'
February 1936

---◀◦▶---

Mrs Clapperton is found dead in her cabin during a holiday cruise and Poirot's solution depends on his most unusual witness ever.

---◀◦▶---

The first note for this story appears in Notebook 66 and is dated January 1935, a year before publication. The elaboration later in the same Notebook includes much of the detail of the completed story:

> Ventriloquist – on boat . . . Col C. very good with cards – says he has been on music hall stage etc. Wife dies in cabin but her voice heard inside after she has been killed

> Man tells steward to lock cabin – body already inside – later comes back and ~~Cabin lock~~ Calls to wife – she answers

apparently (ventriloquist). Hypodermic beside her – and pricks on her bare arm

One point of difference between the notes and the finished story is that the hypodermic as a murder method is replaced by stabbing. While the ventriloquism idea is a clever one it would not have carried a novel and Christie was right to use it only for a short story.

☙ℯ☙

Death on the Nile (novel)
1 November 1937

─────────────◄○►─────────────

When Simon Doyle marries wealthy Linnet Ridgeway, and not Jacqueline de Bellefort, the consequent train of events culminates in triple murder aboard a Nile steamer. Hercule Poirot, also travelling on SS *Karnak*, has observed the tragedy unfolding and investigates one of his most famous cases.

─────────────◄○►─────────────

Although published late in 1937, this classic Poirot title was written up to two years earlier. A letter from Edmund Cork dated 29 April 1936 expressed delight at Christie's news that *Death on the Nile* was finished. Unfortunately, there is no Notebook with notes for the plot of this famous title. We do, however, have, in Notebook 30, a list of potential characters – including one very significant one – and a brief note about possible plot development. Most of the ideas originally intended for inclusion were waylaid into other titles.

Plans

Death on the Nile

Miss Marple?
Mrs P (ex wardress of American prison)
Mathew P son – nice
Mrs Mathew P – nice
Miss P nervy hysterical girl
Master P Boy of 20 – excitable
Dr. Pfeiffer – doctor and toxicologist
Mrs Pfeiffer – recently married to him – 35 – attractive – with past
Marc Tierney – archaeologist – a little apart from the rest
Mrs Van Schuyler – boring American woman elderly snobbish
Mrs Pooper cheap novelist
Miss Harmsworth – girl companion to Miss Van Schuyler
Miss Marple
Rosalie Curtis sickly girl
Mrs Gibson – non stop talker

The first and biggest surprise in this list is the (double) inclusion of Miss Marple – first with, and later without, a question mark – rather than Hercule Poirot. Prior to this, the only novel in which Miss Marple had appeared was *The Murder at the Vicarage* in 1930, and her next novel appearance, *The Body in the Library*, was still a further five years away in 1942. Moreover, the 1932 short story collection *The Thirteen Problems*, set firmly in the parlours of St Mary Mead, could hardly be seen as a preparation for an exotic Egyptian adventure. In 1937 the Nile was as exotic to the majority of Christie readers as Mars is to her current audience: very few travelled abroad for holidays, if, in fact, they took holidays at all, and the days of the package holiday remained a distant mirage. So to transport Miss Marple from the (admittedly relative) safety of St Mary Mead to the banks of the Nile and subsequently to the Temple of Karnak, Abu Simbel and Wadi Haifa may have been seen as a journey too far – hence Poirot was substituted. Miss Marple eventually gets to solve a case abroad but not until almost 30 years later, when her nephew Raymond sends her on a holiday to the fictional island of St Honore. There she solves *A Caribbean Mystery*, her only foreign case.

In contrast, at this stage Poirot was a seasoned traveller – and, of course, a foreigner to begin with. Since his arrival in Britain he had solved cases in a variety of distant locations – France (*The Murder on the Links, The Mystery of the Blue Train, Death in the Clouds*), Yugoslavia (*Murder on the Orient Express*) and Italy (*The Big Four* and 'Triangle at Rhodes'). His most recent case had involved solving a *Murder in Mesopotamia*. Indeed he had already visited Egypt and the Valley of the Kings while solving 'The Adventure of the Egyptian Tomb' in 1923. All things considered, Poirot was a much more likely sleuth to board SS *Karnak* for a particularly blood-soaked journey down the Nile.

Some of the remaining names also provide material for speculation:

Mrs P (ex wardress of American prison)
Mathew P son – nice
Mrs Mathew P – nice
Miss P nervy hysterical girl
Master P Boy of 20 – excitable

In these five characters can be seen the seeds of the Boynton family from 1938's *Appointment with Death* (see Chapter 8). Mrs P is described as a wardress in an American prison exactly as, two years later, the monstrous Mrs Boynton would be; the 'nice' son, Mathew and his wife Mrs Mathew, are the forerunners of Lennox and Nadine Boynton, while the 'nervy and hysterical' Miss P corresponds to Ginevra. Raymond is the last remaining male of the Boynton family although he could hardly be described as an 'excitable boy'. It is interesting that, although Christie decided against using this family in *Death on the Nile*, when she did utilise them she placed them in another foreign setting, this time Petra.

Mrs Van Schuyler – boring American woman elderly snobbish

And in a later note:

Mrs Van Schuyler – a well known confidence trickster
Miss Harmsworth – girl companion to Miss Van Schuyler

The only character to remain as described – with a modification from Mrs to Miss – is Miss Van Schuyler, although her idiosyncrasy changes from confidence trickery to kleptomania. Miss Harmsworth became Cornelia Robson, the unfortunate niece of that ghastly snob.

Mrs Pooper cheap novelist

The unhappily named Mrs Pooper eventually became Salome Otterbourne, who specialised in outspoken novels of love and sex. One of her titles, 'Snow upon the Desert's Face', is almost the same as the early, unpublished non-crime novel written by Agatha Christie herself, *Snow upon the Desert*. This was probably a personal joke inserted by Christie for the amusement of her family.

Rosalie Curtis sickly girl

Rosalie Curtis may well have changed to Rosalie Otterbourne, daughter of the ill-fated Salome.

Some possible plot developments are sketched on the pages following the cast list. Note that 'P', i.e. Poirot ('but P proves that . . .'), has now firmly replaced Miss Marple:

> Dr. Pfeiffer's wife has been recognised – he decides to do away with Mrs. Oger

> Wife of (Dr. Pfeiffer) herself is thief or murderer etc. – makes up story that someone has stolen ring or poison etc. and brooch A.M. seen in glass. She knows that A.M. is in lounge with others at that time but P proves that M.A. is real lettering
>   or
> M.A. idea and yellow dress M.A. has not yellow dress – woman with yellow dress has not initial A.M.

> Dr. Elbes – very ill man – had known her at St. John's prison
> Pfeiffer mentions his researches the castor oil plant
> Now then A. Who killed her?
>   B. Why?

Although the Pfeiffers were never to feature in any Christie work, some of these ideas were to resurface in other books – a stolen ring in *Hickory Dickory Dock* and the prison wardress in *Appointment with Death*.

But the main idea is the symmetrical letters of the alphabet and how confusion can arise depending on whether they are seen directly or through a mirror. A half page of Notebook 30 lists all of these letters, 'H M A W I O T U V Y', and a further list of possible female names starting with each one. (X is omitted presumably on the basis that names beginning with X are rare.) Christie finally settled on Isabel Oger, hence the reference to Mrs Oger above. This idea was eventually incorporated into *Dumb Witness*, also published in 1937, although with completely different names. Whether it was ever in fact intended as a plot device for *Death on the Nile* is debatable, despite the fact that the scenario Christie sketched involved the Pfeiffers from the list of characters for that novel. Adding to this doubt is the fact that there are no characters on the list with either the initials AM or MA.

Almost the final note for this title in Notebook 30 reads:

> The Plan
> Nellie is heard saying 'I wish she were dead – will never be free till she's dead.

Nellie is one of the names appearing on the list of reversible initials ('Helen, Wilhelmina') but the words she utters are very similar to the opening line, overheard by Hercule Poirot, of *Appointment with Death*. 'You do see, don't you, that she's got to be killed?' This, taken in conjunction with the Mrs P's former profession and the make-up of her family, can be seen to form the basis of the later novel.

Four-Fifty from Paddington
4 November 1957

---◄○►---

While travelling to visit her friend Miss Marple, Elspeth McGillicuddy witnesses a murder committed on a train running parallel with hers. During the search for the body, attention focuses on Rutherford Hall, home of the Crackenthorpe family. Miss Marple and her agent Lucy Eylesbarrow investigate.

---◄○►---

All the notes for this title are contained in four Notebooks – 3, 22, 45 and 47 – amounting to 40 pages. *Four-Fifty from Paddington* was received at Collins in late February of 1957. The date at which it is set, and its writing, are contemporaneous. The story opens on 20 December (1956) – 'It was quite dark now, a dark dreary, misty December day – Christmas was only five days away' (Chapter 1) – but apart from Miss Marple attending Christmas dinner at the Vicarage where she discusses local maps with Leonard Clement, the vicar's son, there is no further mention, or atmosphere, of the holiday season.

This book went through more title changes than any other of her books. At various times it was 4.15, 4.30 and 4.54, before eventually becoming *Four-Fifty from Paddington*. The manuscript is headed '4.54 from Paddington', mainly because, as Christie explained in a letter to her Edmund Cork dated 8 April (1957), there was no actual train at that time. She agreed that 'Four-Fifty from Paddington' or even '5 o'clock from Paddington' were better titles.

The extract below from Notebook 47 would seem to pre-date similar notes as this one has no names (apart from Miss Marple), but the basic idea is the one followed in the finished novel. The blackly comic final question is a classic musing of Christie the arch-plotter. A few pages later notes for 'Greenshaw's Folly' and *The Unexpected Guest* are pursued and the train idea is shelved. As 'Greenshaw's Folly' was first published in December 1956, this supports the contention that the notes for *Four-Fifty from Paddington* did not pre-date its composition by very much.

Train – seen from a train? Through window of house. Or vice versa?
  Train idea
  Girl coming down by train to St. Mary Mead sees a murder in another train drawn up alongside – a woman

strangled. Gets home – talks about it to Miss Marple –
Police? Nobody strangled – no body found.

    Why – 2 possible trains one to Manchester – one a slow
local. Where can you push a body off a train

Notebook 3 sketches the basic idea (with Mrs Bantry in place
of Mrs McGillicuddy) but Notebook 45 has a succinct and
accurate version of the opening chapter of the novel:

The Train

Mrs McGillicuddy – a friend of Miss Marple's – going to stay
with her – in train from Paddington – another train on other
line – but same direction – that's overtaken – hang together
for a moment, through window of compartment level with
hers – a man strangling blonde girl – then – train goes on.

    Mrs MG very upset – tells ticket collector – Station
master? Oh! Jane I've seen a murder

Uniquely among Christie's books, we are informed from the
outset of *Four-Fifty from Paddington* that the murderer is a man.
A mere four pages into Chapter 1 the reader is told: 'Standing
with his back to the window and to her was a man. His hands
were round the throat of a woman who faced him and he was
slowly, remorselessly, strangling her.' With such an unequivocal
statement the possibility that the figure seen could have been a
woman in disguise is never seriously considered and Christie
knew her readers well enough to know that they would feel
totally cheated if that transpired to be the solution. Therefore,
with the exception of Emma Crackenthorpe (the motive) and
Lucy Eylesbarrow (the investigator), all the main characters
are male. The problem this presented was to make the men
broadly similar as physical beings while distinguishing them as
characters. She reminds herself of this in Notebook 22:

Must get clear on men

Three dark men – all roughly 5ft 10 to 6 ft Loose jointed

People   Cedric eldest?
　　　Harold married no children
　　　Alfred
　　　Bryan Eastley Ex pilot – Husband of Edith (dead)
Father of Alistair or stepfather?

2 sons of old man – good boy (in Bank) Artist – or scene designer or producer

Cedric – a Robert Graves – rolling stone, uninhibited – (eventually to marry Lucy Eylesbarrow)

Sir Harold Crackenthorpe – busy man – director of Crackenthorpe Ltd. Well to do – not really? On rocks?

Bryan? R.A.F. Wing Command D? At a loose end

Alph[red] Dark slender – the crooked one – black market in war – Ministry of Supply

The 'Robert Graves' reference is to Christie's real-life friend and neighbour, the author of *I, Claudius* among others. Graves was a critical fan and the dedicatee of *Towards Zero*. This reference also clarifies the question left unanswered at the end of the novel – which of the men will Lucy eventually marry?

There were seemingly minor points to consider but ones that impacted on the plot – how to ensure the necessary darkness for the commission of the crime and how to account for the presence in the house of two young boys. The question of possible dates is considered in two Notebooks:

Points to settle

Date of journey possibly Jan 9th or thereabouts
Points to take in – holidays (boys) New Year (Cedric)
Time of getting dark (train)

Dates
Holidays? April – Stobart-West and Malcolm there
So murder end of February? Say – ~~24th~~ 26th

The eventual decision to place the murder just before, and the investigation just after, Christmas answered all the concerns – the early darkness, as well as the presence of the two young boys and Cedric.

But the biggest problem about *Four-Fifty from Paddington* is the identity of the corpse. It is a problem for Miss Marple, the police, the reader and, I suspect, for Agatha Christie herself. We do not know for certain until the novel's closing pages whose murder is actually under investigation. And it must be admitted that it makes what would otherwise have been a Grade A Christie novel, something of a disappointment. It also raises the question of how, divine intervention aside, Miss Marple can possibly know the story behind the murder. The original reader at Collins, who reported on the manuscript, admitted that 'unless I am being very stupid I cannot see how anyone could have known that murderer's motive'. He was not 'being very stupid' as it is not possible to deduce the identity of the killer, or the motive, although, in retrospect, both are perfectly acceptable. The following note shows that Christie had two ideas about the possible identity of the corpse – Anna the dancer or Martine – and, reluctant to abandon either, eventually used aspects of both:

215

Is dead woman Anna the dancer or not?
Is Anne = Mrs Q – or is Anna red herring arranged by Q
Is woman killed because she is Martine and has a son or
  because she is Q's wife and he plans to marry

But the devotion of even the most ardent Christie fan is severely tested when Martine is finally identified.

7

Elephants Can Remember:
Murder in Retrospect

But now, she realised, she had got to remember. She had
got to think back into the past . . . To remember carefully
every slight unimportant seeming incident.

Sparkling Cyanide, Chapter 1Sparkling Cyanide, Chapter 1

SOLUTIONS REVEALEDSOLUTIONS REVEALED

Mrs McGinty's Dead • Ordeal by Innocence • 'Sing a Song of
Sixpence' • Sleeping Murder • Sparkling Cyanide

Some of Agatha Christie's strongest titles feature murder in
the past – the investigation of a case where the detective is
dependent on the memories of those involved, where the
trail has grown cold and clues have disappeared, and where
the uncovering of the truth often awakens a sleeping murderer. She first experimented with this in Dumb Witness,
where Poirot investigates a two-month-old death; six years
later her greatest triumph finds Poirot examining a 16-year-
old case in Five Little Pigs (see Chapter 4); in two other cases,
Mrs McGinty's Dead and Ordeal by Innocence, the verdict is
already handed down and of her last six novels, five of them

217

feature this type of plot. Also in this category we find her historical detective story, *Death Comes as the End*, a daring if not wholly successful experiment from mid-career.

Dumb Witness
5 July 1937

Emily Arundell writes to Hercule Poirot on 17 April but he does not receive the letter until 28 June. And by then she is dead. Poirot goes to Market Basing to investigate her death, where the case involves spiritualism, a brooch, a dog's ball – and another death.

Most of the notes for *Dumb Witness*, roughly 25 pages, are contained in Notebook 30 along with notes for *Death on the Nile* and the newly discovered short story 'The Incident of the Dog's Ball'; the relationship between the novel and its earlier incarnation as the short story (albeit with a vital difference) is considered in detail in the Appendix. *Dumb Witness* was published at the end of 1936 in the US as a *Saturday Evening Post* serial with the title *Poirot Loses a Client*, and as *Mystery at Littlegreen House* in a UK serialisation beginning in February 1937. In connection with the US serialisation, a surviving letter dated June 1936 from Edmund Cork to Christie thanks her for the revised version sent to the *Saturday Evening Post* magazine (who paid $16,000 for it, $2,000 more than *Cards on the Table*). Cork considered it a 'tremendous improvement' and suggested 'using it for Collins also'. This most probably refers to the first four chapters, in which the 'little English village' setting is told in the third person – the rest of the book, in contrast, being narrated by Hastings. In retrospect, the information that they were added at a later stage makes perfect sense.

Dumb Witness is the archetypal Christie village mystery – a mysterious death in a well-to-do household, a collection of impecunious relatives, the village doctor and solicitor, and the arrival of Poirot whose questioning sets village tongues wagging. Once again the red herring of spiritualism is dragged across the investigation. As far back as 'The Adventure of the Egyptian Tomb' in 1923 Christie murderers used this ploy to cover their tracks. And as late as 1961 and *The Pale Horse*, with a more sinister version of *Dumb Witness*'s Tripp sisters, spiritualism is a major plot device.

Unusually, we know from internal evidence – the ending of Chapter 7 – the exact timeline of the novel; Emily Arundell died on 1 May 1936 and Poirot's investigation began on 28 June, although for most of that investigation there is nothing to show that murder has been committed. Reader prejudice is toyed with, and yet again subverted, with the introduction of suspicious foreigner, Dr Tanios. Four previous killers are mentioned – *Death in the Clouds*, *The Mysterious Affair at Styles*, *The Murder of Roger Ackroyd* and *The Mystery of the Blue Train* – and there is an oblique reference to *Murder on the Orient Express* in Chapter 25. The description of Market Basing in Chapter 6 corresponds to that of Wallingford where Christie had, some years earlier, bought Winterbrook House.

The notes, headed with a working title, list the family members and background, although names and details – Charles is not married and his sister is Teresa, not Bella – were to change:

Death of Martha Digby [Emily Arundell]

The Digbys – their family history
Miss Martha – Miss Amelia – Miss Jane – Miss Ethel and
  Mr Thomas
Marriage of Mr Thomas – to a barmaid?

Mr John [Charles] and Miss Daphne (T's children)
John – stock exchange – married – his wife clever woman
Daphne [Bella] marries an Armenian? Dr. Mendeman
   [Tanios] – charming man – his wife quiet, cold

The early chapters of the novel are accurately sketched with only minor differences – the chemist is delayed until Chapter 21 and there is a cryptic reference to painting in connection with Theresa:

General Plan
P. receives letter – he and H[astings] – he writes – then he tears it up – No, we will go – Market Basing – The Lamb . . . Board to be let or sold. Visit to house agents – an order to view – Ellen conversation – rap – rap – rap – a ball drops down staircase terrier wagging his tail

The chemist – his remembrances – they pretend that are writing up a history of the town – he is an amateur archaeologist – the history of the family. P goes to doctor – as a patient (and an archaeologist) doctor comes to dine – a good deal of local gossip – some little mystery about that death? Doctor indignant – perfectly natural causes – he says – well, I should think you'd be satisfied now. P. says 'But she died'

Theresa – flat in Chelsea – painting – her engagement to Dick Donaldson – latter wants to specialise – infection – liver – serum therapeutics

Oddly, there are references to Peggy, rather than (Ara)Bella, in both of the following extracts. This was probably an early name choice for the character, as the clue of the symmetrical letter seen in the mirror, M for Margaret, would still work with it. As we have seen, this device was considered in conjunction with the plotting for *Death on the Nile* (see Chapter 6).

Dr Seber — very ill man — had known her
at St John's prisons.

Pfeiffer mentions his researches.
7 the Cosor of plant.

how then A. who killed her?
        B. why?

    Mrs Van Schuyler.

Mrs Pf. says — a woman in her
Cabin she and her Snd . Oh!
I'm sorry. says it was Joны
Mrs Plenn —

Letters marks.

H. M. A. W. I. O. T. U. V. Y.

Helen.   Margaret. Mary   Henrietta   Antonette
Nellie.   Peggy .   Polly.   Etta .   Nelly
            Greta.   Ettie.

Wilhelmina
  Billie   Isabel   Theodora
  Mina .   Belle.   Dora.

  Winifred   Augusta   Anne
    Freda.   Gussy.   NAN —

*This page of experimentation with symmetrical letters and corresponding
names is from Notebook 30. Note the inclusion here of 'Wilhelmina/ Mina',
the first name of Miss Lawson. The all-important 'Arabella' and 'Teresa'
are arrived at later in the same Notebook.*

Another visit to the terrier – to the Tripps – hallucinations etc. – evidence of the cook – Miss Theresa on stairs that night – a piece of thread – yes, Ellen had found it. Miss Lawson again – money missing from drawer – knew who took it. P. bullies her a bit – she gets rattled – talks about poor Peggy – who has left her husband

Peggy again – about husband – she refuses to say – P. says tell me – I'm going to be in danger – she refuses to say anything. H. says 'she knows something' – asked about dressing gown – says yes – she has a dark blue silk one – Theresa gave it to her. When? When we were all down that weekend, Which day? I can't remember

And a page of letters and names experimenting with symmetrical letters, the vital clue as misinterpreted by Miss Lawson, eventually arrives at the required one:

ARABELLA   A.T.
BELLA   T.A. Arundell

Sparkling Cyanide
3 December 1945

An elegant restaurant, a glamorous birthday party and beautiful Rosemary Barton is poisoned during the toast. A year later, in a macabre reconstruction at the same restaurant and with an almost identical party, there is another death. But who was the intended victim? Colonel Race investigates.

Notes for *Sparkling Cyanide* are scattered over ten Notebooks. Although published in December 1945, the novel was serialised six months earlier in the UK and 18 months earlier in the USA. A copy of the typescript had already been sent to Christie's US agents by January 1944, so this title was completed by the end of 1943. It is a very elaborated version of the short story (and subsequent radio play) 'Yellow Iris', which was first published in July 1937. The basic plot in both is the same but a different murderer is unmasked at the end of the novel.

Sparkling Cyanide is another example of a favourite Christie gambit – a poisoning drama. Its dramatic unexpectedness during a social occasion recalls a similar scene, ten years earlier, in *Three Act Tragedy* and foreshadows another one many years later in *The Mirror Crack'd from Side to Side*. However, some reservation remains as to the feasibility of the scheme. Is it really likely, especially in view of the subsequent investigation, that no one notices the incorrect seating arrangement that is vital to the success of the plot? The preparation and mechanics of this are masterly and the telling of it is very daring (re-read Book I, Chapter 2 and admire the audacity of even the name) but while the concept is undoubtedly clever, the practical application of it is somewhat doubtful.

There are structural similarities to *Five Little Pigs* with the reminiscences of six people of an earlier poisoning, although, unlike the earlier novel, they are not in the form of written accounts. We discover Rosemary Barton through the eyes of the suspects, including her killer, with a different picture emerging in each account. Through individual memories, in the first 70 pages of the book, we see her as wife, sister, niece, lover, friend, adulterer and, finally, victim. While the portrayal is not as full as the earlier novel it is still admirably drawn.

The most concentrated notes appear in Notebooks 13 and 63 with 18 pages each. The other eight Notebooks that feature

Sparkling Cyanide have anywhere between one and six pages of disjointed notes, including a few false starts and some repetition. Despite name changes the characters as sketched in Notebook 35 below are immediately recognisable. As can be seen, the alternative title (under which it was published in the USA) emphasises the 'murder in retrospect' aspect of the novel:

Remembered Death 'Here's Rosemary – that's for
    Remembrance'
Book I
'Sweet as remembered kisses after death'
What must I do to drive away remembrance from my eyes?

Beginning of In Memoriam
Rosemary
Iris . . . shadows – the beginning of it all

Book
Remembered Death – girl's name is Rue

Remembered Death
Rosemary (dead) – husband – George Barton – acts very
    suspiciously – he is a businessman
Stephen Fane [Faraday] – R's lover
Lady Mary Fane – his wife – cold proud clinging jealous
Tony Getty [Tony Morelli aka Anthony Browne] – former
    lover of R's apparently in love with Viola [Iris]
Ruth Chambers [Lessing] – George Barton's sec[retary] –
    efficient girl – may be in love with him
Lucilla Drake – old pussy – cousin – lives with them – has a
    son in S. America – ne'er do well
Murder (of George or V[iola]?) by son who is secretly
    married to Ruth
Col. Race on job

In Notebook 63 we see the novel beginning to take shape, with six characters thinking about Rosemary:

> Remembered Death   Six people are remembering Rosemary Blair [Barton] who had died last November
>
> Sandra – R. her hatred of her – her suspicion that St. doesn't care for her
>
> Iris – puzzling it out – letters etc. – George's manner – Anthony's coming – the Faraways [Faradays]
>
> Stephen – his life – meeting S – calculated advance – the marriage – Rosemary – shock – infatuation – the awakening – her attitude – after the birthday
>
> Anthony Browne – thinking of R – wondering how he could ever have been attracted – her facile loveliness. His name – 'a nice name' – eminently respectable – borne by chamberlain to Henry VIII
>
> Ruth
> It all began with Victor – interview in office with George. Her . . . undesirable relation – my wife – tender-hearted – girlish affection for him – he's got to get out of the country – Argentine cash.
>
> George
> Thinking of his wife – (drinking?) – maudlin – what a pretty thing she was – always knew he wasn't young enough. He'd made up his mind to it – all the same when he'd first had an inkling – the letter – blotting paper – written to whom – that fellow Browne? or that stick Stephen Faraday.

Notebook 21 has a sketch of the table of the first party (Rosemary is included) and, like the reference in the short story version to the location of the first dinner, seems to be set in New York rather than London. It is possible that Boyd Masterson was a forerunner of Colonel Race:

George has had letter – 'Your wife was murdered'

His oldest friend Boyd Masterson – latter consults with Iris – Iris meets Tony – staying with Stephen Fane M.P. and Lady Mary Fane.

The Party
* George Barton
* Iris
* Tony
* Stephen
* Mary [Sandra]
? Carolyn Mercer (R's girlfriend) [dropped, possibly in favour of Ruth]
? Boyd Masterson
? Lucilla Drake (elderly cousin)

N .Y.

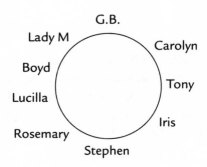

* George Barton

? Iris

* Tony

* Stephen

* Mary

? Carolyn Mercer (Ris synth)

? Boyd Masterman

? Lucilla Drall (Elderly Cousin)

N.Y   Lady M   G.B   Carlyn.

Lucilla! Boyd,

(Rose M -

Ross)

Stephen -

Tony -

Iris

Carolyn has been a mannequist

Sparkling Cyanide's *fatal seating plan – see opposite page.*

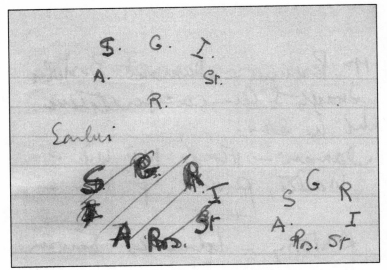

These three cramped drafts, from Notebook 25, of the table from Sparkling Cyanide *show 'Rosemary' in two of them, indicating the first fatal dinner-party.*

Oddly, the following single page is in the middle of the plotting of *Five Little Pigs*, giving the impression that it was dashed down as Christie thought of it. There are two years between publications, but it must be remembered that an empty page was all Christie needed to get her idea down. Chronology was not a factor.

Remembered Death   Possible developments

Black out – snapdragon? At Savoy – performers – indecent song – everyone listens breathlessly – not to miss words. Waiter and drinks – Lights go up – Viola [Iris] gets up to dance – drops bag – young man replaces it on table – on next seat – therefore – a man dies – George Barton

Although Ruth and Victor were always the front-runners for villains, providing, as they do, a more unexpected solution, other characters were also considered. In the second extract below, from an earlier draft, Charles is George Barton and Pauline is Iris Marle:

A. George – kills Rosemary – keep control of money – she is going to leave him. Then Iris because she too will demand money – Lucilla Drake will leave it in her hands. He manufactures letter – work up the 'murdered' idea – ropes in Race

B. Victor Drake – arranges it with Ruth – Ruth to marry George – R. slips cyanide in R's handbag. Victor as waiter puts it in her glass. Iris inherits money – <u>not</u> George – is keen on Gerry – Ruth and Victor (married) decide to act – Victor <u>ostensibly</u> in S. America. Ruth puts cyanide in Stephen's pocket – letter in Iris's bag (from Stephen to Rosemary) – bag replaced wrongly on table – therefore Iris sits down wrong place – George drinks the poison

C. Victor is the man and he is also Gerry Wade [Anthony Browne] – in with Ruth – plot laid between them

Killer could be
Charles – (first death suicide) – has misappropriated P's [Pauline, later Iris] money
    Or
Anthony (really V's lover?) – killed her – Charles finds out – means to separate them – Charles is killed
    Or
Pauline? Killed her sister

229

Death Comes as the End
29 March 1945

———————————◄○►———————————

In Egypt in 2000 BC, wealthy landowner Imhotep
shocks his family by bringing home a new young wife,
Nofret, who antagonises the entire family. Murder soon
follows, but the evil at the heart of the family is not
appeased by a single death and the killer strikes
again . . . and again . . . and again.

———————————◄○►———————————

Long before the current vogue for mysteries set in the past,
Agatha Christie was a pioneer. *Death Comes as the End*, written
in 1943, was an experiment created at the instigation of
Stephen Glanville, professor of Egyptology and a friend of
Max Mallowan. He provided her with much of the basic
information and gave her books to study in order to get
details correct.

Considered purely as a classical detective story this novel
does not pass the key test. There are no clues for the reader
to spot and interpret, thereby arriving at a logical solution.
But as a tense and readable whodunit, it passes with flying
colours. And as a believable picture of a family not sure who
to trust within their own family circle, it is totally believable.
Most of the usual ingredients of her other novels – police
resources and post-mortem analyses, telephones and
telegrams, fingerprints and footprints, formal investigation
and inquests – had to be abandoned. So, while not a first-
class Christie, it is nonetheless a major achievement.

Part of the difficulty interpreting the Notebooks for this
title is the fact that the names of the characters change
throughout the 80-odd pages of the five different Notebooks.

At various times the character who appears in the novel as Nofret is also called Ibunept, Nebet, Ibneb and Tut. And, of course, it is not possible to be sure if the names refer to male or female characters.

Christie writes in her *Autobiography* that 'Houses were far more difficult to find out about than temples or palaces.' And in Notebook 9 we find 16 pages of notes on 'Life and Customs in Ancient Egypt' with details of everyday life (the page references are to some of the volumes borrowed from Stephen Glanville):

Bead bracelets or gold rings with green glazed scarabs P.110 P.46 also

Embalming 21ST D. P.111 and 55

The making of papyrus paper P.114

Description of bow and arrow P.127

Description of Scribe outfit P.14

Description Foundation dynasty P. 51

Description mummification etc. P.55 and P.57

Notebook 46 contains the initial sketch for the family. Although some of the names do not correspond with those in the novel, the characters are all recognisable:

Middle Kingdom Setting   Characters

Ipi – (old mother) Tyrant? Devil? Wise? [Esa]

Father – old fusser – kindly – a nuisance [Imhotep]

Meru – (elder son) Good boy of family – a bit dull – inwardly resentful? [Yahmose]

S – ? Bad boy of family – not at home – Troublemaker [Sobek]

H – Spoilt young son – precocious [Ipy]

Concubine – Victim? Beautiful in danger or Evil – full of power [Nofret]

M's wife – a shrew [Satipy]

S's wife – gentle creature or an Emilia? [Kait]

A daughter – energy – resolve [Renisenb]

N – family friend – shrewd – lawyer like maybe tell in 1st person [Hori – but the '1st person' idea was not pursued]

Hepshut – mischief maker [Henet]

The basic situation is described in Notebook 13:

> Nofret arrives – everyone cruel to her – she is fierce to
> them – her tales of foreign cities – the way she stirs up strife
> – Hori says always there underneath. She writes by scribe
> to Imhotep – Imhotep replies furious to family – he returns –
> settlement of land on her. She dies – scorpion stung her –
> everyone knew – Rensenb troubled – then remembers a
> scene between Nebet and Seneb

The notes for this novel include another example of Christie's system of arranging scenes by allocating letters to them. It is interesting to look at the following page from the Notebooks and compare it to the novel. Although it is headed Chapter 15, the scenes are in fact scattered through Chapters 15, 16 and 17. But her final decision ('A.C.D. – then BB') is followed through. I have added the relevant chapter headings to each scene:

Chapter XV

A Esa and Henet [15 iii]

B Henet and Imhotep [16 i]

C Renisenb and 'Everything is Fear' – meets Aapene – Why do you look at me strangely? Then sees Yahmose – discusses it with him – who could it be? [15 iv]

D ~~Renisenb~~ Yahmose and his father – Y. more authority [15 v]

E Kait and Renisenb [15 vii]

F Renisenb. Teti and Kameni – his eyes on her – strong children [15 vii]

G Renisenb and her father – marriage [17 i]

H Ren. and Kameni – love talk – the amulet – broken – she goes home – looks in box – Henet finds her with it – H's hints [17 ii and iii]

Who dies next?

A.A. Esa – from unguent – or perfumed oil

B.B. Aahene [Ipy]

Yes, B.B. after cheeking Henet [15 vi] who complains to Imhotep

So: A.C.D. – then B.B.

And this is the order as it appears in the published novel:

A Esa and Henet [15 iii]

C Renisenb and 'Everything is Fear' – meets Aapene – Why do you look at me strangely? Then sees Yahmose – discusses it with him – who could it be? [15 iv]

D ~~Renisenb~~ Yahmose and his father – Y. more authority [15 v]

B.B. Aahene [Ipy]. Yes, B.B. after cheeking Henet [15 vi]

The Notebooks offer a solution to at least one tantalising puzzle concerning this novel. In her *Autobiography*, Christie writes:

> *Stephen [Glanville] argued with me a great deal on one point of my denouement and I am sorry to say that I gave in to him in the end . . . If I think I've got a certain thing right in a book – the way it should be – I'm not easily moved from it. In this case, against my better judgement, I did give in. It was a moot point, but I still think now, when I re-read the book, that I would like to re-write the end of it . . . but I was a little hampered by the gratitude I felt to Stephen for all the trouble he had taken and the fact that it had been his idea in the first place.*

It is not entirely clear what she means by 'the end of it' – does she mean the identity of the killer or the manner of revelation? If she means a more dramatic final scene we shall never know, although this would seem unlikely as the setting of the denouement clearly echoes the earlier murders of both Nofret and Satipy. But if she had a different killer in mind, she had already lined up a few candidates:

Henet – hated wife – and all children – eggs on Ibneb – then kills her

Henet – loves old boy – killed first wife – and second 'sister' – determined to destroy Ibneb – pretends to suck up to her

Hori – in league with Ib? She is to gain ascendancy over old woman – Hori has speculated – blame is to be put on Meru

Hori and Ibneb are buddies – he arranges for her to meet old boy – puts him up to deed of settlement by pretending to object – she then rats or is going to – he kills her – then

pretends – she is revenging herself on family – final scene
with Renisenb – <u>you</u> Hori – young cousin rescues her

Son (bad lad) comes in – speaks to concubine – he likes her
– idea is they are in it together

And there was another fascinating idea that never made it
to the printed page at all. In Notebook 13 Christie toys with
the idea of having a modern parallel running alongside the
historical one. Indeed it is possible to see, even in these
brief notes, similarities between the ancient and modern
characters. The old professor and his young wife are
Yahmose and Nofret, Julie is obviously Henet, Regina is a
latter-day Renisenb and Edward and Silas could be Sobek
and Ipy:

Modern start – Old professor or Chancellor – his young wife
– he brings out son and son's wife – widowed daughter and
child

Julie (ancient Mademoiselle who has stayed with them) –
young archaeologist who has stayed with them

Discovery of Tomb Letters – Including one ~~from~~ to dead wife
who is accused of killing Tut

Author's second wife died suddenly – she took drug by
mistake

Young wife dies – quarrel between father and son and wife –
F[ather] says new will – all to Ida

Julie and portrait of Eleanor (first wife) who was going to
come back

Elaborated

235

Dr. ~~Elinor Solomon~~ Oppenheim
Ida – his young wife
Julie the faithful maid and companion ex-governess
Edward Mervyn Oppenheim – dependent on father – is he
    archaeologist
Charlotte – sculptress – or musician (pianist) – or historical
    – or political writer
Charlotte's brother – Richard – the archaeologist
Regina Oppenheim a widow with children – ~~Oscar Walsh~~
Jeremy Walsh – a young writer – psychic – deductive – knows
    too much about people
other son Silas

From the phrase 'Young wife dies', paralleling the death of Nofret, Imhotep's young wife, it would seem that the parallels were to extend to further than family relationships. However, the idea was not pursued any further than these short notes – of course, if it had been it would have meant shorter stories within each period.

These two aspects – the alternative ending and the parallel narrative – make this an even more fascinating novel than heretofore suspected, even without bringing the ground-breaking feature of the historical setting into the discussion. Seemingly complete and interlocking as it is, it would seem that Christie was ready to embroider a few more threads through her narrative. It is entirely probable that had she pursued her present-day parallel, she would have revealed yet another solution; after all, if both branches of the story had arrived at the same destination, a distinct sense of anticlimax would have resulted. So a unique background produced one actual solution, another intended one and a possible third.

Mrs McGinty's Dead
3 March 1952

―◄◦►―

At the request of Superintendent Spence, Poirot agrees to reinvestigate the murder of charwoman Mrs McGinty, found battered to death two months earlier. Although James Bentley has been convicted of her murder, someone in Broadhinny is ready to kill again. And yet, they are all very nice people . . .

―◄◦►―

Continuing a pattern set two years earlier by *A Murder is Announced*, *Mrs McGinty's Dead* is decidedly unglamorous, reflecting the post-war adjustment; it is one of Poirot's rare ventures into the working class. 'The Adventure of the Clapham Cook' in 1923 was his earlier experience. The murder of a charwoman, appalling accommodation, an attempt on Poirot's life and a completely uncharismatic defendant all combine to make *Mrs McGinty's Dead* a particularly dark case.

There are more than 70 pages of notes for this novel. Names, motives, suspects, the earlier cases, the current possibilities all appear in chaotic profusion. As we saw in Chapter 3, the permutations and combinations of the four vitally important early cases and their possible incarnations as current inhabitants of Broadhinny are almost limitless; and all of them are considered.

On the first page Christie sets out the premise of the novel, leaving only the name of the superintendent to be decided:

Inspector ? [sic] old friend retiring worried about case just ending at the Old Bailey (or just ~~sentenced~~ sent for trial).

Not right – evidence all there – motive – opportunity and
clues – but all wrong – his duty to get the facts – sent them
to Public Prosecutor – there his responsibility ended. He
can't do any more . . . Can P do something?

Facts?

No facts. No-one else with motive – as a matter of fact,
they're all very nice people

She eventually settled on Superintendent Spence, Poirot's
partner in investigation from his previous case, *Taken at the
Flood*, four years earlier. This was quite a big gap and the
cover of the first edition of *Mrs McGinty's Dead* is emblazoned
– 'Poirot is Back!'

And over 30 years after her first novel, her powers of invention show no signs of deserting her. She sketches at least
seven possible scenarios before settling on the fourth one
below. It would seem that the title was already decided, probably because it is the name of a children's game, albeit not a
very well known one. It is quoted and described in Chapter 1
but only the title is utilised and there is no attempt to follow
the rest of the verse. This was the one unalterable fact
around which she effortlessly wove these ideas, any one of
which would have made an acceptable plot. As can be seen,
preliminary notes for this case first emerged as early as 1947,
five years before the book's appearance:

Mrs McGinty's Dead
Mrs M is charwoman – middle aged office cleaner – because
of something in wastepaper basket – she pieced together
letters? Had taken something home
Morphia in the morning tea –
Flats! Lawn Road – only super – Mrs M is one of the
cleaners

1947

A. Mrs McGinty's Dead

Start Charwoman found dead in office – Lifted to sofa –
later discovered strangled

Someone goes to break news at her home – real Mrs M is
dead 6 months ago – this one is known to other cleaners
as her sister in law

Why?

Who?

A woman of 50–60 – Hands calloused – feet manicured –
good underclothes

Mrs McGinty's Dead

A. Mrs M is a charwoman. When investigated, it is found
that she has no past history – she bribed former woman
and took her place – her references were forged – 17
Norton St. Birmingham – an accommodation address.
What was she doing in Eleanor Lee's office . . . Evidence
for blackmail?

B. Mrs M is a char – 'does for' the Remington family – lives
in a little house by P.O. – takes a lodger – (James
McBride) her savings broken open – Or hit on head –
blood on James's clothes – he tries to burn them in boiler.

C. Mrs M ~~elderly~~ middle-aged woman – lived with elderly
husband James McGinty. Found killed – JM tells very
peculiar story – (like Wallace) or is he nephew inherits
money. Really young man cultivates her acquaintance –
flatters her up – finally kills her in such a way J is bound
to be suspected – Why?

Ideas for HP (Mrs McGinty)

4 or 5 people in household – one dangerous – P's only clue –
he is pushed at race meeting under horse's hoof or train

etc. by one of them. Mrs McGinty – (housekeeper?) leaves
– is sent away – why? Later he finds her – she is dead

'Wallace' in item C above is a reference to the famous Julia Wallace murder case in Liverpool in 1931. Her husband, whose alibi could never be substantiated, was convicted of her murder but subsequently released. Like Mrs McGinty, Julia Wallace was found in her own sitting room with fatal head injuries.

All of the clues that appear in the book feature in Notebook 43 – the bottle of ink and the letter, the newspaper cutting with its all-important mistake, the coffee cup, the sugar-cutter and Maureen Summerhayes's very daring remark during the party:

Inkstain on the dead woman's finger. Bought bottle of ink that afternoon at PO – no letter found. Newspaper – Daily Newshound or Evening Paper

Sugar cutter – Judge and wife brought them back – Vicarage sale of work

Real clue Robin
E. Kane changed her name to Hope – Evelyn Hope – girl – but not girl – boy. Robin's 'mother' is not his mother – he got her name by deed poll – she was paid to give her name to him – later he kills her – does not want her to tell about past story

Robin's method for second murder – has coffee cup with dregs and lipstick

The slip in paper – child not yet born – therefore sex not – known

Don't like being adopted, do you? (A remark by Maureen
Summerhayes at party)

And then she considers suspects . . .

Now consider each likely household

1. Married couple in late thirties – very vague – like R and A
[Rosalind and Anthony, Christie's daughter and son-in-
law] – do market gardening – (he is son – or she is daughter
of X) [possibly the Summerhayeses]

2. Invalid woman with son – son is artist – or does painted
furniture or a writer – (detective stories?) [Mrs Upward and
Robin]

3. Vaughans – unstable husband (banker or solicitor) quiet
self-effacing wife – children? – one (son) hers by former
marriage?

4. Rich woman – wife very flashy – 2 young men – live
together – (one is son of X) has told stupid rich girl he is son
of Russian Grand Duke

Not all of the previous cases which provide the motivation for
a killer trying to conceal a criminal past appear in the
Notebook as they do in the novel:

Edith Kane [Eva Kane/Evelyn Hope]

Went out that day – he poisoned Wife – a lot of gup in paper
– all about that innocent child – betrayed – she and her child
– the child born later – a daughter – the little daughter who
never knew her father's name. The new life for Edith Kane –
went to Australia – or S. Africa – a new life in a new world.
    She went – yes – but she came back 25 years ago

Janice Remington – acquitted of killing her husband or her lover like Madeleine Smith [Janice Courtland]

Little Lily Waterbrook – took chopper to aunt – detained – only fifteen – released later – Harris? [Lily Gamboll]

Greenwood Case – daughter – changed name – her evidence saved father – thirtyish

Newspaper suspects – Age now
55 Eva Kane (? changed name to Hope – went abroad – had s[on] or d[aughter]
45 Janice Crale – or The Tragic Wife – husband died of morphia – or bath – lover did it – unpleasant man – perverse – took drugs [Janice Courtland]
30 Lily Gamboll – killed aunt

The reference to 'Madeleine Smith' above relates to the case of a woman tried for poisoning her lover Emile L'Engelier in Glasgow in 1857. The verdict against Smith was 'Not Proven'; in reality, it amounted to an acquittal. Like the Wallace case above, it is still the focus of keen speculation.

Appearing together on just one page of Notebook 43, the following would have been added when the plot was well advanced. With the exception of Point B, all these occur in Chapters 13 and 14:

Points to be worked in
A. Mrs Upward sees photo – familiar
B. Mrs Rendell came down to see Mrs Upward that night – couldn't make her hear
C. Maureen talks about being adopted
D. Mrs O sums up Maureen's age and appearance
E. Mrs Rendell asks P about anonymous letters – untrue
F. Poirot told by Mrs O – it was Dr Rendell

In particular, Point C is the main clue that incriminates the killer – although few readers will notice it, so subtly is it inserted. And Point A sets up the second murder in Broadhinny as Mrs Upward plays a very dangerous game with Poirot.

Ordeal by Innocence
3 November 1958

Jacko Argyle died in prison while serving a sentence for the murder of his stepmother. His assertion that he had an alibi for the fatal night was never substantiated – until now. Arthur Calgary arrives at the family home and confirms Jacko's alibi. This means that the real killer is still living among the family and is ready to kill again.

Notebook 28 contains all of the notes for this novel, amounting to almost 40 pages. On 1 October 1957 Agatha Christie wrote to Edmund Cork, asking him to check on the legal situation if person A were to be tried and convicted of the murder of his stepmother despite his claim that he was with person B at the crucial time of the killing. Person B is never found and A dies in prison six months into his incarceration. Then B, who has been abroad for a year, turns up and approaches the police to confirm A's story and provide the alibi. Christie wanted clarification on the situation with regard to a 'free pardon' and the possible reopening of the case. She assured Cork that an early reply would enable her to get to work 'industriously on this projected new book'. The date 'Oct 6th' appears on page 20 of Notebook 28, confirming that the novel was planned and written the year before publication.

'This is easily the best non-branded [Poirot or Marple] Christie we have had for some time . . . *The Innocent* [as it was then called] is close to achieving a successful blend of the classical detective story and the modern conception of a crime novel.' This was the enthusiastic verdict on 1 May 1958 when Collins received the latest Christie. The reader considered that it could benefit from cutting and mentioned that Agatha Christie proposed to do that. His other reservation was about the title and he suggested some alternatives – 'Viper's Point', 'A Serpent's Tooth', 'The Burden of Innocence' and, prophetically, 'Cat among the Pigeons'. Although no one knew it at the time, this was to be the title of the following year's book.

The short story 'Sing a Song of Sixpence' (see Chapter 4), collected in *The Listerdale Mystery,* contains distinct similarities to this novel. As in the short story, an outside investigator arrives at the home of the murder victim, whose relatives are mutually suspicious, and discovers that the killer is a young man with an emotional connection to the elderly family retainer. Change the 'son' of the short story to 'lover' and the similarities to Kirsten Lindstrom and Jacko in *Ordeal by Innocence*, where Arthur Calgary arrives at the Argyle household, are striking. Although the story first appeared in December 1929, almost 30 years earlier, the parallels to *Ordeal by Innocence* are too many to be mere coincidence – the outsider detective, the elderly matriarch bludgeoned to death for money, the gnawing suspicion and distrust, the eventual disclosure of an unsuspected emotional and criminal partnership.

Ordeal by Innocence remains one of the best of the latter-day Christies. It is a crime novel, as distinct from a classical detective story, with deeply held convictions about truth and justice, guilt and innocence. It is marred only by the inclusion, in the last 20 pages, of two perfunctory crimes, a successful and an attempted murder. Coming, as they do, so near the end of the novel, they do not convince either as an illustration of the killer's panic or

W ith her customary ingenuity, Agatha Christie
resolved the thorny question of legal justice and
moral justice. When *Ordeal by Innocence* was written, many
aspects of life were more clear cut than they have subsequently become. If a character in a Christie novel were
unmasked as a murderer, the reader could be sure that
he or she would pay the ultimate price. With the death
in prison of Jacko while serving a sentence for a crime
he did not commit, Christie could be accused of a disser-
vice to both natural and legal justice. Fifteen years earlier in *Five Little Pigs*, Caroline Crale is wrongly
convicted, but it is with her own collusion in expiation
for an earlier misdemeanour. Again, she dies in prison.
And in *Mrs McGinty's Dead* (1952) the unsympathetic
James Bentley is also wrongly convicted but is saved by
Poirot before his execution. But in *Ordeal by Innocence*
Jacko is finally shown to have been morally responsible,
even if his was not the hand that struck the fatal blow.

as a suspense-building exercise; the Notebooks, however, give
some insight into the inclusion of these murders.

The opening of the novel follows exactly the earliest jottings in Notebook 28, even to the amount of the fare paid to
the boatman. The ferry used by Arthur Calgary is the one
that still runs to this day at the end of Greenway Road just
past the imposing gates of Dame Agatha's summer residence.

Arthur Calgary – Crossing ferry – begins

The ferry came to a grinding halt against the shelving
pebbles – A.C. paid fourpence and stepped ashore

Well, this was it – he could still, he supposed, turn back etc

An early page of Notebook 28 gets straight to the crime. This remains largely the same except for the detail of a poker instead of a sandbag. At this stage the character Jacko that appears in the book is still appearing in the Notebook as Albert:

> Violent quarrel between Albert and Mrs A – he attacks her – she is nearly dead – K. sends him off to obtain an alibi. At 8 o'clock – with her again and kills her or he sticks her with a knife – she gets up – tells about him.
>
> Possible course of real events –
>
> Albert – determined to get money out of Mrs. Argyle makes up to Lindstrom – wants her to marry him – she agrees – Mrs. A – won't help – Leo won't help – he works on her – the sandbag from under the door – at 8.15 a form she does not understand – Mrs A bends over it – K socks her

The family members underwent name changes but are still recognisable, while Mr Argyle, Kirsten and Maureen are substantially the same as the finished novel. The calculation of Tina's age shows that these notes were written in 1958:

> Tina half-caste girl – (5 in 1940 – 23 now) married to local postman? Builder's mason? farmer
>
> Linda – married to a man since paralysed – she lives there [Mary]
>
> Johnnie – a job in Plymouth comes over quite often
>
> Albert – bad lot – unstable ~~hanged~~ convicted of murder of Mrs. Argyll [Jacko]
>
> Mr Argyll – a scholar

Mr Argyle – (or Mr Randolph) Randolph Argyle? Ambrose
Randolph?
Thin – ethereal – surrounded by books

Kirsten?
Her homely face – pancake flat – ~~nose~~ surrounded by
bleached permanent w hair
How much better a nun's coif and wimple? – not a
contemplative lay sister – the kind who inspected you
through a grille before admitting you to the visitor's parlour
– or Mother Superior's presence

Calgary goes and sees – Maureen – (married to him?) – Silly
common little girl – but shrewd – went to family when he
was arrested – they didn't know ~~she~~ he was married.

Mary – Tenement in New York – hatred of it all – mother out
in street – car passed – Mrs A – adoption – then hotel life –
nursery growing up – plans for her – meeting with Philip – no
background – goes off marries him – he sets up in business –
Fails – then polio – Mrs. Argyle – wants them there – he is
quite ready to go – goes into hospital – Mary goes to stay at
Sunny Point

The two subsequent victims are also considered. As the notes
below show, however, the original intention was that *either*
Philip or Tina would be the victim:

Who is killed? Philip poisoned – doesn't wake up or Tina
stabbed – she walks from Kirsty to Mickey – collapses

The poisoning of Philip was discarded in favour of stabbing.
In view of the urgency of the killer's situation, this was a more
expedient course and one easily within the capability of the

character in question. And a possible reason for inclusion of the unsuccessful attempt on Tina is that it provides a witness in the absence of any other proof of guilt. For those readers who doubt the medical possibility of the attempted murder of Tina, who continues to walk despite having been stabbed, there are two editions of the *British Medical Journal*, dated 28 January and 18 February 1956, among Christie's papers with pages dealing with just this type of event. And both articles are marked. A careful reading of a very daring Chapter 22 should be enough to dispose of any accusations of cheating.

There were also a few ideas that never got further than Notebook 28:

> Forged will – forged in favour of real murderer – but forged very badly? Or forged badly in favour of Albert.

> Husband dislikes wife and hated the children. Wanted to marry someone? Or had son of his own.

> She was going to alter will in favour of a foundation for orphans – which cut out husband.

And, finally, two intriguing ideas, both actually variations on the same theme . . .

> Or was Albert her [i.e. Mrs Argyle's] son

> Is Kirsten Albert's real mother?

Both of these would have worked and would, moreover, have made psychological sense. The former would have made a profoundly affecting scenario; the latter would perhaps have been more effective as a motivation for Kirsten (as it did for her counterpart in 'Sing a Song of Sixpence') than the one actually used. However, the possibilities of unacknowledged parenthood as a plot device and a motivation are fully explored in *Hercule Poirot's Christmas, Sad Cypress, Mrs McGinty's Dead* and 'Dead Man's Mirror' among others, so perhaps it was simply a case of avoiding repetition.

✑

Sleeping Murder
11 October 1976

Gwenda Reed's new house evokes disturbing memories and her attendance at a performance of *The Duchess of Malfi* confirms her suspicions that, as a child, she witnessed a murder there. Miss Marple's advice to let sleeping murder lie is ignored and a murderer prepares to kill again.

Although published ten months after Christie's death, *Sleeping Murder* was written during the Second World War and, like *Curtain*, placed in safekeeping to appear only after its author's death. Or so, until the discovery of the Notebooks, we thought . . .

Notes relating to the development of *Sleeping Murder* appear in Notebooks 17, 19, 33, 44, 63 and 66, an indication of its convoluted genesis: it underwent two changes (at least) of title and its history is linked with *Taken at the Flood* (see Chapter 12), which in turn is linked with *They Do It with Mirrors*. The Notebooks also show that at various times it was to involve the motif from the Mr Quin story 'The Dead Harlequin' of a person looking down at a dead body on the floor; it could have been a Poirot title and, even more amazingly, a Tommy and Tuppence novel. And despite the assertion that it was written during the Blitz, the Notebooks reveal a very different timescale for its creation.

The first page of Notebook 19 is headed:

Cover Her Face
The Late Mrs. Dane
They Do It with Mirrors

The promising title 'The Late Mrs. Dane' was not pursued although the name appears in the early sketches for *Sad Cypress* and *The A.B.C. Murders*. *Cover Her Face*, meanwhile, was the one-time title for *Sleeping Murder*. It was originally called *Murder in Retrospect*, as it appears on one of the surviving type-scripts; and as Chapter 5 of the novel asserts. Then the American publishers of *Five Little Pigs* appropriated this title in 1942, so the stored manuscript was renamed *Cover Her Face*. All was well until P.D. James used the latter title in 1964 for her first detective novel. Agatha Christie herself, in a 1972 letter to her agent, suggested *She Died Young*. Eventually the final Miss Marple novel to appear in print was published in 1976 as *Sleeping Murder*. But, as can be recognised from the details in the following extract – the familiar house, the wall-paper, the door – the title *Cover Her Face* appears frequently in the Notebooks in connection with *Sleeping Murder*.

Cover her Face
    The House – recognition – door – Staircase etc. Poirot and girl at Duchess of M – her story

Cover her Face
    . . . in the train – then the house – feeling of knowing it – the wall paper in this room – (inside closet) – ~~the door~~ but it was the door that really shook her

The complex history of this novel is best exemplified by a brief quotation from Notebook 63:

> Helen – Start with the house and the girl and Tuppence (?) or friend – Raymond West and wife – the things happening one by one – then the theatre – Malfi – a T and T story? A Miss M story? An HP story?
>
> Helen Rendall – suicide – hanged herself – her husband sold the house and went abroad.
>
> Now who killed her? – Her brother – eminent surgeon – Doctor? – Husband? shell-shocked – girl's husband? H is P's second wife – young, flighty – a lover – Fergus – chauffeur or lover

The only real certainty in all of this plotting is a girl buying a house that contains memories from her earlier life, and we can see from the above extract that Christie was undecided as to whose case this was to be – Miss Marple, Poirot, even Tommy and Tuppence! Apart from that, there was no clear idea of how to proceed; and, presumably, depending on the detective she chose, a different book and possibly a different plot would have followed. This vacillation about the detective also raises questions about the book being written specifically as Miss Marple's last case; if it was created as her final investigation Miss Marple would have been a given from the start.

Notebook 17 has a clear outline of the plot as far as the first four chapters. The heroine's name, later to change to Gwenda, is here Gilda, although her husband's remains the same:

> Gilda – young married woman arriving Plymouth or Southampton – feels ill – stays night then hires car – drives slowly through Southern England. Feeling of coming home – evening – down into the valley – board up – visit to house

agent – (former owners?). She buys it – writes letter
to husband (or takes it furnished? unfurnished?)
Incidents – the path – the door – the wallpaper – sends
telegram to London – to Giles aunt Miss M? – or to Giles
cousin Miss M is her aunt – or to the Crests – theatre – some
young people – etc. – Cover her face – she rushes out and
home. Joan asks her – Miss M. comes up with hot water
bottles and hot coffee and sugar. The next morning . . .
Gilda tells her all about it – Helen etc.

Notebook 66 begins as Notebook 17 but then diverges briefly
to a different idea before returning to the *Duchess of Malfi*
theme. Also included in this jotting is the notion of a father
in a mental hospital for a murder he may or may not have
committed, an idea which appears in *Sleeping Murder.*

Cover her Face
    Start with girl and friend (f[emale]) find house [in]
Sidmouth – queer things etc.
    Husband comes (or is coming) – A's fear – consults local
doctor – really crook? He advises her to leave neighbourhood
– later window box falls on her – 'the house hates me') – play
– Duchess of Malfi etc. – etc. – Helen. Is her father in loony
bin because he thinks he killed his young wife

Notebook 44 confuses the issue further with mention of a
soldier and Poirot:

Theatre party
    Duchess of Malfi – Cover her Face – girl screams – taken
out – won't go home with fiancé – young soldier – goes with
Poirot. A man looking down at someone dead – the man
with the hand – not only that – familiar house – seen it all
before

And Notebook 33 shows the potential Harlequin connection:

Continuation of Harlequin and Helen?
Girl (Anne) comes down stairs and sees girl dead and
man/woman bending over her – (grey hands) Helen

Eventually, with the plot well in hand and Miss Marple firmly
installed as the detective, Christie is able to follow her alphabetical plan:

A. Love letter in bureau to Musgrave? [mentioned in
Chapter 17 iii by Erskine]
B. Newspaper adv. seen by the ex-servant [Chapter 12]
C. Servant 1? 2? heard that H. afraid of someone [Chapter 14]
D. 3 servants – 1. Nurse flighty – out that night . . . . (She is
C̲ [above])
2. Cook – Mrs. F's servant – very young at time
3. Lily – very young at time – say housemaid –
clothes wrong – saw something out of window?
[Chapter 14]
E. Fane in office – gentle, repressed – never married –
possessive mother [Chapter 13]
F. Miss M and mother – learns about Jackson's boy – also
about man on way out – Major M [Chapter 16]
G. Jackson [Affleck] – left under a cloud – (in Fane's
office?) made good – member of an accounting firm –
2nd murder – Lily? Nurse? [Chapter 21 and 22]
H. Major and Mrs. Musgrave [Erskine] – Gwenda talks to
him – lovely girl – yes, I fell in love with her – my wife –
young children – suppose I did the right thing – came
down to Dilmouth because I wanted to see where she
lived once [Chapter 17]
I. Miss M says – body can always be put where you want it
– in garden – following on J. [Chapter 23]

J. Dr. Kennedy with G. Gil and Miss M – the 3 men –
which? Then subsequent lives – Miss M. asks how a man
would feel – lonely – want to talk [Chapter 23 is the
nearest match]

In a somewhat lacklustre book the alibi for the Lily Kimble
murder shines out as a prime example of Christie ingenuity. And it appears in the book much as outlined in
Notebook 17. As usual with the best Christie ploys it is
simplicity itself:

Circumstances of Lily's killing
Writes (against husband's advice) to Dr. K – He when he
comes to see G[iles] and G[wenda] finds Marple – brings
her letter – says he has asked her to come on Tuesday by
4.30 train changing at Dillmouth Junction. G and G get
there at 4.30. Actually he tells her to come by 2.30 train –
two letters – just the same – except for time

Overall, however, *Sleeping Murder* is not in the same class as
other titles written in the early 1940s – *One, Two, Buckle my
Shoe, Evil under the Sun* or *The Body in the Library*. And, thanks
to the Notebooks, we now have a possible reason why.

Notebook 14 contains the first reference to a date in conjunction with this book, September 1947:

Plans Sept. 1947

Dying Harlequin
Cover her face (Helen)
~~Crooked House (The Alt~~[eration]~~s)~~ Done

And it is this date that completely contradicts all the theories
we have received about the date of the book's creation.

There is no other novel that could possibly fit the description of 'Cover her face (Helen)' so it is definitely a reference to the book that we know as *Sleeping Murder*. But if it was only in the planning stages (and a very early stage to judge by the brevity of the note) in September 1947 the writing of it is placed much later than heretofore presumed.

This complication is underlined on the following page when we find a date more than a year later again, with still only the barest outline of the plot:

Plans Nov. 1948

Cover her Face

The girl (or young wife) has memories – come back – point it – 'Helen' is dead at foot of stairs – 'Grey fingers'. Advertisement for Helen Gilliat (name found in a book) – answered by Dr. Gilliat – a plastic surgeon – it was his sister?

And some of the plot outlined here ('name found in a book – answered by Dr. Gilliat – a plastic surgeon') bears no relation to the plot of *Sleeping Murder*, although the reference to 'Grey fingers' here and 'the man with the hand' above, is reflected in the final confrontation in the book, when their disturbing significance becomes clear. Clearly there was still a lot of planning to complete. So we can move the writing of it nearer to 1950, i.e. almost ten years later than the supposed 1940 date.

There are yet further indications that this book was written several years after the war. In the following extract from Notebook 19 ('girl at theatre – stumbles out' clearly identifies *Sleeping Murder*) we find a reference to 'in the war years', a phrase which would surely be written only long after the war had ended:

Jimmy Peterson comes from U.S.A. to look up Val (who was over there in the war years). Girl at theatre – stumbles out – young man follows her

Two final points support the theory that *Sleeping Murder* was not written during the war. First, why write, in the early 1940s, a 'final' case for Miss Marple when at that point her only full-length case had been *The Murder at the Vicarage*, published in 1930, and *The Body in the Library* was not to appear until 1942? And second, in Chapter 24 i of *Sleeping Murder* Inspector Primer mentions the 'poison pen trouble down near Lymstock', a direct reference to *The Moving Finger*, published in 1943.

Overall, *Sleeping Murder* is a disappointing climax to Miss Marple's career. While a perfectly adequate detective story it is not in the same class as the previous year's technical tour de force, *Curtain: Poirot's Last Case*; or, indeed, *A Murder is Announced*, the real apex of Miss Marple's career. The possibility that it was written much later than previously suspected would go a long way towards explaining why.

EXHIBIT E:
N OR M? – A TITLES QUIZ

The two essentials for a story were a title and a plot – the rest was mere spadework, sometimes the title led to a plot, all by itself as it were, and then all was plain sailing – but in this case the title continued to adorn the top of the page and not the vestige of a plot was forthcoming.

'Mr Eastwood's Adventure'

All of the following were considered, but ultimately discarded, as titles for Christie works. They are drawn from the notebooks, the typescripts or manuscripts, readers' reports and correspondence. Some are more obvious than others and the list includes novels, short stories, plays and a Mary Westmacott.

1. Tragic Weekend
2. Post Mortem Justice
3. Retrospective Death
4. In Memoriam
5. Death of a Games Mistress
6. The Innocent
7. Aftermath
8. Blood Feast
9. The Hand
10. A Death has been Arranged
11. Operation Deadline
12. Return Journey
13. Death is Folly
14. Easeful Death
15. Viper's Point
16. 2nd Innings
17. The Tangled Web
18. Laura Finds a Body
19. The Flowing/Incoming Tide
20. A Serpent's Tooth
21. Cat among the Pigeons
22. The Soul in the Window Seat
23. The Spider's Web
24. The World's Forgetting
25. The Manor House Mystery
26. Shadow in Sunlight

Answers on the following page.

Answers

1. *The Hollow*
2. *Five Little Pigs*
3. *Five Little Pigs*
4. *Sparkling Cyanide*
5. *Cat among the Pigeons*
6. *Ordeal by Innocence*
7. 'Sanctuary'
8. *Hercule Poirot's Christmas*
9. *Sleeping Murder*
10. *A Murder is Announced*
11. *Fiddlers Three*
12. *The Hollow*
13. *Dead Man's Folly*
14. *Hallowe'en Party*
15. *Ordeal by Innocence*
16. *N or M?*
17. *The Moving Finger*
18. *Spider's Web*
19. *Taken at the Flood*
20. *Ordeal by Innocence*
21. *Ordeal by Innocence*
22. *The Rose and the Yew Tree*
23. *The Moving Finger*
24. 'The House at Shiraz'
25. *Three Act Tragedy*
26. *A Caribbean Mystery*

Destination Unknown: Murder Abroad

Everything the same every day – nothing ever happening. Not like St. Mary Mead where something was always happening.

A Caribbean Mystery, Chapter 1

━━━━━◄○►━━━━━

SOLUTIONS REVEALED
Appointment with Death (play) • 'The House at Shiraz' •
The Man in the Brown Suit • *Murder in Mesopotamia* •
'Triangle at Rhodes'

━━━━━◄○►━━━━━

More than any of her contemporaries Agatha Christie used 'abroad' as a background throughout her career. As early as her third title, *The Murder on the Links*, she despatched Poirot to France. In her first decade of writing three further titles – *The Man in the Brown Suit, The Big Four* and *The Mystery of the Blue Train* – feature predominantly foreign settings. And as late as 1964 Miss Marple brought her knitting to the Caribbean. Many of Christie's thrillers have similar backgrounds – *They Came to Baghdad, Destination Unknown, Passenger to Frankfurt.* And Poirot solves some of his most famous cases far away from Whitehaven Mansions – *Death on the Nile, Murder on the Orient*

Express, Murder in Mesopotamia and *Appointment with Death*. All of this reflected Christie's own lifelong love of travel.

The Man in the Brown Suit
22 August 1924

─────────────◄○►─────────────

When she is suddenly orphaned, Anne Beddingfeld comes to London where she witnesses a suspicious death in a Tube station. A further death in the deserted Mill House convinces Anne to investigate and she boards a ship bound for South Africa, where she becomes involved in a breathless adventure.

─────────────◄○►─────────────

Christie's fourth novel drew extensively on her experiences with her first husband Archie when they both travelled the world in 1922. Although it starts in England, much of the novel is set on a ship travelling to South Africa and the climax of the novel takes place in Johannesburg. It is not, strictly speaking, a detective story but it does have a whodunit element. An exciting story featuring murder, stolen jewels, a master criminal, mysterious messages and a shoot-out, it is an apprentice work before Christie found her true profession as a detective novelist. Nevertheless it is a hugely enjoyable read with a surprise solution. And this is why it is an important entry in the Christie canon – it presages her most stunning conjuring trick by two years and does it in a most subtle and ingenious way. And it also adopts the technique of using more than one narrator, a scheme that appears, in various guises, throughout her career in novels as diverse as *The A.B.C. Murders*, *Five Little Pigs* and *The Pale Horse*.

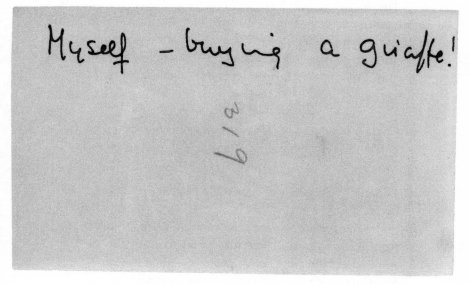

Myself — buying a giraffe!

619

This unpublished photograph, from her 1922 world tour with Archie, shows Agatha Christie buying a wooden giraffe beside a train, exactly as her heroine, Anne, does in Chapter 23 of The Man in the Brown Suit.

The real-life Major Belcher, who employed Archie as a business manager for the round-the-world trip, convinced Christie to include him as a character in her next novel. And he was not satisfied to be just any character; he wanted to be the murderer, whom he considered the most interesting character in a crime novel. He even suggested a title, *Mystery at Mill House*, the name of his own house. In her *Autobiography* she says that although she did create a Sir Eustace Pedler, using some of Belcher's characteristics, he was not actually Belcher.

She also relates in her *Autobiography* that when the serial rights of *The Man in the Brown Suit* were sold to the *Evening News* they changed the title to *Anne the Adventuress*. She thought this 'as silly a title as I had ever heard' – and yet the first page of Notebook 34 is headed 'Adventurous Anne'.

The surviving dozen pages of notes in Notebook 34 reflect the course of the story and represent all that remain of the plotting. Their accuracy suggests that they represent a synopsis of earlier, rougher notes, but as Christie began the notes for this book in South Africa it is understandable that they no longer exist.

Chapter I – Anne – her life with Papa – his friends . . . his death – A left penniless . . . interview with lawyer left with £95.

Chapter II – Accident in Tube – The Man in the Tube – Anne comes home.
Announcement in paper 'Information Wanted' solicitor from Scotland Yard – Inspector coming to interview Anne – her calmness – Brachycephalic – not a doctor. Suggest about being a detective – takes out piece of paper – smells mothballs – realises paper was taken from dead man 17 1 22

III – Visit to Editor (Lord Northcliffe) – takes influential card from hall – her reception – if she makes good. The order to view – Does she find something? Perhaps a roll of films?

V – Walkendale Castle – her researches – The Arundel Castle – Anne makes her passage

VI – Major Sir Eustace Puffin [Pedler] – changing cabins – 13 – to – 17 – general fuss – Eustace, Anne and Dr Phillips and Pratt all laying claim to it

Or man rushes in to ask for aid – after stewardess has come she finds he is stabbed in the shoulder – Doctor enters 'Allow me' – She is suspicious of him – he smiles – in the end man is taken into doctor's cabin and Ship's doctor attends him

The reference to Lord Northcliffe, the famous newspaper-man, suggests that Christie intended to base Lord Nasby, whom Anne visits in Chapter 5 to ask for a job, on him. And both the alternative scenarios involving the changing of cabins and the stabbed man featured in the novel.

'The House at Shiraz'
June 1933

Why has Lady Esther Carr secluded herself in her house in Persia? What really happened to her maid? Parker Pyne investigates.

This short story, from *Parker Pyne Investigates*, is a minor Christie, but it nevertheless features a plot device similar to

'The Companion' in *The Thirteen Problems* and, much later and more elaborately *A Murder is Announced.* There are references in Notebook 63 – all, surprisingly, to a stage adaptation which was never realised as a script. It seems a very unlikely possibility for a stage transformation; but then so, probably, did 'Witness for the Prosecution'! Here Christie toys with various titles, all of which have a relevance to the story:

> The Worlds Forgetting (Play? House at Shiraz)
> Desert Lady

The notes for the adaptation include a sketch for two acts and three scenes:

> Hotel – jumping off places – Lady Esther Carr – scene between her and old lady or old gentleman – globetrotter friend of her mother – the chauffeur – her fury – ran way with him – he left her – old friend says man mad. Conversation between Lady E and girl – Muriel – nice normal girl – or has been nursery governess – she is engaged – chauffeur – a pilot – hard-bitten young man. At the interview he talks to other girl – likes her – they get friendly.

> Act II The house in the Desert – native servants – Lady E – all in Arab dress. Sends him off on errand to Damascus – will be away for a month – then turns on her slave – tells girl she won't be allowed to see Alan – M retorts – turns on her – as tall and as strong as you – she walks backwards – falls. New British Consul is due to call – she throws over breakfast tray – puts on ring – lets him in – receives him as Lady E.

The major difference between the original and the proposed adaptation is that information we are given in the short story through conversation between Pyne and the English Consul is played out on stage. The first scene sets the background to the story and the second shows the accident that precipitates the masquerade. This means that the audience is fully aware earlier of the revelation at the end of the story. But we have no way of knowing if Christie had another surprise in mind – there are no notes for a last act.

'Problem at Pollensa Bay'
November 1935

Mrs Adela Chester asks Parker Pyne to convince her son, Basil, to abandon his girlfriend Betty, whom she considers unsuitable.

There are brief notes in Notebooks 66 and 20 for this light-hearted Parker Pyne short story. The only question was where to set it. A non-crime trifle, it was obviously written for the magazine market:

Excited woman wants M PP to stop her son marrying a girl – they won't be happy – son asks whether PP will help him.

Corsica? Majorca?
A mother and her son – a girl he likes – parents – trousers – Madeleine comes out – this scene – the boy distracted

'Triangle at Rhodes'
May 1936

━━━━━━━━━━━━━◀○▶━━━━━━━━━━━━━

Despite warning the protagonists, Hercule Poirot is unable
to prevent a murder in his Rhodes holiday hotel. But he
can solve it by correctly interpreting the fatal triangle.

━━━━━━━━━━━━━◀○▶━━━━━━━━━━━━━

The genesis of this short story is complicated. There are variant texts in the US and the UK appearances, while there are
copious notes for its dramatisation. And as it was expanded
and altered for the novel *Evil under the Sun,* some of the notes
overlap and intersect. It is not possible to date the Notebooks
accurately, but the following in Notebook 20 succinctly sum-
marises the plot:

> The triangle – Valerie C. loved by Commander C. and
> Douglas Golding

It went through a few changes before arriving at the version
we know. These notes, complete with Christie's sketches of
the various 'eternal triangles', are on either side of those for
'Problem at Pollensa Bay'. To complicate matters even more,
two separate and totally different settings and sets of characters are listed:

> Soviet Russia
>
> Room at hotel –
> In train –

The Triangle

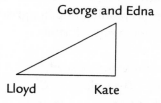

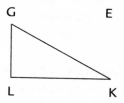

Anna and Ivan
The Gordons – Lloyd and Jessica

Rhodes – Bathing – Emily Renault (Joan Heaslip)

The Courtneys – beautiful – faded – empty-headed
The Goldings arrive – man – plain wife – a shock to discover
they are on honeymoon – his devotion to Mrs C – bowled
over – antagonism between him and C – a quarrel at dinner
– everyone talking about it.

Quiet woman comes to PP . . . what shall she do? He says
leave the island at once – you are in danger – (PP says to
himself where has he seen her – remembrance of murder
trial). Lee a chemist – Golding has his usual drink – gin and
ginger tonic – Mrs Golding drinks it instead and dies

The setting of Soviet Russia (perhaps inspired by a brief foray
there while returning from Ur in 1931) would have been
unique for Christie and very unusual for crime fiction in general at the time. It is perhaps not surprising that this version
was never developed. The other scenario is nearer to the
published version, but it was still to go through further
refinements. Note also that this early draft has it as a case for
Parker Pyne.

Eventually in Notebook 66 we arrive at the 'real' version.
The short précis below of the plot is in the middle of the notes

for *The A.B.C. Murders*, a position which tallies with the publication dates of each. That this plot and setting should suddenly appear, fully formed, while Christie was plotting one her greatest novels is yet another example of her creative fertility.

> Poirot story – Chantries – she beautiful, empty headed,
> he a strong silent man of personality – The Goldings – G
> infatuated with Mrs C – Mrs G in despair comes to Poirot –
> you are in danger. Various scenes if book – actually Chantries
> and Mrs G are lovers – the gin and tonic – Gold – is supposed
> to want to kill C – Mrs C drinks it instead – and dies

Note the words in the middle of this jotting – 'Various scenes if book'. She obviously thought, and correctly, that this situation had great potential for elaboration. And she did just that a few years later in *Evil under the Sun*, although the plots are quite different. Both feature a triangle situation in a beach setting and neither triangle is the one the reader has anticipated, but the motivation for the crimes is different and the eternal triangle theme is given yet another variation in the later work. There is also a distinct similarity to the method of poisoning adopted by the killer in *The Mirror Crack'd from Side to Side*, over 25 years later.

Finally, the following in Notebook 58 may seem like a rough note for 'Triangle at Rhodes', although it actually occurs in the middle of the jottings for *A Caribbean Mystery*:

> Triangle idea (Rhodes)
> Lovely siren – her husband – devoted, dark, cynical –
> little brown mouse, nice little woman, wife – plain stupid
> husband – dark husband really has liaison with mouse.
> They plan to do away with siren – stupid husband is to
> be suspected

There are similarities between the two – the quartet of two husbands and wives in an exotic beach setting. But in fact it is included at this point in the Notebook as a plot resumé to herself as she considered possibilities for her new Caribbean quartet.

∽ℒ℘

Murder in Mesopotamia
6 July 1936

---◄○►---

When Amy Leatheran accepts a nursing job on an archae-ological dig looking after the neurotic Mrs Leidner she little suspects that she will be involved in the investigation of her patient's murder. But how did the killer gain access to his victim when the room was under constant observation?

---◄○►---

From the time of her marriage to Max Mallowan, Christie accompanied him annually to Iraq on his archaeological expeditions. These travels gave her background for her for-eign travel novels but the one that most closely matches her own experiences is *Murder in Mesopotamia*. The setting is an archaeological dig and, apart from the detective plot, there is much detail of day-to-day living, written from first-hand experience.

The surviving notes are not extensive, less than 15 pages in total scattered over four Notebooks. Notebook 66 has a one-line jotting in a list dated January 1935; she wrote the novel during that year with hardback publication in July 1936:

Dig murder 1st person Hospital Nurse?

A list of characters given in Notebook 20 tallies with the published novel (although some of the men are not definitely recognisable), as does the basic situation outlined immediately following:

The People
1. Dr. L[eidner]
2. Mrs L[eidner]
3. Architect B. man of 35 taciturn attractive [Richard Carey]
4. Epigraphist P. moody man – hypochondriac or Priest (not really a priest!) [Fr. Lavigny]
5. Young man R. inclined to be garrulous or naïve [David Emmott]
6. Miss Johnson – middle aged – devoted to L.
7. A wife – not archaeological – pretty – frivolous [Mrs. Mercado]
8. A dour young man G. [Carl Reiter]

The wife – very queer – Is she being doped against her own knowledge? Atmosphere gradually develops of intensity – a bomb may explode any minute

It is a pity there are not more detailed notes for the plot mechanics, especially in view of Christie's reminder to herself at the start of the following extract:

Can we work in the window idea?

Victim	X	Miss J	P

Little Arab boy washing pots

The 'window idea' is undoubtedly one of her most ingenious and original ploys, and like all of her best plots it is so simple – in retrospect. That said, when Miss Johnson stands on the roof in Chapter 23 and says 'I've seen how someone could come in from outside – and no one would ever guess,' this is not exactly the truth. It would have been more strictly accurate to say 'I've seen how someone could commit this murder – and no one would ever guess.' The murderer did not come in from outside – he was already present; and although Miss Johnson realised how he had managed to commit the murder without ever leaving the roof, this is not the same thing.

And despite the reference to the vital 'window idea', the accompanying diagram is not really relevant to it as it represents part of the ground floor plan of the Expedition House, although a different one to that included in the finished novel.

Although Christie experimented briefly with other possible killers, the front-runner always seems to have been the one eventually unmasked:

Possible gambits – Mrs. L's past life – Some man she has injured – husband or someone she betrayed – hate her – pursued her – she gets more and more nervous

Development
　A. Mrs. L is killed
　B. Somebody else is killed in mistake for her – really she engineers it and persecution story is an invention

Dr. L murders Mrs. L
Then a second murder – someone who knew something – Miss Johnson?

Miss J original wife – her revenge?
Or – a trumped up story by wife – and husband killed?
Or Dr. L the villain

Murder in Mesopotamia misses being a first-class Christie due to the unbelievable revelation, during Poirot's explanation, of an unsuspected relationship. The mechanics of the murder are extremely ingenious, the setting and the characters are better drawn than usual and the identity of the killer is undoubtedly a surprise. But the reason for the crime beggars belief; how Christie (or her editor) ever thought this was a likely, or even a credible, scenario is difficult to imagine. Apart from the intrinsic dissatisfaction, it also spoils one of the few examples of Christie's attempt at the 'impossible crime'. This is a sub-genre of the detective novel where the interest lies not only in the identity of the killer but also in the means by which he committed his crime. In the 'impossible crime' detective novel victims are found in the middle of snow-covered lawns with no footprints, in a room under constant observation (as here) or a room with all the doors and windows locked from the inside. Her great contemporary John Dickson Carr, Master of the Locked Room, brought it to full flower. When it is a feature of a Christie plot it is almost as an afterthought; it was never the main focus of her plot. She used it in only three other novels – *Hercule Poirot's Christmas, Why Didn't They Ask Evans?* and *Curtain* – as well as a handful of short stories.

Finally, Notebook 47 reveals that Christie considered using *Murder in Mesopotamia* as the basis for a play. However, she rejects the idea of using the novel's characters or plot as a basis (despite the 'troublemaking attractive woman', a similar character to Mrs Leidner) in sketching a possible scenario:

Play on a dig? Possible characters from Murder in
Mesopot[amia]

Director American – ~~with a troublemaking wife~~ – in love with
a troublemaking attractive woman – widow of an inventor –
or atom scientist – imprisoned for Communist activities –
(after Hiss idea?) Ten years ago – he's in prison – she has
divorced him – in love with Deirdre? Married to him – is
~~Really~~ on point of having affair with middle-aged architect –
two doctors from medical conference Baghdad come along
– one a friend of expedition – the other a plastic surgeon –
he gets killed – then she does

Alger Hiss was a US State Department official accused of
spying and jailed in 1950, but for perjury. His guilt or innocence of the spying accusation is still a matter of debate. He
died in 1992.

The above outline seems an unlikely subject for a stage
play, but some of these ideas did eventually turn up in
Destination Unknown.

Appointment with Death
2 May 1938

---◄○►---

The appalling Mrs Boynton terrorises her family even
while they are on holiday in Petra. When she is found dead
at their camp more than one person is relieved. Hercule
Poirot, while sympathising with the family, has 24 hours
to find the killer.

---◄○►---

There are notes for both the novel and stage versions of this title. Over 60 pages of notes for the latter are contained in four Notebooks and 20 for the novel in Notebook 61, just ahead of preliminary notes for *Hercule Poirot's Christmas* and extended notes for *Akhnaton*. Although published in May 1938, there was an earlier serialisation that January in the *Daily Mail*, where it was called *A Date with Death*, and it appeared at the end of the previous year in the USA. In an essay heralding the serialisation of the novel, Christie wrote that three points of this case appealed to Poirot – the 24 hour deadline, the psychology of the dead woman and the fact that he was asked to investigate by a man with a passion for the truth similar to his own, Colonel Carbury.

In *Appointment with Death* Christie sets herself another technical challenge. The investigation takes place in just 24 hours (although the set-up takes considerably longer) in the spectacular setting of Petra, far removed from the facilities of Scotland Yard. There are no fingerprints, no outsiders, no Hastings; just Hercule Poirot and the suspects – although it has to be said that parts of the solution can be explained only by divine intervention – for example. how can Poirot know about the earlier life of the killer? Tellingly, when Christie adapted this for the stage she completely changed the ending and presented the audience with a more plausible and psychologically compelling solution.

The first page of Notebook 61 is headed 'The Petra Murder'. This is immediately followed by a list of characters and brief descriptions, whose forerunners can clearly be seen in the notes for *Death on the Nile* (see Chapter 6). The name Boynton does not appear at this stage, however, and the family are referred to throughout as Platt:

Characters
Roy – young, neurotic (26?)
Nadine   (22?)
Lucia – Mrs P's own daughter?
Jefferson – eldest son
Prunella (his wife – clear, balanced hair
Sarah Grant (Sybil Grey) a young doctor – interested in
    mental psychology [Sarah King]
Lady Westholme M.P. (a possible future Prime Minister)
Dr Gerard (French?)
Mrs Gibson (very distraught talker)? [Miss Price]

When she returns six pages later (after a quick detour to jot down notes for 'Dead Man's Mirror', *Sad Cypress* and *Curtain*), Christie amends her characters – as usual, some are later renamed, while others do not appear in the novel – and proceeds with her system of assigning letters to scenes. She plots A to L without hesitation or deviation (which may indicate that she had already worked on this elsewhere), even though the order will change quite considerably. The novel's opening sentence, the most arresting of any Christie novel ('You do see, don't you, that she's got to be killed'), does not appear until Scene L in the notes. The fact that Poirot is mentioned in conjunction with this statement may account for its being brought forward.

Petra Murder

The Platt family at Mena House – then on boat to Palestine

People
Mrs Platt [Mrs Boynton]
Jefferson Platt [replaced by Lennox]
Nadine his wife
Marcia [Carol]

Lennox [becomes Raymond in the novel]
Ginevra
Sarah Grey [Sarah King]
Amos Cope (in love with Nadine) [becomes Jefferson Cope in the novel]
Lady Westholme M.P.
Dr Gerard – French doctor
Sir Charles Westholme [does not appear]

A. Sarah Grey and Gerard discuss Mrs Platt – S says sadistic [Part I Chapter 6]
B. Marcia and Lennox – 'It can't go on – Why shouldn't it? It always has – She'll die some day – There's no one to help us. [Part I Chapter 1]
C. Mrs Platt and Ginevra – you're tired tonight my dear – ill – she forces her to be ill [Part I Chapter 4]
D. Nadine and Amos – Why are you here? Leave it all [Part I Chapter 5]
E. Nadine and Jefferson – she begs him – he cries Don't leave me [Part I Chapter 8]
F. Nadine and Mrs Platt – She does not feel spell [Part I Chapter 8]
G. N and Marcia who has overheard conversation – I wouldn't blame you if you did go
H. Amos and Mrs P – latter says she is ill – can only have her own family – a snub [Part I Chapter 5]
I. Marcia and Sarah Grey [Part I Chapter 7]
J. Lennox and Sarah – she tells him to leave – I can't – I'm weak – I'm no good to you [Part I Chapter 9]
K. Sarah and Gerard she admits I've fallen for him [Part I Chapter 9]
L. Lennox and Marcia – we've got to kill her – It would – it would set us all free – HP overhears that last sentence [Part I Chapter 1]

Interestingly, both *Appointment with Death* and the following book, *Hercule Poirot's Christmas,* published six months later, feature Christie's most monstrous creations, Mrs Boynton and Simeon Lee respectively. Both of them bully their family, although in neither case is their tyranny the motivation for their murders. The alternate solution propounded in the stage version of *Appointment with Death* takes the domination to new heights. This novel also features an early example of a young professional woman in Christie, Dr Sarah King. There had been independent young women in earlier novels – apart from Tuppence Beresford there is Emily Trefusis in *The Sittaford Mystery*, Frankie in *Why Didn't They Ask Evans?* and Anne Beddingfeld in *The Man in the Brown Suit* – but Dr King is the first of her profession.

There is much speculation in the notes as to the method of murder, lending strength to the argument that this was a character-driven, rather than a plot-driven, book. And it is not insignificant that in the stage version it is not only a different villain that is unmasked but also a totally different method adopted by the villain. As can be seen, Christie considered quite a few poisons before settling on digitoxin:

Method of Crime etc.

Sarah's drug stolen

Abricine – Sarah's stolen – sudden violent illness of Mrs Pl[att]
Prussic acid in smelling salts?
Digitalin
Narcotic at lunch

> One servant takes up genuine drink (tea?) – One Lady M
> who takes false tea
> If poison – Coniine – Digitoxin – Coramine
> If coniine or coramine – did Lady MacMartin and Miss
> Pierce go up and speak to her – she did not answer
> If insulin Mrs P injected herself
> Point of coniine (or coramine) the muscular paralysis

> The old woman sits – each of family goes up and speaks to
> her – they all see she is dead – but no one says so

The stage adaptation, up to the denouement, is largely the same as the novel. However, as with some of the other stage plays – *The Hollow, Death on the Nile, Go Back for Murder/Five Little Pigs* and *Cards on the Table* (although not dramatised by Christie) – Poirot is dropped. The major difference is the new ending but there is also a discussion in Act II, Scene I of Mrs Boynton's previous career as a wardress. Both of these are discussed in the notes. And it is the seemingly insignificant Miss Price who supplies the vital information leading to the solution, as Christie sketches the revelatory dialogue:

> Do you know – have you done perhaps done rescue work? A
> wardress. Miss P uncomfortable – gets up goes away. Sarah
> who is sitting nearby – then breaks in – 'That explains a lot
> of things – you didn't give up your job when you married –
> you've carried on with it. The need to dominate etc.'

> To be a drug addict – so very sad for the family
> S: Miss Pierce what are you saying
> Miss P: Nothing – nothing at all
> S: Are you saying that Mrs. Boynton took drugs
> Miss P: I found out – quite by accident – of course. I knew it
> was far worse

278

S: But that means . . . Mrs. Boynton was a drug addict
Miss P: Yes dear, I know
S: Tell me – you've got to tell me
Miss P: No, I shall say nothing. The poor woman is dead and . . .
S: Tell me – what did you see or hear –
Miss P tells what she saw – put into stick. Sarah calls Col.
    Carbury – all come – takes out from stick

∾⥼⥽

A Caribbean Mystery
16 November 1964

───────◄○►───────

While holidaying in the West Indies, Miss Marple is subjected
to the endless reminiscences of Major Palgrave. After his
sudden death she regrets not paying more attention when
he talked about a murderer he knew. Is it possible that the
same killer is planning another crime on St Honore?

───────◄○►───────

In *A Caribbean Mystery* Christie used memories of a holiday in
Barbados from a few years earlier. It is Miss Marple's only foreign case, although sending her abroad had been considered
shortly before Christie began *Four-Fifty from Paddington*:

Miss Marple – somewhere on travels – or at seaside

The notes for *A Caribbean Mystery* are scattered over 14
Notebooks, although many of these are no more than jottings of isolated ideas that Christie subsumed into *A Caribbean
Mystery* when she came to write it in 1963. Notebook 4 shows
early musings and in Notebook 48 we find speculation about
two couples:

279

1961 Projects

Carribean [sic] – Miss M – after illness – Raymond and Wife
– Daughter – or son? Bogus major Taylor – like a frog – he
squints.

Idea A Couples Lucky and Greg Evelyn and Rupert [Edward]
    Greg very rich American – Lucky wants to marry young
chap – however pretends it is Rupert – has affair with him.
Point is to be R. kills Greg or Evelyn kills G by mistake for R.
Really it is young man kills Greg

Despite the presence of two couples with almost identical
names in the novel, none of the various permutations and
combinations considered here found their way into *A
Caribbean Mystery*. And in Notebook 35 she lists what were to
become three novels, although the alphabetical sequence is
odd. Perhaps this is the order in which she intended to write
them, although they were actually published in the order
below:

1962 Notes for 3 books
Y. The Clocks (?)
Z. Carribean [sic] Mystery
X. Gypsy's Acre

Some of the ideas Christie jotted down in the various
Notebooks – the frog-faced Major, someone telling long-
winded stories about murder, the administration of hallu-
cinogenic drugs and a husband who 'saves' his wife a few
times only to 'fail' to save her at some later stage – do appear
in the novel. She also reminds herself a few times about 'The
Cretan Bull' from *The Labours of Hercules* and its use of hallu-
cinogenic drugs:

Look up datura poisoning as administered by Indian wives to husbands – and re-read Cretan Bull

Book about Cretan Bull idea – insanity induced by doses of Belladonna

Play or Book – depending on root idea of Murder Made [sic] Easy or Cretan Bull – everything closing round <u>one</u> person gradually – engineered by someone else

A man's wife hangs herself – he cuts her down in time. Really man is preparing the way for her suicide . . . Does this tie in with what doctor or other officer remembers of another case – same man

Story about – woman hanged herself – husband cut her down in time – hushed up

One fact strikingly revealed by the Notebooks is how different a story *A Caribbean Mystery* could have been. In early drafts in Notebook 3 we see the germ of a bizarre idea, not pursued, which is elaborated in Notebook 18. Note also the early possibility of including Hercule Poirot. I can only speculate that Poirot was dropped in favour of Miss Marple as Christie, now as elderly a lady as her creation, had spent a happy holiday in the Caribbean:

(Happy idea) West Indian book – Miss M? Poirot
    Girl crippled by polio – has given up her young man – goes out to where they were going on their honeymoon – she has nurse with her – a rather doubtful character – girl kills anyone who is happy

West Indies
    Miss Marple and possibly Jean Brent – Polio victim and a hospital nurse Doran Watson (Miss? Mrs.?)

Could start with the girl – Jean – crippled – tells fiancé she must give him up – he protests – everyone applauds her – then given a trip because she wishes she could get away. Raymond must perhaps make an arrangement with Mrs. Watson who is going with an old Mr. Van Dieman (rich) – (to give him massage every day?) . . .
If a warped Jean who hates to hear other people's happiness is the murderer – how does she bring it about.
Poison? Narcotic? Tranquillisers? Substitution of same Pep pills – What drug

Combine Polio Jean – (or car accident) sacrifice with frog faced Major (West Indies)

Three consecutive pages in Notebook 3 contain three important elements of *A Caribbean Mystery*:

Book about Cretan Bull idea – insanity induced by doses of Belladonna.
2 pairs husband and wife – B and E apparently devoted – actually B and G (Georgina) have had an affair for years – Brian, G's husband doesn't know? Really it is a different husband and wife – husband is a wife killer. Old 'frog' Major knows – has seen him before – he is killed

And it is in Notebook 18 that we get the main source of misdirection (even though it is mentioned frequently) – the idea of the glass eye:

A different story by Major P – his glass eye rests on ? (1) ?
(2) but really on Jean and Nurse Boscombe

Interestingly, in the original typescript at the end of Chapter 23 and after the 'Evil Eye . . . Eye . . . Eye' clue, there is an extra sentence – '*Miss Marple gasped.*' This may have been considered too daring and does not appear in the published version. And in Notebook 23 we get a rough sketch, literally, of the all-important scene, with the Major looking over Miss Marple's shoulder. Here Christie draws, probably for her own clarification, the physical set-up as Miss Marple listens to the Major's story and misinterprets his gaze:

After lunch Miss Marple talking to Maj –
verandah steps

            Miss M   Mollie Tim

    Quartette   Maj.

Tim doing accounts with Mollie – Maj. talking – pulls out
snap look up and sees the man in the snap

           Left eye R. eye

Notebook 58 is still considering very basic character setting and a slightly different version of the story told by Major Palgrave. Here, the CID man who investigated the crimes tells the story directly to Miss Marple. At this stage in the planning there is no mention of the hotel owners – just the quartet. But there was to be a Christiean twist, not adopted for the novel, even with this limited field of suspects.

Carribean [sic] Mystery

A quartet [of] friends
Mr and Mrs R. Rupert and Emily – English – friends of many
years standing – one pair app[ear] very devoted. One day –
wife confides they never speak to each other in private –
husband (to girl) says wonderful life together – which is lying?

The CID man is in County district in England – man's phone broken down – he walks into town – (car at garage) for doctor – they get back – wife is dead – heart? – man terribly upset – it worries CID man – remembers man – has seen him before – remembers – in France – and his wife had died – same thing in Canada – then marries an American woman – comes to Tobago – CID man found dead

But is it really the woman – The dog it was that died
   The wrong man or wrong woman dies – of heart trouble so that you suspect the wrong pair – really Mrs Rupert is the one with her fads and illnesses – she and chap are having an affair

Finally, we can see the amount of thought that went into the Major and his story, elements of which appear in three Notebooks:

Problem of Major P

Points   Why did Major not recognise his murderer before?
   No new comers to the island – Edward, Greg, Van D Jackson all known to him
   Answer by Miss M? – Major had not seen the man himself – this was a story told him – he had only glanced at snap – then kept it as a curiosity – he takes it out preparatory to showing it to her looks at it – looks up, seeing suddenly the man in the photograph – hastily stuffs it back again

Possibilities   (1) Major had several murderer stories that he had picked up in course of travel
                (2) Could Miss M – (or Esther) have misunderstood
                (3) (Not supported!) Esther lied – why?

The murderer story is different – could be either a man or a woman.

Does Kelly tell Miss M – how Palgrave told him a story – this indicates that it was a woman

Miss M with Jenny in West Indies

The frog faced Major – his gossip – glass eye – appears to be looking different direction from what he really is – 3 husband and wives applicable – Chuck and Patty (affair?) – Greg and ~~Sarah~~ Evelyn

Once more, we can see how the fertility of Christie's imagination might have created a very different novel from the one we have.

In a Glass Darkly:
The Unknown Christie

'... that is to say UN Owen. Or by a slight stretch of fancy:
UNKNOWN'

Ten Little Niggers, Chapter 3

Apart from Agatha Christie's enormous known output there
is also a number of works that are largely unknown, except to
the most ardent fans. These titles are all scripts, either for the
stage or radio, and have all been either performed or published. And all of these titles feature in the Notebooks, some
of them to a large degree.

Agatha Christie is still the only crime novelist to have had
an equally successful career as a playwright. Indeed, arguably
the greatest monument to her success is a play, *The Mousetrap*.
The majority of her plays are well known but there are still a
few surprises.

Akhnaton is a non-crime script from 1937 based on the real-
life Pharoah Akhnaton of Egypt. The little-known *Rule of
Three* contains three utterly contrasting one-act plays,
Christie's only venture into this form. And the final title in
this chapter is the last play that she wrote, *Fiddlers Three*.
Neither play received encouraging reviews, although both
contain much interesting material.

For future consideration are the totally unknown radio plays *Personal Call* and *Butter in a Lordly Dish*, and *Chimneys*. The latter is her own adaptation, and reworking with a new villain, of the 1925 novel *The Secret of Chimneys*; the former two original plays written directly for radio. None of the three is currently available in any form.

Rule of Three
20 December 1962

Over 40 years after her career began Christie was still experimenting when *Rule of Three* was first presented at the Duchess Theatre, London. Reviews were not good however and apart from *Fiddlers Three*, which never had a West End run, it lowered the curtain on her golden age of theatre. It is now an unknown Christie because it has seldom been staged since. But *Rule of Three* shows that, even after a lifetime of hoodwinking her audience, she still had the ability to surprise and entertain. Each of the three plays represents a different aspect of Christie and, moreover, aspects that are very unexpected and atypical. Of the three plays, *Afternoon at the Seaside* is the most unlikely play ever to have come from the pen of Agatha Christie; *The Rats* is not a whodunit but a claustrophobic will-they-get-away-with-it; while *The Patient* is the essence of Christie.

As early as 1955, seven years before its first presentation, in Notebook 3 Christie was including *Rule of Three* in a list of 'Projects'. The same list also anticipates what were to become *Four-Fifty from Paddington* ('New Book Miss M?' below) and the next Westmacott novel, eventually titled *The Burden*. At that stage the three projected plays were to be adaptations of existing, and mutually contrasting, stories; both 'Accident' and 'The Rajah's Emerald' are from *The Listerdale Mystery* and

'S.O.S.' is included in *The Hound of Death*. It is worth noting that 'The Rajah's Emerald' has a thematic connection – the disappearance of jewels on a beach – with the play eventually decided upon, *Afternoon at the Seaside*; and both are light-hearted in tone. The grim poisoning short story 'Accident' had already been adapted in 1939 by Margery Vosper as *Tea for Three*.

General Projects 1955

Angle of Attack   Mary Westmacott

The Unexpected Guest   Play 3 Acts

Three Plays (Rule of Three?)

1.   Accident?
2.   Rajah's Emerald?
3.   S.O.S.?

New Book   Miss M?   P? –

By Notebook 24, two of the eventual titles, C and B below, were included in the following jotting, 'S.O.S.' (although with a question mark) still remaining as the third. Inexplicably, they are listed on the page in reverse alphabetical order; when presented *The Rats* is performed first, followed by *Afternoon at the Seaside*, and culminating with *The Patient*.

Rule of Three   3 1-Act plays for P.S.

C. The Patient
B. Seaside Holiday – I do like to be beside the seaside
A. S.O.S.? [sic]
  The Locket
  Christmas Roses
  Green Paint Or Telephone Call –

'P.S.' was Peter Saunders, her long-time producer. Though the remaining references are elusive, the 'telephone call' in the second list is probably the seed of *The Rats*, where the telephone sets the trap into which the rats are lured; and 'Green Paint' may be a cryptic reference to the proposed innovation she had in mind for the end of *The Patient* (see below).

The Rats

Adulterous lovers Sandra and David each receive a phone call inviting them to the flat of a mutual acquaintance. When they try to leave they discover that they are locked in – and there is a dead body in the Kuwait Chest.

The Rats is not a whodunit although there are a few mysterious deaths, explained by the end of the play. The most obvious similarity is to the Poirot story 'The Mystery of the Baghdad Chest', and its later and more elaborate version, 'The Mystery of the Spanish Chest'. In that story a suspicious husband hides in the chest hoping to catch his wife and her lover in flagrante; in *The Rats*, when the Sandra and David realise that they have been lured to the flat, they suspect a similar trap. But the play develops in a more macabre fashion. It does retain the clue of the little heap of sawdust beneath the chest that gives Poirot 'furiously to think' in the short story. Notebook 24 contains almost five pages of notes:

The Rats

Flat belongs to the Torrances – rather bare – a Kuwait chest is centre – high up into roof – built in cupboards – a dark divan covered with curtains etc. – a long ply wood table –

some modern chairs – one or two pieces of Persian pottery –
a big Arab long nosed beak nosed coffee pot

Body in ~~cupboard~~ – Baghdad Chest – Oh! My God – It's
Robert – Police will come – girl and man discover body of
her husband – Alec arrives – a Mischa like person – says he
got phone call

Although there have been gay characters in Christie before
this (Mr Pye in *The Moving Finger*, Murgatroyd and Hinchcliffe
in *A Murder is Announced* and Horace Bundler in 'Greenshaw's
Folly'), Alec in *The Rats* is the most unequivocal and stereotyp-
ical example and far more sinister than, for example,
Christopher Wren in *The Mousetrap*. He is described in the
script as 'the pansy type, very elegant, amusing, inclined to be
spiteful' and his love for Sandra's former husband is openly
discussed. The Mischa reference, above, is puzzling.

Afternoon at the Seaside

――――――◄○►――――――

A family afternoon on the beach culminates in the capture
of a jewel thief and some unexpected revelations – and a
resolve to go elsewhere for next year's holiday.

――――――◄○►――――――

Of the three plays in *Rule of Three, Afternoon at the Seaside* is the
most unlikely for Agatha Christie to have written. It has been
compared to a saucy seaside English postcard, set as it is
entirely on a beach and involving, at one stage, a female character changing into her swimsuit onstage. The plot, for
Christie, is slight and the humour is at times forced. It is definitely Christie on autopilot – but there is one surprise, repre-
senting a new variation on an old Christie theme. Ironically

the notes for it are extensive, extending to almost 40 pages, albeit with a lot of repetition. There is much speculation about the naming both of the families (the aptly named Mr and Mrs Sour, described as 'whiners', become Mr and Mrs Crum) and the beach huts:

Sea View	(Mon Repos)	Wee Nook
Mrs. Montressor	Mr Wills Mrs Wills	Genevieve Batat

At the Seaside

Iniskillen	Bide a Wee	Mon Repos
Mr Sour	Wilkinson	~~Arlette~~
Child	~~Mr Robbins~~	~~Incognita~~
Mrs Sour	~~Mrs. Robbins~~	Yvonne
(Whiners)	Wilkinson	

But further into the notes there are flashes of the Queen of Crime in the unmasking, not of the villain, but of the police-man – or to be strictly accurate, the policewoman:

Read in paper – robbery at Aga Khan – emeralds/sapphires –

Beach
Mon Desir
Policewoman Alice Jones acting as vamp
Young man and his girl quarrel – another young man and
    they bring down deck chairs –

Some ideas are reminiscent of the Christie of old, even for this short, untypical effort. And, obviously, her ability to spin variations on a theme has not deserted her. The 'switch of trousers' idea has distinct echoes of 'The Rajah's Emerald' from *The Listerdale Mystery*:

Does detective arrive – search the huts? Find emeralds?
Or does old Grubb find it in bucket?
Or child kick pile of sand – Grubb picks out emeralds
God bless my soul

Reasonable possible ideas
Or switch of trousers – Percy gets in the wrong ones
Somers (weakly and gentlemanly – really cat burglar)
Or counterfeit money
Or put into wrong hut
Does Percy get hit with beach ball
Or blackmail

The Patient

Mrs Wingfield is paralysed as a result of a fall from the
balcony of her home. Her doctor has found a way to
communicate with her and is about to do so in the
presence of her family. But someone doesn't want her
to tell the truth of that fateful afternoon.

It is a shame that so few Christie fans are familiar with *The Patient,* as, in many ways, it is the essence of Christie – a closed setting, a limited family circle of suspects, a crafty distribution of suspicion; and all in 40 minutes. It also contains one of her most artfully concealed clues. Unlike the other two plays in this trilogy, it is a pure whodunit with a stunning curtain line. Yes, it is contrived (an immobilised patient communicating via a once-for-Yes-twice-for-No light switch) but so are many other detective plots, including some of her own best titles. Notes for the play appear in Notebooks 22 and 24:

The Patient

Nursing Home – Doctor and Nurse (Patient there? Or wheeled in later)
  Is latter the one who has established communication –

Sales talk by Inspector – jewellery disappeared
  Mrs. X badly injured – paralysed – unable to communicate – ingenious nurse pressure of fingers – apparatus with red bulb – Patient wheeled in –

Patient wheeled in – nurse by her (Bond) or interne
Questions spelled out Murder
          Mirror
          Bathroom
Saw someone   Yes
Someone you knew   Yes
Is that person in the room now   Yes
Spell out the name   A – B
B –   Yes
Collapse reported by nurse? interne? –

Take off the mask – I know well enough who you are
Curtain falls – My God – you!

Alternative end – gloves – coated in phosphorescent paint – hold up your hands – Lights out – Guilty Hands!

Even at this late stage in her theatrical career Christie was experimenting, as the last two notes above show. Incredibly, she wanted the curtain to fall, or the lights to black out, *before* the murderer was unmasked. This, if it had been allowed to continue, would have been the ultimate Christie twist – though the shock was to be somewhat mitigated by a recording of her own voice asking the audience whom they thought the killer was.

The Patient -
Room in Nursing Home. Enlby of doctor
& relations(?). Psychological - nothing organic
       Nurse - her contains the patient
Conscious - (Black nurse?)
       N - says she thinks -
S.O.S. idea - Man (relation? police)
believes that she thinks
       S.O.S. He asks her — once for
Yes - Twice for No ..

       Po m
          Possible ending .
A nurse introduced - really Police woman -
apparently spiritual -

Possible scene

Patient lies, murderer -
       shoots him .

N - Is it Nurse who really was
relation & killed husband .

A sketch and notes for The Patient *from Notebook 64. Note the reference
to 'S.O.S.' the short story from* The Hound of Death *that, like*
The Patient, *also features an unusual method of communication.*

Not surprisingly, however, the idea was not a winner. It was abandoned after a flurry of telegrams to the author, who was abroad during the pre-London tryout in Aberdeen. With a track record of glittering theatrical success behind her, it does seem a very odd concept to have introduced; it would be like reading one of her novels and finding the last chapter missing.

❦

Fiddlers Three
3 August 1972

────────────◄○►────────────

It is very important that businessman Jonathan Panhacker should live until Wednesday 18th as he has made a financial arrangement with his son, Henry, to inherit £100,000 on that date. When he unexpectedly dies, the Fiddlers Three conspire to make sure he is still 'alive' for a few more days.

────────────◄○►────────────

This is the last play written by Agatha Christie and the only one not to receive a West End run. After a glorious and record-breaking playwriting career, this last work was a sad curtain call. Her previous dramatic offering, *Rule of Three* (see above), was not particularly well received and it was ten years before she again felt tempted to try a script. *Fiddlers Three* is a two-act comedy thriller but, unfortunately, it has not enough of either to be a successful blend and falls between two uneasy extremes. It has a complicated history. In its first incarnation, *Fiddlers Five*, it premiered on 7 June 1971; the following year on 3 August a revamped version was presented as *Fiddlers Three*. In the intervening year

Christie amalgamated some characters to reduce the number of Fiddlers.

The set-up is relatively straightforward. If Jonathan Panhacker lives until Wednesday 18th his financial arrangement with his son, Henry, to inherit £100,000 on that date will come to pass. In his turn, Henry has promised to invest the money in a business scheme with Sam Fletcher and Sam Bogosian. When Jonathan suddenly drops dead, Henry, Sam and his secretary, Sally, the Fiddlers Three of the title, scheme to keep him 'alive' until the 18th. This involves a double impersonation, a dubious death certificate and a revelation about an earlier murder. Complications arise in the second act when various people who knew Jonathan arrive at their hideaway hotel demanding to see him.

Like many of Christie's later, and weaker, titles it contains good ideas but her earlier genius for exploiting them has deserted her; if she had written this play 20 years before she would have developed the plot in a more convincing manner. There is an unlikely impersonation and some unconvincing business with pill bottles before the play culminates in the unmasking of an improbable murderer. It cannot be coincidence that many of her later plays – *Spider's Web*, *The Unexpected Guest*, *Verdict*, *The Rats* and *Fiddlers Three* – feature this type of a will-they-get-away-with-it situation even if she frequently manages to reveal a murderer also.

Unsurprisingly, her producer Peter Saunders was not anxious to present it in the West End, correctly presuming that it would receive a critical mauling. As it was, the local press was hardly kinder and phrases such as 'entertaining, amusing but undemanding play', 'lightest vein – bordering on farce' and 'the plot is predictable, witless and shallow' peppered what reviews there were.

As early as October 1958, the first seeds were sown in Notebook 15, although it would be over a dozen years before she began to cultivate it seriously. Obviously, even this late in her career, she was revisiting her faithful Notebooks to find exploitable ideas:

Oct. 1958

Projects

A Play – light-hearted (a Spider's Web type) Where? – girl's school?
    Or Cheating Death parties? Pretending a death? or smuggling away a natural death – devoted fluffy secretary? – a silly type deliberately chosen? Boardroom – K. doubles as wife and corpse – wig etc. – Grand muddle –

The 'girl's school' idea surfaced as *Cat among the Pigeons*, published the following year. And the 'Cheating Death parties' was briefly pursued in Notebook 39 below. 'Smuggling away a natural death' was the one that provided the basis of *Fiddlers Three*.

Notebook 4 contains most of the plotting, but, as with the later book titles, the notes themselves are vague and unfocussed although the list of characters is accurate. A minor mystery about this play is the naming of the two main characters; Panhacker and Bogosian are two of the most unusual names in the entire Christie output.

Scene – an office
Mr Willis Stanley a bit off – story
His friend Mr. Bogosian
Nellie (M) devoted rather talkative and scatty

The Penthouse owner – Very rich man lives in W. Indies
His son ~~or nephew?~~ Make over all his English assets
Going to finance – only a fortnight to go

Then goes up after lunch – or is lift out of order – so he
comes in here – sits in other room – found dead

M. says it will be her husband or brother – Go out to buy me
    an onion [to induce tears]
Jeremy ~~Brooker~~ Brown

That's all right – he's got to be alive – Geraldine – Go on
upstairs with things

Gina
Sally Lee
Sam Fletcher
Jan Bogosian
Henry Panhacker
Solomon Panhacker
An Air Hostess
Detective Inspector Wylie
Mr. Moss

Various titles were considered and *This Mortal Coil* appears on
an early script:

This Mortal Coil
Operation Deadline
Sixpence Off
Deadline
Fiddle de Death

In Notebook 39, under the mysterious heading 'M and J
Play', we find two attempts at a 'death duties' play. The first
sketch has echoes of 'Jane in Search of a Job', originally published in August 1924 and collected ten years later in *The
Listerdale Mystery*:

> Death duties – girl is dead – great fortune is coming to her – idea is she has to appear alive for one more week. Man advertises for young lady – 5ft 7in, fair – hair slight build, blue eyes etc. First scene interesting girls whittled down – one is chosen to impersonate girl – J

The second is nearer to the eventual plot, but this was not developed until Notebook 4 where it becomes recognisably *Fiddlers Three*.

> Death Duties – a natural death body has to be hidden for a week – impersonation by M or J – undertaker helps. Office – M and her two employers
> Mr Leonard – big, bouncy, common
> Mr Arkwright – melancholy – dreary
> They are in a jam – what to do
> Sally!

Akhnaton
Published 14 May 1973

Spanning a period of 16 years, the play concerns the attempts of the young King Akhnaton to introduce a new religion to Egypt. His failure spells tragedy for himself, his queen and, ultimately, Egypt.

There are almost 50 pages of notes for this title, mainly in Notebook 61. Called by Christie's husband, Sir Max Mallowan, 'the most beautiful play' she ever wrote, it is based on the real-life Pharoah Akhnaton of Egypt in 1375 BC.

Although written in 1937 it was not published until 1973, with a blurb written by Agatha Christie herself. Shortly after its completion Christie sent it to the actor (later Sir) John Gielgud. His reply, which she kept, expressed his admiration for the play while declining to become involved in a production. In fact *Akhnaton* was never professionally produced, but it was seen in the Westcliff Agatha Christie Theatre Festival in 2001; the one-off presentation used a minimum of setting and props and was, in essence, an elaborate reading.

Although by no means a typical Agatha Christie play, it does contain Christie-like elements – there is a death by poisoning, masterminded by an unsuspected villain using an innocent party.

There are 40 pages of notes for this play. These include extensive background material as well as sketches for the play itself. The very first page of notes begins with a cast list (in the published version Mutnezmet, Nefertiti's sister, has become Nezzemut), and this is followed by a sketch of the opening scene:

Queen Tyi
Horemheb
Eye
Nefertiti
Mutnezmet
Tutankhamun
The father of Tyi
The mother of Tyi
The High Priest of Amon
The High Priest of Re
A Priest of Ptah

Act I Scene I
Amenhotep the Magnificent is near to death – the king of
Mitanni sends the image of Ishtar of Niniveh to Egypt
(second time such a procedure happened) in hopes that the
Goddess might exorcise the evil spirits which were causing
the King's infirmity. The Goddess passes through. ~~Horemheb~~
~~talks with~~ the father and mother of Tyi talk together. The
High Priest of Ammon talks to Horemheb – on evils of
foreign marriage – Queen Tyi appears with her son. –

The early pages of Notebook 61 show seven scenes for Act I,
four for Act II and two for Act III. A redrafting ten pages later
brings it closer to the published version, which has three
scenes each for the first two Acts and four for the third with
an Epilogue. The notes show this Epilogue as the last scene
of the play.

In between the drafts there are notes on

Indulgences – A verdict of acquittal sold by Scribes – pardoned
names inserted in the blanks.

Heart scarab – 'O my heart rise not up against me as a
witness'

Gold collars as gifts –

The book *From Fetish to God* by Budge is also mentioned on
the very first page and there are page references to it
throughout the notes. This research is similar to that undertaken by Christie for *Death Comes as the End* from books
loaned to her by Stephen Glanville, the dedicatee (see
Chapter 7):

Visit by Tyi in 12th year of A's reign – description of clothes
   P.155
Tribute? – A scene showing it being brought' P.151
Description of Palace for scene P.138

One of the earliest quotations, presumably from this book, is reproduced with minor variations to form almost the closing lines of the play. The last traces of Akhnaton are erased, soon to be replaced by 'the divine Amon, King of Gods':

How bountiful are the possessions of him who knows the gifts of that God (Amon). Wise is he who knows him. Favoured is he who serves him, there is protection for him who follows him.

EXHIBIT F:
THE HOUSE OF DREAMS: UNUSED IDEAS

'Unless I get a rough sketch of my idea down, it will go'
Mrs McGinty's Dead, Chapter 24

SOLUTIONS REVEALED
Four-Fifty from Paddington • 'Jewel Robbery at the Grand
Metropolitan' • 'Miss Marple Tells a Story'

There is a story, possibly apocryphal, that detective novelist Nicholas Blake (in real life the Poet Laureate Cecil Day Lewis) offered to buy some plot ideas from Christie but she replied that she intended using them all herself. The Notebooks are littered with such ideas and what follows are some of those that never got further than the page on which they appeared. Some haunted her – the non-identical twins, the chamber-maid, the arty friends – as they appeared again and again.

Twins – point is not identical – Twins identical – one killed in railway smash?

Identical twins – claimant assumes identity of sister (killed in railway smash) rich widow

These are just two of the ten versions of the 'twins' idea that litter the Notebooks. A railway smash and a false identity are minor features of *Murder in Mesopotamia*. Twin sisters also feature in *Elephants Can Remember* and on a more light-hearted note, twins are the solution to one of Tommy and Tuppence's *Partners in Crime* cases.

———•◆•———

Mirrors
    Man or woman – she gets post or chums up with another woman – they come to hotel together.
    Background of one is all right – cathedral town etc. Have been in A.R.P. together – they give alibi to man

———•◆•———

The heading 'Mirrors' confirms what a diffuse history *They Do it with Mirrors* had. The only tenuous connection to that novel is the idea of giving an alibi to someone.

Nitro benzene – point is – it sinks to bottom of glass – woman takes sip from it – then gives it to husband

Camphor in capsule

Murder by lipstick – lip burnt first – cigarette given wrong end first

Strychnine or drug absorbed through skin

Influenza depression virus – Stolen? Cabinet Minister?

Lanolin poison? Strychnine? The poison that makes everything yellow (applied to dress – very misleading as another girl had yellow dress (1931)

Lanoline rubbed into skin

Mirrors

Man & woman –

She gets post or dum up
with another woman –
They come to Hotel together –
Back [illegible] of [illegible] all right –
Cathedral Prom etc –
[illegible] then A.R.P. together –

They sive alibi to

Man –

Despite its heading, this page from Notebook 19 has no connection with any 'Mirrors' title. It is the page open on Christie's lap in this 1946 photograph.

These are just a few of the ideas using various forms of poison, Christie's favourite method of despatch throughout her career. 'Murder by lipstick' is particularly imaginative.

———•◆•———

Chambermaid in hotel accomplice of man – evidence always accepted and clinches case

Chambermaid story – a hotel – Torquay? Riviera? Spain? Majorca? English better

The chambermaid idea, of which the above are just two examples, appears ten times in the Notebooks. Evidently the idea of a dishonest chambermaid was one that held possibilities for Christie as she utilised it in both 'The Jewel Robbery at the Grand Metropolitan' and 'Miss Marple Tells a Story'. But neither of those fits the plot device of any of the above. The second one is vague enough to fit anything.

———•◆•———

Legless man – sometimes tall – sometimes short

The 'legless man' motif is another idea that appears in ten Notebooks although nothing was ever made of it. The idea behind this device was that such a person could alter his appearance very dramatically, thereby making identification difficult. Christie's fellow detective novelist John Dickson Carr used this plot device definitively in his 1938 novel *The Crooked Hinge*.

———•◆•———

Stabbed through eye with hat pin

This very gruesome idea is untypical of Christie, its attraction probably the difficulty of spotting the means of death. It also appears in three other Notebooks.

———•◆•———

Isotope idea – Carbon 14 – hypodermic injection (for typhoid?) normal procedure. He (?) is going abroad – appointment with local doctor – his place is taken by impostor who gives so-called typhoid injection.

This idea, inspired by a visit to a laboratory during a US visit in the 1960s, has strong echoes of *One, Two, Buckle my Shoe* in the impersonation of a doctor in order to poison a patient.

————•◆•————

Committee crime – Mr Llewellyn – tiresome woman – makes speech – drinks glass of water

Glass of water – Dr Haydock . . . Suicide because of anonymous letter? At Harton Parva – the vicar's sister – vinegary woman – the school teacher – at village shop vicar's sister gets groceries – lays down letters – girl slips one in

These jottings appear in the same Notebook, the first one in a list of projected Miss Marple short stories. And it seems very much Miss Marple's territory. The seeds of *The Moving Finger* can be seen in the 'suicide because of anonymous letters' idea and the method of inserting a letter in an otherwise innocent bundle appears in Chapter 13 of that novel.

————•◆•————

Disappearance of actress – strange behaviour of head gardener

This wonderfully enigmatic combination of ideas appears in Notebook 65 alongside the notes for *Ten Little Niggers*, although it dates from much earlier in Christie's career. The suspicious head gardener, very much Miss Marple territory, does make a brief appearance in 'Ingots of Gold' from *The Thirteen Problems*.

————•◆•————

A blonde millionaire's daughter kidnaps herself so as to get
away to marry young man

This surfaces three times in the Notebooks, each time speci-
fying a blonde perpetrator. It sounds relatively non-criminal
and may have been intended as a light-hearted story, not
unlike one of Tommy and Tuppence's early adventures –
'A Pot of Tea'.

———•◆•———

Tom, Dick or Harry come to Bridge – point – none of them
existed!

Tempting though it is to believe that this is a reference to
Cards on the Table, it appears in a list headed 'Ideas 1940', four
years after that title. It is difficult to see what Christie had in
mind here.

———•◆•———

Infra Red photograph

This unusual idea may have been inspired by her interest in
photography during her archaeological work with Sir Max
Mallowan. It appears in a list of possible Miss Marple stories,
although it would not appear to be one with which Miss
Marple might be familiar.

———•◆•———

Dangerous drugs stolen from car – doctor very upset –
excitement in village

Dangerous drugs stolen from doctor's car – X goes touring
in car – follows a doctor in strange town – or Doctor himself
is criminal – later marries dead patient's wife or daughter

Although it never appears as a plot device in its own right,
this scenario is one of those mentioned in *Hickory Dickory*

Dock as a means of getting hold of poison. Our old friend the doctor (statistically the most homicidal profession in Christie) resurfaces here and although the idea was jotted down in the late 1930s, the second note may be the inspiration for Dr Quimper in *Four-Fifty from Paddington*. This idea appears in five Notebooks.

———•◆•———

A false Hercule P. – he is in some hotel lunching re-growing one of his moustaches which have been burnt – wild out of the way spot

The 'wild out of the way spot' may be the setting of 'The Erymanthian Boar', the snowbound top of a Swiss mountain, but the moustache regrowing was never explored despite its appearance in two other Notebooks.

10

Sanctuary: A Holiday for Murder

'Well – to put it plainly – do you come to places expecting a
holiday from crime – and find instead bodies cropping up?'
'It has happened, yes; more than once.'
Appointment with Death, Part II Chapter 1

SOLUTIONS REVEALED
*At Bertram's Hotel • Evil under the Sun • Hallowe'en Party •
Hercule Poirot's Christmas • Peril at End House •
Sad Cypress • Towards Zero*

◄○►

Holidays and festivals have provided backgrounds for a
number of Christie stories. Some of them – *Peril at End House,
Evil under the Sun* – interrupt Poirot's summer holiday; others
disrupt his Christmas – *Hercule Poirot's Christmas* – while
Hallowe'en and Guy Fawkes Day also proved a suitable dramatic backdrop for murder. Some of his more exotic holidays
in Petra – *Appointment with Death* – and Egypt – *Death on the
Nile* – can be found in Chapters 8 and 6 respectively while
Miss Marple's holiday in the Caribbean is discussed in
Chapter 8. The other unmistakable family holiday, *Afternoon
at the Seaside*, is discussed in Chapter 9.

Peril at End House
7 February 1932

―――――――――◄○►―――――――――

While holidaying in St Loo Poirot and Hastings meet Nick Buckley, the impoverished owner of End House. When she tells them that she has had three close brushes with death, Poirot investigates, but is unable to avert a real tragedy at End House.

―――――――――◄○►―――――――――

Peril at End House was published on both sides of the Atlantic in early February 1932 with a serialisation in both places some months earlier. This, in turn, would mean that it was written most probably during late 1930/early 1931. The plotting for it is contained in two Notebooks, 59 and 68. Notebook 68 is a very small pocket-diary sized notebook and, apart from a detailed listing of train times from Stockport to Torquay, is devoted entirely to this novel. Notebook 59 also contains extensive notes for the Mr Quin story 'The Bird with the Broken Wing', first published in *The Mysterious Mr Quin* in April 1930, and for 'Manx Gold' (see Chapter 5), the treasure hunt story/competition that appeared in May 1930.

Peril at End House is a magnificent example of the Golden Age detective story. It is rarely mentioned in any discussion of Christie's best titles and yet it embodies all of the virtues of the detective story in its prime: it is told with succinct clarity, enviable readability and scrupulous fairness in clueing. Every single fact the reader needs in order to arrive at the correct solution is given with superb sleight of hand. And like all of the best detective stories the secret of the plot (a mistake in names) is simple – when you know. On page 3 of Notebook 59 Christie uses a telling phrase – 'conversation without having a point' – referring to the early conversation between Poirot and Hastings in the garden of the hotel. At this point in her career virtually every conversation in a novel has a 'point' – the delineation of an important character trait (the silk stockings episode in *Cards on the Table*), a hint about motivation (Major Burnaby gruffly discussing crosswords and acrostics in Chapter 1 of *The Sittaford Mystery*), a major clue (the difficulty established in Chapter 2 of getting a sleeping berth on the normally half-empty Orient Express) or the confirmation of a previously suspected fact (the picnic in *Evil under the Sun*). And although she refers to a conversation without having a point, there is a mention of the missing airman (the motive) in the actual conversation to which the notes allude.

Peril at End House is interesting not just because of its own virtues but also because of the number of themes and ideas that Christie went on to exploit in later titles:

* The murder in *Peril at End House* takes place during a fireworks display when the sound of a gunshot is camouflaged by the sound of fireworks; this idea was to be an important plot feature of the 1936 novella 'Murder in the Mews'. In fact, it is one of the refinements added to the original version of this story, 'The Market Basing Mystery' (see below).
* The use of names as a device to fool the reader makes an early appearance in this novel. It was to reappear in *Dumb Witness, Mrs McGinty's Dead, A Murder is Announced* and, with an international twist, in *Murder on the Orient Express*.
* A murder method that involves sending poisoned chocolates to a patient in hospital resurfaces three years

---

As usual some of the names change – Lucy Bartlett becomes Maggie Buckley, while Walter Buckhampton is Charles Vyse and the Curtises become the Crofts – but much of the notes tally with the finished novel, leading once more to the suspicion that earlier notes have not survived. Interestingly, in Notebook 59 the character of Nick Buckley is referred to throughout as Egg – the future nickname of Mary Lytton-Gore in *Three Act Tragedy*; although it is odd that the surname Beresford – already in use for Tommy and Tupppence – is chosen.

> Poirot and Hastings sitting in Imperial Hotel – H reads from paper about Polar expedition – a letter from Home Secretary begging Poirot to do something. H urges him to do so – P

later in *Three Act Tragedy*, when it is used to despatch the unfortunate Mrs de Rushbridger.

* A vital and poignant clue from the contents of a letter posted by the victim shortly before her death and subsequently forwarded by the recipient to Poirot appears again (and arguably in an even more ingenious form) the following year in *Lord Edgware Dies*.
* The use of cocaine by the 'smart set' of the 1930s is revisited in *Death in the Clouds* when Lady Horbury is found to have cocaine in her dressing-case.
* Apart from the letter clue above there are other strong similarities to *Lord Edgware Dies* – an attractive and ruthless female draws Poirot, for her own purposes, into the case.
* Subterfuge concerning wills was also to be a feature of *Sad Cypress*, *A Murder is Announced*, *Taken at the Flood* and *Hallowe'en Party*.

refuses – no longer any wish for kudos. The garden – girl – someone calls 'Egg' – Poirot goes down stairs – falls – girl picks him up – she and Hastings assist him to verandah – he thanks her suggests cocktail. H is sent to get them – returns to find pair firm friends

People in this story
Egg Beresford – owner of End House
Cousin Lucy – a distant cousin – 2nd or 3rd cousin – Lucy
   Bartlett
Egg's cousin Walter Buckhampton – son of her mother's
   sister – he works in a solicitor's office in St. Loo – he loves
   Egg
Mr and Mrs Curtis – old friends who live next door – he is an
   invalid who came down there years ago – they seem
   pleasant and jovial
Freddie – Frederica Rice – a friend – parasite who lives on
   Egg and admits it frankly
Lazarus – has a big car – often down there – a member of an
   antique firm in London

The hotel where Poirot and Hastings sit is a real Torquay hotel, the Imperial, with a verandah overlooking Torquay Bay; in the book it is re-imagined as the Majestic Hotel in St Loo. The rest of the cast is recognisable and the opening of the book follows the above plan exactly.

The plot is developed further in Notebook 68; I have indicated the chapters in which the following scenes occur:

At End House they pass Lodge and cottage – man gardening
– bald head old fashioned spectacles – stares – admitted to
End House – they wait for Nick – old pictures – gloom –
damp – decay. Nick enters – slight surprise – Poirot talks to
her – shows her bullet [Chapter 2]

They return to Hotel – Freddie Rice talks to Poirot – suggests Nick is an amazing little liar – likes to invent things. Poirot presses her – such as – she talks about brakes of car [Chapter 2]

P asks her if she will send for a woman friend – she suggests 'My cousin Maggie' – she was to come to me next month – I could ask her to come now – second cousin really – there's a large family of them – Maggie is the second – she's a nice girl – but perhaps a bit dull [Chapter 3]

A call upon Mr Vyse – a reference to legal advice – P mentions he called yesterday at 12 – but Mr. Vyse was out – Mr Vyse agrees [Chapter 6]

The fireworks – they go over to the Point – Nick and Maggie are to follow – they all watch – they're a long time. Poirot and H go back – fall over body in scarlet shawl – then see Nick coming – it's Maggie – Nick with traces of tears on her face [Chapter 7]

'Murder in the Mews'/'The Market Basing Mystery'
December 1936/October 1923

A quill pen, a dressing case, a game of golf and a cuff link all combine to make Hercule Poirot suspicious of a Guy Fawkes Night suicide.

The ploy of murder disguised as suicide is given the Christie treatment in the novella 'Murder in the Mews', an early proof of her ingenuity at ringing the changes on a clichéd plot. This ploy first appeared over ten years earlier in the short story 'The Market Basing Mystery', and when she came to elaborate it in the mid-1930s she retained the original idea and added a few refinements. It remains a handbook in detective story writing technique with the main clue brought to the reader's attention again and again.

As the Notebooks reveal, the 5 November background was originally to have been a very different plot. Among a list of plot ideas in Notebook 20 that included *Sad Cypress*, 'Triangle at Rhodes' and 'Problem at Sea' we find the following:

> Murderer leaves body just before he finds it (officially)! It has been dead for two hours so he has alibi
> Nov. 5th – fireworks going off. Book?

But the only aspect of this jotting that she subsequently used was in 'Murder in the Mews', where she adopted the Guy Fawkes connection; echoing *Peril at End House* four years earlier, it is used as a camouflage for the gunshot. Most of the plotting is in Notebook 30:

> Adaptation of Market Basing Mystery
> Mrs Allen – young woman living in Mews – engaged to be married – her friend, Jane Petersham – quiet dark girl

> The Mews Murder
> P and Japp Guy Fawkes day – little boy – back to Japp's room – a call – young woman shot – in Mayfair
> Mrs. Allen – Miss Jane Plenderleith – she arrived home that morning – found her friend dead

> Locked cupboard (with golf clubs in) tennis balls – and a couple of empty suitcases.

Pistol in hand too loose – wrist watch on right wrist –
blotting paper torn off – stubs of two different cigarettes

Typically, the pages are scattered throughout the Notebook
and are interspersed with ideas for stories with a British
Museum and National Gallery background, the death of a
fortune-teller and much of the plotting for *Dumb Witness*. Not
surprisingly in a novella more than six times the length of the
original, most of the material above is new; only the wrist-
watch clue and the cigarettes are imported from the earlier
story. And the characters and background in the two versions
are totally different.

∾⁓

Hercule Poirot's Christmas
19 December 1938

————————◄○►————————

Simeon Lee is a wealthy and horrible old man who enjoys
tormenting his family. When he gathers them together for
Christmas he sets in motion a train of events that culminates
in his own murder. Luckily Hercule Poirot is staying with the
Chief Constable and is on hand to investigate.

————————◄○►————————

Published originally during Christmas week, with a serialisation on both sides of the Atlantic a month earlier, this is
Christie at her most ingenious. Expert misdirection, scrupulous clueing, an unexpected murderer all coalesce to produce
one of the all-time classic titles. Despite its title and publication date, however, there is no Christmas atmosphere whatever, even before the murder occurs. 'The Adventure of the
Christmas Pudding', an inferior story from every viewpoint, is

far more festive. An earlier case, *Three Act Tragedy*, is discussed in Part III, 'December 24th', and a foreshadowing of *They Do It with Mirrors* appears in Part VI, 'December 27th', while the biblical reference to Jael two pages later is the basis of *Butter in a Lordly Dish.*

There are two pages of Notebook 61 that contain rough notes for what was to become *Hercule Poirot's Christmas.* The pages follow immediately after those for *Appointment with Death*, published six months earlier:

Blood Feast

Inspector Jones – comes to see old Silas ~~Faraday~~ Chamberlayne – diamond king from S.A.

Characters

A family such as
Arthur – the good stay at home one
Lydia – clever nervy wife
Mervyn – son still at home dilettante artist
Hilda – his very young wife – rather common
David – very mean – sensitive
Dorothy – his articulate wife
Regina – unhappy woman – separated from husband
Caroline – her daughter – fascinating – reportedly bad
Edward – her devoted husband – bad lot

Although some names are accurate – Lydia, Hilda, David – the personality traits are not reflected in the eventual characters; and the last three listed have no equivalents. The policeman's name changes although Simeon Lee did make his fortune in South Africa.

Of the 65 pages of existing notes, however, most of them are in Notebook 21. Christie opens with the beginning of a quotation from Shakespeare's *Macbeth*, which may have been intended as a title, and quickly follows this with sketches of the Lee family. She breaks off to write brief notes for what were to become *Curtain* and *Sad Cypress* and then returns to *Hercule Poirot's Christmas*. The first draft of the characters is immediately recognisable, apart from the Nurse, who does not appear in the novel:

A. Who would have thought [the old man to have had so much blood in him?]

Old Simeon Lee – A horrid old man

Alfred – the good son – (a prig) bores his father
Lydia – Alfred's clever well-bred bitter wife – she makes gardens
Harry? – The Prodigal son – he comes home and the old man likes him
Stephen Fane – A young man from S. Africa – son of Simeon's partner – (he cheated him!) – S. is really Simeon's son
Juanita Simeon's grand-daughter [Pilar] – back from Spain – his daughter ran away with a Spaniard and J. is really not grand-daughter – latter was killed in revolution – J was her friend
The Nurse – says old man was going to leave her all his money – wanted to marry her. She was married already – her husband is in New Zealand

The course of the story is outlined in the extract below, the novel following this synopsis closely:

Possible course of story

1. Stephen in train going up to Midcourt – this drab people – his impatience – the sun he comes from – then his first sight of Pilar – exotic – different – reads label

2. Pilar in train – thinking – keyed up – her nervousness – handsome looking man – conversation – about Spain – the war – finally he reads label
3. Alfred and Lydia – conversation – she is like a greyhound – mention of her gardens – telephone call – Patterson – Horbury – she doesn't like that man
4. George and Magdalene – or David and Hilda strong motherly woman

    If G and M – his pomposity – and earnestness – his wife's impatience – her vagueness at some point about a letter (she has a lover) – he says better off when my father dies – they must go for Xmas important not to offend old man – he has written saying he would like to have all his children round him at Xmas – sounds quite sentimental
5. David and H

    He gets letter – nervous – neurotic passionately fond of his mother – won't go to the house – she, wise and motherly, persuades him – he goes off and plays piano violently
6. Harry Hugo arrives – cheery word to old Patterson – the prodigal – I could do with a drink – greeting from Lydia – she likes him
7. Old man himself – Horbury – he asks about his family – then goes and gets out diamonds – his face devilish glee

Interview with Alfred

Interview with Harry

Talk about prodigal son to Horbury

There were still significant clues to be inserted, while she also paid attention to the description, given by various characters, of the 'scream' establishing the time of death – or so we are led to think – heard in the murder room:

Scenes to work in
(A) Portrait of old Lee P looks at it – found by someone
(B) Passport dropped out of window
(C) Statues in recess
(D) P. buys moustache
(E) Balloon

Screams
Alfred A man in mortal agony
Lydia Like a soul in hell
Harry Like killing a pig
David Like a soul in hell

Although the plotting follows closely the course of the novel with relatively few deviations, Christie did try a few variations, the main ones being the presence of a co-conspiring nurse or a criminal husband-and-wife. At this stage 'Drew' is the forerunner of Sugden, the investigating officer, but there is no mention of his being a policeman:

Who is murderer?

~~Nurse – a fairly good looking young woman of thirty (actually his daughter) – her desire for revenge~~

Drew is the man – Why? Illegitimate son – then Nurse is his sister – the two of them planned it

or – like Macbeth – a man and his wife do this – son of an earlier marriage?
   Possibly his second marriage was illegal – he makes a will so worded that the children of his second marriage inherit even if not legitimate – that will is destroyed – a draft is prduced by Nurse leaving it to her.

A new idea – is Nurse married to one of the sons? – the gay prodigal? – he manages to pull a string at the right moment

321

As suggested by her crossing-out of the idea here, Christie did not utilise the nurse in this novel. But the homicidal nurse was to resurface two years later in *Sad Cypress*.

∽↺↻

Evil under the Sun
9 June 1941

───────◀○▶───────

Beautiful vamp Arlena Marshall is murdered while staying at the same glamorous hotel on Smuggler's Island where Hercule Poirot is holidaying. He investigates her murder, which involves a typewriter, a bottle of suntan lotion, a skein of wool and a packet of candles.

───────◀○▶───────

Evil under the Sun was written during 1938 and received, and read, by Edmund Cork by 17 February 1939. It had first appeared, in the USA, as a serial towards the end of 1940. At first glance *Evil under the Sun* and 'Triangle at Rhodes' (see Chapter 8) appear to be the same story. Both feature Hercule Poirot, a beach setting and two couples as the main protagonists. In each case, one couple consists of a vamp and a quiet husband, the other a charmer and a 'mouse' (in Christie's own word). And both stories exemplify perfectly Christie's fertility of plot invention because, despite these not insignificant similarities, the solutions and killers are completely different. In each case the triangle the reader is encouraged to envisage is completely wrong – and also completely different. In both cases clever stage-management forces the reader to look in the wrong direction despite, in the case of the novel, abundant clues to the truth.

There are 60 pages of Notebook showing its origins, and thanks to these we can see the detailed working-out that went into one of Christie's most ingenious novels. The setting exists in reality as Burgh Island, off the coast of Devon, a venue well known to Christie as she stayed at the hotel there on a few occasions. The island is cut off from the mainland twice a day at high tide and is reached by a sea-tractor. She utilises its geography to suit her purposes in creating a perfect alibi.

That storehouse of plot devices, *The Thirteen Problems*, yet again provided the rough basis for this novel. 'A Christmas Tragedy' features two people, the murderer and a witness (in this case Miss Marple herself), 'finding' a dead body before it has been murdered, thereby providing the killer with an impeccable alibi. In the case of the short story the body is that of a natural death victim, conveniently dead two hours earlier, but in the novel it is the live body of the killer's accomplice. Both plots feature a large and camouflaging hat (also a feature of *Dead Man's Folly*). Many refinements were obviously possible in the course of a novel – a larger cast of suspects, the added complication of a triangle situation, a warm beach to confuse the time of death instead of a hotel room and a more elaborate alibi for the killer. But it is essentially the same plot.

Right from the first page of Notebook 39 Christie seems to have the plot, the main characters and the setting already well advanced. This may be because she was developing an earlier short story. Names were to change but this description was to form the basis of the book:

Seaside Mystery

H.P. is at seaside – comments on bodies everywhere – makes old-fashioned remarks. Main idea of crime – G an ordinary rather 'simple' man is apparently bowled over by a well-worn siren. His wife is very unhappy about it – shows

distinct jealousy. He has alibi all morning (with H.P.)
goes with a woman for a walk and discovers body of siren –
distinctive bathing dress – Chinese 'hat' – and red auburn
curl. Suggest to woman to stay with body – she flinches –
he finally says he will and she goes for police. Part of
'dead woman' is acted by (wife?) or (woman he really
cares about?). Immediately after woman has gone for help –
siren appears from other direction – he kills her (strangled?)
and places her in same position

Therefore characters are:
George Redfern – quiet bank manager etc.
Mary Redfern – white skin / not (tanned) dark
Gloria Tracy – Siren very rich – mad on men
Edward Tracy – Husband
Rosemary Weston – in love with Edward

Scene Hotel on island – Bigbury [Burgh Island]

If the names were not exactly the same as those in the published novel – the first names of the Redferns became Patrick and Christine, while Gloria and Edward Tracy became Arlena and Kenneth Marshall, and Rosemary Weston is Rosamund Darnley – the differences are not significant enough to prevent recognition.

A few pages later, several details have been established:

Beginning

House – built by a sea captain sold first when bathing came in

Hercule Poirot – with whom?
The American in Appointment with Death [Jefferson Cope]
Major Blount [Barry] or Miss Tough [Brewster] looking at
    everyone

Arlena King – red haired lovely – husband – an author and
    playwright – Arlena left a fortune a year or two previously
Jean [Linda] – her daughter – athletic girl – hates stepmother
Middle aged spinster – sister of Arlena's husband – says
    she's a bad lot

People?

Kenneth ~~Leslie~~ Marshall
Arlena ~~Leslie~~ Marshall
Linda ~~Leslie~~ Marshall
Patrick ~~Desmond Redfern~~ –
Cristina   " or McGrane
Mr and Mrs Gardiner (Americans)
Or (Bev) (gone with Desmond) [Possibly Irene, the
    Gardiners' far-off daughter]
Rosemary Darley
H.P.
Or Mrs Barrett   [not used]
The Reverend Stephen Mannerton [Lane]
Horace Blatt (red faced magnate)
Miss Porter [Miss Brewster]
Mrs Springfelt [not used]
Major Barry

The reference to *Appointment with Death* above is slightly mys-
tifying; there is no reference to this book in *Evil under the
Sun* and no character in common, apart from Poirot.
Christie may have toyed with the idea of introducing
Jefferson Cope from the earlier novel and perhaps aban-
doned it in case it spoiled the reader's enjoyment of
Appointment with Death. The Gardeners, the compromise
American characters she instead created, provide light relief
throughout the novel.

She also utilises her alphabetical sequencing, here in working out short scenes of encounters rather than plot development. Although she does not follow the sequence exactly, the only scene not to appear in any form is E. Scene B is the all-important one that Poirot remembers in Chapter 11 ii when he muses on five significant remarks uttered there:

Beginning
A. House built by etc. [Chapter 1 i]
B. H.P. watches bodies – Mrs Gardiner – reciting Beverly etc.
   – her husband says Yes, darling – Mr Barrett, Miss Porter
   and Miss Springer. Arlena – pushes off on her float.
   Major Barry – these red-headed gals – I remember in
   Poonah [Chapter 1 ii and iv]
C. The Marshalls arrive – Kenneth and Rosemary – an
   encounter
D. Linda thinks – her face – breakfast [Chapter 2 ii]
E. Miss Porter and Miss Springer – latter tells her friend what
   she overheard. You were with Desmond and Cristina and
   H.P. and Mrs Kane
F. Rosemary and H.P. – taste in wives [Chapter 2 i]
G. Christine Redfern and Desmond
H. Rosamund and Kenneth [Chapter 3 i]

One particularly intriguing element of the notes to this novel relates to the complicated alibis Christie attempted to provide for most of the characters. This caused much crossing-out and rearranging and she changed the details quite considerably before she arrived at a version that pleased her. Two of her favourite unused ideas, the dishonest, collusive chambermaid and the two 'arty' friends, surfaced briefly before being discarded and returned to the 'unused' category, while she also experimented with other solutions before returning to the thoughts she had initially set out:

Alternative Plan

Arlena dies Christine disappears
   Desmond and Christine go out on a float – early – or in
their boat – Japanese sunshade. You do believe me, darling,
when I tell you there's nothing in it at all. No one sees them
come back

Alternatives

A. Desmond kills Christine
      First arranges body – then drowns her – gets rid of
      other woman – puts C's body on rocks as though fallen
      from above – right spot indicated by stone (peculiar
      colour marking etc.) the night before.

B. Desmond and Gladys Springett do murder – (Christine is,
      perhaps, only fiancée?). Gladys and 'friend' are at Gull
      Cove – latter sketching – forever looking for flowers (or
      shells?). Goes through cave – acts the part of 'the body'
      and returns

C. Christine and Desmond are a pair of crooks. Money –
      banked in her name – her story of blackmail coming out
      when questioned by the Police

D. Is the chambermaid Desmond's wife? ALL her stories
      false – about blackmail – about seeing Christine etc. –
      alters Linda's watch

Where is everyone?
Blatt – out in boat – later sails found in a cave
Major Barry – drive his car into Lostwitch – business –
   market day – early closing – lots of people on beach

327

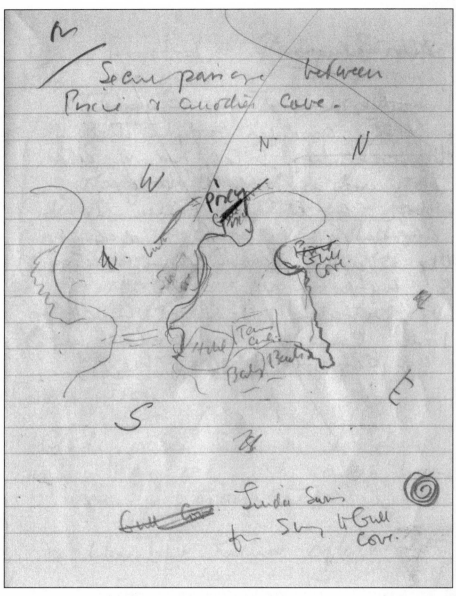

This sketch from Notebook 39 shows the mainland and the island (complete with compass points) and the route between the two. Also shown are the Hotel and Tennis Court, the Bathing Beach as well as Pixy Cove and Gull Cove. Note the change of mind about the last two locations.

The Gardiners – on beach (she goes up to get wool or he
    gets it for her)
Babcock – to church – signs book – but it could be previous
    day
Kenneth? Typing in room
Rosamund? Bathing? On float
Tennis – Christine, Rosamund, Kenneth, Gardiner

And many of the clues that feature in the novel (the bath that
no one will admit taking, the candles, the sun-tan lotion
bottle) appear in the Notebooks:

About Linda – Packet of candles – calendar – other things
    she remembers – green?
Bath?
Kenneth – typing at middle table
Bottle thrown from window

◌⟋◌

Towards Zero
3 July 1944

———————————◄○►———————————

Before murder interrupts a holiday weekend in Lady
Tressilian's house in Gull's Point, we meet a disparate
group of people. All of their destinies are inextricably
linked as zero hour approaches. Superintendent Battle
investigates a case where the solution seems obvious.
But is it too obvious?

———————————◄○►———————————

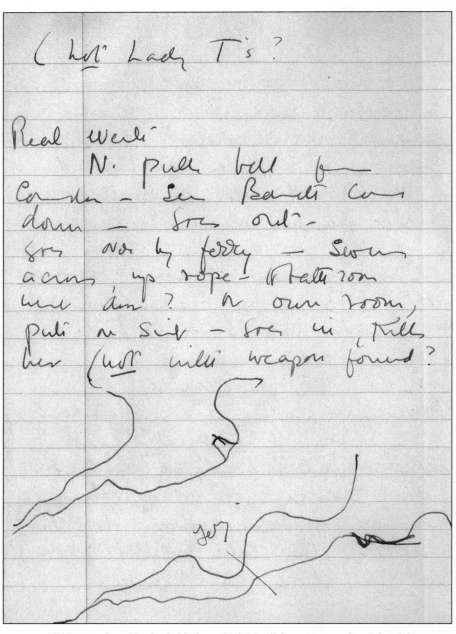

(*not* Lady T's ?

Real ending
    N. pulls bell for
Candida — See Bandit come
down — goes out —
goes over by ferry — Swims
across, up rope — (Bathroom
wet dinner? In own room,
puts on suit — goes in, Kills
her (*not* until weapon found ?

This page from Notebook 32 shows both Neville's actions on the night of the murder in Towards Zero, *and a rough diagram of the local geography, including the scene of his alibi-breaking swim.*

Towards Zero is superb Christie. The plot resembles a series of Russian dolls with one concealed inside the other. The reader is presented with one solution and within that is another, and behind that yet another. The motivation and clue laying are masterly because the whole plot is predicated on the 'wrong' solution being uncovered and then disproved and the subsequent one being discovered. And there is yet another solution behind that.

Nine months before Zero Hour we meet, in a series of vignettes, a group of people; at first they seem totally disconnected. Then we realise that, for various reasons, they are all converging on Lady Tressilian's house in September.

Sharing a plot device used years earlier in *The Murder at the Vicarage* and more recently in 'Murder in the Mews', this is a dark and emotional crime novel as well as a very clever detective story with subtle clueing and better-than-usual characterisations. Twelve years after its publication the novel was presented on stage with a slightly altered ending (although the same killer), but it was not one of Christie's major stage successes.

The plotting for this novel is contained in two Notebooks, the majority of it in Notebook 32 and with a further ten pages in Notebook 63. Its genesis seems to have been painless and clear from the start, as the notes follow the finished book very closely and very little of the plotting from the Notebooks is not included. As can be seen from below, the notes are quite detailed and accurate. Even here, however, Christie came up with a few ideas that did not appear.

On the first page of the notes the all-important story that Mr Treves tells is clearly stated. Apart from the importance of the homicidal tendency of its main protagonist, it also includes the important clue of the (unspecified) 'physical trait', a distinction shared by all the suspects:

Story about 2 children – bows and arrows – one kills the
   other – or shotgun?
One child practiced – narrator – old man – says he would
   know that child again by a physical trait

Yes, so many people all converging from different points – all
   Towards Zero

There is an alphabetical list of scenes, although it does not
tally exactly with the novel. It would seem that there was to be
a Sir Marcus and a Mr Trevelyan; in the novel they are amalgamated into Mr Treves. None of the members of the house
party are included. The listing of 'The Cleaners' is at first
puzzling until we remember that a dry-cleaning firm with
mixed-up suits provides one of the main clues to the mystery.
Their omission from the opening scenes is a shame as it
would have been a fascinating puzzle for the reader trying to
fit a dry-cleaners' into the jigsaw.

A. MacWhirter – suicide – his rescue – fall off cliff – arrested
   by tree
B. Sir Marcus – holding forth in his chambers after acquittal
   of client
D. The murderer – his mind – the date
E. Superintendent Battle
F. Mr. Trevelyan – looking at hotel folders
G. The Cleaners

The list of characters is also very close to the novel. As usual,
however, the names were to change, although not as totally as
other novels (Nevil, Judy and Clare/Audrey Crane become
Nevile, Kay and Audrey Strange):

People
Lady Tressillian
Mary Aldin or Kate Aldin
Barrett (lady's maid)
Thomas Royde
Adrian Royde
Nevil Crane – well known tennis player and athlete
Judy Crane – formerly Judy Rodgers
Ted Latimer – wastrel – lives on his wits
Clare Crane or Audrey Crane – formerly Audrey Standish
MacWhirter

Towards Zero
Nevill (or Noel) Crane – tennis player – athlete sportsman
Audrey his first wife 'Snow White' – frozen – fractured –
    hysterical childhood etc.
Judy his second wife – a glamorous girl – suffused with
    vitality – pagan – Rose Red

The events of the fatal night are worked out:

Night of Tragedy

Neville and Lady T – quarrel overheard by butler – then he
goes – rings bell for Barret (old maid). He has also put
narcotic in her milk – she sees him go out – goes to Lady T
who denies ringing bell. B feeling very confused and queer
gets back to bed and passes out. Lady T discovered in
morning.

A few interesting ideas that never made it into the novel
show that some of the detail was not self-evident. It must be
remembered of course that the 'victim' below is not the real
victim and is only a means to an end in this labyrinthine

plot. Although none of the detail appears quite as outlined, the series of dated vignettes that opens the novel could indeed be seen, in retrospect, as sketches of eventual witnesses. The victim is not related to Judy/Kay and Audrey has not remarried, thus paving the way for a romance at the end of the novel:

> Towards Zero
> Series of vignettes of various people – witnesses at murder trial which takes place in last chapter?
>
> Who is victim? Judy's stepmother? Her father – very rich man – left the money to 2nd wife (chorus girl or shop girl) she has it for life – Judy wants the money
>
> Audrey quickly remarries her quiet doctor – a biologist – or archaeologist – they are happy but poor – she wants stepmother's money for research

But one of the most tantalising notes in Notebook 63 concerns a 'new end' to *Towards Zero*. The page references are, presumably, to those of the publishers' proofs, and one interesting point is that in the novel it is McWhirter who carries out all of the actions here attributed to Thomas Royde. Unfortunately we will never know what the original draft was – the Notebook then continues to list the events that appear in the published novel just before the section 'Zero Hour':

> New End to Zero starting P. 243
>
> Thomas and little girl acquaintance – Dog and fish – Goes to cleaner – (lost slip) quarrel about suit – Royde – ever so sorry – thought you said Boyd – Easthampton Hotel – gets

suit – takes it home – smell on shoulder – takes it back –
or rings up. Goes to Easthampton Hotel – no Boyd staying
there – goes up to cliff – Audrey – afraid of being hanged.

P. 255 the police come – Battle talks to the others ending
with Royde – then goes to house – Mary comes across him
in attic – Or Kay? Wet rope

269? Royde speaks to B privately – B comes out – A taken
off – then B looks over house – finds rope – Mary? Or Kaye?
Finds him there – it would be strong enough to hang a man!

In September 1956 a stage version of the novel opened in
London, dramatised by Gerald Verner and Christie. Some of
the notes for this adaptation appear in the Notebooks,
although they are not comprehensive and consist mainly of a
list of scenes without any elaboration. But the opening scene
in Notebook 17 corresponds closely with the play itself:

Act I
Royde alone on stage – looking out of window – takes
up Audrey's photo – looks at it – puts it down – walks to
window – Kay rushes in (tennis racquet) agitated – picks up
Audrey's photo – dashes it down into grate – Royde turns –
she looks like guilty child.
    Oh! Who are you? I know who you are – the man from
Malaya
    R. Yes, I'm the man from Malay

At Bertram's Hotel
15 November 1965

────────◄○►────────

Miss Marple's nephew treats her to a stay in Bertram's
Hotel, a relic of Edwardian decency in London. While
enjoying its old-fashioned, and somewhat suspicious,
charm, she becomes involved in a disappearance,
robbery and murder.

────────◄○►────────

At Bertram's Hotel was the second Marple novel in as many
years. Like its predecessor, *A Caribbean Mystery*, the title page
included the reminder 'Featuring Miss Marple The Original
Character as created by Agatha Christie'. This appeared as a
result of the recent incarnations of the character on screen
in the Margaret Rutherford travesties.

While the setting of this novel is typical Christie and
Marple, our expectations are confounded in the denouement when an even more breathtaking conspiracy than that
of *Murder on the Orient Express* is revealed. The notes for this
novel are evenly divided between three Notebooks. Notebook
27 has two dated pages, 'October 30th' and 'November 17th'
(1964), and the first page of Notebook 36 is dated 'October
'64'. Notebook 23 would seem to pre-date the notes in the
other two, as the following extract shows:

Bertram's Hotel

Description of it – Mayfair St. etc. – Edwardian comfort –
fires – porters . . . Tea and muffins – 'Only get muffins at
Bertrams'. Points about hotel – a nucleus of 'landed gentry'
– old style Miss Marple points out later – 'pockets' left over

really no-one like that left – No, 'Bertrams' hotel belongs to two Americans – (never seen!). They cash in by deliberately recreating the nucleus (at low prices) to give the right atmosphere – then Americans and Australians etc. come at large prices.

Meg Gresham [Bess Sedgwick] – her career – well born? rich? Ran away with Irish groom. Then married Parker Whitworth – enormous man – then Duke of Nottingham – then Count Stanislaus Vronsky – Dirk Chester – film star – or Op. singer

Amalgamate this with frog-faced old major Ronnie Anstruther and Miss Marple – staying a week in London. His talk about murder – same chap – saw him again – different name – same kind of death – medical fellers seemed satisfied – quite all right – only different name again – Looks at someone coming

The general set-up is the same as the novel but the mention of the 'frog-faced Major' (possibly a forerunner of Colonel Luscombe, the guardian of Bess's daughter, Elvira, although without the unflattering description) and his talk about an earlier murder had appeared in 1964 in *A Caribbean Mystery*, so these notes were probably written prior to that. Or it may be Christie's general description of retired Army men! Despite this, much of the plot is accurately sketched; but it is sketched at least three times in the course of the notes, each adding little or nothing to the earlier, possibly an indication that her powers of weaving variations were waning.

Ideas
Bertram's is a HQ – of a crime organization – mainly bank robberies? Train robberies? No real violence – Money is

taken in respectable luggage to Bertram's. Certain people take it there – rehearsed beforehand – they are usually actors – character actors and they double for certain people – Canon Penneyfather, General Lynde, Fergus Mainwaring – country girl – Mr and Mrs Hamilton Clayton? – Contessa Vivary – Ralph Winston

Resume of story
Bess Sedgwick – an outlaw rich loves dangerously – Resistance – racing car falls for foreign criminal – handsome – attractive Stan Lasky. She combines with him and they plan robberies on a colossal scale – this has now been going on for (5 years?) (longer?) HQ is Bertram's Hotel which changes hands – has a lot of money spent on it and people of the gang are infiltrated into it. Henry is its controlling brain and Bess is his partner – the Americans are its titular owner – but really a façade for Henry – there is a shuttle service – jewels or bank notes pass through Bertram's in the hands of old fashioned 'clients', elderly ladies – clerics – lawyers – Admirals and Colonels – pass out next day – with rich American to Continent

While there is very little in any of the Notebooks about the murder of Michael Gorman, the commissionaire at Bertram's and an important figure from Bess Sedgwick's past, our old friend the chambermaid gets yet another outing. Although the setting of a hotel would seem to be perfect for this idea, however, a satisfactory solution eluded her – again:

Circumstances of murder?
Meg – breakfast tray by bed – Kidneys, mushrooms, bacon, tea – chambermaid – evidence – as to conversation between Meg and husband (Chester? Stanislaus?) Anything the matter? She is opening letters. 'No, nothing' – This evidence

clears husband – also chambermaid collects tray – not waiter –

Bertrams   Points
Murder – woman in bed – chambermaid's evidence – took her breakfast in bed – quite all right then (9 a.m.) body not found until 12 – really killed – at 8.30. Man (in evening dress) as waiter takes in breakfast tray – strangles her – knifes her – shot? Then goes down and out. In it are chambermaid and Richards

Hallowe'en Party
10 November 1969

A bobbing-for-apples game goes horribly wrong at Lucilla Drake's teenage party. One of the guests, Mrs Oliver, approaches her friend Hercule Poirot who subsequently visits Woodleigh Common and, in the course of his investigation, uncovers a long-forgotten crime as well as the killer at the Hallowe'en party.

The notes for *Hallowe'en Party* provide the clearest example in the whole of the Notebooks of a definite starting and finishing date for a title. The first page of Notebook 16, with the notes for *Hallowe'en Party*, is headed 'Jan. 1st 1969' and 45 pages later we read:

July 7th Halloween Party completed

Chapter 1 to 21 inc. ending p. 280 to be sent or taken to H[ughes] M[assie]. 3 or 4 chapters to go to Mrs Jolly [her typist] on Dictaphone rolls 1 to 9. Continue corrections and revisions in them commencing P. 281 and send on to H. M.

At this time Agatha Christie was 78 and although six months for a full-length novel is not unreasonable, it is a long way from the 1930s and 1940s when she finished two or three novels a year. It is entirely possible that the idea for this novel was hatched during a visit to America in late 1966, where Hallowe'en was a bigger holiday, when she accompanied Sir Max Mallowan on a lecture tour. She toyed with the idea of an eleven-plus, rather than a Hallowe'en, party for young teenagers. But the basic plot device was set from the beginning. Yet again Mrs Oliver appears, as she does in four of the final dozen titles that Christie wrote. Also making a reappearance is the policeman Spence from *Mrs McGinty's Dead* and *Taken at the Flood*; and he was to appear again three years later in *Elephants Can Remember*.

Themes, ideas and plots from earlier titles abound. There are strong echoes throughout of *Dead Man's Folly*. In both we have a child murdered during a game, witnesses to an earlier murder presenting a danger to a hitherto safe killer and the creation of a thing of beauty as a grave – a folly in one novel and a garden in the other. As we shall see, a short story from 35 years earlier, 'How Does Your Garden Grow?' was also in her mind. *Dead Man's Folly*, *Mrs McGinty's Dead* and *The Labours of Hercules* are specifically mentioned in Chapter 4, 5 and 11 respectively; the inspiration for *Butter in a Lordly Dish* is referred to in Chapter 11, Miss Bulstrode from *Cat among the Pigeons* is recalled in Chapter 10 and a brief allusion towards the end of Chapter 16 may have provided the basis for *Nemesis*, two years later. Mrs Drake's looking over the staircase (Chapter 10) has distinct similarities to Marina Gregg's in *The Mirror Crack'd from Side to Side*. And the opening line of Chapter 17 is almost identical to that in 'The Case of the Perfect Maid'.

Like many of the late titles, both the notes for *Hallowe'en Party* and the book itself are diffuse and unfocussed. There are some new ideas as well as those from earlier titles but there are also too many meandering conversations. The uneasy mix does not coalesce into a coherent and ingenious detective novel. Compare the set-up with similar titles from earlier decades – *Dumb Witness, Taken at the Flood* and *Mrs McGinty's Dead* – where Poirot arrives in a small town to investigate a suspicious death and we can appreciate the deterioration in the quality of the titles from *Endless Night* onwards. Apart from *Passenger to Frankfurt* all of the titles after 1967 are journeys into the past, each one weaker than the previous. But they are all predicated on a compelling basic idea.

Apart from name changes, the following extracts outline the basic situation that sets the plot in motion, although it has to be asked why Miranda (Mifanwy in the notes) does not admit earlier that she, and not Joyce, was the original witness. And the later revelation of her parenthood in the novel beggars belief.

Jenny Butcher – Mrs. O's friend on Hellenic cruise – widow – husband was (leukaemia?) or polio victim – contracted it abroad – a scholar? Man of intellect – child Mifanwy eleven or twelve – did father die at Ephesus? Stroke?

Is it Mifanwy who saw murder? Her father's? or her father kill Jenny's lover? Or – her father – or mother – or mother's sister still alive and living in Woodlawn Common kills brother (or mental defective). Anyway Mifanwy saw a murder – tells her older friend Joyce. Joyce boasts about this at party as her adventure. Mifanwy was not at party – ill that day – cold?

Mrs Oliver is at Party – helping a friend – friend is: Jean Buckley? Or Gwenda Roberts ?

Her family consists of: Daughter of 14 – Twin boys Henry and Thomas 12 – A husband – Doctor? G.P.

Bobbing for apples? Looking glass? (future husband) Snap Dragon – talk about origins of these rites – snapdragon – should be Christmas

The following significant passage from Notebook 16 appears almost verbatim in Chapter 1. Here we see resonances of an earlier Christie as she teases and taunts the reader with hints of an earlier crime:

Joyce – 'Oo-er – I saw a murder once'
Grown up – 'Don't say silly things, Joyce'
Beatrice 'Did you really – really and truly?
Joan 'Of course she didn't – she's just making it up'
Joyce 'I did see a murder – I did – I did'
Ann 'Why didn't you go to the police about it, then'?
Joyce 'Because I didn't know it was a murder'

With the usual name changes – Mary Drake becomes Rowena and Sonia Karova is Olga Seminoff – she lists some of the characters:

Possible characters

Mary Drake – Giver of party (?)
Mother or step-mother of Joyce [Mrs Reynolds]
Alistair Drake – fair – good-looking – vague
Sonia Karova – Au pair girl came to Barrets Green four or
    five years earlier
The Drake – old Miss or Mrs. Kellway an Aunt lived with
    them – dies suddenly – left a will hand written, leaving
    money to Sonia – former wills left money to Alistair

Girl ran away – never found – or – girl's body found – or au
   pair girl disappeared – went off with a young man
A school teacher – Miss Emlyn – her body found – seen with
   a man

The notes indicate that much of the plot eluded Christie for
a long time, as again and again she tried to get a coherent
outline:

A garden made out of a quarry by Mrs. Llewellyn Browne –
rich eccentric elderly woman mad on gardens – sunk gardens
– saw one in N. Ireland – spent a lot of money.

David McArdle – young, artistic landscape planner –
rumoured to be an elderly woman's fancy – to make money
out of them.

Also au pair girl Alenka – looked after old lady – she was
keen on David – (refer to *Cornish Mystery* – she thinks
husband is giving her arsenic)

Au pair girl – looked after old Mrs. Wilberforce – Aunt dies –
her will found later – hidden in Chinese jar – (under carpet?)
– money left to Olga – A supposedly written by her – but it
was a forgery

Mary Drake – rich runs place – husband – Julian – polio
victim? – weak – works on board of hospital – draws
beautifully – forges – or – is Mr. Drake her second husband –
first one was polio victim – did she kill him? In order to
marry No. 2

But eventually she settled on a scenario that pleased her, and
on pages headed 'May 20th' and '31st' (1969) we find the
following:

Idea – Sonia (Olga) (Katrina) was friends with John Leslie Ferrier – he had a conviction for forgery. Michael induces Leslie to forge will – offers him money – Leslie then killed (knifed by Michael) – Or – Hit and Run by car. Mary in with him her husband killed (hit and run) Soon after he inherits – man in car – car was pushed from somewhere 15 miles away, Michael at a meeting in London

Sequence –
A. Mrs. L.B. makes will or codicil – Michael hears about it (from Olga)
B. Gets Leslie to forge a codicil – pays him money – knifes him after a row between jealous girls.
C. Death of Mrs. L.B. (overdose)
D. Death of polio nephew – his wife adored him – Mrs. Mary had people playing bridge.
E. Mrs. L.B. had written draft codicil of my will. She had written it – or shown it to girl – then changed its position (work out details). Possibly in library.

Ideas and Points May 31st

A. Cleaning woman goes to Mrs. Oliver about seeing codicil
B. Poirot opens letter – Hungarian Herzoslovakian friend – has visited family – Olga Seminova – young man Olga was going to marry
C. Poirot and Michael Wright – in wood – he was with Miranda.
D. Miss Byways and hedges – Doctor dispensary – has cooked up prescription – little bottle of pills
E. Leonard or Leopold was near Michael and Miranda – sly – knows something – nasty little eavesdropper – is Leopold the next victim? Leopold – scientific bent – eavesdropper – possible juvenile blackmailer – or his sister Ann

This is, in fact, the plot she adopted, although why Mrs Llewellyn-Smythe should have written a codicil and then hidden it is never fully explained in the novel. And is it at all likely that Leopold, an 11-year-old, should blackmail a double murderer, thereby becoming another victim?

The short story 'How Does Your Garden Grow?' hovers over the novel, as the extract below shows. Both feature an elderly lady ignoring her family to leave her fortune to a foreign companion and the subsequent scapegoating of the legatee. The 'shells' is a reference to the plot of the earlier story, where strychnine is concealed in an oyster and the shells later hidden in plain sight as a decoration in the garden:

What did Joyce see? Mary Drake comes out from back door – shells – sticks them by path

11

Poirot Investigates:
The Labours of Hercules

. . . a passion for getting at the truth. In all the world there is nothing so curious, and so interesting and so beautiful as the truth . . .

Three Act Tragedy, Act III Chapter 5

―◦―

SOLUTIONS REVEALED
'The Affair at the Bungalow' • *After the Funeral* • *Appointment with Death* • *At Bertram's Hotel* • 'The Companion' • *Death in the Clouds* • *Elephants Can Remember* • *Murder on the Orient Express* • 'The Mystery of Hunter's Lodge' • *The Mystery of the Blue Train* • *Sparkling Cyanide* • *Taken at the Flood* • *Three Act Tragedy* • Plot details of most of the Labours are also revealed.

―◦―

The Labours of Hercules
8 September 1947

The Labours of Hercules is not just Agatha Christie's greatest short story collection; it is one of the greatest collections in the entire crime fiction genre. It is brilliant in concept, design and execution. As he once again plans his retirement and the consequent cultivation of vegetable marrows, Poirot is attracted to the idea of a few well-chosen cases as his swan song. He decides to accept only cases similar to those undertaken by his mythological namesake, with the stipulation that his will be metaphorical equivalents.

All but one of the stories were published originally in *The Strand* magazine over a period of almost a year. 'The Nemean Lion' appeared in November 1939 and the rest of the tales followed in the same order as the book until 'The Apples of the Hesperides' in September 1940. The final story, 'The Capture of Cerberus', did not appear in *The Strand* and has a more complicated history, which is discussed, with the original version of that story, in the Appendix to this volume.

In August 1948 Penguin Books made publishing history when they issued one million Agatha Christie books on the same day – 100,000 copies each of ten titles. The venture was such a success that it was repeated five years later. This time they were titles of her own choosing, and for each she wrote a special Foreword giving some background information. One of this second batch was *The Labours of Hercules* and in its Foreword Christie explains that Poirot's Christian name was the inspiration that prompted her to write these stories. She goes on to explain that some of the tales, 'The Lernean Hydra' and 'The Cretan Bull', for instance, were straightforward and, indeed, these are very typical Christie village-murder-mystery Poirot cases. 'The Erymanthian Boar' and 'The Girdle of Hyppolita', she reveals, gave her more trouble – and 'The Capture of Cerberus' almost defeated her.

The metaphors throughout are inspired – wagging tongues represent the multi-headed viper in 'The Lernean Hydra', a sleazy tabloid newspaper stands for the polluted Augean Stables and 'The Apples of the Hesperides' are those on a priceless Cellini chalice. The stories themselves range

347

from the domestic mystery in 'The Lernean Hydra' and the nostalgic love story, albeit with a Christie twist, in 'The Arcadian Deer', to the brutal thriller in 'The Erymanthian Boar'. Amusing scenes – Poirot suffering in a hotel in the west of Ireland – alternate with terrifying scenes – Poirot helpless at the approach of a razor-wielding criminal – and poignant ones – Poirot convincing a terminally ill ballerina to return to her true love.

In many of the stories she manages to work in a second example of symbolism apart from the main one. 'The Erymanthian Boar' features a dangerous criminal in snowy surroundings, mirroring the physical setting as well as the metaphorical animal; 'The Cretan Bull' has a man of magnificent physique as well as, literally, basinfuls of blood; in 'The Apples of the Hesperides' Poirot is helped by the tipster Atlas who, like his famous namesake, takes the weight of Poirot on his shoulders; and the clamouring schoolgirls at the end of 'The Girdle of Hyppolita' are compared to the Amazons from the fable. Hercules' castanets of bronze in the original are replaced by the modern telegraph in 'The Stymphalean Birds'; the golden horns of 'The Arcadian Deer' appear as the golden hair of Katrina and in the mythical version Hercules does not kill the deer but returns it safely, as does Hercule Poirot with the love of Ted Williamson's life.

There are copious notes for this inventive collection. This in itself is unusual, as there are relatively few notes for most of Christie's short stories. This is probably because the writing of this collection involved extra research into the originals and more working out of detail than normally associated with the writing of a short story. Also, these stories were written as part of a collection and not, as before, individual stories for sporadic publication. Most of these notes are included in Notebook 44 with some minor notes scattered over three others, Notebooks 28, 39 and 62.

Notebook 44 contains some of the background to the Greek myths that Christie used as a basis for the tales:

Hydra of Lernea – 9 heads burnt out in flames – last head cut off and buried

The Deer with feet of bronze – horns of gold – feet of bronze – dedicated to Artemis – a year to find her

Boar of Erymanthe – Combined with centaurs of Pholoe – trapped on precipice of snow and captured alive

Augean Stables – River through breach in wall

Birds of Stymphalia – Birds of prey eat human flesh. H drives them out with bronze castanets and shoots them

Cretan Bull – mad bull

Horses of Diomedes (Mares) – savage – chained to mangers – H tames them

Girdle of Hyppolita – Hera spreads rumour and Amazons revolt

Troupeau of Geryon – giant with 3 bodies or with 3 heads – guarded by 2-headed dog Ortho and Eurython

Apples of Hesperides – H holds up sky while A[tlas] gets apples – A wants table then H asks for cushion for shoulder – hands back to A and goes off. Golden apples given by Immo to Jupiter for nuptials – apples delivered – are given back to Hesperides

Cerberus – Descent into underworld – no weapon – Cerberus returns to underworld

She toyed with a few ideas before getting down to the serious plotting and many of these were incorporated into the finished product. Eight of the stories follow, with only minor variations, these initial notes, although she made changes to 'The Horses of Diomedes'. Notice, though, how the two stories that she admitted gave her some trouble, 'The Erymanthian Boar' and 'The Girdle of Hyppolita', change quite considerably and the one that 'almost defeated' her, 'The Capture of Cerberus', is totally different in the published collection:

Lion of Nemea – Peke dog kidnapped

Hydra of Lernea – Poison Pen – or scandal in country place – one person at bottom of it
   Lernean Hydra – Woman suspected of killing husband – (verdict was accident!)

Deer of Arcadia – Dancer who disappears – young man – could P find her

Erymanthian Boar – Criminal traced and taken – race gang?

Stymphalean Birds – Young man blackmailed . . . by two women

Augean Stables – Political scandal – HP to distract attention – gets medical student to produce dead body Sham murder? Party funds or archaeological theft?

Cretan Bull – Mad killer?

Horses of Diomedes – taming of his children – boys? By introducing them to police work

Girdle of Hyppolita – a head mistress? Oxford don?
A priceless manuscript?

Geryon Cattle – Strange sect – leader unmasked – perhaps the flock of some pastor – a new sect – religious enthusiast
Geryon from Orient – eastern Religion

Apple of Hesperides – Treasure in a convent – disappeared many years ago – stolen – given by thief to convent

Cerberus – A dog story? Or somebody dead – brought back from the dead – or been murdered?

'The Nemean Lion'

The kidnapping of a Pekingese dog provides Poirot with his first Labour.

As can be seen, the notes for 'The Nemean Lion' are extensive and follow closely the published version. It may well have been the case that, as the first story in the series, Christie gave it a lot of thought and careful consideration. It is also the longest story in the collection. There is a lone note in Notebook 39 that foreshadows this plot; although it does not generally resemble the published version of 'The Nemean Lion', the story does feature the important fact of Miss Carnaby's inheritance of a Peke from a former employer:

Companion left Peke – she goes as housemaid – gives different names alternate places? She and friend – latter gets reward

The next extract, from Notebook 44, is an accurate precis of the published story:

HP summoned by Joseph Hoggin – old boy very upset – his wife lost her Pekingese – received a demand for £200, which she paid and dog was returned. HP has interview with Mrs J and Miss Carnaby – the companion – foolish talkative woman. Facts are as follows – Amy and Ching went to park – A saw baby in his pram – just speaking to Nurse but Ching gone – lead cut – she fetches lead – HP admits it is cut – the women look at him breathlessly – then letter comes – the money to be sent in £1 notes.

In the end P instructs Georges to find flat between certain limits – he asks Sir J – remind him of manufacturer in Liege who poisoned his wife to marry a blonde secretary. P's visit to flat on Miss A's day out – Augustus barks and tries to keep him out. The invalid sister – P knows all – her defence – no pension – old age – no home and no education – a trade union. Ching left at flat – Augustus taken – can always find his way home. How often? Ten times.

There is more to this story than at first meets the eye. Amy Carnaby is a delightful but poignant creation. Her situation – elderly untrained companion facing a bleak future in her old age – is similar to that of Dora Bunner in *A Murder is Announced* when Miss Blacklock rescues her. Miss Carnaby's criminal brain is, however, a major asset and Poirot, in 'The Flock of Geryon', calls her 'one of the most successful criminals that I have ever encountered'. The plot, a very clever one, is also particularly rich for a 20-page short story. There is the main plot involving the Pekinese dog/Nemean Lion but also a sub-plot involving the soap manufacturer poisoner in Belgium years earlier. And it is not fanciful to see, in the switch-of-dogs idea, the forerunner of *Evil under the Sun*, which appeared two years later. Poirot also mentions this case in Chapter 14 of *The Clocks*.

'The Lernean Hydra'

—◄◦►—

Ugly rumours bring Poirot to a small village to investigate
the death of the doctor's wife.

—◄◦►—

The plot of this story is largely contained on two pages in
Notebook 44, the only difference being the change of name
from Nurse Carpenter to Harrison:

> Doctor comes to P – embarrassed – no good going to police –
> wife dead – rumours – practice falling off – doesn't know how
> to combat it. P asks – who is the woman? Doctor angry –
> leaves – P says must have truth. Girl dispenser – admits will
> marry her – wife a difficult invalid – details of her death
> consistent with poisoning arsenic. P warns him – I shall get at
> truth. P sees girl – honest – frank – says old Miss L is worst. P.
> sees Miss L – etc. etc. Tracked down to Nurse – Handsome
> middle-aged woman – Nurse Carpenter? – She did it. He finds
> nurse – her Madonna face – he presses her – autopsy – she
> says no – no indeed – she <u>was</u> murdered – morphia pills

And ten pages later . . .

> Lernean Hydra Cont.
> P talks of Home Office – she says yes – because Mrs O <u>was</u>
> murdered. P gets them to announce engagement – Jean gets
> abusive letter. The morphia pills – v – opium pills – Doctor
> called in – orders opium pills – which Jean supplies

The intervening pages include preliminary notes for four of
the other Labours as well as two pages of chemical formulae,
possibly of potential poisons. This outline is generally in

keeping with the published story; note however that the idea, in the second extract, of announcing an engagement and a consequent abusive letter is not pursued. In many ways this is the most typically Christiean of all the Labours – Poirot goes to a small village to investigate a mysterious death, in this case the possible poisoning of a wife, whose husband is under suspicion. The short stories 'The Cornish Mystery' and 'How Does Your Garden Grow?', and the novels *Dumb Witness* and *Mrs McGinty's Dead*, as well as the Marple novel *The Moving Finger*, all have similar set-ups. And this short story has distinct parallels with the earlier story 'The Blue Geranium' from *The Thirteen Problems*.

'The Arcadian Deer'

◄o►

Poirot penetrates an impersonation in an effort to reunite
two lovers before it is too late.

◄o►

'The Arcadian Deer' is an idyllic story, as befits one set in Arcady, and does not feature a crime. There is however a Christiean twist in the final words of the first extract – and one that she uses a few times elsewhere in her work, although usually for a sinister purpose. The impersonation of an attendant (maid, butler, waiter, steward) is used here for non-criminal reasons, unlike its use in *Death in the Clouds*, *Appointment with Death*, *Three Act Tragedy*, *Sparkling Cyanide*, *Elephants Can Remember* and *At Bertram's Hotel*. And its reverse (the impersonation by a domestic of a 'real person') is a feature of *Taken at the Flood*, *The Mystery of the Blue Train*, *After the Funeral* and *Murder on the Orient Express*. Short stories 'The Affair at the Bungalow' and 'The Companion' from *The Thirteen Problems* and 'The Mystery of Hunter's Lodge' from *Poirot Investigates* also feature this ploy.

There are two sketches for the opening scene of this story, the second of which is the more detailed. Both versions are accurate, although Ted's beloved, Mary Brown in the first draft, has become in the second the more romantic Marie and, ultimately, 'Nita – Incognita – Juanita':

Young man in country village – car breaks down – appeals to him – find his sweetheart Mary Brown – gone to London and vanished – if in trouble will see her through. Was MB down there with a rich lady – MB was servant – really the dancer herself (kept by Lord Masterfield?) or wife of a rich polo playing young American. P sees her – a hard faced Young woman – she tells him she has not maid's address. The maid – a coarse looking girl. P knows it is the girl herself

Begging your pardon Sir – the young man – simple – handsome as a god – his persistence. Recognised HP from photo in Tatler – couldn't be another moustache like that – P softens. P has dinner at Inn – young man comes up there – find this girl – Marie – doesn't know other name. Switzerland – the girl – he hardly remembers her – so changed – her maid – Yes – remembers her – that other – do you mean Juanita – replaced maid when latter was away – P says Yes – what happened to her – she died young – Arcady. P explains – mystery about maid – blackmailed Sir George – his wife – Nita – Incognita – Juanita

'The Erymanthian Boar'

A violent criminal and an isolated setting combine to make this fourth Labour a very dangerous one.

As befits its origins, this is the most bloodthirsty of the Labours and is in many ways a very atypical Christie story. A gangster arranging a rendezvous on a Swiss mountaintop is not a regular feature of her output. The image of Hercule Poirot hopping out of bed to relieve three thugs of their firearms while someone else holds them at bay is one that sits badly with the great detective of the square eggs and the blackcurrant sirop. That said, it contains a twisting plot with multiple impersonations crammed into a mere 20 pages. This is also a use of the plastic surgeon idea, which is mentioned a few times in the Notebooks, including the early, unused notes for *Sleeping Murder*, as well as those for *Crooked House* and the tentative dramatisation of *Murder in Mesopotamia*.

The following notes accurately reflect, if somewhat cryptically, the course of a rather complicated story:

> Switzerland – HP leaves World's End – goes to Zermatt and up from there to hotel at top – something happens to funicular. Has HP first received telegram – or note – from M. Belex who saw him – the notorious Marascaud – believed to be up there – Inspector Drouet – certain people went up in funicular with him.
>
> Schwab – lonely American
> Dr. Karl Lutz (~~nervous physician~~) or Austrian Jewish doctor – facial surgeon
> 3 horsey men – cardsharpers
> Nervous English doctor
> Already there?
> The waiter – Gustave – introduces himself to HP as Inspector Drouet
> Manager – terribly nervous – has been bribed by Gust[ave]
> Mysterious patient

Marascaud bookmaker – took cash – share out in this lonely place. Gustave said 'It's one of them' – G is 'attacked' in night – doctor attends on him – speaks to P. P sees him – his face smothered in bandages. Who attacked him – 3 men – they get drunk – attack P – Schwab – saves him with pistol

Christie's preliminary notes for this story are partly utilised as the criminal Marrascaud is 'traced and taken' alive – an important point, as Poirot underlines in the last line of the story; the 'race gang' element, however, is not pursued.

'The Augean Stables'

◄○►

The fifth Labour presents Poirot with one of the most unusual cases of his entire career.

◄○►

The plot for this story – involving some elements from Christie's preliminary notes, though not the 'dead body' – is summarised in Notebook 62:

Hercule Poirot and Prime Minister – P looks at him – as old Scotch chemistry Professor has said he's a good man. P explains why Dagmar always hated her father – clean up the Augean stables – P sees Mrs NP – still beautiful woman – her reaction – P says certain cryptic things to her.

P and Dashett (young newspaper man) – says you have to turn the Thames and wash out Houses of Parliament. Sydney Cox – editor of This Week's Garbage – nasty little man – HP comes to them – pleads – threatens – finally begs. Paragraph – The Honey Bee – in Little Bedchester – in the Tube – Mrs NP leaves London for Scotland. Libel trial – Miss Greta Handersohn – a waitress in a café in Copenhagen –

approached by a journalist. P says a very old idea – Queen's Necklace – to discredit Marie Antoinette.

This story follows the notes very closely, but there is one puzzling feature – the use of the initials 'NP' throughout in reference to the Prime Minister. There is no equivalent in the story, where the Prime Minister is Edward Ferrier. Although it is an enjoyable story with an inspired symbolism, it is one that is in the highest degree unlikely both in the mechanics of the story and in its outcome. One can't help wondering if Christie's unpleasant experiences in the aftermath of her 1926 disappearance were, to some degree, responsible for this swipe at the tabloid newspaper industry. This case is mentioned in the 'Maids in the Kitchen' chapter of *One, Two, Buckle My Shoe* when Poirot refers to it as 'ingenious'.

'The Stymphalean Birds'

<o>

A good deed has horrifying consequences for an innocent abroad.

<o>

The first attempt at this story, with its domestic setting, does not figure at all in the published version although it is possible to discern the germ of the subsequent idea – two women, an abusive husband, a young man emotionally blackmailed into helping:

Mrs Garland and Mrs Richardson – latter married – terrified of husband – latter gets a gun out – young woman parks herself in Gary's apartment – he is young, married, a solicitor. Husband comes and browbeats him – threatens divorce – a womanish creature – Or – mother pleads also – an aging creature

A second outline, however, is followed almost exactly with Poirot making a very belated appearance in just the last four pages. The change of setting to a fictional foreign country, Herzoslovakia (scene of *The Secret of Chimneys*), is in keeping with many of the other Labours:

> Harold – his friendship with Nora Raymond – two women – Poles – look like birds. Her husband is studying architecture – her mother – worried – anxious. She comes into his room – for help – husband rushes in – swings something at her – she dodges – rushes out – man rushes after her – into her room – she fires – he falls – she gets him out of room – someone might come. Mother comes – says he's dead. Advices [sic] HP – he speaks to him – or – hotel manager – kept quiet – he goes out and wires for money – gives it to them – police come – everything hushed up – then mother in agony again – the women in room next door have heard

Even here, though, there are differences. In the published version there is no mention of Nora Raymond and a paperweight achieves the 'death', not the gun suggested by the notes ('she fires – he falls'). This change makes sense; the story is set in a hotel, and a gunshot in such a location would have attracted attention and made the plot unworkable.

'The Cretan Bull'

—◄◦►—

Is Poirot's seventh Labour merely a case of bad heredity or is it something more sinister?

—◄◦►—

There are relatively few notes about the seventh Labour, 'The Cretan Bull'. The main problem seems to have been the choice of poison – Christie finally settled on atropine (also the poison of choice in 'The Thumb Mark of St Peter' from *The Thirteen Problems*). The story shares an untypical emphasis on blood – the 'mad killer' idea – with 'The Erymanthian Boar'. But as in other Christie titles – *Hercule Poirot's Christmas* and 'The Importance of a Leg of Mutton' from *The Big Four*, for example – this is an important part of the plot:

> P asked down – country squire and old friend fear that squire's boy is mad – madness in family – boy has been in Navy – (got out of that) – squire never got over wife's death – boating accident or car accident –
> (Does HP enquire about that as though he thinks car had been tampered with by crony? Wife only with him by afterthought says husband – asked, friend blusters – said first he had heard of that – make him sound suspicious. Boy marvellously handsome – girl there in love with him – he himself believes he is mad. Drug – eyes? Scopolamine – hyoscyamine – atropine – or aconite – ointment smeared on – hallucinations. Final attempt to kill girl

This story shares a plot device with *A Caribbean Mystery* and is in fact referenced during the plotting of the later novel. The most interesting few words in the above extract are undoubtedly 'make him sound suspicious'. This was the strategy on which Christie built her career – the presentation of a story in such a way as to make the innocent seem guilty and vice versa. Few people reading this story will not single out George Frobisher as the villain of the piece, which is exactly what Christie intended.

'The Horses of Diomedes'

―◁◦▷―

Poirot tackles the scourge of drug-pushers.

―◁◦▷―

There are two distinct sets of notes for this eighth Labour. Despite the fact that Notebook 44 contains the 'correct' notes for most of the other Labours, the relevant notes for this story are those from Notebook 62:

P on trail of drug racket – County place – (not county) – rich manufacturers etc –
Old General Boynton – Gout – choleric – swollen leg. Daughters – wild girls – one gets herself into a mess – not daughter at all?
Gang – Old Boy the head of the racket – Girls turn on him

Stillingfleet – calls on Poirot – the drug racket – turns decent people into wild beasts – you asked me to keep my eyes open – girl in a fire – mews – hashish – he got girl out of it. The other sister – used to be decent kids – father an Old General. P sees them – sullen girl – hard boiled – says Stillingfleet is a good sort. P says will look her father up – look of alarm in her eyes – P says will be discreet.
S[tillingfleet] and P – says very young – 18 – damned shame they aren't better looked after – P goes down to Norfolk – the General – Gout – temper – worried about his girls. P says: Who are their friends?
Dalloway – man like a horse – slow etc. – Mrs Larkin – at her house P sees the others – dartboard etc. –
Hylda – vague girl – Cummings – young doctor – assistant to older man – sandwich box (belonging to Dalloway) in hall – P gets note (look in S. Box) – he does

361

There are a few minor changes – Dr Stillingfleet (possibly of 'The Dream' and *Third Girl*) changes to Dr Stoddart, the sandwich box becomes a hunting flask and there is no mention of a dartboard.

There are notes in Notebook 44 relating to this story, but they present different, and in one case, rather outlandish speculations:

> The Mares of Diomedes
>   Old racing man – his 'gals' very wild – what can P do? –
> Bloomsbury – one of them shoots someone – (Mrs Barney?)
> – unlike twin idea – woman servant one of them – NO!!
>   OR
> P pays a young man to be 'killed' by one of them – Or –
> Secret service – Jacinta?

The idea of 'the old General and his wild girls', from the first extract, is retained (note the change from 'boys', in the preliminary notes, to 'girls' here) but the rather bizarre idea of Poirot paying someone to allow himself to be killed, presumably as a ruse, was abandoned. The reference to Mrs Barney is to an infamous London murder case when the glamorous Elvira Barney was tried, and subsequently acquitted, for the shooting of her lover Michael Scott Stephen in May 1932.

The potent symbolism of the mythical horses that feed on human flesh transmuting into dope peddlers who carry out a similar loathsome trade is undeniable. But there is an element of sermonising in the story that tends to detract from its plot. Once again Christie trades on our misperception, this time of the seemingly typical retired army stereotype, a not infrequent character in her fiction – Colonel Protheroe in *The Murder at the Vicarage,* Major Porter in *Taken at the Flood,* Major Palgrave in *A Caribbean Mystery,* General Macarthur in *Ten Little Niggers* and Major Burnaby in *The Sittaford Mystery.*

And there are many more examples. But they are not always to be trusted . . .

The allusion to the unlike twin is to an idea that crops up again and again throughout the Notebooks (see 'The House of Dreams', page 303). As shown by its constant reappearance, Christie never successfully tackled this idea and here was no exception. A certain amount of exasperation is detectable in the exhortation, 'NO!!', to herself.

'The Girdle of Hyppolita'

————◄o►————

Two seemingly disparate cases, an art robbery and a missing schoolgirl, are brought together in the ninth Labour.

————◄o►————

This is another story that is considerably changed from Christie's early conception of it, although traces of the 'head mistress' idea are still visible. As can be seen, with this story Christie gave free rein to her considerable inventiveness. There are quite a number of sketches both for the development of the story and for the interpretation of the original myth – a manuscript, an archaeological find and a picture were all considered. And even after the picture was adopted, she still considered some other scenarios:

P at Oganis or Lestranges – very super girl's finishing school – the frightening Miss Beddingfeld

Is girl there really a crook? Or is she missing millionaire's daughter who is being hunted for everywhere?

A precious manuscript? A picture? An archaeological find? A stolen picture? Painted over by one of the girls (crook)

and presented to Head Mistress – latter therefore taken it
into the right country – custom's Pass – etc.

Kidnapped schoolgirl – she is new – delivered over to Miss
Nortress – dull with plate [plaits?] – wire on teeth –
miserable skinny looking object – they go to Paris – girl
disappears on train – (really emerges from lavatory and joins
man – all made up – very actressy – in mink coat. On way
back from lunch – slips into lavatory – man comes out – hat
found on line. Girl found a day later at Amiens – unhurt –
dazed.

Theft of famous picture (G of H). It is to be smuggled
into France – to dealer there? – crook? Acc[tress] takes
employment with 'elder sister' – meets child – and takes her
to Victoria – knock out drops – false actress becomes kid –
once in France changes in lavatory – arrives with man –
very smart.

Pictures in exhibition with other girls work – P as conjuror –
wipes it off with turpentine – exposes the Girdle of
Hyppolita

This is another Labour that is rich in plot with two seemingly
disparate ideas, the disappearance of a schoolgirl and a
stolen painting, neatly tied together. There is a certain similarity to the book that she was to write 20 years later – *Cat
among the Pigeons* – in the smuggling of a valuable item in a
schoolgirl's luggage. The masquerade of an adult as a young
girl is also a plot feature of that book, as well as of the short
story 'The Regatta Mystery'.

'The Flock of Geryon'

───────────◄○►───────────

A protagonist from 'The Nemean Lion' returns to help
Poirot investigate a series of odd deaths.

───────────◄○►───────────

'The Flock of Geryon' is the weakest story in the series, and
this is reflected in the paucity of notes; those that exist are
vague enough to have been developed in almost any way. The
following is from Notebook 44, and the sect suggested in the
preliminary notes is one of the starting-off points:

> P is visited by Miss? (Amelia) – little annuity – exercises
> people's dogs – has been reading German book – criminal
> impulses – sublimation. Could she work for P? A case – her
> friend – strange sect – down in Devon. Young millionaire's
> son – there? Or middle-aged daughter of very rich man?
> Or rich man's widow?

There is no particular ingenuity in either the story or the
symbolism. It is rescued only by the presence of the enterprising and entertaining Amy Carnaby from 'The Nemean Lion'.
Oddly, there is no mention in the notes of Carnaby's name.
'Miss? (Amelia)' may be Christie's own shorthand (although
it is not very short!) or it may simply be that she had no copy
of *The Strand* to hand to check the earlier name. There is a
brief reference to Hitler in this story (see also 'The Capture
of Cerberus' in the Appendix).

'The Apples of the Hesperides'

―――――――――◄○►―――――――――

A remote setting provides Poirot with the final clue in a
case that really began centuries earlier.

―――――――――◄○►―――――――――

There are fewer notes for 'The Apples of the Hesperides'
than for any other Labour. The plot is not involved and
required little in the way of planning once the main clue of
the nun was planted. The basic outline reflects the final
version:

> Millionaire – gold chalice stolen from him – no clue. P talks
> to American detective – Pat Ryan – a wild fellow – a decent
> wife – but wouldn't get him to run straight – she went back
> to Ireland – or daughter – a nun. Ireland – the convent – P
> arrives there – tramp with bottle of brandy – world in my
> hands

> Little tipster in bar in Ireland – 'Atlas' is his pseudonym – HP
> says doesn't look it (horse to back – 'The World' by Greek
> Hero out of Geography). You have not to hold up the World
> – only Hercule Poirot

Some minor details are different – the horse to back is
Hercules rather than the more elaborate one of the notes;
and there is no tramp.

Like the earlier 'The Erymanthian Boar', this case takes
Poirot to a remote and beautiful location, this time on the
west coast of Ireland. Apart from mentioning a coach tour
holiday of Irish gardens in Chapter 11 of *Hallowe'en Party*, this
is his only visit to Ireland and is memorable to him for all the
wrong reasons.

Like Sir Joseph Hoggin in 'The Nemean Lion', Emery Power loses financially as a result of Poirot's investigation although in his case there is a spiritual benefit. (There is a minor error of fact when Poirot promises him that 'the nuns will say Masses for your soul'. Nuns can't say mass and mass for the soul is celebrated only after a person's death.) The final scene, in the isolated convent on the edge of the Atlantic, is a particularly poignant one with a wise and telling exchange.

'The Capture of Cerberus'

<o>

Is the Countess Vera's nightclub the scene of more than just harmless revelry?

<o>

The following extracts refer to the version of the story collected in *The Labours of Hercules* in 1948 (for the newly discovered version see the Appendix). It is further proof of Christie's fecundity with plot that she was able to imagine a second allegorical interpretation of the last Labour of Hercules. In the original Greek myth Hercules has to pass into Hell, overcoming the ferocious hound that guards the gates; in the Poirot Labour Hell is a nightclub with a large dog in the entrance foyer. The steps down into the club are labelled 'I meant well' and 'I can give up any time I like', an amusing take on the old saying 'The path to Hell is paved with good intentions'. And the hound, originally intended as a nightclub 'gimmick', plays a vital part in the plot.

As often happens, names were changed, but the following outline is otherwise accurately reflected in the published version:

Cerberus

Raid – blackout for 2 minutes – has it happened? And J tells P?
Combed the place inside out – jewels – no, drugs – no jewels
    but 5 or 6 people noticed weren't there –
Secret exit – whole grill moves out – house next door –
    Cabinet Minister etc.
We were in the clear – Jimmy Mullins – wanted – Battersea
    Murderer – has given the place a write up –
But this time we've <u>got</u> to succeed –
P talks to dog man –
The fatal evening – Is P there? – Or does he hear?

He comes over wall – black out etc. – how many people
    come out
Mr Vitamian Crusoe –
Miss Sylvia Elkins
~~Giuseppe~~ Martacendi – cook's boy
Paul Varesco
Two packets – the emeralds – the other – cocaine

This is a more light-hearted interpretation of the myth than the original unpublished version, with the naming of both the nightclub itself and the amusing use of the steps into it. And we also get a glimpse of Miss Lemon's hitherto unsuspected feminine instincts in the closing lines. On 'the fatal evening' Poirot is at the club but leaves early and Christie adopts the idea of Japp recounting the details to him ('or does he hear?'). None of the early part of this story, Poirot's meeting with the Countess in the London Underground and his subsequent visit to her nightclub, features in the Notebooks.

EXHIBIT G:
MURDER IS EASY: SEEDS OF INSPIRATION

'I'm never at a loss for a plot'
Cards on the Table, Chapter 4

SOLUTIONS REVEALED
'The Case of the Perfect Maid' • *The Sittaford Mystery*

These short jottings are perfect examples of Christie's imaginative cultivation of even the smallest seed of an idea into a fully formed bloom – and often, with her customary good sense, she used that idea more than once. These ideas often appear in a list of similar ideas but sometimes on a page in the middle of notes for another title, as inspiration struck. And all of them appear separately from the plotting of the story in which they ultimately appeared.

* Poor little rich girl – house on hill – luxury gadgets etc. – original owner

This appears on a list of a dozen ideas for possible Miss Marple stories. It probably dates from the early days of the Second World War as it is surrounded by notes for *N or M?* and *Curtain*. This idea is incorporated into 'The Case of the Caretaker', which first appeared in January 1942. And 25 years later much of that story was reworked for the 1967 novel *Endless Night*.

✳ Hargreaves case – young man and girl – she suspected – swears to him she is innocent – he warns her – her innocence is proven – she then admits she is guilty

This idea, which has strong echoes of one of her greatest short story (and subsequent stage) successes – 'Witness for the Prosecution', appears two pages after a page dated June 1944. It is included while she is sketching ideas for a 'play on moral issue involving husband and wife'.

✳ Witness in murder case – quite unimportant – offered post abroad – hears indirectly it is a fake offer – or servant – cook?

Appearing in a list of 'Ideas A–U' and dating from the early 1940s, this device had already been used in the early Mr Quin story 'The Sign in the Sky', first published in July 1924, and briefly in Chapter 6 of *Why Didn't They Ask Evans?*. And in the early stages of *The Big Four* this ploy is used on Poirot himself.

✳ Invisible ink – written (will?) Or print a different document

'Motive Vs. Opportunity' from *The Thirteen Problems* and 'The Case of the Missing Will' from *Poirot Investigates* both feature this idea. But as those two stories had originally appeared in the 1920s this jotting, from the late 1930s, cannot be their starting point. It appears on a long list a few pages before the notes for the stories that were to become *The Labours of Hercules*.

✳ Not identical twins – one sister pretends to be 2 – totally different looking woman – (invalid) pretends to be maid – really 2 of them

The idea of non-identical twins appears again and again in the Notebooks – featuring in both used and unused ideas – and this variation on it appears four times, twice in one Notebook. As outlined above, this device is the main one in 'The Case of the Perfect Maid'.

> ✳ Spoof butler

This idea is difficult to date but seems to have been a possibility Christie considered for one of Tommy and Tuppence's *Partners in Crime* adventures, although the rest of Notebook 65, where it appears, is taken up with *Ten Little Niggers*. The short story 'The Listerdale Mystery', published in December 1925, concerns a 'spoof butler' but this note is unlikely to refer to that early story. It seems more likely that it became *Three Act Tragedy*, where such a butler is one of the major plot devices of that brilliant novel.

> ✳ Or Japp – unhappy with D.P.P. A case – yes – not happy – asks Poirot will he check up on it. Young man – bitter – difficult

This note, appearing just ahead of a page dated September 1947, eventually became *Mrs McGinty's Dead*, but not with Japp (who had long disappeared) but Superintendent Spence from *Taken at the Flood*. The bitter young man is the already convicted James Bentley.

> ✳ Short Marple Stories A. Poison Pen – big hearty girl is it

This appears on a lengthy list of similar cryptic ideas for short Marples, sandwiched between the plotting of *Sparkling Cyanide* and *N or M?*. It is obviously the germ of *The Moving Finger*, although a 'big hearty girl' is not unmasked at the end of that novel.

✳ . . . with teeth projecting, discoloured or white and even
(better for short story)

The teeth of the victim are one of the first anomalies noticed
by Miss Marple when she views *The Body in the Library*.

✳ Stamp idea – man realises fortune – puts it on old letter –
a Trinidad stamp on a Fiji letter

The 'stamp idea' appears frequently – at least eight times
with minor variations. It is used in the Marple story 'Strange
Jest' and is also a plot feature of *Spider's Web*.

✳ See a pin and pick it up all the day you'll have good luck
(dressmaker has been already – comes again – woman is
dead)

This is the basis of 'Village Murder'/'Tape-Measure Murder'
and a ploy of Poirot's in 'The Under Dog'. The idea of a murderer returning and 'discovering' the body also featured in
The Sittaford Mystery.

✳ Old lady in train – tells girl (or man) she is going to
Scotland Yard – a murderer at work – she knows next
victim will be the vicar – Girl takes job in village etc.

This jotting, which appears in a list dated January 1935, is the
basis for *Murder Is Easy*, although without a murdered vicar or
a girl taking a village job. The novel itself is one of the few for
which there are no notes.

12

The Body in the Library:
Murder by Quotation

There was a long shuddering sigh, and then two voices spoke in turn. Strangely enough, the words they uttered were both quotations. David Lee said: 'The Mills of God grind slowly . . .'

Lydia's voice came like a fluttering whisper: 'Who would have thought the old man to have had so much blood in him?'

Hercule Poirot's Christmas, Book III

◄○►

SOLUTIONS REVEALED

Death on the Nile, Endless Night • The Hollow • The Man in the Brown Suit • The Mirror Crack'd from Side to Side • The Murder of Roger Ackroyd • The Mysterious Affair at Styles • The Pale Horse • Sad Cypress • Taken at the Flood

◄○►

Throughout her life Agatha Christie was a voracious reader. Her childhood was filled with books and *Postern of Fate* discusses them at length – *The Cuckoo Clock, Four Winds Farm, Winnie the Pooh, Little Grey Hen, The Red Cockade, The Prisoner of Zenda*. Her Notebooks are littered with lists of books, which apart from many crime titles, included novels by Graham

Greene, Alan Sillitoe, Muriel Spark, Rumer Godden, John Steinbeck and Nevil Shute. So it is not surprising that some of her titles, including those of the Mary Westmacotts, derive from quotations from a variety of sources – Shakespeare, Flecker, Tennyson, Blake, Eliot. Apart from titles, extracts appear throughout her books, and some novels (*The Mirror Crack'd from Side to Side* and *Appointment with Death*) end poignantly with appropriate quotations.

Sad Cypress
4 March 1940

> *Come away, come away, death*
> *And in sad cypress let me be laid*
> *Fly away, fly away breath!*
> *I am slain by a fair, cruel maid.*

Shakespeare, Twelfth Night

Elinor Carlisle is on trial for the murder of Mary Gerard. The case against her seems foolproof as only she had the means, motive and opportunity to introduce poison at the fatal lunch. Dr Lord thinks there is more to it than meets the eye and approaches Hercule Poirot.

Although published in March 1940, *Sad Cypress* had appeared in serial form in the USA at the end of the previous year. It is another example of a novel with characters more carefully drawn than many other novels, and although there is a clever plot device at the core there is less emphasis

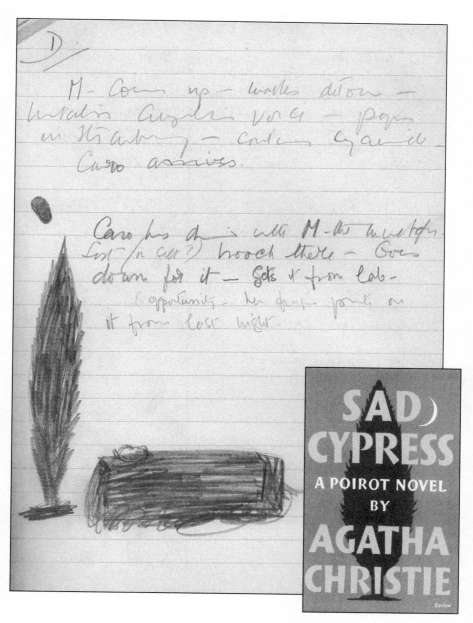

This sketch appears, inexplicably, in Notebook 35 during the plotting of Five Little Pigs *(1943) but is unmistakably the cover design for* Sad Cypress *(1940). Alongside the tree is, possibly, a coffin – of cypress wood perhaps, as per the quotation?*

on clues and timetables and the minutiae of detection. As other commentators have pointed out, however, there is also a flaw in the plot; and there is a second problem.

Notebook 20 has a version of the plot device of *Sad Cypress* and it is unequivocally stated, and dated, in Notebook 66. As early as this 1935 date, note that the murderer was to be female:

> Rose without thorns – a thornless white rose mentioned by front door – later apomorphine injected by murderer into herself

> Jan 1935
> A. Rose without thorn mentioned by front door – later murderess injects apomorphine into herself – draws attention to prick as having been caused by thorn

Four pages later in the same Notebook we find a second reference to it showing that, over two years later, it was still in the planning process:

> Feb 1937
> A (as before)
> A. Illegitimate daughter – Begins hospital nurse attending old wealthy woman – (she learns about daughter supposedly d[aughter] of gardener) then kills off patient by sweets sent from niece – later niece and Mary antagonistic over a young man – nurse poisons Mary – Evelyn (niece) thought to have done it.

Notebook 21 adds some detail, while item G on an alphabetical list in Notebook 66 also includes a similar plot device – but in a very different setting:

Retired hospital nurse – apomorphine stunt – Evelyn Dane –
inherits from Aunt – Mary is really daughter – actually
companion – Jeremy is cousin who has loved Evelyn and
now loves Mary – Nurse pretends to be surprised to see Mrs.
D's picture – she attended her for the birth of a child etc.

Poison – man injects apomorphine after sharing some
dish – small tube with morphia on it found later – really
apomorphine. Family reunion – old father killed – who did it?
– he has whisky and soda for tea – others have tea – ~~fresh tea~~

The family reunion mentioned in the latter extract was
changed but the idea of disguising the poison in freshly
brewed tea was retained.

Like some other works, the Notebooks contain little that is
different from the finished novel, leading to the suspicion
that there were discarded notes that no longer exist. Apart
from some name changes – Roger becomes Roddy, Mrs
Dacres is changed to Mrs Welman and the first Nurse
becomes O'Brien – the notes follow the course and detail of
the novel almost exactly:

Beginning
Elinor in London – anonymous letter – accusing undue
influence – Elinor about to destroy it – then rings up Roger

Old Mrs. Dacres very ill – nurses in charge of case – gossip
~~Mrs~~. Nurse Chaplin – a local nurse – Nurse Hopkins – they
talk together – A photograph Mrs. D – asks for – signed
Lewis – her husband's name was ~~Roger~~ Henry

Somewhat sudden death of old lady – suspicious absence of
morphine? – Nurses not sure – she dies intestate

The characters also were settled early on and, apart from their names, did not change. The eternal triangle too was defined from the beginning:

> The relations – in house
>   Mary Dane [Gerrard] – daughter of gardener – acted as companion
>   Evelyn her niece arrives – and Roger Dacres – nephew by marriage
>   She is a real character – hard up – fascinating – antagonism between her and Mary
>
> Roger falls in love with Mary – Eve gives her a sum of money – Mary comes to life – Nurse Chaplin advises her to make a will
>
> Dr. Lord – good-looking young man – fall in love with Elinor?
>
> The nurses – Moira O'Brien resides in house – Nurse Hopkins from village – comes every morning to give a hand. As Nurse C leaves – Mary accompanies her – says her Auntie in Australia is a hospital Nurse
>
> Mary's death? She is at cottage – Elinor asks her to come up to the house for lunch – a cold lunch – Sandwiches – Nurse offers to make them a nice cup of tea – (apomorphine in kitchen) – the sandwiches – Mary to have salmon ones as she is a Catholic – gets her excited and then drowsy – Nurse Hopkins doesn't like the look of her – sends for doctor – difficult to get him – morphine poisoning

One of the flaws in the plot of *Sad Cypress* is that at the fatal lunch the killer cannot know that Elinor Carlisle will not also drink the poisoned tea along with Mary. The short note in

Notebook 21 to the effect that 'Mary to have salmon ones as she is a Catholic' may have been an early solution to the problem of ensuring that only the intended victim ingested the poison, by attempting to guarantee that Mary would be limited in the type of sandwich (assumed erroneously to be the means of poisoning) she could eat. However, as the murder occurs on a Thursday (Chapter 7), Mary would not, in fact, be limited in her choice; the restriction on eating meat applied only to Fridays. And, in the event, the killer did not prepare the supposedly poisoned sandwiches anyway, so could not have stage-managed that aspect of the scene. It does seem as if this is a definite problem.

But there is a further problem, also of a practical nature – how could Nurse Hopkins have known that Elinor would call herself and Mary from the Lodge to the house for the fatal lunch? And how did she have a hypodermic and apomorphine with her? Her original plan to poison Mary in her own (Hopkins') cottage, as surmised by Poirot in the final chapter, does not answer the question either, as that scenario, even if it were to include Elinor, would be so unlikely as to be suspicious. Unfortunately the Notebooks give no indication as to whether Christie considered this difficulty.

The aftermath of the murder is also accurately reflected in Notebook 21, with little deviation from the finished novel:

Death of old lady – no will – her fortune goes to Elinor as next of kin

E and Roger – a little stiffness – she says it doesn't matter which of us has it – he again feels there is a coolness between them.

R. and Mary – incipient love affair – she is pleased – Mary's young man Edmund is angry – they quarrel

Elinor sees them together – R. is ringing her

Elinor gives Mary £1000 pounds – she accepts

And ultimately . . .

> Dr. Lord comes to Poirot – insists it wasn't her – can't be
> Hopkins she had nothing to do with sandwiches – just made
> tea which they both drank – little bit of paper with morphine
> under the stove – the kitchen – it was open – someone could
> have got in there while the others were down in the Lodge

The Moving Finger
14 June 1943

The Moving Finger writes; and, having writ moves on
The Rubaiyat of Omar Khayyam

Shortly after Jerry Burton and his sister move to the idyllic
village of Lymstock, a series of anonymous letters horrifies
the inhabitants and culminates in the death of the local
solicitor's wife. The vicar's wife decides to send for an
expert in wickedness – Miss Marple.

This is another example of a novel narrated by a male. Apart
from the Hastings novels, seven other titles (*The Murder of
Roger Ackroyd, The Murder at the Vicarage, The Moving Finger,
Crooked House, Endless Night*; and both *The Pale Horse* and *The
Clocks* are partly male-narrated) have male narrators while
only two (*Murder in Mesopotamia* and, for the most part, *The
Man in the Brown Suit*) have female ones. While it is by no
means extraordinary for a female writer to write as a male,
this may have been dictated from the beginning of Christie's
career when, having created Hastings as Poirot's chronicler,

she grew accustomed to the idea of telling the story as a male. It would have been inconceivable for Poirot to have a close female friend with whom he lived and shared his cases. And equally inconceivable, but for different reasons, is the possibility that they would be recounted by his wife! In *The Moving Finger* it is also odd that Jerry Burton narrates the entire story without ever telling us anything about his background or that of his sister. Apart from the fact that he was a pilot and that Joanna has a busy social life we learn nothing about them.

Not only was *The Moving Finger* published almost a year earlier in the USA but the US and UK editions are significantly different, although this did not come to light until the mid-1950s. When Penguin Books published the title in 1953 a flurry of correspondence drew Edmund Cork's attention to these discrepancies. He had supplied Penguin with a US edition for their reprint, as the agent's own file copy of the UK edition had been a war casualty. When he contacted Christie's US agent in July 1953 seeking an explanation of the inconsistencies it was difficult, even then, to say how the mistake happened. The most likely explanation, according to them, was that the US publishers had worked from a copy used by the publishers of the serial, *Colliers Magazine*, who had 'cut' the manuscript. The mistake has been perpetuated ever since. While the basic story remains the same, many minor characters have disappeared from the US edition and some passages, including the opening scene, are significantly different. Apart from puzzling references to characters who do not (seemingly) exist the overall effect is to leave the US edition a shorter book.

The same situation, and probable explanation, applies to *Murder is Easy*.

Miss Marple was indicated as the detective from the beginning, which makes her non-appearance until Chapter 10 (of the UK edition) all the more peculiar. It is almost a cameo appearance, less than a dozen pages. The setting, however, is very much Miss Marple territory and Lymstock is the typical English village associated with Agatha Christie. Apart from St Mary Mead the number of similar villages in Christie novels is actually surprisingly small, despite the common perception that they are all set in such surroundings.

The Moving Finger also has the most unusual denouement of any Christie novel. We learn who the killer is before Miss Marple's explanation. The ploy to trap the murderer is known to the reader as we watch him attempt another killing. This is at variance with similar ruses in, for example, *The Body in the Library, Cards on the Table* and *Towards Zero,* where the reader is unaware of the identity of the victim of the trap.

There are only 15 pages of Notebook devoted to *The Moving Finger* and, apart from a few fleeting references elsewhere, most of these pages are in Notebook 62. It does not seem to have presented many technical problems and the plotting progresses smoothly. And she follows her (then) normal pattern of assigning letters to scenes.

The initial appearance is dated, although not very precisely, 1940:

Ideas (1940)
Poison pen – letters in village – 'repressed spinster' indicated – really plot by someone to discredit her – (a resourceful mother?) Miss Marple

Although the 'repressed spinster' as the source of the anonymous letters is much discussed in Lymstock as, indeed, the killer hoped, the 'discrediting' idea was abandoned; perhaps it had too many echoes of the recent *Murder is Easy*, where the killer hoped that the murders would discredit the real target, a person with a strong motives for removing all of the victims.

Christie began work on the novel the following year, as shown by a subsequent note, and the general set-up closely follows Notebook 62. In a typical piece of Christie misdirection, she uses the minor crime of anonymous letters as camouflage for the more deadly crime of murder. This is the same principle of camouflage adopted by the killer in *The A.B.C. Murders*, although in that novel a series of murders is used to camouflage one particular killing. The town, the people and their names, the events and the first murder all appear in the book as they do in the Notebook:

Anonymous letters – deliberate – finally woman commits suicide as a result of letter – really killed (by husband?)

Books 1941 Miss M? or told in 1st person
    Poison Pen – all round village – unhappiness etc. – wife of lawyer (?) gets one – kills herself – really is killed by husband – and he then puts letter in her pocket – its subject matter is untrue

Suspected of writing letters – Vicar's ~~sister?~~ wife – schoolmistress – doctor's ~~wife~~ sister? – Hearty spinster – maidservant – maidservant is next killed because she saw something or knew something

Description of town – market town known better days – they take bungalow – the letters come – not sister – wonders if there is much of this sort of thing about – what about if a shot in the dark hits the bulls eye?

Resume of people they meet
   Dr. Thomas – his sister – dark fierce 'manly looking'
woman – little Mr Pye – Vicar – his wife – goes home to find
Mrs. Symmington calling

In the notes for this novel we again see the method of assigning letters to scenes, although in this case no rearrangement
of them is specified in the Notebook:

Progress   Moving Finger   Points

A. J[erry] discovers book of sermons cut out pages
   [Chapter 9 v]
B. Megan goes home [Chapter 7 ii]
C. Maid knows something – scene between her and Elsie
   H[olland] – Joanna overhears comes back and tells J?
   Did she come back that afternoon? Does she come and
   ask advice from Partridge? She is killed – deliberate
   [Chapter 7, but not exactly as described here]
D. Tea with Miss Emily – big raw-boned dragon looks after
   her [Chapter 7 iv]
E. Vicar? His wife – vague – slightly bats? Hits nail on head –
   poor Aimee very unhappy woman [Chapter 5 i]
F. Institute? Someone typing – J goes in – finds Aimee who
   'heard' someone leave [Chapter 10 ii]
G. J going off to sleep 'No S[moke] W[ithout] F[ire]' –
   smoke – smoke screen – War – 'scrap of paper' Nurse
   told him as little boy – etc [Chapter 8 i]
H. Spiteful rumour about – Elsie means to be No. 2
   [Chapter 9 ii]
I. The posted letters – Aimee's written at Institute – one of
   them is IT – substituted – (did she drop them and pick
   them up in High St. – S[ymmington] there) (E[mily]
   B[arton] at Institute too) [Chapter 13 ii]

As can be seen, the order changed considerably – the muti-lated book of sermons (scene A) is not discovered until Chapter 9 – and the scenes are scattered through the book. Scene C is an ingenious twist on the person who 'knows something' and then becomes the next victim. Here, instead of knowing or seeing something dangerous to the killer, the maid 'knows something' because she saw nothing. It is the fact that she saw *nothing* when she should actually have seen *something* that seals her fate.

The Moving Finger is another title that Christie considered dramatising. Notebook 45 consists of rough preliminary notes including a list of the characters of the novel and tentative set-tings. But the novel is very 'mobile', with many scenes set in the streets and houses of Lymstock. The multiple potential settings, as shown by the note below, created immediate prob-lems in devising a successful dramatisation of this title:

Scene?
Maisonette or divided house?
Garden of same used by both
Room in police station
Symmington's house

The Hollow
25 November 1946

I hate the dreadful hollow behind the little wood
Its lips in the field above are dabbled with blood red heath,
The red ribb'd ledges drip with a silent horror of blood
And Echo there, whatever is ask'd her, answers 'Death'.

Tennyson, *Maud*

<hr>

Poirot is not amused by the scene at the swimming pool –
the sprawled man and the woman with the revolver standing over him. He assumes that it has been arranged for his
benefit until he realises that it is not a tableau and that he
is looking at a dying man . . .

<hr>

Poirot quotes the Tennyson poem in Chapter 18 and
although it is more blood-drenched than the novel,
Henrietta sees the relevant symbolism. Interestingly, the last
line of the poem also appears in Notebook 3 in an entry
dated October 1972, when Christie was planning what was to
be her final novel.

The very earliest glimmering of the plot of *The Hollow*
can be seen in a throwaway line in Notebook 13 – 'Poirot
asks to go down to country – finds a house and various fantastic details' – hidden among an A–Z list of other ideas.
The very fact of Poirot going 'down to country' is the first
clue but the fantastic details are the elements of the
tableau that greets him when he calls to The Hollow – the
dying man sprawled by the swimming pool, the blood drip-
ping into the pool itself, the woman standing over him
holding the revolver, and the other onlookers in the
drama, one holding a basket of eggs and another holding a
basket of dahlia heads.

Described in somewhat unexciting terms on the original
blurb as 'a human story about human people', *The Hollow* is
almost a Mary Westmacott title. It resembles a 'straight' novel
more than a detective story and, indeed, has less in the way of
clues and detection than almost any other Poirot title. In an
article for the Ministry of Information in 1945 Christie wrote:
'Naturally one's methods alter. I have been more interested

as the years go by in the preliminaries of crime. The interplay of character upon character, the deep smouldering resentments and dissatisfactions that do not always come to the surface but which may suddenly explode into violence.' This is the template of *The Hollow* – a weekend of smouldering and complicated emotions erupting into murder. The character drawing in this novel is the most searching she has done to date. *Five Little Pigs* and *Sad Cypress* paved the way but in *The Hollow*, her powers of characterisation reached full flower – to the detriment, unfortunately, of the detective plot. *Five Little Pigs* is the most perfect example of the marrying of the two, *Sad Cypress* still has a distinct detective plot with clues and alibis; but in *The Hollow*, the detection is minimal and Poirot is almost surplus to requirements.

When, some years later, Christie came to dramatise *The Hollow* for the stage, she dropped Hercule Poirot from it. And it is difficult not to agree with this decision. Of all his cases, he does not fit in here. It is inconceivable that he would have bought a house in the country and at no subsequent time is it even mentioned. And as this case involves little in the way of physical clues, he is almost entirely dependent on the characters. When Christie says in her *Autobiography* that he doesn't fit, she is quite right. It was probably pressure from her publishers that caused her to insert him into this milieu; he hadn't appeared in a novel since *Five Little Pigs*, three years earlier. He doesn't enter the novel until almost 100 pages into it and, even more peculiarly, his French idioms are almost completely absent. Also dropped from the stage version is the character David Angkatell, who is completely superfluous and whose absence from the novel would have had no adverse effect either.

The notes in Notebook 13 are preceded by *Death Comes as the End* and followed by *Taken at the Flood*, a sequence reflected in the order of publication. The first point of interest in Notebook 13 is the fact that two alternate titles were under consideration for *The Hollow*. Both of them reflect elements of the finished novel. The events take place over what proves, indeed, to be a tragic weekend and the poignant memories of happier early days – a motif that runs throughout the novel – dominate the lives of many of the characters:

Tragic Weekend
Return Journey

Elizabeth Savarnake [Henrietta]
Lucy Angkatell
Gwenda – her niece [Midge]
John Christow/Ridgeway
Gerda Ridgeway
Veronica Cray
Edward
Henry Angkatell

Lady Angkatell in early morning – Gwenda – poor Gerda etc [Chapter I]

H.P. next door

The Hollow features strong echoes of Greenway in the descriptions of Ainswick, the Angkatell family home that dominates both the book and the lives of many of the characters. It is described in Chapter 18 as 'the white graceful house, the big magnolia growing up it, the whole set in an amphitheatre of wooded hills'; and in Chapter 6: 'the final turn in through the gate and up through the woods till you came out into the open and there the house was – big and white and welcoming'.

Note that the niece's name, Gwenda, was abandoned (perhaps because of its similarity to Gerda) in favour of Midge. But it is also possible that there is a connection with Gwenda from *Sleeping Murder*, in view of the new timeline for the writing of that novel (see Chapter 7). And the alternative that was considered for (Dr) John Christow's name, Ridgeway, was to become the name of the disease on which he was working.

The salient elements of the plot are succinctly captured in a half-dozen pages of Notebook 13:

> John at consulting desk – gear changing – annoyance with G.
>   – E. and her wonderful knack with cars
> E. in studio
> Edward – his nervousness – sly, clever creature
>
> Points
>
> Gerda in straightforward fashion because discovers liaison
>   of John
> Lady A – sheer vagueness
> Edward – in love with Eliz.
> Eliz. [Henrietta] – very cleverly tries to shield G
> Bit of clay pointing to herself
> Ends by Gerda trying to kill Eliz.

More practical details are teased out in Notebook 31:

> Now strict mechanics
>
> G. takes revolvers – shoots John – puts revolver in knitting
> bag – or puts revolver in fox cape and purse down below
> settee. Henrietta finds it – puts it back in collection
>   Inspector comes to Sir Henry – asks about revolver. Is
> another missing?
>   Sir H. stalls – finally says it is

Was it in a holster?

Yes

Holster found in road near V's cottage – in bush?

Gerda takes out 2 revolvers – ~~shoots him with one~~ puts holster in V's fur then shoots him – drops it in knitting bag and other by John's body or follows John to cottage – drops holster – comes back after him to pool – shoots him – back at home hides revolver?

Recovers it at inquest? Gudgeon takes revolver from eggs – puts it in study

Henrietta does indeed try to shield Gerda, although she doesn't resort to the piece-of-clay gambit. Nor is there an attempt to incriminate Veronica Cray by placing the gun in her fur cape, although in the stage adaptation the gun is found in Veronica's handbag. With her customary fertility of invention, Christie sketches a few possible scenarios for the disposal of the incriminating gun and holster, elements from each of which – the two revolvers, Sir Henry's missing revolver, Gudgeon and the eggs – she subsumed into the novel.

Christie introduces, in Notebook 32, an already reordered alphabetical sequence (but without, for some reason, any F, G or I) although it is not followed exactly in the novel. Note that here she is referring to the story as 'Echo', reflecting the last line of the Tennyson quotation:

End of Echo

H.P. on seat around pool – Inspector's men crashing about – Grant comes to him – making a monkey of him

A. Must find pistol fired just before – Mrs. C no time to hide it – must have hidden it near [Chapter 26]

B. All of them with motive – Lady A and David – Edmund and Henrietta. P. says solution – away not towards –

from not to. G[rant] says sometimes I think they all know – P says They do know. [Chapter 26]

C. Lady A – about truth – would be satisfied [Chapter 27]
H. Midge breaks off engagement [Chapter 27]
D. P. at home – Inspector – they find pistol [Chapter 26]
E. Midge and Edward and gas [Chapter 28]
J. P and Henrietta find leather holster [Chapter 29]

Taken at the Flood
12 November 1948

There is a tide in the affairs of men,
Which, taken at the flood, leads on to fortune . . .

Shakespeare, *Julius Caesar*

―――――――――◄○►―――――――――

Gordon Cloade is killed in an air raid and his new young wife, Rosaleen, inherits a fortune. When a mysterious death brings Hercule Poirot to Warmsley Vale he realises that the Cloade family, badly in need of money, has good reason to kill her. So why was it not Rosaleen who died?

―――――――――◄○►―――――――――

Taken at the Flood was another novel (like *Four-Fifty from Paddington* and *Ordeal by Innocence*) whose title gave trouble. The original suggestions were *The Incoming Tide* or *There is a Tide,* until it was discovered that the new Taylor Caldwell novel was called *There is a Time.* This probably explains why not once, in the course of 30 pages of notes, scattered across 13 Notebooks, is the title *Taken at the Flood* (or its eventual US equivalent *There is a Tide*) mentioned. In the body of the

391

novel the quotation appears in Book II, Chapter 16. In fact, the genesis of the title and, indeed, the book itself, is far more complicated. In a letter dated September 1947 Christie's agent refers to a 'revised' version of *Taken at the Flood* and the 'marvellous job in altering it'. This tantalising reference must remain a mystery, as there is nothing in either the Notebooks or the surviving correspondence to clarify it.

The plot of *Taken at the Flood* is one of Christie's most intricate. To begin with, none of the deaths are as they initially seem. The first death, presumed a murder, is an accident; the second, presumed a suicide, is in fact a suicide (although seasoned Christie readers will suspect murder); and the third, presumed suicide, is a murder. This combination of explanations is unique in the Christie output.

What's more, both Frances and Rowley Cloade, independently of each other, complicate the real killer's plan with sub-plots of their own, each of which ends with the violent death of their co-conspirators. Then there is confusion about the identity of the first corpse. Is he Enoch Arden? Is Robert Underhay still alive? Is he the man found dead in the Blue Boar? And if he isn't, who is that corpse? This plot device is shared, brilliantly, in *One, Two Buckle my Shoe*, and much less successfully in *Four-Fifty from Paddington*.

Some of this complexity is mirrored in the notes, due mainly to the fact that they are intertwined for much of the time with those for *They Do It with Mirrors* and *Sleeping Murder*. In the notes, the working title for *Taken at the Flood* hovered between 'Cover Her Face', the one-time title for *Sleeping Murder*, and 'Mirrors', shorthand for *They Do It with Mirrors*. Each is used three times but in all cases with the character names and plot of *Taken at the Flood*. It is worth remembering that none of the three titles is very specific; all could, with minimal tweaking, apply to any Christie title, whereas titles such as *Murder on the Orient Express* or *Lord Edgware Dies* are precise and could not be considered interchangeable.

In the opening pages of Notebooks 19 and 30 we find the genesis of the Cloade family situation:

Cover her Face

Characters

The Cloades

Nathaniel – solicitor – embezzling money [Jeremy]
Frances – His wife daughter of – Lord Edward Hatherly father Lady Angarethick – says her family are all crooks
Jeremy – ex-pilot – lawless – daring [probably the origin of David Hunter]
Jane Brown – Girl of character engaged to Jeremy? [Lynn]
Susan Cloade – (or a widow?) Cool – discerning [Adela or Katherine]

Rosaleen Hunter
Nathaniel Clode
Frances Clode – (aristocratic wife)
Susan Ridgeway
A Cloade – war widow – breeds dogs

As usual, however, names were to change. The example above, from Notebook 30, is the only use of the name 'Rosaleen' anywhere in the notes and it is used with her Hunter, rather than Cloade, surname. Throughout the Notebooks she is referred to as Lena, itself a diminution of Rosaleen. The 'Cloade war widow' who breeds dogs may have been inspired by Christie's own daughter Rosalind, a devoted dog lover and breeder, whose first husband, Hubert Prichard, perished in the war.

Notebook 13 illustrates Christie's frequently adopted alphabetical system:

A. Mrs. Marchmont asks Lena for money – (gets it?) [Book I Chapter 5]
B. Frances asks – David interrupts – her reaction – for the moment he feels afraid
  David and Lena look out of window – sees Lynn. Lena sees too?
  He goes off – interview with Lynn – then him and Lena again [Book I Chapter 6]
C. Hercule Poirot – Aunt Kathie – spirit guidance [Prologue]
D. The farm – Lena and Rowley – he looks at it just as he looks at her – (planning its death?) she goes away – stranger comes – asks way to (?) Furrowtown – goes passed it – face is familiar to Rowley [Book I Chapter 8]
E. Rowley goes up to White Hart – Beatrice the barmaid photo of L. and Edmund – Frances and Jeremy – photo – to get H.P's address [Book I Chapters 11 and 12]
F. David reading letter – get your things packed – go up to London – stay there – I'll deal with this [Book I Chapter 10]
G. David and E.A. – veiled blackmail – D. says get out of here [Book I Chapter 9]
H. Where is money to be paid? London? Tube? Poirot – seat? etc. – Bessie overhears (David goes to London – to see Lena Tube – Rowley in crowd) [not used]
I. Rowley visits Poirot – urges him to come to Warmsley Heath [Book II Chapter 1]
J. Death of E.A. – David suspected – arrested? – button in dead man's hand [Book II Chapter 5]
K. Lena and the Church [Book II Chapter 6]
L. Poirot and Lynn – people much the same – don't change [Book II Chapter 12]

Although most of these, slightly rearranged, appear in the published novel, there are a number of minor differences: scene H does not feature at all; Furrowtown in scene D becomes Furrowbank in the book; it is not a button (scene J) that is found in the room but a cigarette lighter with the initials DH; and scene C in the novel precedes much of the action.

Rosaleen's religion, apart from being a major factor in her personality, is also an important plot device. Her Roman Catholicism, and its attendant guilt, haunts all of her conversation with David. Read again their scenes in light of the solution and much of the dialogue takes on a different meaning. And it is the scene at the church that gives Poirot one of his clues:

> Lena – depressed – says – very worried I've been – wants to see priest – asks him – doesn't go to confession

> Priest – Lena – (or clergyman) Go to confession – I'm in mortal sin

> Lena gets conscience – her letter – ~~planning of death~~ – wickedness – I want to make what reparation I can

> Girl and R[oman] C[atholic] church – P sees her

Taken at the Flood is another novel for which quite a few intriguing ideas were rejected:

> Lena in London – D. telephones her – goes to station – sees station master – Swings out of express as it leaves – returns to White Hart though window – Knifes E.A. – leaves as clue something he has already missed (lighter?) – goes to call box
>   L. telephones Anne 9.18
>   D.   "   "   " (London wants you)

Here we see the set-up of the faked telephone call that establishes Hunter's alibi. But he doesn't knife 'E.A.' (Enoch Arden) as he finds him already dead from a head wound when he gets there. For much of the notes, meanwhile, Rowley is the villain:

> Rowley arranges L's suicide (in London) has to go to see a bull etc
> Does Rowley play the part of Underhay in London – with Lena

While he is not indictable at the end of the novel, Rowley does have two deaths on his conscience. But his playing the part of Underhay in London could be seen as a complication too far. Another suggestion was that Rowley and Frances should work together:

> Rowley – jealous of David – has plans – he and Frances agree to blackmail – but Rowley's idea is to inherit – so Lena must die

In fact Rowley and Frances work independently in the novel, although without any idea of killing Rosaleen.

> Possibly button from Lena's dress found by E.A.'s body – or does Rowley take it away. Shot heard as Anne and R and D are approaching house. Suggested that R could have laid timing fuse to cartridge

A timing fuse to fake a gunshot, thereby confusing the time of death, is a plot device in *The Murder at the Vicarage*, but otherwise Christie depended only rarely on mechanical means to achieve her effects (*The Murder of Roger Ackroyd* being a notable exception) and, thankfully, did not start here.

Although it is preceded by a number of rejected ideas – Nathaniel/Jeremy does not resort to blackmail and murder – the last line of the following note does reflect the reality of the novel. Major Porter, a poignant portrait, agrees, through poverty, to perjure himself but later, in a final futile attempt to regain his self-respect, kills himself:

Cover her Face

Nathaniel who has embezzled a lot of trust funds – wife is Rose – 'county' – shrewd – fond of him but knows his weakness – gallant and sticks to sinking ship. Says at last 'Of course I always knew he was a crook' . . . Family all rather crooked – but Rose is straight – (nice!). Enoch is steady character he has come across – conversation in club inspires him to hire Enoch to sound out Lena and levy blackmail. Enoch turns screws on him – he kills Enoch – (a) tries to fasten crime on Lena – or (b) suicide – then goes to Porter – gets him to identify dead man as Underhay Porter desperately poor agrees.

The following, while an interesting plot twist, would have been a difficult one to carry off:

U. is alive – reads inquest – arrives at Doon – sees – Lena – falls in love with her?

It would mean Underhay falling in love with the woman masquerading as his dead wife and, effectively, robbing his fortune.

But the most intriguing of the ideas Christie rejected concern the book's possible title:

Cover her ~~eyes~~ face – mine eyes dazzle – she died young – outburst by David. Why?

Exactly – why? Why would David Hunter have exclaimed these words? The quotation 'Cover her face – mine eyes dazzle – she died young' is from *The Duchess of Malfi*, and concerns the murder of a sister by a brother. Presumably David would have used it upon the death of Rosaleen – his 'sister'? Now we understand why *Cover Her Face* was considered as a title. Or perhaps it was the other way round – Christie saw it as a good title, which it is, and was anxious to work it in? Whatever is the case, echoing, as it does, the critical scene in Chapter 3 of *Sleeping Murder* (see Chapter 7), it can be seen as further confirmation that *Sleeping Murder* was written later than formerly assumed.

The Pale Horse
6 November 1961

And I looked, and behold a Pale Horse,
And his name that sat on him was Death
Revelation 6:8

―――――◄◌►―――――

A list of names is found on the body of a murdered priest
but what do they have in common? Is there such a thing as
murder by suggestion? Are the elderly women in Much
Deeping really practising black magic?

―――――◄◌►―――――

Although written in 1960 and published the following year, *The Pale Horse* had an inspiration from many years earlier. Mr P was a pharmacist who, almost 50 years earlier, instructed Agatha Christie in the preparation and dispensing of drugs. One day he showed her a dark-coloured lump that he took from his pocket, explaining that it was curare and he carried it around

398

with him because it gave him a feeling of power. As she writes in her *Autobiography*: 'He struck me, in spite of his cherubic appearance, as a possibly dangerous man. His memory remained with me so long that it was still there waiting when I first conceived the idea of writing my book *The Pale Horse*.'

One of the strongest titles of the last 15 years of her career, *The Pale Horse* has a horribly plausible plot, a very unusual poison and a genuine feeling of menace over and above the usual whodunit element. At first it seems as if Agatha Christie has changed literary tracks and is writing black magic but, as with many of her titles, what you think you see is not what you get.

Notebook 58 has two pages of Notes on 'Voodoo' just before the notes for *The Pale Horse*. Phrases such as 'Blood Pact – the sacrifice of a pig – snake vertebrae mingled – the asson or sacred rattle – Legba, the God who removes the barrier – Abobo, a ritual exclamation' are all noted. The application of these researches can be seen in Chapter 6 of the novel.

Although thallium – the murder method in *The Pale Horse* – was used many years earlier by her great contemporary Ngaio Marsh in her novel *Final Curtain*, it was Christie's novel that gained notoriety in the UK in June 1972 when Graham Young was convicted of the murder of two workmates and the attempted murder of two more using the same poison. Both the novel and Agatha Christie were mentioned during the trial. Although Young denied having read *The Pale Horse*, an enterprising reporter contacted Christie to get her reaction. She explained that she had used it in the novel as it was unusual and interesting for a detective novelist, being tasteless and odourless as well as difficult to detect.

Although the notes are scattered over five Notebooks, the basic plot was established early on, as were some of the characters. Notebook 38 contains a sketch of the opening pages although the woman is not found dead, but dies shortly after Father Gorman's ministrations. It seems that from the beginning thallium was to be the murder method. And the coffee bar scene, with the important hair-pulling incident, appears in the novel exactly as it does here:

The Thallium Mystery

Start somehow with a list of names e.g.
Sarah Montfort
Anthony West
Mrs. Evershed
Lilian Beckett –
Jaspar Handingly – All of them dead

A woman – hospital nurse – found dead – the place
    ransacked – she says list – all dead

They are all dead
Begins – coffee bar – the girls fight – one pulls out fistful of
    other one's hair
Police? Girl is good sport – says didn't really hurt

The formula – paid agents – women who go round – report
    on medicine bottles etc. – they do several houses in
    neighbourhood – report on the N.H. service

She then worked on the mechanics of the business of the 'death broker' – a good description – as well as some of his potential 'customers'. She did not pursue the thought of using Poirot but settled for her second possibility – 'plain', in other words not part of a series:

Book
Thallium? Series of poisonings going back over years? Hair
    falling out only symptom in common
Poirot?
Plain?
A 'Death Broker' – you pay – the person concerned goes –
    by various natural causes
Idea like killing off jury (or *Ten Little Niggers*?)
No apparent connection – But there is one. What?

The idea of the Murder Syndicate arranged by (?) Osborne –
a strange dual personality – a respectable family – not a bad
lot – leaves home, wild, comes back the Prodigal Son – but
middle class respectability not enough for him – when
Father dies – well off – opens branches in 3 districts run by
his assistants – he is at other ones always – actually has a
second life abroad?

It is not entirely clear if Dr Corrigan, mentioned in the following extract as a possible partner in crime, was to have
been a relation of Ginger's, but Osborne was the villain of the
piece from the start. And the outline below is accurately
reflected in the published novel, although not all of the elements – Dr C is not 'in it' (he is a police surgeon) and
Venables' name is not on the original list – were incorporated and three 'witches' names were to change:

Ideas
(1) Ginger is Ginger Corrigan – Heiress to money?
    (a) Her would-be killer is in Fete party – man's wife
    (b) Doc. C.[orrigan] is in it – he and Osborne? Object
        – to set up big research unit abroad
(2) Osborne – a double life character – father was
    respectable prosperous old fashioned pharmacist –
    other O. ran off as boy – went on stage – impersonator

401

Rough idea of how the racket is worked – The organisation?
Double life – a chemist (shop)

A rich man – crippled – collects silver – his name will be 'on
list' (false) – his niece or nephew will be framed.
Others – 1st Business man – office – or meet in park
  2nd weird sisters – ritual
  3rd employed person to make enquiries as to medicines
  etc. by victims – Consumer research it – replacing of
  some medicament by thallium

Head man Dr. C? Osbourn
False head adam's apple – Mr Vuillaumy [Venables] Rich
  eccentric

Next:
Samuel disbarred lawyer
3 W[eird] Sis[ters]
Thelma French – Sybil White (or Greek name) – Alison Wilde
  – cook – village witch

Does Osborne come to Fete from Bournemouth – ~~accosts~~ –
  comes to Mark – rang up Dr. Corrigan
or police? Saw the man – describes him – scene in chemist's
  shop at Bournemouth

One intriguing possibility for this novel was the introduction
of Miss Marple. This is not as unlikely as may at first seem.
The novel features quite a number of elderly women in a
small village, as well as her old friend from *The Moving Finger*,
Mrs Dane Calthrop, so Miss Marple would have felt quite at
home. Christie toyed with two ideas for involving her, both
very feasible – as a neighbour of one of the victims or as a
great-aunt to Mark Easterbrook:

The Pale Horse Extra notes

Near Miss Marple one of the 'Names' lives
  Is 'Mark' Miss M's great nephew (Raymond's son)
  Three 'weird' sisters – living at the 'Pale Horse' formerly
an inn – inside is picture framed – formerly the Inn Sign at
end Mark (?) cleans it – the rider skeleton appears – Miss M
gives quotation from Revelations
  Thelma Grey is owner of Pale Horse – her family came
from Ireland – witchcraft – her gr-gr-gr-etc. aunt burnt as a
witch (probably all lies somebody says!). She talks about
witchcraft – and what it is

Finally, Notebook 6 has an unexpected jotting:

Pale Horse Play?

Expresso 2 girls – Andrew startled

That's all – nothing more exists. It is difficult to see how the
novel could have transferred successfully to the stage.
Perhaps the discussion on *Macbeth* and its Three Witches
encouraged Christie to consider an adaptation but, practical
difficulties aside, it was not a suitable case for dramatisation.

The Mirror Crack'd from Side to Side
12 November 1962

Out flew the web and floated wide;
The mirror crack'd from side to side
'The curse has come upon me,' cried
The Lady of Shalott.

Tennyson, *The Lady of Shalott*

---◀◎▶---

What was it that film actress Marina Gregg saw in her home, Gossington Hall in St Mary Mead, that caused her to 'freeze', just before a murder was committed there? Further attempts on Marina's life and three more deaths follow before Miss Marple can explain the look of doom.

---◀◎▶---

The Mirror Crack'd from Side to Side is the last of the village murder mysteries. Christie began work on this in late 1961 and by January of the following year was well advanced. But when the manuscript was submitted, in April 1962, there was a spate of concerned correspondence between her agent and publishers and at one stage it was doubtful if the book would be ready in time for the Christmas market. The early mention of German measles in the first draft was considered such a giveaway, although its complete omission was felt to be unfair, that a rewrite was called for. The first person to read it when the manuscript was received at Collins successfully predicted not only the killer but the motive also, long before the first murder was committed. And after its publication the problem rumbled on with the receipt of a letter from an angry American reader bitterly complaining about the motive and its lack of sensitivity to a tragedy in the life of the well-known actress Gene Tierney. Despite a reply from Edmund Cork to the effect that Agatha Christie knew nothing about this until long afterwards, the accusation is still resurrected from time to time.

The first six pages of Notebook 39 contain an embarrassment of riches in the shape of plot ideas. The first page is confidently headed 'Miss M Book' and in the course of the following pages the plot devices of *The Clocks*, *A Caribbean Mystery* and *The Mirror Crack'd from Side to Side* are all sketched, along with echoes of 'The Case of the Caretaker' (where Dr Haydock encourages her to unravel a 'nice' murder) as well as a short idea – the girl and the nasty fall – that appears as a throwaway scene in Chapter 2 of *The Mirror Crack'd from Side to Side*:

> Dr Haydock – getting old – Miss M says can't knit – Dr H suggest unravel – you've always had an interest in murder to say nothing of more than your fair share of it. Proceeds to tell her a story.

> At the Development – a girl looking over a house has a nasty fall – has man with her pushed her

> Dr H's story – Is it story of Clocks – typist – blind woman – dead man

> Miss M with Jenny in West Indies – the frog faced Major – his gossip – glass eye – appears to be looking different direction from what he really is

Eventually she settles on the 'Development Murder' (as it is referred to throughout) as her next novel and gets down to the serious plotting. This is the 71-year-old Agatha Christie still working at full creative stretch at an age when most people have retired:

> Jessica Knight – M asks her to go to chemist? Then she gets up, slips her coat on and goes for walk. The Development – entering a strange country – scraps of talk – near accident? Man and girl – looking at cottage – her fall – Heather Badcock

Notebook 4 has the germ of the idea that is the main plot device of the book:

The Rubella idea – Reason for crime – child has been born
defective owing to one natal infection – while the 'fan' has
grim determination not to miss meeting her idol

And Notebook 8 develops this further with a rough sketch of
the first few chapters:

Development Murder
Chapter I Miss Marple and Development – her walk – when
old place was Protheroes – the Bantry's – young women who
remind her of various people – then a Hilda Glazebrook –
one of those tiresome gushing women. Patience Considine –
Actress and Film star – Hilda's hero worship – bit about
German measles – no ill effects – P's look – as though frozen

The contentious four words ('bit about German measles')
appear very near the beginning of the notes, indicating
Christie's intention of playing dangerously fair with the
reader. In the event she rewrote this and other similar references, and avoided mentioning German measles until very
near the end of the novel.

The bulk of the plotting of this title is in Notebook 52,
although from the ease of the sequence it would seem that
she already knew where she was going with it. Once the setting of Gossington Hall and its new inhabitant was decided,
and the rubella idea established, the book was smoothly
drafted:

Miss M unravelling – Marina Gregg buys Bantrys old house –
Mrs B in lodge

Her husband Arthur Rossiter (?) quiet intelligent man – dark
horse?

Heather Beasly (?) in a 'development' house – Miss M – out walking – falls down – Heather picks her up – cup of tea – talk etc. about Marina Gregg? Story of H. going with measles etc. – Mr Beasley bank clerk? Insurance agent? House agent? School teacher?

Encounter between M[arina] and H[eather] – husband there (Does Mrs B recount all this later to Miss M?)

Some nonsense H said (first mention of G measles?) – Well M answered her – but there was a minute or two – and she said it quite absent-mindedly and as though she was thinking of something else – mechanically – said it so often before – but her eyes staring – over Heather's head – as though she saw something – something terrible – at what?
   Well – staircase
   Who was coming up

The idea of looking over the shoulder and seeing something amazing/frightening/puzzling features in a few Christie novels and in each case she comes up with a credible and completely different situation. The earliest example is in *The Mysterious Affair at Styles,* followed a few years later by another instance in *The Man in the Brown Suit.* Significant other cases in point are included in *Appointment with Death* and *Death Comes as the End.* Two years after *The Mirror Crack'd from Side to Side,* she presents us, and Miss Marple, with a similar puzzle when Major Palgrave sees something disturbing over Miss Marple's shoulder in *A Caribbean Mystery.* The answer to that riddle is her most daring and original solution to the over-the-shoulder theme and may, indeed, have been inspired by the reference to Nelson in the extract below.

A minor point about *The Mirror Crack'd from Side to Side* is the fact that Mrs Bantry relates all of the dramatic events of the reception back to Miss Marple. Why did Christie not arrange, under some pretext, that Miss Marple attend the party herself? This could have been easily set up and would have overcome the necessity to construe Marina's actions as filtered through a third, and sometimes fourth, person. But perhaps this is the very reason that she did not. Miss Marple would have seen too much and too easily. As it is, the jogging of the arm and the dropping of the sleeping draught into the glass is glossed over, although in reality it would have been difficult to stage-manage. This is also one of the few examples of the use of a fictitious poison in a proprietary medicine.

For the most part the people Christie originally listed (or versions thereof) appear in the finished book:

Now People
Kathleen Leila Carlyn [Margot Bence] – adopted child from
slum family – mother wrote letter – then her own [Marina's]
child comes – she makes settlement on adopted children –
girl and 2 boys –
      Does Lara come to board with Cherry – (a pal her sister
has picked up) or working somewhere as hairdresser or as a
photographer (best?)
      Ella Schwarz [Zeilinsky] – social secretary – in love with
Jason
      Heather's husband Arthur
      Mary Bates –a widow – husband dead in a rather peculiar
way (car accident?)
      Carlton Burrowes – surprise guest – used to know Marina

Who were on stairs or coming up?
      Ms Sage – just over his head – frozen stare – at what – or
whom?
A. Picture on wall – subject? Death of Nelson!!

B. Carlton Burrowes – Alfred Klein – one a friend
C. The other brought by him
D. A photographer girl from Homes and Gardens
E. Ella Schwarz
F. Arthur Badcock
G. Mary Baine
H. Very elderly man

Another unfortunate, and utterly unbelievable, coincidence is presented in this novel. Even the most devoted Christie fan cannot accept that Arthur Badcock, who is portrayed and perceived as a dull and insignificant man, was once the husband of famous, glamorous Marina. In Chapter 8 iii he is described as looking like 'a piece of chewed string. Nice but wet.' True, Marina's first marriage, 'an early one which didn't count', is mentioned in Chapter 3, but to accept that he happens to live in the small village where she happens to buy a house, that neither of them mention it and that no one else is aware of it, is expecting too much of the reader's indulgence. Why this complication was introduced at all is difficult to explain. Christie knew her readers better than to ask them to accept that this implausible revelation would form a part of the solution and so, as Arthur is only briefly, and never convincingly, considered as a possible murderer it would seem a complication too far. For sheer unbelieveability this coincidence ranks with the revelation of Miranda's parentage in *Hallowe'en Party*, the identity of Louise Leidner's first husband in *Murder in Mesopotamia* and that of Stodart-West's mother in *Four-Fifty from Paddington*.

She recovers herself – usual charm to Heather – Dormil –
uses it on her – H. puts it down (to talk) M. puts hers down
– to stretch out both hands turning round – knocks H's
drink – have mine – tomato juice instead

The 'Homes and Gardens' photographer, Margot Bence,
carries echoes of the adopted children in *Ordeal by Innocence*
from four years earlier. And the widow Mary Bates (subsequently listed as Baine) does not figure in the story; Carlton
Burrowes may be an early version of Ardwyck Fenn.

The biggest surprise is the inclusion in the above list of
the 'Death of Nelson' (complete with double exclamation
marks) as the subject of the all-important picture on the
stairs. In the novel it is the Madonna and Child motif of the
painting that causes both Marina to 'freeze' and Miss
Marple's theory to be vindicated. Is it possible that at this
stage in the planning Christie had not decided on the
reason for the look of doom? Unlikely as it might appear,
this would seem to be the case, as some of the other options
for the 'frozen' stare are listed and eventually included in
the novel.

And, finally, Miss Marple explains . . .

Miss M says – I've been very stupid – medical book – shuts it

The Meeting – Miss M wants to stand on stairs – the light –
'I understand better now'
      She took an overdose? Very easy to do – or perhaps
someone gave it to her
      To Dermot – Very simple Doom has come upon me cried
was Heather – doom came on her as a direct result of what
she once did – many years ago – meaning no harm but
lacking consideration – thinking only of what an action
meant to her. She did because she went to an Entertainment

to see and meet Marina Gregg at a time when she was
suffering from German measles

Endless Night
30 October 1967

Every Night and every Morn
Some to Misery are born
Every Morn and every Night
Some are born to Sweet Delight,
Some are born to Sweet Delight,
Some are born to Endless Night.

Blake, *'Auguries of Innocence'*

────────────◄○►────────────

Penniless Michael Rogers woos and marries Ellie, an enor-
mously wealthy American heiress. They build a dream
house in the country but their blissful existence is ruined
by a spate of unpleasant incidents. A fatal accident follows
and a monstrous plot is gradually revealed.

────────────◄○►────────────

The Collins reader, in a report dated 23 May 1967, found
Endless Night 'prodigiously exciting to read. The atmosphere
is doom-laden from the beginning and all the minor tricks
and ornaments are contrived to heighten the effect.' Phrases
such as 'dazzling sleight-of-hand', 'handled with great assurance' and 'Mrs. Christie has, as always, been very clever' are
scattered through the report.

In an interview for *The Times* in the month following publication Christie admitted, 'it's rather different from anything
I've done before – more serious, a tragedy really. In some

families one child seems born to go wrong . . . Usually I spend three or four months on a book but I wrote *Endless Night* in six weeks. If you can write fairly quickly the result can often be more spontaneous. Being Mike wasn't difficult.' She began drafting in America in late 1966 when she accompanied Sir Max, who was on a lecture tour.

Endless Night is Agatha Christie's final triumph. It was the last great novel that she was to write and is the greatest achievement of her last 20 years. It is also an astonishing book to have appeared from a 75-year-old writer at the end of a long and illustrious career. It is astonishing for a few reasons: it is written by an elderly upper middle class woman in the voice of a young working class male; it recycles her most famous trick 40 years after she originated it; it is totally unlike anything else she ever wrote; and finally, it is a return to the multiple death scenarios of *Ten Little Niggers* and *Death Comes as the End*. By the end of the novel all the main protagonists are dead – Ellie, Greta, Mrs Lee, Santonix, Claudia Hardcastle; and Michael is behind bars, at best, for life.

The plot is an amalgam of at least four earlier plot ideas.

First, with a narrator – Michael Rogers – as the villain of the piece, comparisons with *The Murder of Roger Ackroyd* are inevitable. It should be remembered that even before this, Agatha Christie had experimented with the narrator-murderer device in 1924 in *The Man in the Brown Suit*. There, Sir Eustace Pedlar narrates part of the novel through extracts from his diaries, before his eventual unmasking as the villain. The ploy came to fruition in 1926 with *The Murder of Roger Ackroyd*, a village murder mystery narrated by the local doctor, who is unmasked by Poirot as a blackmailer and a murderer. Forty years later she added another twist to it with *Endless Night*.

While *The Murder of Roger Ackroyd* is a whodunit, however, *Endless Night* is most decidedly not. For much of its length it seems to be merely a novel with menacing undertones, and only at its conclusion is it perceived as a carefully plotted crime novel. It is thus utterly unlike anything that Agatha Christie had written before and so, a repetition of the Ackroyd trick was not a possibility that anyone considered. This makes its impact all the more impressive. Nobody expected her to repeat her dazzling trick of 40 years earlier. But it should be remembered that Agatha Christie made a career out of doing what nobody expected.

Second, *Endless Night*'s plot set-up is identical to *Death on the Nile*. Two lovers collude to install a charming villain into the life of a wealthy heiress; the plan is to marry and subsequently kill her. The lovers fake a serious argument and are, to all appearances, at daggers drawn. Although the mechanics of the murder in each case are totally different, the similarities are too obvious to ignore and unlikely to be mere coincidence. In *Endless Night* there is also an unexpected development when Michael begins to harbour unexpected feelings for the ill-fated Ellie.

Oddly, although the Collins reader's report when Christie first submitted *Endless Night* was enthusiastic – finding that 'the difficult gimmick is fairly played', and 'the murder is pretty ingenious' – his fear was that the critics would maul it. This mauling would presumably result from its sheer unexpectedness. In the event he was completely wrong as it received some of the best reviews that Christie had ever received: 'one of the best things Mrs Christie has ever done' (*Sunday Times*); 'Christie at topmost peak' (*Evening Standard*); 'Wickedly ingenious murder mystery' (*Scotsman*); 'the most devastating [surprise] that this surpriseful author has ever brought off' (*Guardian*).

Third, its greatest, and most obvious, similarity is to the Marple short story 'The Case of the Caretaker', first published in January 1942. There we have a wealthy heiress, Louise Laxton, marrying the local ne'er-do-well and being murdered in exactly the same way as Ellie Rogers. (There are two versions of this short story – the second, unpublished version is slightly more elaborate.) In many ways, *Endless Night* is an expanded form of 'The Case of the Caretaker', but told in such a way as to make it a new story.

Fourth, *The Mysterious Affair at Styles* also features a collusive couple who stage a very public argument, thereby convincing listeners, and readers, that they hate each other. They, like their counterparts in *Endless Night*, have doctored the victim's existing medication, allowing both of them to be absent at the time of the crime.

The earliest note below dates from 1961 and appears in a list of ideas that includes *A Caribbean Mystery*, *The Mirror Crack'd from Side to Side* and *The Clocks*:

Husband – wants to marry rich wife – get rid of her – employs someone to threaten her – grudge – he intercepts sweets – etc. saves her life several times – her death in the end comes through fear – running from a 'ghost' – she falls

Although there are strong hints in this jotting of *A Caribbean Mystery* ('saves her life several times'), the idea of marrying a rich wife and employing someone to threaten her is the basis of *Endless Night*.

The following year it is listed with her proposed titles for 1963 and 1964, after *The Mirror Crack'd from Side to Side* had been delivered to Collins. There is no mention yet of the eventual title and the references to it throughout the notes are always as 'Gypsy's Acre', the scene of the legend that seems, from the dedication, to have provided the germ of the book. Nor is there any indication at this early stage of the method of telling – one of the main features of the novel. Note also that 'Gypsy's Acre' is listed as X – an indication, perhaps, that she intended to work on this before the other two, which are listed as Y and Z.

1962
Notes for 3 books
Y. The Clocks (?)
Z. Carribean [sic] Mystery
X. Gypsy's Acre

X Gypsy's Acre
Piece of land and road – tea at pub – story about accidents there – husband plans to kill wife – faked motor accident?

Two years before publication we find a further elaboration. And, indeed, much of this early jotting finds its way into the novel. The gypsy, the story, the horse, the 'accident' and the death are all utilised in *Endless Night*.

The dedication of *Endless Night* is 'To Nora Prichard from whom I first heard the legend of Gypsy's Acre'. Nora Prichard was Mathew Prichard's other grandmother – his father's mother. She lived in the real location of Gypsy's Acre near Pentre-Meyrich in the Vale of Glamorgan in Wales, where many years earlier a nearby gypsy encampment was cleared and the head gypsy cursed the land. After numerous road accidents subsequently occurred in the vicinity, this possibly apocryphal tale gathered support.

> Oct 1st 1965
> A. Gypsy's Acre
> Place where accidents happen – etc. – A woman seen
> (gypsy?) by husband – asks people – really has heard story
> already – but pretends it is the first time – a bit upset – a
> sceptical young fellow – but therefore more easily upset.
> Wife interested – not nervous – then one day, wife sees gypsy
> figure – and so on – working things up. Does gypsy figure
> catch bridle of horse – (stick pin in). Husband at accident –
> someone sees it from window – she is badly injured – shock
> – dies – really morphine

One definite omission from the novel is the reference to the husband as 'a sceptical young fellow'; this is not a description that could ever apply to Michael Rogers. And of course he is not present at Ellie's 'accident'. Note also that at this stage there is still no mention of the husband as the architect of his wife's death, much less as the narrator of the story.

Notebook 28 adds an important plot device or, to be strictly accurate, borrows it from 'The Case of the Caretaker':

> The Cyanide Murder – capsules – the tranquilliser. Someone
> dies (W) – falls down stairs – thrombosis? – heart? – an
> open window. Body found 2 or 3 hours after death. Y – gives
> friend one of her capsules; Z – dead – a link is apparent
> between Z and W – this leads everyone astray

Originally this idea was to have been a different type of book but, as can be seen from below, the cyanide capsule was instead subsumed into *Endless Night*. The jotting also observes the important medical fact that the body must be either in the open air or not seen by a medical person until some time after death, in order for the potassium cyanide fumes to dissipate.

By October 1966 the novel was taking shape in the form in which we know it. Before she settled on Greta, however, Christie experimented with various other female characters, although it is difficult to see either of them as Ellie Rogers, the heiress to a multi-million pound fortune:

1966 – Oct. – (in U.S.A.) Projects – Gypsy's Acre
Adventurer – Jason – good looking – Australian? American?
His meeting with old Mrs. Lee – the story – Accident Mile
or Claire Holloway – teaches at a Girl's School or College –
her old friend Anne – Marie – Claire – cousin – Jason – or
an au pair girl Sidonie – her brother or Hildegarde – point
is Hildegarde and J – are in it together – contrived accident.
H is a Valkyrie girl. Use Pot. Cyanide idea – capsule

The idea of a good-looking foreigner, Jason, is abandoned for Michael Rogers, a drifter from a working class background. I can only speculate that the 75-year-old Christie felt more comfortable narrating in the voice of a fellow-countryman than in that of a 'foreign adventurer'. And as soon as she adopts a change of name from Hildegarde to Greta we have arrived at the lethal pairing at the heart of the novel. In fact, Greta is compared to a Valkyrie a few times in the course of *Endless Night*.

But some ideas were abandoned and never progressed further than the Notebooks:

Gypsy's Acre – up for sale – auction – talk at pub where
auction is held. Auctioneer a stranger to neighbourhood –
hints round about – it goes for very little – auctioneer
puzzled. Old man tells him You'm foreigner here – accidents
– bad luck on it – Old Mrs. Lee
    'Whoever you're acting for, you've done a bad turn to him
– no credit to him – he'll be dead within the year – (They
have been paid by someone wanting to get it cheap)

AGATHA CHRISTIE'S SECRET NOTEBOOKS

There are a few problems with the minutiae of the plot of *Endless Night*, mainly concerning the characters Claudia Hardcastle and the gypsy, Mrs Lee. First, we are expected to believe that Claudia has visited The Folly in the grounds of Gypsy's Acre, for reasons unspecified, and picked up a poisoned capsule carelessly dropped by Michael and Greta when they are doctoring Ellie's capsules (how many did they make?); she takes the capsule and subsequently dies. At the same time Claudia manages to drop a highly identifiable cigarette lighter. Even for the most indulgent Christie fan, this is completely incredible. If Christie had retained her earlier idea of Ellie giving a capsule to a friend (see above) this would have made the situation credible.

Then, on the day of Ellie's death Greta has planned to meet Claudia to spend the day shopping (Chapter 17). We later discover, almost by accident, that this never happened because relatives of Claudia arrived unexpectedly. In Janet Morgan's 1984 biography she mentions that Collins asked Christie to increase the whodunit element by boosting the part played by one of Ellie's trustees. This may account for the unlikely coincidence of the arrival of Cora on the day of Ellie's death. But it also means that Greta's whereabouts are unaccounted for at the time of the death, although this is not mentioned at any stage.

Also, when is Mrs Lee actually killed? And why does Michael draw attention to her disappearance? We know he has killed her (at the end of Chapter 23), so surely it is in his interest to keep the fact of her death quiet? In fact, when does he actually kill her? Four days after his arrival in New York he receives a letter from Major Phillpot informing him that Mrs Lee's body has been found in the quarry and that she has been 'dead some days'. If Phillpot's letter arrived four days after he arrived, that would suggest that it was posted on the day Michael docked in America, which, in turn, suggests that he murdered Mrs Lee just before he left for America. So where was she between that and her disappearance (Chapter 21)?

What is the explanation of the stone with the note wrapped around it saying 'It was a woman who killed your wife' (Chapter 20)? The supposition is that this is another part of the plot (otherwise why mention it at all?) and yet it seems pointless, as it is never again mentioned. And if it is in fact genuine, does it mean that Greta is after all the woman in the red cloak mentioned by the rosy-faced woman in Chapter 18 and at the inquest in Chapter 19? We have been already told (Chapter 16) that she owns a red cloak.

The answer to most of these difficulties may lie with Collins' insistence on an increase in the whodunit element. An earlier, and significantly different, typescript shows that all of these developments were added, in Christie's own handwriting, at a later stage. In this previous draft Mrs Lee does not die but returns to Market Chadwell having spent some time with another band of gypsies elsewhere in the country; Ellie unwittingly gives Claudia, a fellow hay fever sufferer, a capsule (Christie's original idea) from the poisoned batch before Greta and Michael have replaced them with innocent ones; and all references to the red cloak are also handwritten additions. Four paragraphs from 'Four days after my arrival in New York' to 'It seemed like an impossible coincidence' have been inserted, on a handwritten page, into Chapter 22. Also appearing as a handwritten insertion is the line 'I want

continued overleaf

> more than pushing an old woman over a quarry' towards the end of Chapter 23. I have no doubt that all these amendments were made to accommodate an editor's misguided idea that this novel should be a whodunit. Instead, they introduced loose ends into an already watertight plot. The Queen of Crime should have been left to her own devices – literally.

> Does auctioneer have accident getting home – young man with pince-nez like Ed(ward) Bolan – clever – Hotel built? Or flats – with room service or home for old people –? Or old house used for that – Fleet House – girl at house (Mothercare type) hospital nurse – finds old lady dead – from the home

Eventually, we get to the final and vital idea that was to set *Endless Night* apart from virtually everything else that Agatha Christie wrote. Note that originally she intended the narrator to be an architect intent on building a house, but in the novel the role of Ellie's architect was given to the enigmatic Santonix instead:

> Idea? Told in first person – by an architect
> 'I first heard about Gypsy's Acre from old Simon Barlow'
>   etc. looks at it. The perfect house – meets girl
> What do you want
> I want thirty thousand pounds
> What for?
> To build a house

Without its unreliable narrator this would have been a different, and possibly indifferent, novel. After all, the eternal triangle idea, and two sides of that triangle conspiring to kill

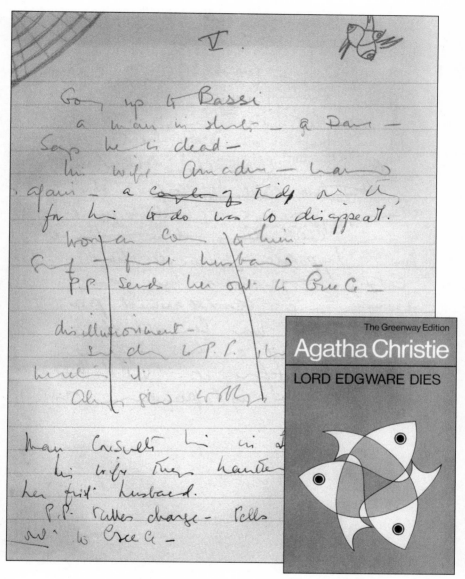

V.

Going up to Bassi
a man in studio — a Dawn —
Says he is dead —
his wife Amadn — man
again — a couple of kids on the
for him to do was to disappear.
woman come to him
first husband —
P.P sends her out to Bruce —

disillusionment —
Say? she to P.P.
bring it
Always plan to try

Man Criswell his wis
his wife They hunter
her first husband.
P.P. takes charge — Tells
out to Bruce —

The Greenway Edition

Agatha Christie

LORD EDGWARE DIES

This page from Notebook 66 is one of many examples in the Notebooks of Agatha doodling the three intertwined fishes, as sketched by Lois Hargreaves in 'The House of Lurking Death' (Partners in Crime). The symbol was subsequently used as the cover design on the Greenway Collected edition of Agatha's books, begun in the late 1960s and published throughout the 1970s.

the third, is new neither to literature in general nor to crime fiction in particular, much less to Agatha Christie. The originality lies in what further trick the writer can weave around it. And just at the end of her career, when everyone assumed that Agatha Christie had played all the tricks she possibly could, she surprised everyone – yet again. If *Endless Night* had been told in the third person much of its devastating impact would have been defused.

APPENDIX

Swan Song – Two Last Stories

THE CAPTURE OF CERBERUS

It has always been a minor mystery to Christie scholars why 'The Capture of Cerberus' did not appear in *The Strand* magazine after the other 11 Labours, as it seemed an inexplicable omission. The discovery of a hitherto unknown and unpublished version of the story, with a completely different setting and plot, may now allow us to solve this puzzle.

In 'The Capture of Cerberus' Poirot once more looks for a missing person, and in this respect his twelfth Labour resembles similar missions in 'The Lernean Hydra' and 'The Girdle of Hyppolita'. But there all similarity ends, as this final task has an unprecedented aspect – his quarry is dead.

Although Collins Crime Club eventually published *The Labours of Hercules* on 8 September 1947, with Christie adding an introductory Foreword to explain the rationale for Poirot's undertaking (see Chapter 11), the twelfth story's non-appearance in *The Strand* remained puzzling. The magazine had always provided a ready market for Christie short stories throughout the 1930s and into the 1940s, with her name emblazoned on the cover as a selling point. Christie herself explicitly mentions this story in the Foreword to the 1953 Penguin edition of *The Labours of Hercules* when she explains that in the writing of the stories, 'over the final *Capture of Cerberus* I gave way completely to despair'. She left it aside for six months and 'then suddenly, one day coming up on the escalator on the Tube the idea came. Thinking excitedly about it, I went up and down on the escalator about eight times.' But, as we shall see, while this may be the truth, it is not the entire truth . . .

When was it written?

Clue No. 1

Labours one to eleven were first published in the UK in *The Strand* magazine beginning in November 1939 ('The Nemean Lion') and culminating in September 1940 ('The Apples of the Hesperides'). On 12 January 1940 Edmund Cork wrote to Christie about the twelfth story, explaining that he thought that *The Strand* would not publish it (at this stage they had already published three of them) and suggesting that she think about writing a replacement for eventual book publication. *The Strand* had already paid £1,200 for the stories as written and if they decided not to publish one of them, as they may have indicated to Edmund Cork, they were not entitled to look for a replacement. On 12 November 1940 (after *The Strand* had appeared without 'Cerberus') she wrote to ask for the return of 'the Cerberus story' in order 'to do a new one'. But it was not until 23 January 1947 (i.e. early in the year of the book's publication) that the second version was finally submitted.

Clue No. 2

Notebook 44 contains most of the notes for all 12 of the stories. At first glance it seems that they were all plotted and finished together, as most of the notes tally with the finished Labours as we know them. But a closer examination, in light of the discovery of the alternative version and this correspondence, shows a potentially different story. The initial notes for the last half-dozen stories all begin, and in some cases finish, on a right-hand page of Notebook 44 with the left-hand page left blank, and follow the sequence of the book. Notes for the first and hitherto unpublished version of 'Cerberus' follow this pattern. But the notes for the collected one are inserted, in different ink and slightly different writing, on a left-hand page, sandwiched, out of sequence, between those for 'The Horses of Diomedes' and 'The Flock Of Geryon'. It is not unreasonable to suppose that, when inspiration for the revamped story struck, Christie went back to her original notes and inserted her new idea as near as she could to the original. Also, the later notes are written in biro, whereas the original notes are, like those for all the other Labours, in pencil.

Why was it never published?

There can be little doubt that the political situation of the time and the poorly disguised picture of Adolf Hitler in section iii was the main (and probably only) reason for the rejection of the story. Unusually for Christie, it is blatantly political from the first page, mentioning not just the impending war but also the previous one: 'The world was in a very disturbed state – every nation alert and tense. At any minute the blow might fall – and Europe once more be plunged in war.' Later in the story we are told about 'August Hertzlein . . . [who] was the dictator of dictators. His warlike utterances had rallied the youth of his country and of allied countries. It was he who had set Central Europe ablaze . . .' And in case there is any lingering doubt he is later described as having 'a bullet head and a little dark moustache'.

This would have been considered much too close to the actual state of the world and one of its inhabitants in 1939 to be considered escapist reading. Why Christie chose to write this story will never be known, as there is little evidence elsewhere in her work that she was particularly political. And the

Cerberus.

Read — blackout for 2 minutes
Has it happened? Ans J. tells P?
Combed the place inside out — Jewels
in the soup? No drugs No drugs
No jewels — but 5 or 6 people
notched wearing them —
    Secret Serv — whole grill moves
out — house next door — Cabinet
Minister etc   we are in the
clear — Juny Mullins — wanted —
Battersea Murderer —   Has given her
place a write up —
    But this time we've got to
succeed —
    P calls to Dog man —
    then rings up Japp.
The fatal evening.
        Is P there?
            or does he hear?

Cerberus -

Pink + Vera Ronaloff -
Says he found "the
people back from the dead."

Dr Hershattz -
Hitler made a marvellous
speech. - I am willing to die -
And falls shot - a boy -
... been each side of him - Saving
him - revolver in hand -
The Boy was my Son.
I want him brought back to life -

Father Lavallois
His consort - He planned to open
a Great Meeting - To propose
International Disarmament -

*. . . to the newly-discovered earlier version included in the Appendix.
Note the difference in handwriting over the almost 10-year period.*

rejection by *The Strand* may have rankled more than she cared to admit as this very assassination scenario is utilized in the 'Good Fat Hen' chapter of *One, Two, Buckle My Shoe*, published the following year while the Countess Vera is fondly recalled by Poirot in the 'Maids Are Courting' chapter of the same novel. The writing of novel and short story would have been contemporaneous.

In an interview for her Italian publishers, Mondadori, conducted soon after the publication of *Passenger to Frankfurt* in 1970, she writes, 'I have never been in the least interested in politics.' So why did she not simply tone down the portrait and change the name? Ironically, Chapter 17 of that novel contains more than a passing reference to the main idea of the short story. Is it possible that, 30 years after it had been rejected, Agatha Christie unearthed her idea and inserted it into a very different book? And that, long after *The Strand* had ceased publication, she had the last laugh?

'The Capture of Cerberus'
(unpublished version) in the Notebooks

There are notes to the unpublished version of the story in Notebooks 44 and 62:

Cerberus
Does Poirot go to look for 2 friends supposedly dead
~~Lenin – Trotsky – Stalin~~
~~George II – Queen Anne –~~
Must go unarmed (like Max Carrados in room story)

Poirot and Vera Rossakoff – says to a friend – 'he brings people back from the dead'
    Dr Hershaltz
    Hitler made a marvellous speech – I am willing to die –

and falls shot – a boy. Two men each side of him – surprise him – revolver in hand. The boy was my son – I want him brought back to life.

Father Lavallois – his convert – he planned to speak – a great meeting – to propose International Disarmament. Dr Karl Hansberg – compiles stastistics – letter of introduction from . . . medical authorities in Berlin – doctor in charge lured away by religion – nurse tries to prevent him. Herr Hitler – hands him a card.

While the similarities to Hitler are quite clear in the story, there is no mention of the actual name – until we read Notebook 62. But the 'hands him a card' at the end is mystifying; and some of the other references are equally mysterious. If, as is almost certain, this was written in 1939 why are Lenin, Trotsky and Stalin listed? Lenin died in 1924 but Trotsky lived until 1940 and Stalin until 1953; and the other two historical figures were long dead. Moreover, none of them could be considered friends. All the names are crossed out in Notebook 44 but their presence at all is inexplicable. The Max Carrados reference is to the detective created by Ernest Bramah and the story 'The Game Played in the Dark'; this character and story had already been pastiched in the Tommy and Tuppence collection *Partners in Crime,* where Tommy emulates the blind detective in the story 'Blindman's Buff'.

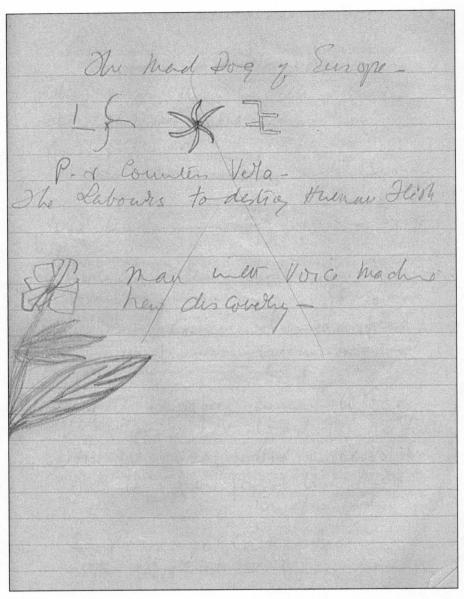

This page from Notebook 62, during the original plotting of 'The Capture of Cerberus' (despite the reference to 'destroy human flesh' and its echo of 'The Horses of Diomedes'), may represent Christie's doodles of a variation on the Swastika.

The Capture of Cerberus
(The Labours of Hercules XII)

i

Hercule Poirot sipped his *apéritif* and looked out across the Lake of Geneva.[1]

He sighed.

He had spent his morning talking to certain diplomatic personages, all in a state of high agitation, and he was tired. For he had been unable to offer them any comfort in their difficulties.

The world was in a very disturbed state – every nation alert and tense. At any minute the blow might fall – and Europe once more be plunged into war.

Hercule Poirot sighed. He remembered 1914 only too well. He had no illusions about war. It settled nothing. The peace it brought in its wake was usually only the peace of exhaustion – not a constructive peace.

He thought sadly to himself:

'If only a man could arise who would set enthusiasm for peace flaming through the world – as men have aroused enthusiasm for victory and conquest by force.'

Then he reflected, with Latin commonsense, that these ideas of his were unprofitable. They accomplished nothing. To arouse enthusiasm was not his gift and never had been.

433

Brains, he thought with his usual lack of modesty, were his speciality. And men with great brains were seldom great leaders or great orators. Possibly because they were too astute to be taken in by themselves.

'Ah well, one must be a philosopher,' said Hercule Poirot to himself. 'The deluge, it has not yet arrived. In the meantime this *apéritif* is good, the sun shines, the Lake is blue, and the orchestra plays not badly. Is that not enough?'

But he felt that it was not. He thought with a sudden smile:

'There is one little thing needed to complete the harmony of the passing moment. A woman. *Une femme du monde – chic*, well-dressed, sympathetic, *spirituelle!*'[2]

There were many beautiful and well-dressed women round him, but to Hercule Poirot they were subtly unsatisfactory. He demanded more ample curves, a richer and more flamboyant appeal.

And even as his eyes roamed in dissatisfaction round the terrace, he saw what he had been hoping to see. A woman at a table nearby, a woman so full of flamboyant form, her luxuriant henna-red hair crowned by a small round of black to which was attached a positive platoon of brilliantly feathered little birds.

The woman turned her head, her eyes rested casually on Poirot, then opened – her vivid scarlet mouth opened too. She rose to her feet, ignoring her companion at the table, and with all the impulsiveness of her Russian nature, she surged towards Hercule Poirot – a galleon in full sail. Her hands were outstretched, her rich voice boomed out.

'Ah, but it is! It *is*! *Mon cher Hercule Poirot*! After how many years – how many years – we will not say how many! It is unlucky.'

Poirot rose to his feet, he bent his head gallantly over the Countess Vera Rossakoff's hand. It is the misfortune of small precise men to hanker after large and flamboyant women.

Poirot had never been able to rid himself of the fatal fascination the Countess had for him. Now, it was true, the Countess was far from young. Her makeup resembled a sunset, her eyelashes dripped with mascara. The original woman underneath the makeup had long been hidden from sight. Nevertheless, to Hercule Poirot, she still represented the sumptuous, the alluring. The bourgeois in him was thrilled by the aristocrat. The old fascination stole over him. He remembered the adroit way in which she had stolen jewellery on the occasion of their first meeting, and the magnificent aplomb with which she had admitted the fact when taxed with it.[3]

He said:

'*Madame, enchanté* –' and sounded as though the phrase were more than a commonplace politeness.

The Countess sat down at his table. She cried:

'You are here in Geneva? Why? To hunt down some wretched criminal? Ah! If so, he has no chance against you – none at all. You are the man who always wins! There is no one like you – no one in the world!'

If Hercule Poirot had been a cat he would have purred. As it was he twirled his moustaches.

'And you, Madame? What is it that you do here?'

She laughed. She said:

'I am not afraid of you. For once I am on the side of the angels! I lead here the most virtuous of existences. I endeavour to amuse myself, but everyone is very dull. Nichevo?'

The man who had been sitting with the Countess at her table had come over and stood hesitating beside them. The countess looked up.

'Bon Dieu!' she exclaimed. 'I forgot you. Let me present you. Herr Doktor Keiserbach – and this – this is the most marvellous man in the world – M. Hercule Poirot.'

The tall man with the brown beard and the keen blue eyes clicked his heels and bowed. He said:

'I have heard of you, M. Poirot.'

Countess Vera overbore Poirot's polite rejoinder. She cried:

'But you cannot possibly know how wonderful he is! He knows everything! He can *do* anything! Murderers hang themselves to save time when they know he is on their track. He is a genius, I tell you. He never fails.'

'No, no, Madame, do not say that.'

'But it is *true*! Do not be modest. It is stupid to be modest.' She turned to the other man. 'I tell you, he can do miracles. He can even bring the dead back to life.'[4]

Something leaped – a startled flash – into the blue eyes behind the glasses. Herr Keiserbach said:

'So?'

Hercule Poirot said:

'Ah, by the way, Madame, how is your son?'

'The beloved angel! So big now – such shoulders – so handsome! He is in America. He builds there – bridges, banks, hotels, department stores, railways – anything the Americans want.'

Poirot looked slightly puzzled. He murmured:

'He is then an engineer, or an architect?'

'What does it matter?' demanded the Countess Rossakoff. 'He is adorable. He is wrapped up in iron girders and things called stresses. The kind of things I have never understood nor cared about. But we adore each other.'[5]

Herr Keiserbach took his leave. He asked of Poirot:

'You are staying here, M. Poirot? Good. Then we may meet again.'

Poirot asked the lady:

'You will have an *apéritif* with me?'

'Yes, yes. We will drink vodka together and be very gay.'

The idea seemed to Hercule Poirot a good one.[6]

ii

It was on the following evening that Dr Keiserbach invited Hercule Poirot to his rooms.

They sipped a fine brandy together and indulged in a little desultory conversation together.

Then Keiserbach said:

'I was interested, M. Poirot, by something that our charming friend said about you yesterday.'

'Yes?'

'She used these words. *He can even bring the dead back to life.*'

Hercule Poirot sat up a little in his chair. His eyebrows rose. He said:

'That interests you?'

'Very much.'

'Why?'

'Because I feel those words may have been an omen.'

Hercule Poirot said sharply:

'Are you asking me to bring the dead to life?'

'Perhaps. What would you say if I did?'

Hercule Poirot shrugged his shoulders. He said:

'After all, death is death, Monsieur.'

'Not always.'

Hercule Poirot's eyes grew sharp and green. He said:

'You want me to bring a person who is dead to life again. A man or a woman?'

'A man.'

'Who is it?'

'You do not appear appalled by the task?'

Poirot smiled faintly. He said:

'You are not mad. You are a sane and reasonable individual. Bringing the dead to life is a phrase susceptible of many meanings. It may be treated figuratively or symbolically.'

The other said:

'In a minute you will understand. To begin with, my name is not Keiserbach. I adopted that name so that I should pass unnoticed. My own name is too well-known. That is, it has been too well-known for the last month.

'Lutzmann.'

He spoke it significantly. His eyes searched Poirot closely. Poirot said sharply:

'Lutzmann?' He paused and then said in a different tone. 'Hans Lutzmann?'

The other man said in a hard dry voice:

'*Hans Lutzmann was my son . . .*'

iii

If, a month previously, you had asked any Englishman who was responsible for the general condition of European unrest, the reply would almost inevitably have been 'Hertzlein'.

There was, it was true, also Bondolini,[7] but it was upon August Hertzlein that popular imagination fastened. He was the dictator of dictators. His warlike utterances had rallied the youth of his own country and of allied countries. It was he who had set central Europe ablaze and kept it ablaze.

On the occasion of his public speeches he was able to set huge crowds rocking with frenzied enthusiasm. His high strangely tuned voice had a power all its own.

People in the know explained learnedly how Hertzlein was not really the supreme power in the Central Empires. They mentioned other names – Golstamm, Von Emmen. These, they said were the executive brains. Hertzlein was only the figurehead. Nevertheless it continued to be Hertzlein who loomed in the public eye.

Hopeful rumours went about. Hertzlein had an incurable cancer. He could not live longer than six months. Hertzlein had valvular disease of the heart. He might drop down dead any day. Hertzlein had had one stroke already and might have another any moment. Hertzlein after violently persecuting the Catholic Church had been converted by the famous Bavarian monk, Father Ludwig. He would shortly enter a monastery. Hertzlein had fallen in love with a Russian Jewess, the wife of a doctor. He was going to leave the Central Empires and settle down with her in Sweden.

And in spite of all the rumours, Hertzlein neither had a stroke, nor died of cancer, nor went into a monastery, nor eloped with a Russian Jewess. He continued to make rousing speeches amidst scenes of the greatest enthusiasm and at judicious intervals he added various territories to the Central Empires. And daily the shadow of war grew darker over Europe.

Desperately people repeated all the hopeful rumours even more hopefully. Or demanded fiercely:

'Why doesn't someone assassinate him? If only he were out of the way . . .'

There came a peaceful week when Hertzlein made no public utterances and when hopes of each of the separate rumours increased tenfold.

And then, on a fateful Thursday, Herr Hertzlein addressed a monster meeting of the Brothers of Youth.

People said afterwards that his face was drawn and strained, that even his voice held a different note, that there was about him a prescience of what was to come – but there are always people who say such things afterwards.

The speech began much as usual. Salvation would come through sacrifice and through the force of arms. Men must die for their country – if not they were unworthy to live for it. The democratic nations were afraid of war – cowardly – unworthy to survive. Let them go – be swept away – by the glorious force of the Young. Fight – fight and again fight – for Victory, and to inherit the earth.

Hertzlein, in his enthusiasm stepped out from behind his bulletproof shelter. Immediately a shot rang out – and the great dictator fell, a bullet through his head.

In the third rank of the listening people, a young man was literally torn to pieces by the mob, the smoking pistol still grasped in his hand. That young man was a student named Hans Lutzmann.

For a few days the hopes of the democratic world rose high. The Dictator was dead. Now perhaps, the reign of peace would come. That hope died almost immediately. For the dead man became a symbol, a martyr, a Saint. Those moderates whom he had failed to sway living, he swayed dead. A great wave of warlike enthusiasm swept over the Central Empires. Their Leader had been killed – but his dead spirit should lead them on. The Central Empires should dominate the world – and sweep away democracy.

With dismay, the peace lovers realised that Hertzlein's death had accomplished nothing. Rather it had hastened the evil day. Lutzmann's act had accomplished less than nothing.

iv

The dry middle-aged voice said:

'*Hans Lutzmann was my son.*'

Poirot said:

'I do not yet understand you. Your son killed Hertzlein –'

He stopped. The other was slowly shaking his head. He said:

'My son did *not* kill Hertzlein. He and I did not think alike. I tell you he loved that man. He worshipped him. He believed in him. He would never have drawn a pistol against him. He was a Nazi[8] through and through – in all his young enthusiasm.'

'Then if not – who did?'
The elder Lutzmann said:
'That is what I want you to find out.'
Hercule Poirot said:
'You have an idea . . .'
Lutzmann said hoarsely:
'I may be wrong.'
Hercule Poirot said steadily:
'Tell me what you think.'
Keiserbach leaned forward.

v

Dr Otto Schultz readjusted his tortoiseshell rimmed glasses.
His thin face beamed with scientific enthusiasm. He said in
pleasant nasal accents:
'I guess, Mr Poirot, that with what you've told me I'll be
able to go right ahead.'
'You have the schedule?'
'Why, certainly, I shall work to it very carefully. As I see it,
perfect timing is essential to the success of your plan.'
Hercule Poirot bestowed a glance of approval. He said:
'Order and method. That is the pleasure of dealing with a
scientific mind.'
Dr Schultz said:
'You can count on me,' and wringing him warmly by the
hand he went out.

vi

George, Poirot's invaluable manservant, came softly in.
He inquired in a low deferential voice:
'Will there be any more gentlemen coming, sir?'
'No, Georges, that was the last of them.'

Hercule Poirot looked tired. He had been very busy since he had returned from Bavaria the week before. He leaned back in his chair and shaded his eyes with his hand. He said:

'When all this is over, I shall go for a long rest.'

'Yes, sir. I think it would be advisable, sir.'

Poirot murmured:

'The Last Labour of Hercules.' Do you know, Georges, what that was?'

'I couldn't say, I'm sure, sir. I don't vote Labour myself.'

Poirot said:

'Those young men that you have seen here today – I have sent them on a special mission – they have gone to the place of departed spirits. In this Labour there can be no force employed. All must be done by guile.'

'They seemed very competent looking gentlemen, if I may say so, sir.'

Hercule Poirot said:

'I chose them very carefully.'

He sighed and shook his head. He said:

'The world is very sick.'

George said:

'It looks like war whichever way you turn. Everybody's very depressed sir. And as for trade it's just awful. We can't go on like this.'

Hercule Poirot murmured:

'We sit in the Twilight of the Gods.'

vii

Dr Schultz paused before a property surrounded by a high wall. It was situated about eight miles from Strasbourg.

He rang the gate bell. In the distance he heard the deep baying of a dog and the rattle of a chain.

The gate-keeper appeared and Dr Otto Schultz presented his card.

'I wish to see the Herr Doktor Weingartner.'

'Alas, Monsieur, the doctor has been called away only an hour ago by telegram.'

Schultz frowned.

'Can I then see his second in command?'

'Dr Neumann? But certainly.'

Dr Neumann was a pleasant-faced young man, with an ingenuous open countenance.

Dr Schultz produced his credentials – a letter of introduction from one of the leading alienists in Berlin. He himself, he explained, was the author of a publication dealing with certain aspects of lunacy and mental degeneracy.

The other's face lighted up and he replied that he knew Dr Schultz's publications and was very much interested in his theories. What a regrettable thing that Dr Weingartner should be absent!

The two men began to talk shop, comparing conditions in America and Europe and finally becoming technical. They discussed individual patients. Schultz recounted some recent results of a new treatment for paranoia.

He said with a laugh:

'By that means we have cured three Hertzleins, four Bondolinis, five President Roosevelts and seven Supreme Deities.'

Neumann laughed.

Presently the two men went upstairs and visited the wards. It was a small mental home for private patients. There were only about twelve occupants.

Schultz said:

'You understand I'm principally interested in your paranoiac cases. I believe you have a case admitted quite recently which has some peculiarly interesting features.'

viii

Poirot looked from the telegram lying on his desk to the face of his visitor.

The telegram consisted simply of an address. Villa Eugenie Strasbourg. It was followed by the words 'Beware of the Dog'.

The visitor was an odoriferous gentleman of middle-age with a red and swollen nose, an unshaven chin and a deep husky voice which seemed to rise from his unprepossessing looking boots.[9]

He said hoarsely:

'You can trust me, guv'nor. Do anything with dogs, I can.'

'So I have been told. It will be necessary for you to travel to France – to Alsace.'

Mr Higgs looked interested.

'That where them Alsatian dogs come from? Never been out of England I 'aven't. England's good enough for me, that's what I say.'

Poirot said:

'You will need a passport.'

He produced a form.

'Now fill this up. I will assist you.'

They went laboriously through it. Mr Higgs said:

'I had my photo took, as you said. Not that I liked the idea of that much – might be dangerous in my profession.'

Mr Higgs' profession was that of a dog stealer, but that fact was glossed over in the conversation.

'Your photograph,' said Poirot, 'will be signed on the back by a magistrate, a clergyman, or a public official who will vouch for you as being a proper person to have a passport.'

A grin overspread Mr Higgs' face.

'That's rare, that is,' he said. 'That's rare. A beak saying as I'm a fit and proper person to have a passport.'

Hercule Poirot said:

'In desperate times, one must use desperate means!'

'Meaning me?' said Mr Higgs.

'You and your colleague.'

They started for France two days later. Poirot, Mr Higgs, and a slim young man, in a checked suit and a bright pink shirt, who was a highly successful cat burglar.

ix

It was not Hercule Poirot's custom to indulge in activities in his proper person, but for once he broke through his rule. It was past one in the morning when, shivering slightly in spite of his overcoat, he was laboriously hoisted to the top of a wall by the help of his two assistants.

Mr Higgs prepared to drop from the wall into the grounds inside. There was a violent baying of a dog and suddenly an enormous creature rushed out from under the trees.[10]

Hercule Poirot ejaculated:

'*Mon Dieu*, but it is a monster! Are you sure –?'

Mr Higgs patted his pocket with complete assurance.

'Don't you worry, guv'nor. What I've got here is the right stuff. Any dog'll follow me to hell for it.'

'In this case,' murmured Hercule Poirot, 'he has to follow you out of hell.'

'Same thing,' said Mr Higgs, and dropped off the wall into the garden.

They heard his voice.

'Here you are, Fido. Have a sniff of this . . . That's right. You come along of me . . .'

His voice died away into the night. The garden was dark and peaceful. The slim young man assisted Poirot down from the wall.[11] They came to the house. Poirot said:

'That is the window there, the second to the left.'

The young man nodded. He examined the wall first,

smiled in satisfaction over a convenient pipe, and then easily and seemingly without effort he disappeared up the wall. Presently, very faintly, Poirot heard the sound of a file being used on the barred window.

Time passed. Then something dropped at Poirot's feet. It was the end of a silk ladder. Someone was coming down the ladder. A short man with a bullet head and a little dark moustache.

He came down slowly and clumsily. At last he reached the ground. Hercule Poirot stepped forward into the moonlight.

He said politely:

'*Herr Hertzlein, I presume.*'

x

Hertzlein said:

'How did you find me?'

They were in the compartment of a second class sleeper bound for Paris.

Poirot, as was his fashion, answered the question meticulously.

He said:

'At Geneva, I became acquainted with a gentleman called Lutzmann. It was his son who was supposed to have fired the shot that killed you and as a result young Lutzmann was torn to death by the crowd. His father, however, was firmly convinced that his son had never fired that shot. It seemed therefore as though Herr Hertzlein had been shot by one of the two men who were on either side of Lutzmann and that the pistol was forced into his hand and those two men had fallen upon him at once crying out that he was the murderer. But there was another point. Lutzmann assured me that in these mass meetings the front ranks were always packed with ardent supporters – that is to say by thoroughly trustworthy persons.

'Now the Central Empire administration is very good. Its organisation is so perfect that it seemed incredible that such a disaster could have occurred. Moreover there were two small but significant points. Hertzlein, at the critical moment, came out from his bulletproof shelter and his voice had sounded different that evening. Appearance is nothing. It would be easy for someone to carry out an impersonation on a public platform – but the subtle intonation of a voice is a thing more difficult to copy. That evening Herr Hertzlein's voice had lacked its usual intoxicating quality. It was hardly noticed because he was shot only a very few minutes after he had started to speak.

'Suppose, then, that it was *not* Herr Hertzlein speaking, and consequently *not* Herr Hertzlein who had been shot? Could there be a theory that would account for those very extraordinary happenings?

'I thought that that was possible. Amongst all the various rumours that circulate in a time of stress, there is usually a foundation of truth beneath at least one of them. Supposing that that rumour was true that declared that Hertzlein had lately fallen under the influence of that fervent preacher, Father Ludwig.'

Poirot went on, speaking slowly:

'I thought it possible, Excellency, that you, a man of ideals, a visionary, might have come suddenly to realise that a new vista, a vista of peace and brotherhood, was open to humanity, and that you were the man to set their feet upon that path.'

Hertzlein nodded violently. He said in his soft husky thrilling voice:

'You are right. The scales fell from my eyes. Father Ludwig was the appointed means to show me my true destiny. Peace! Peace is what the world wants. We must lead youth forward to live in brotherhood. The youth of the world must join together, to plan a great campaign, a campaign of peace. And

447

I shall lead them! *I* am the means appointed by God to give peace to the world!'

The compelling voice ceased. Hercule Poirot nodded to himself, registering with interest his own aroused emotion.

He went on drily:

'Unfortunately, Excellency, this vast project of yours did not please certain executive authorities in the Central Empires. On the contrary it filled them with dismay.'

'Because they knew that where I led, the people would follow.'

'Exactly. So they kidnapped you without more ado. But they were then in a dilemma. If they gave out that you were dead, awkward questions might arise. Too many people would be in the secret. And also, with you dead, the warlike emotions you had aroused might die with you. They hit instead upon a spectacular end. A man was prevailed upon to represent you at the Monster meeting.'

'Perhaps Schwartz. He took my place sometimes in public processions.'

'Possibly. He himself had no idea of the end planned for him. He thought only that he was to read a speech because you yourself were ill. He was instructed at a given moment to step out from the bulletproof shelter – to show how completely he trusted his people. He never suspected any danger. But the two storm troopers had their orders. One of them shot him and the two of them fell on the young man standing between them and cried out that it was his hand that had fired the shot. They knew their crowd psychology.

'The result was as they had hoped. A frenzy of national patriotism and a rigid adherence to the programme of force by arms!'

Hertzlein said:

'But you still do not tell me how you found me?'

448

Hercule Poirot smiled.

'That was easy – for a person, that is, of my mental capacity! Granted that they had not killed you (and I did not think that they could kill you. Someday you might be useful to them alive, especially if they could prevail upon you to readopt your former views). Where could they take you? Out of the Central Empires – but not too far – and there was only one place where you could be safely hidden – in an asylum or a mental home – the place where a man might declare tirelessly all day and all night that he was Herr Hertzlein and where such a statement would be accepted as quite natural. Paranoics are always convinced that they are great men. In every mental institution there are Napoleons, Hertzleins, Julius Caesars – often many examples of *le bon Dieu* himself!

'I decided that you would most probably be in a small institution in Alsace or Lorraine where German speaking patients would be natural; and probably only one person would be in the secret – the medical director himself.

'To discover where you were I enlisted the services of some five or six *bona fide* medical men. These men obtained letters of introduction from an eminent alienist in Berlin. At each institution they visited the director was, by a curious coincidence, called away by telegram about an hour before the visitor's arrival. One of my agents, an intelligent young American doctor, was allotted the Villa Eugenie and when visiting the paranoic patients he had little difficulty in recognising the genuine article when he saw you. For the rest, you know it.'

Hertzlein was silent a moment.

Then he said, and his voice held once again that moving and appealing note:

'You have done a greater thing than you know. This is the beginning of peace – peace over Europe – peace in all the world! It is my destiny to lead mankind to Peace and Brotherhood.'

Hercule Poirot said softly:

'Amen to that . . .'

xi

Hercule Poirot sat on the terrace of a hotel at Geneva. A pile of newspapers lay beside him. Their headlines were big and black.

The amazing news had run like wildfire all over the world. HERTZLEIN IS NOT DEAD.

There had been rumours, announcements, counter-announcements – violent denials by the Central Empire Governments.

And then, in the great public square of the capital city, Hertzlein had spoken to a vast mass of people – and there had been no doubt possible. The voice, the magnetism, the power . . . He had played upon them until he had them crying out in a frenzy.

They had gone home shouting their new catchwords.

Peace . . . Love . . . Brotherhood . . . The Young are to save the World.

There was a rustle beside Poirot and the smell of an exotic perfume.

Countess Vera Rossakoff plumped down beside him. She said:

'Is it all real? Can it work?'

'Why not?'

'Can there be such a thing as brotherhood in men's hearts?'

'There can be the belief in it.'

She nodded thoughtfully. She said:

'Yes, I see.'

Then, with a quick gesture she said:

'But they won't let him go on with it. They'll kill him. Really kill him this time.'

Poirot said:

'But his legend – the new legend – will live after him. Death is never an end.'

Vera Rossakoff said:

'Poor Hans Lutzmann.'

'His death was not useless either.'

Vera Rossakoff said:

'You are not afraid of death, I see. I am! I do not want to talk about it. Let us be gay and sit in the sun and drink vodka.'

'Very willingly, Madame. The more so since we have now got hope in our hearts.'

He added:

'I have a present for you, if you will deign to accept it.'

'A present for me? But how charming.'

'Excuse me a moment.'

Hercule Poirot went into the hotel. He came back a few seconds later. He brought with him an enormous dog of singular ugliness.

The Countess clapped her hands.

'What a monster! How adorable! I like everything large – immense! Never have I seen such a big dog! And he is for me?'

'If it pleases you to accept him.'

'I shall adore him.' She snapped her fingers. The large hound laid a trusting muzzle in her hand. 'See, he is as gentle as a lamb with me! He is like the big fierce dogs we had in Russia in my father's house.'

Poirot stood back a little. His head went on one side. Artistically he was pleased. The savage dog, the flamboyant woman – yes, the tableau was perfect.

The Countess inquired:

'What's his name?'

Hercule Poirot replied, with the sigh of one whose labours are completed:

'Call him Cerberus.'

Notes

1. Unlike the collected version, which is set unequivocally in London, the previously unpublished version has, like many other Labours, an international flavour. From the first sentence we are 'abroad' and, for the third time in the Labours, in Switzerland (perhaps significantly a neutral country). Poirot has already visited the country during 'The Arcadian Deer' and 'The Erymanthian Boar'.

2. A most unlikely and almost unique thought for Poirot!

3. This is a reference to the first meeting of Vera Rossakoff and Poirot in 'The Double Clue', published in December 1923, when he unmasked her as a jewel thief. They subsequently met four years later in *The Big Four*.

4. This is a reference to *The Big Four* when Poirot arranges the return to the Countess of the small son she had thought long dead.

5. The passage about the Countess's son is almost word-for-word the same as in the collected version of the story.

6. It seems odd that Poirot would look forward to drinking vodka.

7. Although he sounds like a character from the world of operetta, it is difficult not to think of Mussolini.

8. Despite the unavoidable allegory throughout the story, this is the only unequivocal reference to the Nazis.

9. The dog handler is called Mr Higgs, and described as 'odoriferous' in both versions of the story.

10. Such is the political flavour, the eponymous Hound is almost forgotten and he plays a much smaller role than his counterpart in the collected story.

11. In the course of this story we see a different Poirot, one who longs for the company of a woman, drinks vodka and now climbs over a wall, although this is a feat he has already performed in the course of the eleventh Labour, 'The Apples of the Hesperides'. Indeed, the tracking down and eventual discovery of August Hertzlein is reminiscent of a similar procedure involving the Cellini chalice in that story.

THE INCIDENT OF THE DOG'S BALL

In this story we have a recognisable, and in many ways, a typical Christie setting – a small village, a wealthy old lady and her avaricious relatives. It is immediately apparent, even from the title, that there are strong links to the 1937 novel *Dumb Witness*. She retains the basic situation and it is possible to see the germs of ideas that she expanded – the brief mention of the Pym spiritualists, the all-important accident on the stairs – into larger parts in the novel. But unlike some other occasions when she reused an earlier idea or short story ('The Mystery of the Baghdad Chest' for example), here she gives us a different murderer and explanation.

The plot device of Poirot receiving a plea for help from someone who dies before Poirot can talk to them is one that she had used on a few previous occasions. As early as *The Murder on the Links* (1923) his correspondent is already dead when Poirot arrives in France. Subsequently it is used in 'How Does your Garden Grow?' and 'The Cornish Mystery'.

When was it written?

Of the Poirot and Hastings short stories, all with the exception of 'Double Sin' (September 1928) and 'The Mystery of the Baghdad Chest' (January 1932) were published in

453

1923/24. All the Poirot short stories after 1932 feature Poirot alone. No notes for any of those early stories survive and where Christie refers to them in the Notebooks, it is only as a reminder to herself of the possibility of expanding or reusing them. In many ways 'The Incident of the Dog's Ball' is similar in style, setting and tone to many others dating from the early 1920s and published in *Poirot Investigates* and *Poirot's Early Cases*. But if it was written early in Christie's career, this in turn raises the question of why it would have lain for almost 20 years without appearing in print. It does not appear in her agent's records of work received by them and offered for sale. I hope to show that it dates from later in her career.

In Notebook 30 it is included in a list (illustrated on the jacket of this book) which may help us to establish more accurately its date of composition:

Ideas
A. Dog's Ball
B. Death on the Nile
C. Strychnine absorbed through skin?
D. Double Alibi e.g. A and B murder C but – A is accused of trying to murder B at same time.
E. Figurehead woman. Man back from Africa.
F. Second Gong elaborated
G. Mescaline
H. Illegitimate daughter – apomorphine idea?
Ideas to be incorporated
    Brownie camera idea
    Brooch with AO or OA on it AM. MA

If we apply some of Poirot's own methods we may be able to arrive at a timetable.

Ideas

A. Paris Ball.

B. Death on the Nile.

C. Strychnine absorbed through skin?

D. Double alibi e.g. A & B murder C. but — A is accused of trying to murder B at same time.

E. Fishing woman. Man back from Africa.

F. Second Gong elaborated.

G. Mescaid.

H. Illegitimate daughter. sponsorship idea?

Ideas to be incorporated

Brownie Camera idea.

Brown with A O or O A or it A.M. M.A.

Wife of (Dr. _____?) herself is thief
or murderer etc — makes up
story that someone has written
threatening or poison etc. + words
A.M. seen in glass. She knows this

Clue No. 1

There are a number of immediately recognisable stories here: *Dumb Witness* or 'The Incident of the Dog's Ball' (A), *Death on the Nile* (B), *They Do it with Mirrors* (D) and *Sad Cypress* (H). 'The Second Gong' (F) was first published in June 1932 and both *Dumb Witness* and *Death on the Nile* in 1937, the former in July and the latter in November of that year. So it is reasonable to assume that the list was written between those dates, i.e. after 'The Second Gong' in June 1932 and before *Dumb Witness* in July 1937.

Clue No. 2

Unlike Item F on the list, 'Second Gong elaborated', there is no mention of elaboration in connection with 'Dog's Ball', lending support to the theory that it did not then exist as a short story.

Clue No. 3

In the Christie Archive there are two letters from her agent Edmund Cork. One, dated 26 June 1936, acknowledges receipt of a revised version of *Dumb Witness*; another, dated 29 April 1936, expresses delight at her news that *Death on the Nile* was finished. We now have two new limits – later than June 1932 and before April 1936. Can we do better? I think so.

Clue No. 4

It is not unreasonable to suppose that the writing of *Death on the Nile* and *Dumb Witness*, both of them among her longest books, took over a year, which would bring our latest date back to April 1935. Our new dates are now June 1932 and April 1935. And if we add two items of conjecture to the equation . . .

Clue No. 5
In the change from 'The Incident of the Dog's Ball' to *Dumb Witness*, the setting moves from Little Hemel, in the county of Kent, to Market Basing, Berkshire:

> General Plan P. receives letter – he and H – he writes – then he tears it up – No, we will go – Market Basing – The Lamb

Market Basing is commonly assumed to bear more than a passing resemblance to Wallingford where Agatha Christie lived. She bought her house there in 1934 and this may account for the change of setting for the novel. There is evidence for this in the reference to The Lamb, a Wallingford pub, in Notebook 63. This is, admittedly, conjecture but as Poirot would say, 'It gives one furiously to think, does it not?'

Clue No. 6
Miss Matilda Wheeler writes to Poirot on 12 April, a Wednesday, according to Poirot's exposition: 'Consider the dates, Hastings' (section v). The 12th of April fell on a Wednesday in 1933.

Conclusion?
So we may conclude that 'The Incident of the Dog's Ball' was written, in all likelihood, in 1933.

Why was it never published?

Agatha Christie was now a household name. By the mid-1930s and *Three Act Tragedy* she was selling 10,000 hardbacks in the first year of a new title; she was one of the first writers to appear in paperback; her books had been dramatised and filmed. Why would any magazine not jump at the chance to publish a little gem of a new Poirot story, with its guarantee of increased sales? If it was offered to them . . . Again, we are in the realms of speculation, but I think the reason it never appeared in print is disappointingly mundane: it was never published because she never offered it to her agent. Because, in turn, she decided to turn it into a novel. Consider the evidence:

Clue No. 1

Her production of short stories had decreased from the multiple appearances of earlier years – 27 in 1923 and 34 in 1924 – to a mere half-dozen in 1933 and seven the following year. As she said when she refused to contribute to the Detection Club's collaborative novels, 'the energy to devise a series is much better employed in writing a couple of books'. She may well have thought the same about this short story and decided to turn it into a complete new Poirot book.

Clue No. 2

The Edmund Cork letter referred to above, dated 26 June 1936, acknowledges receipt of a revised version of *Dumb Witness*. This seems to refer to the first four chapters, a domestic English village setting, which were added to help ensure a US serialisation sale (it was serialised in the *Saturday Evening Post* in November/December 1936) and would lend support to the idea that it was an expansion of 'The Incident of the Dog's Ball'. In the novel Hastings begins his first-person narration only at Chapter 5; up to then the story is told in the omniscient third person with the assurance from Hastings, when he begins his narrative, that he did not witness the earlier events personally but that he 'has set them down accurately enough'. And the opening scenes of both the short story and Chapter 5 are, apart from the month of the year, identical.

Clue No. 3

This not-offered-for-sale theory may also account for the major oversight involving the dates within the story. In section i Poirot says 'No, April the 12th is the date [on which the letter was written] assuredly' but in section iv he refers to August as the month when Miss Wheeler wrote the letter. An agent and/or an editor would surely have noticed a mistake of this magnitude, and one so germane to the plot.

Conclusion

In conclusion, it is entirely possible that 'The Incident of the Dog's Ball' was written in 1933 and never offered for publication but, instead, transformed, in 1935/36, into the novel *Dumb Witness*.

'The Incident of the Dog's Ball' in the Notebooks

The story is referred to in two Notebooks, but in Notebook 30 it is mentioned only in passing as Idea A in the list above. In Notebook 66 we find more detail with resemblance to the short story rather than the novel:

Dog's Ball   People

Mrs Grant – typical old lady
Miss Lawson – twittery companion
Mollie Davidson – Niece – earns living in a beauty parlour
Her young man – a ne'er do well
Journalist – Ted Weedon – has been in prison for forgery –
    forged uncle's name in City office –
owing to girl pressing him for money – some actress
James Grant – prim . . . respectable gentleman –
Engaged to hospital nurse – Miss O'Gorman
Ellen
Cook

The niece's name – Mollie Davidson – remains the same, as does her occupation; and that name appears nowhere else in the notes for *Dumb Witness*. The nephew's is amended only slightly to Graham, although that of the victim changes substantially from Mrs Grant to Miss Wheeler. Neither Mollie's young man or James Grant's fiancée features in the short story although Ted Weedon's proclivity for forgery is transferred to Charles Arundell, the rechristened nephew in the novel.

The Incident of the Dogs Ball[1]
(From the notes of Captain Arthur Hastings O.B.E.)

i

I always look back upon the case of Miss Matilda Wheeler with special interest simply because of the curious way it worked itself out – from nothing at all as it were!

I remember that it was a particularly hot airless day in August. I was sitting in my friend Poirot's rooms wishing for the hundredth time that we could be in the country and not in London. The post had just been brought in. I remember the sound of each envelope in turn being opened neatly, as Poirot did everything, by means of a little paper-cutter. Then would come his murmured comment and the letter in question would be allotted to its proper pile. It was an orderly monotonous business.

And then suddenly there came a difference. A longer pause, a letter not read once but twice. A letter that was not docketed in the usual way but which remained in the recipient's hand. I looked across at my friend. The letter now lay on his knee. He was staring thoughtfully across the room.

'Anything of interest, Poirot?' I asked.

'*Cela dépend.* Possibly you would not think so. It is a letter from an old lady, Hastings, and it says nothing – but nothing at all.'

'Very useful,' I commented sarcastically.

'*N'est ce pas*? It is the way of old ladies, that. Round and round the point they go! But see for yourself. I shall be interested to know what you make of it.'

He tossed me the letter. I unfolded it and made a slight grimace. It consisted of four closely written pages in a spiky and shaky handwriting with numerous alterations, erasions, and copious underlining.

'Must I really read it?' I asked plaintively. 'What is it about?'

'It is, as I told you just now, about nothing.'

Hardly encouraged by this remark I embarked unwillingly on my task. I will confess that I did not read it very carefully. The writing was difficult and I was content to take guesses on the context.

The writer seemed to be a Miss Matilda Wheeler of The Laburnums, Little Hemel. After much doubt and indecision, she wrote, she had felt herself emboldened to write to M. Poirot. At some length she went on to state exactly how and where she had heard M. Poirot's name mentioned. The matter was such, she said, that she found it extremely difficult to consult anyone in Little Hemel – and of course there was the possibility that she might be completely mistaken – that she was attaching a most ridiculous significance to perfectly natural incidents. In fact she had chided herself unsparingly for fancifulness, but ever since the incident of the dog's ball she had felt most uneasy. She could only hope to hear from M. Poirot if he did not think the whole thing was a mare's nest. Also, perhaps, he would be so kind as to let her know what his fee would be? The matter, she knew, was very trivial and unimportant, but her health was bad and her nerves not what they had been and worry of this kind was very bad for her, and the more she thought of it, the more she was *convinced* that she was right, though, of course, she would not *dream* of saying anything.[2]

That was more or less the gist of the thing. I put it down with a sigh of exasperation.

'Why can't the woman say what she's talking about? Of all the idiotic letters!'

'*N'est ce pas?* A regrettable failure to employ order and method in the mental process.'

'What do you think she does mean? Not that it matters much. Some upset to her pet dog, I suppose. Anyway, it's not worth taking seriously.'

'You think not, my friend?'

'My dear Poirot, I cannot see why you are so intrigued by this letter.'

'No, you have not seen. The most interesting point in that letter – you have passed it by unnoticed.'

'What is the interesting point?'

'*The date, mon ami.*'

I looked at the heading of the letter again.

'April 12th,' I said slowly.

'*C'est curieux, n'est ce pas?*' Nearly three months ago.'[3]

'I don't suppose it has any significance. She probably meant to put August 12th.'

'No, no, Hastings. Look at the colour of the ink. That letter was written a good time ago. No, April 12th is the date assuredly. But why was it not sent? And if the writer changed her mind about sending it, why did she keep it and send it now?'

He rose.

'*Mon ami* – the day is hot. In London one stifles, is it not so? Then how say you to a little expedition into the country? To be exact, to Little Hemel which is, I see, in the County of Kent.'

I was only too willing and then and there we started off on our visit of exploration.

ii

Little Hemel we found to be a charming village, untouched in the miraculous way that villages can be when they are two miles from a main road. There was a hostelry called The George, and there we had lunch – a bad lunch I regret to say, as is the way at country inns.

An elderly waiter attended to us, a heavy breathing man, and as he brought us two cups of a doubtful fluid called coffee, Poirot started his campaign.

'A house called The Laburnums,' he said. 'You know it? The house of a Miss Wheeler.'

'That's right, sir. Just past the church. You can't miss it. Three Miss Wheelers there were, old-fashioned ladies, born and brought up here. Ah! well, they're all gone now and the house is up for sale.'

He shook his head sadly.

'So the Miss Wheelers are all dead?' said Poirot.

'Yes, sir. Miss Amelia and Miss Caroline twelve years ago and Miss Matilda just a month or two ago. You thinking of buying the house, sir – if I may ask?'

'The idea had occurred to me,' said Poirot mendaciously. 'But I believe it is in a very bad state.'

'It's old-fashioned, sir. Never been modernised as the saying goes. But it's in good condition – roof and drains and all that. Never grudged money on repairs, Miss Wheeler didn't, and the garden was always a picture.'

'She was well off?'

'Oh! very comfortably off indeed, sir. A very well-to-do family.'

'I suppose the house has been left to someone who has no use for it? A niece or nephew or some distant relative?'

'No, sir, she left it to her companion, Miss Lawson. But Miss Lawson doesn't fancy living in it, and so it's up for sale. But it's a bad time for selling houses, they say.'

'Whenever one has to sell anything it is always a bad time,' said Poirot smiling, as he paid the bill and added a handsome tip. 'When exactly did you say Miss Matilda Wheeler died?'

'Just the beginning of May, sir – thank you, sir – or was it the end of April? She'd not been in good health for a long time.'

'You have a good doctor here?'

'Yes, sir, Dr Lawrence. He's getting on now, but he's well thought of down here. Always very pleasant-spoken and careful.'

Poirot nodded and presently we strolled out into the hot August sunshine and made our way along the street in the direction of the church.

Before we got to it, however, we passed an old-fashioned house set a little way back, with a brass plate on the gate inscribed with the name of Dr Lawrence.

'Excellent,' said Poirot. 'We will make a call here. At this hour we shall make sure of finding the doctor at home.'

'My dear Poirot! But what on earth are you going to say? And anyway what are you driving at?'

'For your first question, *mon ami*, the answer is simple – I shall have to invent. Fortunately I have the imagination fertile. For your second question – *eh bien*, after we have conversed with the doctor, it may be that I shall find I am not driving at anything.'

iii

Dr Lawrence proved to be a man of about sixty. I put him down as an unambitious kindly sort of fellow, not particularly brilliant mentally, but quite sound.

Poirot is a past master in the art of mendacity. In five minutes we were all chatting together in the most friendly fashion – it being somehow taken for granted that we were old and dear friends of Miss Matilda Wheeler.

'Her death, it is a great shock to me. Most sad,' said Poirot. 'She had the stroke? No?'

'Oh! no, my dear fellow. Yellow atrophy of the liver. Been coming on for a long time. She had a very bad attack of jaundice a year ago. She was pretty well through the winter except for digestive trouble. Then she had jaundice again the end of April and died of it. A great loss to us – one of the real old-fashioned kind.'

'Ah! yes, indeed,' sighed Poirot. 'And the companion, Miss Lawson – ?'

He paused and rather to our surprise the doctor responded promptly.

'I can guess what you're after, and I don't mind telling you that you've my entire sympathy. But if you're coming to me for any hope of "undue influence" it's no good. Miss Wheeler was perfectly capable of making a will – not only when she did – but right up to the day of her death. It's no good hoping that I can say anything different because I can't.'

'But your sympathy –'

'My sympathy is with James Graham and Miss Mollie. I've always felt strongly that money shouldn't be left away from the family to an outsider. I daresay there might be some sort of case that Miss Lawson obtained an ascendency over Miss Wheeler owing to spiritualistic tomfoolery – but I doubt if there's anything that you could take into court. Only run yourself in for terrific expense. Avoid the law, wherever you can, is my motto. And certainly medically I can't help you. Miss Wheeler's mind was perfectly clear.'

He shook hands with us and we passed out into the sunlight.

'Well!' I said. 'That was rather unexpected!'

'Truly. We begin to learn a little about my correspondent. She has at least two relatives – James Graham and a girl called Mollie. They ought to have inherited her money but did not do so. By a will clearly not made very long ago, the whole amount has gone to the companion, Miss Lawson. There is also a very significant mention of spiritualism.'

'You think that significant?'

'Obviously. A credulous old lady – the spirits tell her to leave her money to a particular person – she obeys. Something of that kind occurs to one as a possibility, does it not?'

iv

We had arrived at The Laburnums. It was a fair sized Georgian house, standing a little way back from the street with a large garden behind. There was a board stuck up with For Sale on it.

Poirot rang the bell. His efforts were rewarded by a fierce barking within. Presently the door was opened by a neat middle-aged woman who held a barking wire-haired terrier by the collar.

'Good afternoon,' said Poirot. 'The house is for sale, I understand, so Mr James Graham told me.'

'Oh! yes, sir. You would like to see over it?'

'If you please.'

'You needn't be afraid of Bob, sir. He barks if anyone comes to the door, but he's as gentle as a lamb really.'

True enough, as soon as we were inside, the terrier jumped up and licked our hands. We were shown over the house – pathetic as an empty house always is, with the marks of pictures showing on the walls, and the bare uncarpeted floors. We found the woman only too ready and willing to talk to friends of the family as she supposed us to be. By his mention of James Graham, Poirot created this impression very cleverly.

Ellen, for such was our guide's name, had clearly been very attached to her late mistress. She entered with the gusto of her class into a description of her illness and death.

'Taken sudden she was. And suffered! Poor dear! Delirious at the end. All sorts of queer things she'd say. How long was it? Well, it must have been three days from the time she was took bad. But poor dear, she'd suffered for many years on and off. Jaundice last year she had – and her food never agreed with her well. She'd take digestion tablets after nearly every meal. Oh! yes, she suffered a good deal one way or another. Sleeplessness for one thing. Used to get up and walk about the house at night, she did, her eyesight being too bad for much reading.'

It was at this point that Poirot produced from his pocket the letter. He held it out to her.

'Do you recognise this by any chance?' he asked.

He was watching her narrowly. She gave an exclamation of surprise.

'Well, now, I do declare! And is it you that's the gentleman it's written to?'

Poirot nodded.

'Tell me how you came to post it to me?' he said.

'Well, sir, I didn't know what to do – and that's the truth. When the furniture was all cleared out, Miss Lawson she gave me several little odds and ends that had been the mistress's. And among them was a mother of pearl blotter that I'd always admired. I put it by in a drawer, and it was only yesterday that I took it out and was putting new blotting paper in it when I found this letter slipped inside the pocket. It was the mistress's handwriting and I saw as she'd meant to post it and slipped it in there and forgot – which was the kind of thing she did many a time, poor dear. Absent-minded as you might say. Well, I didn't know what to do. I didn't like to put it in the fire and I couldn't take it upon myself to open it and I didn't see as it was any business of Miss Lawson's, so I just put a stamp on it and ran out to the post box and posted it.'

Ellen paused for breath and the terrier uttered a sharp staccato bark. It was so peremptory in sound that Poirot's attention was momentarily diverted. He looked down at the dog who was sitting with his nose lifted entreatingly towards the empty mantelpiece of the drawing-room where we were at the time.

'But what is it that he regards so fixedly?' asked Poirot. Ellen laughed.

'It's his ball, sir. It used to be put in a jar on the mantelpiece and he thinks it ought somehow or other to be there still.'

'I see,' said Poirot. 'His ball . . .' He remained thoughtful for a moment or two.

'Tell me,' he said. 'Did your mistress ever mention to you something about the dog and his ball? Something that perturbed her greatly?'

'Now it's odd your saying that, sir. She never said anything about a ball, but I do believe there was something about Bob here that was on her mind – for she tried to say something just as she was dying. "The dog," she said. "The dog –" and then something about a picture ajar – nothing that made sense but there, poor soul, she was delirious and didn't know what she was saying.'

'You will comprehend,' said Poirot, 'that this letter not reaching me when it should have done, I am greatly intrigued about many things and much in the dark. There are several questions that I should wish to ask.'

By this time Ellen would have taken for granted any statement that Poirot had chosen to make. We adjourned to her somewhat overcrowded sitting-room and having pacified Bob by giving him the desired ball which he retired under a table to chew, Poirot began his interrogations.

'First of all,' he said, 'I comprehend that Miss Wheeler's nearest relations were only two in number?'

'That's right, sir. Mr James – Mr James Graham whom

469

you mentioned just now – and Miss Davidson. They were first cousins and niece and nephew to Miss Wheeler. There were five Miss Wheelers, you see, and only two of them married.'

'And Miss Lawson was no relation at all?'

'No, indeed – nothing but a paid companion.'

Scorn was uppermost in Ellen's voice.

'Did you like Miss Lawson, Ellen?'

'Well, sir, she wasn't one you could dislike, so to speak. Neither one thing nor the other, she wasn't, a poor sort of creature, and full of nonsense about spirits. Used to sit in the dark, they did, she and Miss Wheeler and the two Miss Pyms. A sayance, they called it. Why they were at it the very night she was taken bad. And if you ask me, it was that wicked nonsense that made Miss Wheeler leave her money away from her own flesh and blood.'

'When exactly did she make the new will? But perhaps you do not know that.'

'Oh! yes, I do. Sent for the lawyer she did while she was still laid up.'

'Laid up?'

'Yes, sir – from a fall she had. Down the stairs. Bob here had left his ball on top of the stairs and she slipped on it and fell. In the night it was. As I tell you, she used to get up and walk about.'

'Who was in the house at the time?'

'Mr James and Miss Mollie were here for the weekend. Easter it was, and it was the night of Bank Holiday. There was cook and me and Miss Lawson and Mr James and Miss Mollie and what with the fall and the scream we all came out. Cut her head, she did, and strained her back. She had to lie up for nearly a week. Yes, she was still in bed – it was the following Friday – when she sent for Mr Halliday. And the gardener had to come in and witness it, because for some reason I couldn't on account of her having remembered me in it, and cook alone wasn't enough.'

'Bank holiday was the 10th of August,'[4] said Poirot. He looked at me meaningfully. 'Friday would be the 14th. And what next? Did Miss Wheeler get up again?'

'Oh! yes, sir. She got up on the Saturday, and Miss Mollie and Mr James they came down again, being anxious about her, you see. Mr James he even came down the weekend after that.'

'The weekend of the 22nd?'

'Yes, sir.'

'And when was Miss Wheeler finally taken ill?'

'It was the 25th, sir. Mr James had left the day before. And Miss Wheeler seemed as well as she'd ever been – bar her indigestion, of course, but that was chronic. Taken sudden after the sayance, she was. They had a sayance after dinner, you know, so the Miss Pyms went home and Miss Lawson and I got her to bed and sent for Dr Lawrence.'

Poirot sat frowning for a moment or two, then he asked Ellen for the address of Miss Davidson and Mr Graham and also for that of Miss Lawson.

All three proved to be in London. James Graham was junior partner in some chemical dye works,[5] Miss Davidson worked in a beauty parlour in Dover Street. Miss Lawson had taken a flat near High Street, Kensington.

As we left, Bob, the dog, rushed up to the top of the staircase, lay down and carefully nosed his ball over the edge so that it bumped down the stairs. He remained, wagging his tail, until it was thrown up to him again.

'The incident of the dog's ball,' murmured Poirot under his breath.

v

A minute or two later we were out in the sunshine again.

'Well,' I said with a laugh. 'The dog's ball incident did not amount to much after all. We now know exactly what it was. The dog left his ball at the top of the stairs and the old lady tripped over it and fell. So much for that!'

'Yes, Hastings, as you say – the incident is simple enough. What we do not know – and what I should like to know – and what I *mean* to know – is why the old lady was so perturbed by it?'

'Do you think there is anything in that?'

'Consider the dates, Hastings. On Monday night, the fall. On Wednesday the letter written to me. On Friday the altered will. There is something curious there. Something that I should like to know. And ten days afterwards Miss Wheeler dies. If it had been a sudden death, one of these mysterious deaths due to "heart failure" – I confess I should have been suspicious. But her death appears to have been perfectly natural and due to disease of long standing. *Tout de même –*'

He went off into a brown study. Finally he said unexpectedly:

'If you really wished to kill someone, Hastings, how would you set about it?'

'Well – I don't know. I can't imagine myself –'

'One can always imagine. Think, for instance, of a particularly repellent money-lender, of an innocent girl in his clutches.'

'Yes,' I said slowly. 'I suppose one might always see red and knock a fellow out.'

Poirot sighed.

'*Mais oui*, it would be that way with you! But I seek to imagine the mind of someone very different. A cold-blooded but cautious murderer, reasonably intelligent. What would he try first? Well, there is accident. A well staged accident –

that is very difficult for the police to bring home to the perpetrator. But it has its disadvantages – it may disable but not kill. And then, possibly, the victim might be suspicious. Accident cannot be tried again. Suicide? Unless a convenient piece of writing with an ambiguous meaning can be obtained from the victim, suicide would be very uncertain. Then murder – recognised as such. For that you want a scapegoat or an alibi.'

'But Miss Wheeler wasn't murdered. Really, Poirot –'

'I know. I know. *But she died*, Hastings. Do not forget – *she died*. She makes a will – and ten days later she dies. And the only two people in the house with her (for I except the cook) both benefit by her death.'

'I think,' I said, 'that you have a bee in your bonnet.'

'Very possibly. Coincidences do happen. But she wrote to me, *mon ami*, she wrote to me, and until I know what made her write I cannot rest in peace.'

vi

It was about a week later that we had three interviews.

Exactly what Poirot wrote to them I do not know, but Mollie Davidson and James Graham came together by appointment, and certainly displayed no resentment. The letter from Miss Wheeler lay on the table in a conspicuous position. From the conversation that followed, I gathered that Poirot had taken considerable liberties in his account of the subject matter.

'We have come here in answer to your request, but I am sorry to say that I do not understand in the least what you are driving at, M. Poirot,' said Graham with some irritation as he laid down his hat and stick.

He was a tall thin man, looking older than his years, with pinched lips and deep-set grey eyes. Miss Davidson was a handsome fair-haired girl of twenty-nine or so. She seemed puzzled, but unresentful.

'It is that I seek to aid you,' said Poirot. 'Your inheritance it has been wrested from you! It has gone to a stranger!'

'Well, that's over and done with,' said Graham. 'I've taken legal advice and it seems there's nothing to be done. And I really cannot see where it concerns *you*, M. Poirot.'

'I think James, that that is not very fair to M. Poirot,' said Mollie Davidson. 'He is a busy man, but he is going out of his way to help us. I wish he could. All the same, I'm afraid nothing can be done. We simply can't afford to go to law.'

'Can't afford. Can't afford. We haven't got a leg to stand upon,' said her cousin irritably.

'That is where I come in,' said Poirot. 'This letter' – he tapped it with a finger-nail – has suggested a possible idea to me. Your aunt, I understand, had originally made a will leaving her property to be divided between you. Suddenly, on the 14th April she makes another will. Did you know of that will, by the way?'

It was to Graham he put the question.

Graham flushed and hesitated a moment.

'Yes,' he said. 'I knew of it. My aunt told me of it.'

'What?' A cry of astonishment came from the girl.

Poirot wheeled round upon her.

'You did not know of it, Mademoiselle?'

'No, it came as a great shock to me. I thought it did to my cousin also. When did Auntie tell you, James?'

'That next weekend – the one after Easter.'

'And I was there and you never told me?'

'No – I – well, I thought it better to keep it to myself.'

'How extraordinary of you!'

'What exactly did your aunt say to you, Mr Graham?' asked Poirot in his most silky tone.

Graham clearly disliked answering the question. He spoke stiffly.

'She said that she thought it only fair to let me know that she had made a new will leaving everything to Miss Lawson.'

'Did she give any reason?'

'None whatever.'

'I think you ought to have told me,' said Miss Davidson.

'I thought better not,' said her cousin stiffly.

'*Eh bien*,' said Poirot. 'It is all very curious. I am not at liberty to tell you what was written to me in this letter, but I will give you some advice. I would apply, if I were you, for an order of exhumation.'

They both stared at him without speaking for a minute or two.

'Oh! no,' cried Mollie Davidson.

'This is outrageous,' cried Graham. 'I shall certainly not do anything of the sort. The suggestion is preposterous.'

'You refuse?'

'Absolutely.'

Poirot turned to the girl.

'And you, Mademoiselle? Do you refuse?'

'I – No, I would not say I refused. But I do not like the idea.'

'Well, I do refuse,' said Graham angrily. 'Come on, Mollie. We've had enough of this charlatan.'

He fumbled for the door. Poirot sprang forward to help him. As he did so a rubber ball fell out of his pocket and bounced on the floor.

'Ah!' cried Poirot. 'The ball!'

He blushed and appeared uncomfortable. I guessed that he had not meant the ball to be seen.

'Come on, Mollie,' shouted Graham now in a towering passion.

The girl had retrieved the ball and handed it to Poirot.

'I did not know that you kept a dog, M. Poirot,' she said.

'I do not, Mademoiselle,' said Poirot.

The girl followed her cousin out of the room. Poirot turned to me.

'Quick, *mon ami*,' he said. 'Let us visit the companion, the now rich Miss Lawson. I wish to see her before she is in any way put upon her guard.'

'If it wasn't for the fact that James Graham knew about the new will, I should be inclined to suspect him of having a hand in this business. He was down that last weekend. However, since he knew that the old lady's death would not benefit him – well, that puts him out of court.'

'Since he knew –' murmured Poirot thoughtfully.

'Why, yes, he admitted as much,' I said impatiently.

'Mademoiselle was quite surprised at his knowing. Strange that he should not tell her at the time. Unfortunate. Yes, unfortunate.'

Exactly what Poirot was getting at I did not quite know, but knew from his tone that there was something. However, soon after, we arrived at Clanroyden Mansions.

vii

Miss Lawson was very much as I had pictured her. A middle-aged woman, rather stout, with an eager but somewhat foolish face. Her hair was untidy and she wore pince-nez. Her conversation consisted of gasps and was distinctly spasmodic.

'So good of you to come,' she said. 'Sit here, won't you? A cushion. Oh! dear, I'm afraid that chair isn't comfortable. That table's in your way. We're just a little crowded here.' (This was undeniable. There was twice as much furniture in the room as there should have been, and the walls were covered with photographs and pictures.) 'This flat is really too small. But so central. I've always longed to have a little place of my own. But there, I never thought I should. So good of dear Miss Wheeler. Not that I feel at all comfortable about it.

No, indeed I don't. My conscience, M. Poirot. *Is it right?* I ask myself. And really I don't know what to say. Sometimes I think that Miss Wheeler meant me to have the money and so it must be all right. And other times – well, flesh and blood is flesh and blood – I feel very badly when I think of Mollie Davidson. Very badly indeed!'

'And when you think of Mr James Graham?'

Miss Lawson flushed and drew herself up.

'That is very different. Mr Graham has been very rude – most insulting. I can assure you, M. Poirot – there was no undue influence. I had no idea of anything of the kind. A complete shock to me.'

'Miss Wheeler did not tell you of her intentions?'

'No, indeed. A complete shock.'

'You had not, in any way, found it necessary to – shall we say, open the eyes – of Miss Wheeler in regard to her nephew's shortcomings?'

'What an idea, M. Poirot! Certainly not. What put that idea into your head, if I may ask?'

'Mademoiselle, I have many curious ideas in my head.'

Miss Lawson looked at him uncertainly. Her face, I reflected, was really singularly foolish. The way the mouth hung open for instance. And yet the eyes behind the glasses seemed more intelligent than one would have suspected.

Poirot took something from his pocket.

'You recognise this, Mademoiselle?'

'Why, it's Bob's ball!'

'No,' said Poirot. 'It is a ball I bought at Woolworth's.'

'Well, of course, that's where Bob's balls do come from. Dear Bob.'

'You are fond of him?'

'Oh! yes, indeed, dear little doggie. He always slept in my room. I'd like to have him in London, but dogs aren't really happy in town, are they, M. Poirot?'

'Me, I have seen some very happy ones in the Park,' returned my friend gravely.

'Oh! yes, of course, the Park,' said Miss Lawson vaguely. 'But it's very difficult to exercise them properly. He's much happier with Ellen, I feel sure, at the dear Laburnums. Ah! what a tragedy it all was!'

'Will you recount to me, Mademoiselle, just what happened on that evening when Miss Wheeler was taken ill?'

'Nothing out of the usual. At least, oh! of course, we held a séance – with distinct phenomena – distinct phenomena. You will laugh, M. Poirot. I feel you are a sceptic. But oh! the joy of hearing the voices of those who have passed over.'

'No, I do not laugh,' said Poirot gently.

He was watching her flushed excited face.

'You know, it was most curious – really *most* curious. There was a kind of halo – a luminous haze – all round dear Miss Wheeler's head. We all saw it distinctly.'

'A luminous haze?' said Poirot sharply.

'Yes. Really most remarkable. In view of what happened, I felt, M. Poirot, that already she was *marked*, so to speak, for the other world.'

'Yes,' said Poirot. 'I think she was – marked for the other world.' He added, completely incongruously it seemed to me, 'Has Dr Lawrence got a keen sense of smell?'

'Now it's curious you should say that. "Smell this, doctor," I said, and held up a great bunch of lilies of the valley to him. And would you believe it, he couldn't smell a thing. Ever since influenza three years ago, he said. Ah! me – physician, heal thyself is so true, isn't it?'

Poirot had risen and was prowling round the room. He stopped and stared at a picture on the wall. I joined him.

It was rather an ugly needlework picture done in drab wools, and represented a bulldog sitting on the steps of a house. Below it, in crooked letters, were the words '*Out all night and no key!*'[6]

Poirot drew a deep breath.

'This picture, it comes from The Laburnums?'

'Yes. It used to hang over the mantelpiece in the drawing-room. Dear Miss Wheeler did it when she was a girl.'

'Ah!' said Poirot. His voice was entirely changed. It held a note that I knew well.

He crossed to Miss Lawson.

'You remember Bank Holiday? Easter Monday. The night that Miss Wheeler fell down the stairs? *Eh bien,* the little Bob, he was out that night, was he not? He did not come in.'

'Why, yes, M. Poirot, however did you know that? Yes, Bob was very naughty. He was let out at nine o'clock as usual, and he never came back. I didn't tell Miss Wheeler – she would have been anxious. That is to say, I told her the next day, of course. When he was safely back. Five in the morning it was. He came and barked underneath my window and I went down and let him in.'

'So that was it! *Enfin!*' He held out his hand. 'Goodbye, Mademoiselle. Ah! Just one more little point. Miss Wheeler took digestive tablets after meals always, did she not? What make were they?'

'Dr Carlton's After Dinner Tablets. Very efficacious, M. Poirot.'

'Efficacious! *Mon Dieu!*' murmured Poirot, as we left. 'No, do not question me, Hastings. Not yet. There are still one or two little matters to see to.'

He dived into a chemist's and reappeared holding a white wrapped bottle.

vii

He unwrapped it when we got home. It was a bottle of Dr Carlton's After Dinner Tablets.

'You see, Hastings. There are at least fifty tablets in that bottle – perhaps more.'

He went to the bookshelf and pulled out a very large volume. For ten minutes he did not speak, then he looked up and shut the book with a bang.

'But yes, my friend, now you may question. Now I know – everything.'

'She was poisoned?'

'Yes, my friend. Phosphorus poisoning.'

'Phosphorus?'

'Ah! *mais oui* – that is where the diabolical cleverness came in! *Miss Wheeler had already suffered from jaundice. The symptoms of phosphorus poisoning would only look like another attack of the same complaint.* Now listen, very often the symptoms of phosphorus poisoning are delayed from one to six hours. It says here' (he opened the book again) '"*The person's breath may be phosphorescent before he feels in any way affected.*" That is what Miss Lawson saw in the dark – Miss Wheeler's phosphorescent breath – "a luminous haze". And here I will read you again. "*The jaundice having thoroughly pronounced itself, the system may be considered as not only under the influence of the toxic action of phosphorus, but as suffering in addition from all the accidents incidental to the retention of the biliary secretion in the blood, nor is there from this point any special difference between phosphorus poisoning and certain affections of the liver – such, for example as yellow atrophy.*"[7]

'Oh! it was well planned, Hastings! Foreign matches – vermin paste. It is not difficult to get hold of phosphorus, and a very small dose will kill. The medicinal dose is from $1/100$ to $1/30$ grain. Even .116 of a grain has been known to kill. To make a tablet resembling one of these in the bottle – that too would not be too difficult. One can buy a tablet-making machine, and Miss Wheeler she would not observe closely. A tablet placed at the bottom of this bottle – one day, sooner or later, Miss Wheeler will take it, and the person who put it there will have a perfect alibi, for she will not have been near the house for ten days.'

'She?'

'Mollie Davidson. Ah! *mon ami*, you did not see her eyes when that ball bounced from my pocket. The irate M. Graham, it meant nothing to him – but to her. "I did not know you kept a dog, M. Poirot." Why a *dog*? Why not a child? A child, too, plays with balls. But that – it is not evidence, you say. It is only the impression of Hercule Poirot. Yes, but everything fits in. M. Graham is furious at the idea of an exhumation – he shows it. But she is more careful. She is afraid to seem unwilling. And the surprise and indignation she cannot conceal when she learns that her cousin has known of the will all along! He knew – and he did not tell her. Her crime had been in vain. Do you remember my saying it was unfortunate he didn't tell her? Unfortunate for the poor Miss Wheeler. It meant her death sentence and all the good precautions she had taken, such as the will, were in vain.'

'You mean the will – no, I don't see.'

'Why did she make that will? The incident of the dog's ball, *mon ami*.

'Imagine, Hastings, that you wish to cause the death of an old lady. You devise a simple accident. The old lady, before now, has slipped over the dog's ball. She moves about the house in the night. *Bien*, you place the dog's ball on the top of the stairs and perhaps also you place a strong thread or fine string. The old lady trips and goes headlong with a scream. Everyone rushes out. You detach your broken string while everyone else is crowding round the old lady. When they come to look for the cause of the fall, they find – the dog's ball where he so often left it.

'But, Hastings, now we come to something else. Suppose the old lady earlier in the evening after playing with the dog, puts the ball away in its usual place, and the dog goes out –

and stays out. That is what she learns from Miss Lawson on the following day. She realises that *it cannot be the dog who left the ball at the top of the stairs.* She suspects the truth – but she suspects the wrong person. She suspects her nephew, James Graham, whose personality is not of the most charming. What does she do? First she writes to me – to investigate the matter. Then she changes her will *and tells James Graham that she has done so.* She counts on his telling Mollie though it is James she suspects. They will know that her death will bring them nothing! *C'est bien imaginé* for an old lady.

'And that, *mon ami,* was the meaning of her dying words. I comprehend well enough the English to know that it is a *door* that is ajar, not a *picture.* The old lady is trying to tell Ellen of her suspicions. The dog – the picture above the jar on the mantelpiece with its subject – 'Out all night' and the ball put away in the jar. That is the only ground for suspicion she has. She probably thinks her illness is natural – but at the last minute has an intuition that it is not.'

He was silent for a moment or two.

'Ah! if only she had posted that letter. I could have saved her. Now –'

He took up a pen and drew some notepaper towards him.

'What are you going to do?'

'I am going to write a full and explicit account of what happened and post it to Miss Mollie Davidson with a hint that an exhumation will be applied for.'

'And then?'

'If she is innocent – nothing –' said Poirot gravely. 'If she is not innocent – we shall see.'

viii

Two days later there was a notice in the paper stating that a Miss Mollie Davidson had died of an overdose of sleeping draught. I was rather horrified.[8] Poirot was quite composed.

'But no, it has all arranged itself very happily. No ugly scandal and trial for murder – Miss Wheeler she would not want that. She would have desired the privacy. On the other hand one must not leave a murderess – what do you say? – at loose. Or sooner or later, there will be another murder. Always a murderer repeats his crime. No,' he went on dreamily 'it has all arranged itself very well. It only remains to work upon the feelings of Miss Lawson – a task which Miss Davidson was attempting very successfully – until she reaches the pitch of handing over half her fortune to Mr James Graham who is, after all, entitled to the money. Since he was deprived of it under a misapprehension.'

He drew from his pocket the brightly coloured rubber ball.

'Shall we send this to our friend Bob? Or shall we keep it on the mantelpiece? It is a reminder, *n'est ce pas, mon ami*, that nothing is too trivial to be neglected? At one end, Murder, at the other only – the incident of the dog's ball . . .'

Notes

1. The exact wording of the title appears, more than once, in Chapter 9 of *Dumb Witness* and also in Miss Arundell's letter in Chapter 5.

2. This letter is very similar to that sent by Miss Amelia Barrowby, another elderly lady living in a small village who is subsequently poisoned, in 'How Does Your Garden Grow?'

3. If the letter was written on 12 April and received by Poirot in early August, this should read 'nearly four months ago'.

4. This should read 'April'.

5. Oddly, this very specific occupation, suspicious in the context of a poisoning mystery, is never mentioned again.

6. This picture (it changes to a jar with similar wording in Chapter 8 of the novel) can be seen in Greenway House and may have been part of Christie's inspiration. She was a dog-lover and lifelong dog-owner.

7. This scientific explanation appears verbatim in Chapter 23 of *Dumb Witness.*

8. This somewhat questionable procedure, with Poirot taking the law into his own hands, is also adopted in the novel.

Select Bibliography

Of the many books written about Agatha Christie, the following have been most helpful:

Barnard, Robert, *A Talent to Deceive* (1980)
Campbell, Mark, *The Pocket Essentials Guide to Agatha Christie* (2006)
Morgan, Janet, *Agatha Christie* (1984)
Osborne, Charles, *The Life and Crimes of Agatha Christie* (1982)
Sanders, Dennis and Lovallo, Len, *The Agatha Christie Companion* (1984)
Sova, Dawn B., *Agatha Christie A to Z* (1996)
Thompson, Laura, *Agatha Christie, An English Mystery* (2007)
Toye, Randall, *The Agatha Christie Who's Who* (1980)

Index of Titles